HEBREWS

WISDOM COMMENTARY

Volume 54

Hebrews

Mary Ann Beavis and HyeRan Kim-Cragg

Linda Maloney

Volume Editor

Barbara E. Reid, OP

General Editor

A Michael Glazier Book

LITURGICAL PRESS

Collegeville, Minnesota

www.litpress.org

A Michael Glazier Book published by Liturgical Press

Cover design by Ann Blattner. *Chapter Letter 'W'*, *Acts of the Apostles, Chapter 4*, Donald Jackson, Copyright 2002, *The Saint John's Bible*, Saint John's University, Collegeville, Minnesota USA. Used by permission. All rights reserved.

1   2   3   4   5   6   7   8   9

Library of Congress Cataloging-in-Publication Data

Beavis, Mary Ann.
    Hebrews / Mary Ann Beavis and HyeRan Kim-Cragg ; Linda Maloney volume editor ; Barbara E. Reid, OP, general editor.
        pages cm. — (Wisdom commentary ; Volume 54)
    "A Michael Glazier book."
    Includes bibliographical references and index.
    ISBN 978-0-8146-8204-3 — ISBN 978-0-8146-8229-6 (ebook)
    1. Bible. Hebrews—Commentaries.   I. Title.

BS2775.53.B43   2015
227'.87077—dc23   2015018831

Contents

Abbreviations

1 En.	1 Enoch
11Q13	Melchizedek Scroll from Qumran Cave 11
Ant.	Flavius Josephus, *Jewish Antiquities*
AB	Anchor Bible
Abr.	*De Abrahamo*
AsJT	*Asia Journal of Theology*
Ann.	Tacitus, *Annals*
ANTC	Abingdon New Testament Commentaries
Antichr.	Hippolytus, *On the Antichrist*
Apol.	*Apologia*
As. Mos.	Assumption of Moses
ASV	American Standard Version
AV	Authorized Version
B.J.	Flavius Josephus, *Bellum Judaicum*
BA	*Biblical Archaeologist*
BDAG	Walter Bauer, W. F. Arndt, and F. W. Gingrich (3rd ed., rev. by F. W. Danker), *Greek–English Lexicon of the NT*
BibInt	Biblical Interpretation Series
BSac	*Bibliotheca Sacra*

BTB	*Biblical Theology Bulletin*
CBQ	*Catholic Biblical Quarterly*
CBQMS	Catholic Biblical Quarterly Monograph Series
CEB	Common English Bible
Cherabim	Philo, *On the Cherubim*
CSCA	Centre for the Study of Christianity in Asia
EAPR	*East Asian Pastoral Review*
Ebr.	Philo, *De Ebrietate*
Ep.	Pliny, *Epistles*
FCB	Feminist Companion to the Bible
FCNTECW	Feminist Companion to the New Testament and Early Christian Writings
Fr. Matt.	Origen, *Fragments on Matthew*
FemT	*Feminist Theology*
GIPS	Gender Issues in Philippine Society
Haer.	*Adversus Haereses*
HTR	*Harvard Theological Review*
HUCA	*Hebrew Union College Annual*
IFRT	Institute of Formation and Religious Studies
IFT	Introductions in Feminist Theology
IG	*Image and Gender*
IO	*Institutio Oratoria*
JFSR	*Journal of Feminist Studies in Religion*
JSNTSup	Journal for the Study of the New Testament Supplement Series
JSOT	*Journal for the Study of the Old Testament*
JSOTSup	Journal for the Study of the Old Testament Supplement Series
JSP	*Journal for the Study of the Pseudepigrapha*
JSQ	*Jewish Studies Quarterly*
Jub.	Jubilees

LCR	*Lutheran Church Review*
Leg. All.	*Legum allegoriae*
LNTS	Library of New Testament Studies
LP	*Living Pulpit*
LXX	Septuagint
Mart. Isa.	Martyrdom of Isaiah
Meg.	Megillah
Midr.	Midrash
MJTM	*McMaster Journal of Theology and Ministry*
Mos.	*De Vita Mosis*
MS	Maryhill Studies
MT	Masoretic Text
NASB	New American Standard Bible
NCV	New Century Version
NIGTC	New International Greek Testament Commentary
NIV	New International Version
NJB	New Jerusalem Bible
NLV	New Life Version
NRM	New Religious Movement
NTL	New Testament Library
NTS	*New Testament Studies*
OQR	*Oberlin Quarterly Review*
RBS	Resources for Biblical Study
ResQ	*Restoration Quarterly*
RevExp	*Review and Expositor*
RWS	*Review of Women's Studies*
SBL	Society of Biblical Literature
SBLDS	Society of Biblical Literature Dissertation Series
SBLSymS	Society of Biblical Literature Symposium Series
SemeiaSt	Semeia Studies

SJT	*Scottish Journal of Theology*
SNTSMS	Studiorum Novi Testamenti Societas Monograph Series
SP	Sacra Pagina
StPatr	Studia Patristica
Spec.	*De specialibus legibus*
T.Ab.	Testament of Abraham
TBT	*The Bible Today*
T.Levi	Testament of Levi
UNESCO	United Nations Educational, Scientific and Cultural Organization
UNICEF	United Nations Children's Fund
UPIC	University Parish International Community

Contributors

Marie Annharte Baker is a First Nations poet, essayist, and activist in Winnipeg, Manitoba, Canada.

Dr. Mary Ann Beavis is professor in the Department of Religion and Culture, St. Thomas More College, University of Saskatchewan. She is the author of many articles and several books in the subject areas of biblical studies and religious studies.

Rev. Dr. HyeRan Kim-Cragg is Lydia Gruchy Professor of Pastoral Studies, St. Andrew's College, University of Saskatchewan. She is the author of many articles and several books in the subject areas of religious education and worship.

Rev. Dr. Nancy Calvert-Koyzis is currently manager of supportive care at the Dr. Bob Kemp Hospice in Hamilton, Ontario. She taught for over twenty years, full-time and part-time, at colleges, universities, and theological colleges. She is the author or editor of three books and many articles in the area of biblical studies.

Dr. Ma. Maricel S. Ibita earned her doctorate from the Faculty of Theology and Religious Studies, Katholieke Universiteit Leuven, Belgium. Her publications and research interests on the Bible employ historical-critical method, literary analysis, approaches that use human sciences, and contextual approaches. She brings this expertise along with her advocacy for justice, peace, and integrity of creation as she returns to her home country, the Philippines.

Dr. Ma. Marilou S. Ibita is a postdoctoral researcher at the Katholieke Universiteit Leuven (Leuven, Belgium) and a guest lecturer at the Institute of Formation and Religious Studies (Quezon City, Philippines). Her research interests include, among others, New Testament hermeneutics, hospitality and meals in the New Testament, and the role of the Bible in popular culture and religious education.

Dr. Justin Jaron Lewis is associate professor in the Department of Religion and Judaic Studies Program, University of Manitoba. He is the author of *Imagining Holiness: Classic Hasidic Tales in Modern Times* (McGill-Queens University Press, 2009) and other work on Jewish storytelling and imaginative interpretation of Scripture.

Foreword

"Come Eat of My Bread . . . and Walk in the Ways of Wisdom"

Elisabeth Schüssler Fiorenza
Harvard University Divinity School

Jewish feminist writer Asphodel Long has likened the Bible to

> a magnificent garden of brilliant plants, some flowering, some fruiting,
> some in seed, some in bud, shaded by trees of age old, luxurious growth.
> Yet in the very soil which gives it life the poison has been inserted. . . .
> This poison is that of misogyny, the hatred of women, half the human
> race.[1]

To see Scripture as such a beautiful garden containing poisonous ivy
requires that one identify and name this poison and place on all biblical
texts the label "Caution! Could be dangerous to your health and survival!"
As critical feminist interpretation for well-being this Wisdom Commentary seeks to elaborate the beauty and fecundity of this Scripture-garden

---

1. Asphodel Long, *In a Chariot Drawn by Lions: The Search for the Female in the Deity*
(London: Women's Press, 1992), 195.

and at the same time points to the harm it can do when one submits to its world of vision. Thus, feminist biblical interpretation engages two seemingly contradictory insights: The Bible is written in kyriocentric (i.e., lord/master/father/husband-elite male) language, originated in the patri-kyriarchal cultures of antiquity, and has functioned to inculcate misogynist mind-sets and oppressive values. At the same time it also asserts that the Bible as Sacred Scripture has functioned to inspire and authorize wo/men[2] in our struggles against dehumanizing oppression. The hermeneutical lens of wisdom/Wisdom empowers the commentary writers to do so.

In biblical as well as in contemporary religious discourse the word *wisdom* has a double meaning: It can either refer to the quality of life and of people and/or it can refer to a figuration of the Divine. Wisdom in both senses of the word is not a prerogative of the biblical traditions but is found in the imagination and writings of all known religions. Wisdom is transcultural, international, and interreligious. Wisdom is practical knowledge gained through experience and daily living as well as through the study of creation and human nature. Both word meanings, that of capability (wisdom) and that of female personification (Wisdom), are crucial for this Wisdom Commentary series that seeks to enable biblical readers to become critical subjects of interpretation.

Wisdom is a state of the human mind and spirit characterized by deep understanding and profound insight. It is elaborated as a quality possessed by the sages but also treasured as folk wisdom and wit. Wisdom is the power of discernment, deeper understanding, and creativity; it is the ability to move and to dance, to make the connections, to savor life, and to learn from experience. Wisdom is intelligence shaped by experience and sharpened by critical analysis. It is the ability to make sound choices and incisive decisions. Its root meaning comes to the fore in its Latin form *sapientia*, which is derived from the verb *sapere*, to taste and to savor something. Hence, this series of commentaries invites readers to taste, to evaluate, and to imagine.

In the figure of *Chokmah-Sophia-Sapientia-Wisdom*, ancient Jewish scriptures seek to hold together belief in the "one" G*d[3] of Israel with both masculine and feminine language and metaphors of the Divine.

---

2. I use wo/man, s/he, fe/male and not the grammatical standard "man" as inclusive terms and make this visible by adding /.

3. I use the * asterisk in order to alert readers to a problem to explore and think about.

In distinction to traditional Scripture reading, which is often individualistic and privatized, the practice and space of Wisdom commentary is public. Wisdom's spiraling presence (*Shekinah*) is global, embracing all creation. Her voice is a public, radical democratic voice rather than a "feminine," privatized one. To become one of Her justice-seeking friends, one needs to imagine the work of this feminist commentary series as the spiraling circle dance of wisdom/Wisdom.[4] To imagine the feminist work of this commentary series as a Spirit/spiritual intellectual movement in the open space of wisdom/Wisdom who calls readers to critically analyze, debate, and reimagine biblical texts and their commentaries as wisdom/Wisdom texts inspired by visions of justice and well-being for everyone and everything. Wisdom-Sophia-imagination engenders a different understanding of Jesus and the movement around him. It understands him as the child and prophet of Divine Wisdom and as Wisdom herself instead of imagining him as ruling King and Lord who has only subalterns but not friends. To approach the N*T[5] and the whole Bible as Wisdom's invitation of cosmic dimensions means to acknowledge its multivalence and its openness to change. As bread—not stone.

In short, this commentary series is inspired by the feminist vision of the open cosmic house of Divine Wisdom-Sophia as it is found in biblical Wisdom literatures, which include the N*T:

> Wisdom has built Her house
> She has set up Her seven pillars . . .
> She has mixed Her wine,
> She also has set Her table.
> She has sent out Her wo/men ministers
> to call from the highest places in the town . . .
> "Come eat of my bread
> and drink of the wine I have mixed.
> Leave immaturity, and live,
> And walk in the way of Wisdom." (Prov 9:1-3, 5-6)

4. I have elaborated such a Wisdom dance in terms of biblical hermeneutics in my book *Wisdom Ways*. Its seven steps are a hermeneutics of experience, of domination, of suspicion, of evaluation, of remembering or historical reconstruction, of imagination, and of transformation. However, such Wisdom strategies of meaning making are not restricted to the Bible. Rather, I have used them in workshops in Brazil and Ecuador to explore the workings of power, Condomblé, Christology, imagining a the*logical wo/men's center, or engaging the national icon of Mary.

5. See the discussion about nomenclature of the two testaments in the introduction, pages xxxii–xxxiii.

Editor's Introduction to Wisdom Commentary

"She Is a Breath of the Power of God" (Wis 7:25)

Barbara E. Reid, OP

General Editor

Wisdom Commentary is the first series to offer detailed feminist interpretation of every book of the Bible. The fruit of collaborative work by an ecumenical and interreligious team of scholars, the volumes provide serious, scholarly engagement with the whole biblical text, not only those texts that explicitly mention women. The series is intended for clergy, teachers, ministers, and all serious students of the Bible. Designed to be both accessible and informed by the various approaches of biblical scholarship, it pays particular attention to the world in front of the text, that is, how the text is heard and appropriated. At the same time, this series aims to be faithful to the ancient text and its earliest audiences; thus the volumes also explicate the worlds behind the text and within it. While issues of gender are primary in this project, the volumes also address the intersecting issues of power, authority, ethnicity, race, class, and religious belief and practice. The fifty-eight volumes include the books regarded as canonical by Jews (i.e., the Tanakh); Protestants (the "Hebrew Bible" and the New Testament); and Roman Catholic, Anglican, and Eastern Orthodox Communions (i.e.,

Tobit, Judith, 1 and 2 Maccabees, Wisdom of Solomon, Sirach/Ecclesiasticus, Baruch, including the Letter of Jeremiah, the additions to Esther, and Susanna and Bel and the Dragon in Daniel).

A Symphony of Diverse Voices

Included in the Wisdom Commentary series are voices from scholars of many different religious traditions, of diverse ages, differing sexual identities, and varying cultural, racial, ethnic, and social contexts. Some have been pioneers in feminist biblical interpretation; others are newer contributors from a younger generation. A further distinctive feature of this series is that each volume incorporates voices other than that of the lead author(s). These voices appear alongside the commentary of the lead author(s), in the grayscale inserts. At times, a contributor may offer an alternative interpretation or a critique of the position taken by the lead author(s). At other times, she or he may offer a complementary interpretation from a different cultural context or subject position. Occasionally, portions of previously published material bring in other views. The diverse voices are not intended to be contestants in a debate or a cacophony of discordant notes. The multiple voices reflect that there is no single definitive feminist interpretation of a text. In addition, they show the importance of subject position in the process of interpretation. In this regard, the Wisdom Commentary series takes inspiration from the Talmud and from *The Torah: A Women's Commentary* (ed. Tamara Cohn Eskenazi and Andrea L. Weiss; New York: Women of Reform Judaism, Federation of Temple Sisterhood, 2008), in which many voices, even conflicting ones, are included and not harmonized.

Contributors include biblical scholars, theologians, and readers of Scripture from outside the scholarly and religious guilds. At times, their comments pertain to a particular text. In some instances they address a theme or topic that arises from the text.

Another feature that highlights the collaborative nature of feminist biblical interpretation is that a number of the volumes have two lead authors who have worked in tandem from the inception of the project and whose voices interweave throughout the commentary.

Woman Wisdom

The title, Wisdom Commentary, reflects both the importance to feminists of the figure of Woman Wisdom in the Scriptures and the distinct wisdom that feminist women and men bring to the interpretive process. In the Scriptures, Woman Wisdom appears as "a breath of the power of God, and a pure emanation of the glory of the Almighty" (Wis 7:25), who was present and active in fashioning all that exists (Prov 8:22-31; Wis 8:6). She is a spirit who pervades and penetrates all things (Wis 7:22-23), and she provides guidance and nourishment at her all-inclusive table (Prov 9:1-5). In both postexilic biblical and nonbiblical Jewish sources, Woman Wisdom is often equated with Torah, e.g., Sir 24:23-34; Bar 3:9–4:4; 38:2; 46:4-5; 2 Bar 48:33, 36; 4 Ezra 5:9-10; 13:55; 14:40; 1 Enoch 42.

The New Testament frequently portrays Jesus as Wisdom incarnate. He invites his followers, "take my yoke upon you and learn from me" (Matt 11:29), just as Ben Sira advises, "put your neck under her [Wisdom's] yoke and let your souls receive instruction" (Sir 51:26). Just as Wisdom experiences rejection (Prov 1:23-25; Sir 15:7-8; Wis 10:3; Bar 3:12), so too does Jesus (Mark 8:31; John 1:10-11). Only some accept his invitation to his all-inclusive banquet (Matt 22:1-14; Luke 14:15-24; compare Prov 1:20-21; 9:3-5). Yet, "wisdom is vindicated by her deeds" (Matt 11:19, speaking of Jesus and John the Baptist; in the Lucan parallel at 7:35 they are called "wisdom's children"). There are numerous parallels between what is said of Wisdom and of the *Logos* in the Prologue of the Fourth Gospel (John 1:1-18). These are only a few of many examples. This female embodiment of divine presence and power is an apt image to guide the work of this series.

Feminism

There are many different understandings of the term "feminism." The various meanings, aims, and methods have developed exponentially in recent decades. Feminism is a perspective and a movement that springs from a recognition of inequities toward women, and it advocates for changes in whatever structures prevent full human flourishing. Three waves of feminism in the United States are commonly recognized. The first, arising in the mid-nineteenth century and lasting into the early twentieth, was sparked by women's efforts to be involved in the public sphere and to win the right to vote. In the 1960s and 1970s, the second wave focused on civil rights and equality for women. With the third wave, from the 1980s forward, came global feminism and the emphasis on the contextual nature of interpretation. As feminism has matured, it has recognized that inequities based on gender are interwoven with power imbalances based on race, class, ethnicity, religion, sexual identity, physical ability, and a host of other social markers.

Feminist Women and Men

Men who choose to identify with and partner with feminist women in the work of deconstructing systems of domination and building structures of equality are rightly regarded as feminists. Some men readily identify with experiences of women who are discriminated against on the basis of sex/gender, having themselves had comparable experiences; others who may not have faced direct discrimination or stereotyping recognize that inequity and problematic characterization still occur, and they seek correction. This series is pleased to include feminist men both as lead authors and as contributing voices.

Feminist Biblical Interpretation

Women interpreting the Bible from the lenses of their own experience is nothing new. Throughout the ages women have recounted the biblical stories, teaching them to their children and others, all the while interpreting them afresh for their time and circumstances.[1] Following is a very brief sketch of select foremothers who laid the groundwork for contemporary feminist biblical interpretation.

One of the earliest known Christian women who challenged patriarchal interpretations of Scripture was a consecrated virgin named Helie, who lived in the second century CE. When she refused to marry, her parents brought her before a judge, who quoted to her Paul's admonition, "It is better to marry than to be aflame with passion" (1 Cor 7:9). In response, Helie first acknowledges that this is what Scripture says, but then she retorts, "but not for everyone, that is, not for holy virgins."[2] She is one of the first to question the notion that a text has one meaning that is applicable in all situations.

A Jewish woman who also lived in the second century CE, Beruriah, is said to have had "profound knowledge of biblical exegesis and out-

---

1. For fuller treatments of this history, see chap. 7, "One Thousand Years of Feminist Bible Criticism," in Gerda Lerner, *Creation of Feminist Consciousness: From the Middle Ages to Eighteen-Seventy* (New York: Oxford University Press, 1993), 138–66; Susanne Scholz, "From the 'Woman's Bible' to the 'Women's Bible,' The History of Feminist Approaches to the Hebrew Bible," in *Introducing the Women's Hebrew Bible*, IFT 13 (New York: T & T Clark, 2007), 12–32; Marion Ann Taylor and Agnes Choi, eds., *Handbook of Women Biblical Interpreters: A Historical and Biographical Guide* (Grand Rapids, MI: Baker Academic, 2012).

2. Madrid, Escorial MS, a II 9, f. 90 v., as cited in Lerner, *Feminist Consciousness*, 140.

standing intelligence."[3] One story preserved in the Talmud (b. Berachot 10a) tells of how she challenged her husband, Rabbi Meir, when he prayed for the destruction of a sinner. Proffering an alternate interpretation, she argued that Psalm 104:35 advocated praying for the destruction of sin, not the sinner.

In medieval times the first written commentaries on Scripture from a critical feminist point of view emerge. While others may have been produced and passed on orally, they are for the most part lost to us now. Among the earliest preserved feminist writings are those of Hildegard of Bingen (1098–1179), German writer, mystic, and abbess of a Benedictine monastery. She reinterpreted the Genesis narratives in a way that presented women and men as complementary and interdependent. She frequently wrote about feminine aspects of the Divine.[4] Along with other women mystics of the time, such as Julian of Norwich (1342–ca. 1416), she spoke authoritatively from her personal experiences of God's revelation in prayer.

In this era, women were also among the scribes who copied biblical manuscripts. Notable among them is Paula Dei Mansi of Verona, from a distinguished family of Jewish scribes. In 1288, she translated from Hebrew into Italian a collection of Bible commentaries written by her father and added her own explanations.[5]

Another pioneer, Christine de Pizan (1365–ca.1430), was a French court writer and prolific poet. She used allegory and common sense to subvert misogynist readings of Scripture and celebrated the accomplishments of female biblical figures to argue for women's active roles in building society.[6]

By the seventeenth century, there were women who asserted that the biblical text needs to be understood and interpreted in its historical context. For example, Rachel Speght (1597–ca.1630), a Calvinist English poet, elaborates on the historical situation in first-century Corinth that prompted Paul to say, "It is well for a man not to touch a woman" (1 Cor 7:1). Her aim

3. See Judith R. Baskin, "Women and Post-Biblical Commentary," in *The Torah: A Women's Commentary*, ed. Tamara Cohn Eskenazi and Andrea L. Weiss (New York: Women of Reform Judaism, Federation of Temple Sisterhood, 2008), xlix–lv, here lii.

4. Hildegard of Bingen, *De Operatione Dei*, 1.4.100; PL 197:885bc, as cited in Lerner, *Feminist Consciousness*, 142–43. See also Barbara Newman, *Sister of Wisdom: St. Hildegard's Theology of the Feminine* (Berkeley: University of California Press, 1987).

5. Emily Taitz, Sondra Henry, Cheryl Tallan, eds., *JPS Guide to Jewish Women 600 B.C.E.–1900 C.E.* (Philadelphia: JPS, 2003), 110–11.

6. See further Taylor and Choi, *Handbook of Women Biblical Interpreters*, 127–32.

was to show that the biblical texts should not be applied in a literal fashion to all times and circumstances. Similarly, Margaret Fell (1614–1702), one of the founders of the Religious Society of Friends (Quakers) in Britain, addressed the Pauline prohibitions against women speaking in church by insisting that they do not have universal validity. Rather, they need to be understood in their historical context, as addressed to a local church in particular time-bound circumstances.[7]

Along with analyzing the historical context of the biblical writings, women in the eighteenth and nineteenth centuries began to attend to misogynistic interpretations based on faulty translations. One of the first to do so was British feminist Mary Astell (1666–1731).[8] In the United States, the Grimké sisters, Sarah (1792–1873) and Angelina (1805–1879), Quaker women from a slaveholding family in South Carolina, learned biblical Greek and Hebrew so that they could interpret the Bible for themselves. They were prompted to do so after men sought to silence them from speaking out against slavery and for women's rights by claiming that the Bible (e.g., 1 Cor 14:34) prevented women from speaking in public.[9] Another prominent abolitionist, Sojourner Truth (ca. 1797–1883), a former slave, quoted the Bible liberally in her speeches[10] and in so doing challenged cultural assumptions and biblical interpretations that undergird gender inequities.

Another monumental work that emerged in nineteenth-century England was that of Jewish theologian Grace Aguilar (1816–1847), *The Women of Israel*,[11] published in 1845. Aguilar's approach was to make connections between the biblical women and contemporary Jewish women's concerns. She aimed to counter the widespread notion that women were degraded in Jewish law and that only in Christianity were women's

---

7. Her major work, *Women's Speaking Justified, Proved and Allowed by the Scriptures*, published in London in 1667, gave a systematic feminist reading of all biblical texts pertaining to women.

8. Mary Astell, *Some Reflections upon Marriage* (New York: Source Book Press, 1970, reprint of the 1730 edition; earliest edition of this work is 1700), 103–4.

9. See further Sarah Grimké, *Letters on the Equality of the Sexes and the Condition of Woman* (Boston: Isaac Knapp, 1838).

10. See, for example, her most famous speech, "Ain't I a Woman?," delivered in 1851 at the Ohio Women's Rights Convention in Akron, OH; http://www.fordham.edu/halsall/mod/sojtruth-woman.asp.

11. The full title is *The Women of Israel or Characters and Sketches from the Holy Scriptures and Jewish History Illustrative of the Past History, Present Duty, and Future Destiny of the Hebrew Females, as Based on the Word of God*.

dignity and value upheld. Her intent was to help Jewish women find strength and encouragement by seeing the evidence of God's compassionate love in the history of every woman in the Bible. While not a full commentary on the Bible, Aguilar's work stands out for its comprehensive treatment of every female biblical character, including even the most obscure references.[12]

The first person to produce a full-blown feminist commentary on the Bible was Elizabeth Cady Stanton (1815–1902). A leading proponent in the United States for women's right to vote, she found that whenever women tried to make inroads into politics, education, or the work world, the Bible was quoted against them. Along with a team of like-minded women, she produced her own commentary on every text of the Bible that concerned women. Her pioneering two-volume project, *The Woman's Bible*, published in 1895 and 1898, urges women to recognize that texts that degrade women come from the men who wrote the texts, not from God, and to use their common sense to rethink what has been presented to them as sacred.

Nearly a century later, *The Women's Bible Commentary*, edited by Sharon Ringe and Carol Newsom (Westminster John Knox Press, 1992), appeared. This one-volume commentary features North American feminist scholarship on each book of the Protestant canon. Like Cady Stanton's commentary, it does not contain comments on every section of the biblical text but only on those passages deemed relevant to women. It was revised and expanded in 1998 to include the Apocrypha/Deuterocanonical books, and the contributors to this new volume reflect the global face of contemporary feminist scholarship. The revisions made in the third edition, which appeared in 2012, represent the profound advances in feminist biblical scholarship and include newer voices. In both the second and third editions, *The* has been dropped from the title.

Also appearing at the centennial of Cady Stanton's *The Woman's Bible* were two volumes edited by Elisabeth Schüssler Fiorenza with the assistance of Shelly Matthews. The first, *Searching the Scriptures: A Feminist Introduction* (New York: Crossroad, 1993), charts a comprehensive approach to feminist interpretation from ecumenical, interreligious, and multicultural perspectives. The second volume, published in 1994, provides critical feminist commentary on each book of the New Testament

---

12. See further Eskenazi and Weiss, *The Torah: A Women's Commentary*, xxxviii; Taylor and Choi, *Handbook of Women Biblical Interpreters*, 31–37.

as well as on three books of Jewish Pseudepigrapha and eleven other early Christian writings.

In Europe, similar endeavors have been undertaken, such as the one-volume *Kompendium Feministische Bibelauslegung*, edited by Luise Schottroff and Marie-Theres Wacker (Gütersloh, Gütersloher Verlagshaus, 2007), featuring German feminist biblical interpretation of each book of the Bible, along with apocryphal books, and several extrabiblical writings. This work, now in its third edition, has recently been translated into English.[13] A multivolume project, *The Bible and Women: An Encylopaedia of Exegesis and Cultural History*, edited by Irmtraud Fischer, Adriana Valerio, Mercedes Navarro Puerto, and Christiana de Groot, is currently in production. This project presents a history of the reception of the Bible as embedded in Western cultural history and focuses particularly on gender-relevant biblical themes, biblical female characters, and women recipients of the Bible. The volumes are published in English, Spanish, Italian, and German.[14]

Another groundbreaking work is the collection The Feminist Companion to the Bible Series, edited by Athalya Brenner (Sheffield: Sheffield Academic Press, 1993–2001). To date, nineteen volumes of commentaries on the Old Testament have been published, with more in production. The parallel series, Feminist Companion to the New Testament and Early Christian Writings, edited by Amy-Jill Levine with Marianne Blickenstaff and Maria Mayo Robbins (Sheffield: Sheffield Academic Press, 2001–2009), contains thirteen volumes with one more planned. These two series are not full commentaries on the biblical books but comprise collected essays on discrete biblical texts.

Works by individual feminist biblical scholars in all parts of the world abound, and they are now too numerous to list in this introduction. Feminist biblical interpretation has reached a level of maturity that now makes possible a commentary series on every book of the Bible. In recent decades, women have had greater access to formal theological education, have been able to learn critical analytical tools, have put their own in-

---

13. *Feminist Biblical Interpretation: A Compendium of Critical Commentary on the Books of the Bible and Related Literature*, trans. Lisa E. Dahill, Everett R. Kalin, Nancy Lukens, Linda M. Maloney, Barbara Rumscheidt, Martin Rumscheidt, and Tina Steiner (Grand Rapids, MI: Eerdmans, 2012).

14. The first volume, on the Torah, appeared in Spanish in 2009, in German and Italian in 2010, and in English in 2011 (Atlanta, GA: SBL). For further information, see http://www.bibleandwomen.org.

terpretations into writing, and have developed new methods of biblical interpretation. Until recent decades the work of feminist biblical interpreters was largely unknown, both to other women and to their brothers in the synagogue, church, and academy. Feminists now have taken their place in the professional world of biblical scholars, where they build on the work of their foremothers and connect with one another across the globe in ways not previously possible. In a few short decades, feminist biblical criticism has become an integral part of the academy.

Methodologies

Feminist biblical scholars use a variety of methods and often employ a number of them together.[15] In the Wisdom Commentary series, the authors will explain their understanding of feminism and the feminist reading strategies used in their commentary. Each volume treats the biblical text in blocks of material, not an analysis verse by verse. The entire text is considered, not only those passages that feature female characters or that speak specifically about women. When women are not apparent in the narrative, feminist lenses are used to analyze the dynamics in the text between male characters, the models of power, binary ways of thinking, and dynamics of imperialism. Attention is given to how the whole text functions and how it was and is heard, both in its original context and today. Issues of particular concern to women—e.g., poverty, food, health, the environment, water—come to the fore.

One of the approaches used by early feminists and still popular today is to lift up the overlooked and forgotten stories of women in the Bible. Studies of women in each of the Testaments have been done, and there are also studies on women in particular biblical books.[16] Feminists

15. See the seventeen essays in Caroline Vander Stichele and Todd Penner, eds., *Her Master's Tools? Feminist and Postcolonial Engagements of Historical-Critical Discourse* (Atlanta, GA: SBL, 2005), which show the complementarity of various approaches.

16. See, e.g., Alice Bach, ed., *Women in the Hebrew Bible: A Reader* (New York: Routledge, 1998); Tikva Frymer-Kensky, *Reading the Women of the Bible* (New York: Schocken, 2002); Carol Meyers, Toni Craven, and Ross S. Kraemer, *Women in Scripture* (Grand Rapids, MI: Eerdmans, 2000); Irene Nowell, *Women in the Old Testament* (Collegeville, MN: Liturgical Press, 1997); Katharine Doob Sakenfeld, *Just Wives? Stories of Power and Survival in the Old Testament and Today* (Louisville, KY: Westminster John Knox, 2003); Mary Ann Getty-Sullivan, *Women in the New Testament* (Collegeville, MN: Liturgical Press, 2001); Bonnie Thurston, *Women in the New Testament* (New York: Crossroad, 1998).

recognize that the examples of biblical characters can be both empowering
and problematic. The point of the feminist enterprise is not to serve as an
apologetic for women; it is rather, in part, to recover women's history and
literary roles in all their complexity and to learn from that recovery.

Retrieving the submerged history of biblical women is a crucial step
for constructing the story of the past so as to lead to liberative possibilities for the present and future. There are, however, some pitfalls to this
approach. Sometimes depictions of biblical women have been naïve and
romantic. Some commentators exalt the virtues of both biblical and
contemporary women and paint women as superior to men. Such reverse
discrimination inhibits movement toward equality for all. In addition,
some feminists challenge the idea that one can "pluck positive images
out of an admittedly androcentric text, separating literary characteriza-
tions from the androcentric interests they were created to serve."[17] Still
other feminists find these images to have enormous value.

One other danger with seeking the submerged history of women is
the tendency for Christian feminists to paint Jesus and even Paul as
liberators of women in a way that demonizes Judaism.[18] Wisdom Commentary aims to enhance understanding of Jesus as well as Paul as Jews
of their day and to forge solidarity among Jewish and Christian
feminists.

Feminist scholars who use historical-critical methods analyze the
world behind the text; they seek to understand the historical context
from which the text emerged and the circumstances of the communities
to whom it was addressed. In bringing feminist lenses to this approach,
the aim is not to impose modern expectations on ancient cultures but to
unmask the ways that ideologically problematic mind-sets that produced
the ancient texts are still promulgated through the text. Feminist biblical
scholars aim not only to deconstruct but also to reclaim and reconstruct
biblical history as women's history, in which women were central and

17. Cheryl Exum, "Second Thoughts about Secondary Characters: Women in
Exodus 1.8–2.10," in *A Feminist Companion to Exodus to Deuteronomy*, FCB 6 (Sheffield:
Sheffield Academic Press, 1994), 75–97, here 76.

18. See Judith Plaskow, "Anti-Judaism in Feminist Christian Interpretation," in
Searching the Scriptures: A Feminist Introduction (New York: Crossroad, 1993), 1:117–29;
Amy-Jill Levine, "The New Testament and Anti-Judaism," in *The Misunderstood Jew:
The Church and the Scandal of the Jewish Jesus* (San Francisco: HarperSanFrancisco,
2006), 87–117.

active agents in creating religious heritage.[19] A further step is to construct meaning for contemporary women and men in a liberative movement toward transformation of social, political, economic, and religious structures.[20] In recent years, some feminists have embraced new historicism, which accents the creative role of the interpreter in any construction of history and exposes the power struggles to which the text witnesses.[21]

Literary critics analyze the world of the text: its form, language patterns, and rhetorical function.[22] They do not attempt to separate layers of tradition and redaction but focus on the text holistically, as it is in its present form. They examine how meaning is created in the interaction between the text and its reader in multiple contexts. Within the arena of literary approaches are reader-oriented approaches, narrative, rhetorical, structuralist, post-structuralist, deconstructive, ideological, autobiographical, and performance criticism.[23] Narrative critics study the interrelation

---

19. See, for example, Phyllis A. Bird, *Missing Persons and Mistaken Identities: Women and Gender in Ancient Israel* (Minneapolis: Fortress Press, 1997); Elisabeth Schüssler Fiorenza, *In Memory of Her: A Feminist Theological Reconstruction of Christian Origins* (New York: Crossroad, 1984); Ross Shepard Kraemer and Mary Rose D'Angelo, eds., *Women and Christian Origins* (New York: Oxford University Press, 1999).

20. See, e.g., Sandra M. Schneiders, *The Revelatory Text: Interpreting the New Testament as Sacred Scripture*, rev. ed. (Collegeville, MN: Liturgical Press, 1999), whose aim is to engage in biblical interpretation not only for intellectual enlightenment but, even more important, for personal and communal transformation. Elisabeth Schüssler Fiorenza (*Wisdom Ways: Introducing Feminist Biblical Interpretation* [Maryknoll, NY: Orbis Books, 2001]) envisions the work of feminist biblical interpretation as a dance of Wisdom that consists of seven steps that interweave in spiral movements toward liberation, the final one being transformative action for change.

21. See Gina Hens Piazza, *The New Historicism*, Guides to Biblical Scholarship, Old Testament Series (Minneapolis: Fortress Press, 2002).

22. Phyllis Trible was among the first to employ this method with texts from Genesis and Ruth in her groundbreaking book *God and the Rhetoric of Sexuality*, Overtures to Biblical Theology (Philadelphia: Fortress Press, 1978). Another pioneer in feminist literary criticism is Mieke Bal (*Lethal Love: Feminist Literary Readings of Biblical Love Stories* [Bloomington: Indiana University Press, 1987]). For surveys of recent developments in literary methods, see Terry Eagleton, *Literary Theory: An Introduction*, 3rd ed. (Minneapolis: University of Minnesota Press, 2008); Janice Capel Anderson and Stephen D. Moore, eds., *Mark and Method: New Approaches in Biblical Studies*, 2nd ed. (Minneapolis: Fortress Press, 2008).

23. See, e.g., J. Cheryl Exum and David J. A. Clines, eds., *The New Literary Criticism and the Hebrew Bible* (Valley Forge, PA: Trinity Press International, 1993); Edgar V. McKnight and Elizabeth Struthers Malbon, eds., *The New Literary Criticism and the New Testament* (Valley Forge, PA: Trinity Press International, 1994).

among author, text, and audience through investigation of settings, both spatial and temporal; characters; plot; and narrative techniques (e.g., irony, parody, intertextual allusions). Reader-response critics attend to the impact that the text has on the reader or hearer. They recognize that when a text is detrimental toward women there is the choice either to affirm the text or to read against the grain toward a liberative end. Rhetorical criticism analyzes the style of argumentation and attends to how the author is attempting to shape the thinking or actions of the hearer. Structuralist critics analyze the complex patterns of binary oppositions in the text to derive its meaning.[24] Post-structuralist approaches challenge the notion that there are fixed meanings to any biblical text or that there is one universal truth. They engage in close readings of the text and often engage in intertextual analysis.[25] Within this approach is deconstructionist criticism, which views the text as a site of conflict, with competing narratives. The interpreter aims to expose the fault lines and overturn and reconfigure binaries by elevating the underling of a pair and foregrounding it.[26] Feminists also use other postmodern approaches, such as ideological and autobiographical criticism. The former analyzes the system of ideas that underlies the power and values concealed in the text as well as that of the interpreter.[27] The latter involves deliberate self-disclosure while reading the text as a critical exegete.[28] Performance criticism attends to how the text was passed on orally, usually in communal settings, and

24. See, e.g., David Jobling, *The Sense of Biblical Narrative: Three Structural Analyses in the Old Testament*, JSOTSup 7 (Sheffield: Sheffield University, 1978).

25. See, e.g., Stephen D. Moore, *Poststructuralism and the New Testament: Derrida and Foucault at the Foot of the Cross* (Minneapolis: Fortress Press, 1994); *The Bible in Theory: Critical and Postcritical Essays* (Atlanta, GA: SBL, 2010); Yvonne Sherwood, *A Biblical Text and Its Afterlives: The Survival of Jonah in Western Culture* (Cambridge: Cambridge University Press, 2000).

26. David Penchansky, "Deconstruction," in *The Oxford Encyclopedia of Biblical Interpretation*, ed. Steven McKenzie (New York: Oxford University Press, 2013), 196–205. See, for example, Danna Nolan Fewell and David M. Gunn, *Gender, Power, and Promise: The Subject of the Bible's First Story* (Nashville, TN: Abingdon, 1993); David Rutledge, *Reading Marginally: Feminism, Deconstruction and the Bible*, BibInt 21 (Leiden: Brill, 1996).

27. See Tina Pippin, ed., *Ideological Criticism of Biblical Texts: Semeia* 59 (1992); Terry Eagleton, *Ideology: An Introduction* (London: Verso, 2007).

28. See, e.g., Ingrid Rose Kitzberger, ed., *Autobiographical Biblical Interpretation: Between Text and Self* (Leiden: Deo, 2002); P. J. W. Schutte, "When *They, We*, and the Passive Become *I*—Introducing Autobiographical Biblical Criticism," *HTS Teologiese Studies / Theological Studies* vol. 61 (2005): 401–16.

to the verbal and nonverbal interactions between the performer and the audience.[29]

From the beginning, feminists have understood that interpreting the Bible is an act of power. In recent decades, feminist biblical scholars have developed hermeneutical theories of the ethics and politics of biblical interpretation to challenge the claims to value neutrality of most academic biblical scholarship. Feminist biblical scholars have also turned their attention to how some biblical writings were shaped by the power of empire and how this still shapes readers' self-understandings today. They have developed hermeneutical approaches that reveal, critique, and evaluate the interactions depicted in the text against the context of empire, and they consider implications for contemporary contexts.[30] Feminists also analyze the dynamics of colonization and the mentalities of colonized peoples in the exercise of biblical interpretation. As Kwok Pui-lan explains, "A postcolonial feminist interpretation of the Bible needs to investigate the deployment of gender in the narration of identity, the negotiation of power differentials between the colonizers and the colonized, and the reinforcement of patriarchal control over spheres where these elites could exercise control."[31] Methods and models from sociology and cultural anthropology are used by feminists to investigate women's everyday lives, their experiences of marriage, childrearing, labor, money, illness, etc.[32]

29. See, e.g., Holly Hearon and Philip Ruge-Jones, eds., *The Bible in Ancient and Modern Media: Story and Performance* (Eugene, OR: Cascade Books, 2009).

30. E.g., Gale Yee, ed., *Judges and Method: New Approaches in Biblical Studies* (Minneapolis: Fortress Press, 1995); Warren Carter, *The Gospel of Matthew in Its Roman Imperial Context* (London: T & T Clark, 2005); *The Roman Empire and the New Testament: An Essential Guide* (Nashville, TN: Abingdon, 2006); Elisabeth Schüssler Fiorenza, *The Power of the Word: Scripture and the Rhetoric of Empire* (Minneapolis: Fortress, 2007); Judith E. McKinlay, *Reframing Her: Biblical Women in Postcolonial Focus* (Sheffield: Sheffield Phoenix Press, 2004).

31. Kwok Pui-lan, *Postcolonial Imagination and Feminist Theology* (Louisville, KY: Westminster John Knox, 2005), 9. See also Musa W. Dube, ed., *Postcolonial Feminist Interpretation of the Bible* (St. Louis, MO: Chalice, 2000); Cristl M. Maier and Carolyn J. Sharp, *Prophecy and Power: Jeremiah in Feminist and Postcolonial Perspective* (London: Bloomsbury, 2013).

32. See, for example, Carol Meyers, *Discovering Eve: Ancient Israelite Women in Context* (New York: Oxford University Press, 1991); Luise Schottroff, *Lydia's Impatient Sisters: A Feminist Social History of Early Christianity*, trans. Barbara and Martin Rumscheidt (Louisville, KY: Westminster John Knox, 1995); Susan Niditch, *"My Brother Esau Is a Hairy Man": Hair and Identity in Ancient Israel* (Oxford: Oxford University Press, 2008).

As feminists have examined the construction of gender from varying cultural perspectives, they have become ever more cognizant that the way gender roles are defined within differing cultures varies radically. As Mary Ann Tolbert observes, "Attempts to isolate some universal role that cross-culturally defines 'woman' have run into contradictory evidence at every turn."[33] Some women have coined new terms to highlight the particularities of their socio-cultural context. Many African American feminists, for example, call themselves *womanists* to draw attention to the double oppression of racism and sexism they experience.[34] Similarly, many US Hispanic feminists speak of themselves as *mujeristas* (*mujer* is Spanish for "woman").[35] Others prefer to be called "Latina feminists."[36] Both groups emphasize that the context for their theologizing is *mestizaje* and *mulatez* (racial and cultural mixture), done *en conjunto* (in community), with *lo cotidiano* (everyday lived experience) of Hispanic women as starting points for theological reflection and the encounter with the divine. Intercultural analysis has become an indispensable tool for working toward justice for women at the global level.[37]

Some feminists are among those who have developed lesbian, gay, bisexual, and transgender (LGBT) interpretation. This approach focuses on issues of sexual identity and uses various reading strategies. Some point out the ways in which categories that emerged in recent centuries are applied anachronistically to biblical texts to make modern-day judgments. Others show how the Bible is silent on contemporary issues about

---

33. Mary Ann Tolbert, "Social, Sociological, and Anthropological Methods," in *Searching the Scriptures*, 1:255–71, here 265.

34. Alice Walker coined the term (*In Search of Our Mothers' Gardens: Womanist Prose* [New York: Harcourt Brace Jovanovich, 1967, 1983]). See also Katie G. Cannon, "The Emergence of Black Feminist Consciousness," in *Feminist Interpretation of the Bible*, ed. Letty M. Russell (Philadelphia: Westminster, 1985), 30–40; Nyasha Junior, "Womanist Biblical Interpretation," in *Engaging the Bible in a Gendered World: An Introduction to Feminist Biblical Interpretation in Honor of Katharine Doob Sakenfeld*, ed. Linda Day and Carolyn Pressler (Louisville, KY: Westminster John Knox, 2006), 37–46; Renita Weems, *Just a Sister Away: A Womanist Vision of Women's Relationships in the Bible* (San Diego: Lura Media, 1988).

35. Ada María Isasi-Díaz (*Mujerista Theology: A Theology for the Twenty-first Century* [Maryknoll, NY: Orbis Books, 1996]) is credited with coining the term.

36. E.g., María Pilar Aquino, Daisy L. Machado, and Jeanette Rodríguez, eds., *A Reader in Latina Feminist Theology* (Austin: University of Texas Press, 2002).

37. See, e.g., María Pilar Aquino and María José Rosado-Nunes, eds., *Feminist Intercultural Theology: Latina Explorations for a Just World*, Studies in Latino/a Catholicism (Maryknoll, NY: Orbis Books, 2007).

sexual identity. Still others examine same-sex relationships in the Bible by figures such as Ruth and Naomi or David and Jonathan. In recent years, queer theory has emerged; it emphasizes the blurriness of boundaries not just of sexual identity but also of gender roles. Queer critics often focus on texts in which figures transgress what is traditionally considered proper gender behavior.[38]

Feminists also recognize that the struggle for women's equality and dignity is intimately connected with the struggle for respect for Earth and for the whole of the cosmos. Ecofeminists interpret Scripture in ways that highlight the link between human domination of nature and male subjugation of women. They show how anthropocentric ways of interpreting the Bible have overlooked or dismissed Earth and Earth community. They invite readers to identify not only with human characters in the biblical narrative but also with other Earth creatures and domains of nature, especially those that are the object of injustice. Some use creative imagination to retrieve the interests of Earth implicit in the narrative and enable Earth to speak.[39]

Biblical Authority

By the late nineteenth century, some feminists, such as Elizabeth Cady Stanton, began to question openly whether the Bible could continue to be regarded as authoritative for women. They viewed the Bible itself as the source of women's oppression, and some rejected its sacred origin and saving claims. Some decided that the Bible and the religious traditions that enshrine it are too thoroughly saturated with androcentrism and patriarchy to be redeemable.[40]

---

38. See, e.g., Bernadette J. Brooten, *Love between Women: Early Christian Responses to Female Homoeroticism* (Chicago and London: University of Chicago Press, 1996); Mary Rose D'Angelo, "Women Partners in the New Testament," *JFSR* 6 (1990): 65–86; Deirdre J. Good, "Reading Strategies for Biblical Passages on Same-Sex Relations," *Theology and Sexuality* 7 (1997): 70–82; Deryn Guest, *When Deborah Met Jael: Lesbian Feminist Hermeneutics* (London: SCM, 2011); Teresa Hornsby and Ken Stone, eds., *Bible Trouble: Queer Readings at the Boundaries of Biblical Scholarship* (Atlanta, GA: SBL, 2011).

39. E.g., Norman C. Habel and Peter Trudinger, *Exploring Ecological Hermeneutics*, SBLSymS 46 (Atlanta, GA: SBL, 2008); Mary Judith Ress, *Ecofeminism in Latin America*, Women from the Margins (Maryknoll, NY: Orbis Books, 2006).

40. E.g., Mary Daly, *Beyond God the Father: A Philosophy of Women's Liberation* (London: The Women's Press, 1986).

In the Wisdom Commentary series, questions such as these may be raised, but the aim of this series is not to lead readers to reject the authority of the biblical text. Rather, the aim is to promote better understanding of the contexts from which the text arose and of the rhetorical effects it has on women and men in contemporary contexts. Such understanding can lead to a deepening of faith, with the Bible serving as an aid to bring flourishing of life.

Language for God

Because of the ways in which the term "God" has been used to symbolize the divine in predominantly male, patriarchal, and monarchical modes, feminists have designed new ways of speaking of the divine. Some have called attention to the inadequacy of the term *God* by trying to visually destabilize our ways of thinking and speaking of the divine. Rosemary Radford Ruether proposed *God/ess*, as an unpronounceable term pointing to the unnameable understanding of the divine that transcends patriarchal limitations.[41] Some have followed traditional Jewish practice, writing *G-d*. Elisabeth Schüssler Fiorenza has adopted *G*d*.[42] Others draw on the biblical tradition to mine female and non-gender-specific metaphors and symbols.[43] In Wisdom Commentary, there is not one standard way of expressing the divine; each author will use her or his preferred ways. The one exception is that when the tetragrammaton, YHWH, the name revealed to Moses in Exodus 3:14, is used, it will be without vowels, respecting the Jewish custom of avoiding pronouncing the divine name out of reverence.

Nomenclature for the Two Testaments

In recent decades, some biblical scholars have begun to call the two Testaments of the Bible by names other than the traditional nomencla-

41. Rosemary Radford Ruether, *Sexism and God-Talk: Toward a Feminist Theology* (Boston: Beacon, 1983).

42. Elisabeth Schüssler Fiorenza, *Jesus: Miriam's Child, Sophia's Prophet; Critical Issues in Feminist Christology* (New York: Continuum, 1994), 191 n. 3.

43. E.g., Sallie McFague, *Models of God: Theology for an Ecological, Nuclear Age* (Philadelphia: Fortress Press, 1987); Catherine LaCugna, *God for Us: The Trinity and Christian Life* (San Francisco: Harper Collins, 1991); Elizabeth A. Johnson, *She Who Is: The Mystery of God in Feminist Theological Discourse* (New York: Crossroad, 1992). See further Elizabeth A. Johnson, "God," in *Dictionary of Feminist Theologies*, 128–30.

ture: Old and New Testament. Some regard "Old" as derogatory, implying that it is no longer relevant or that it has been superseded.
Consequently, terms like Hebrew Bible, First Testament, and Jewish
Scriptures and, correspondingly, Christian Scriptures or Second Testament have come into use. There are a number of difficulties with these
designations. The term "Hebrew Bible" does not take into account that
parts of the Old Testament are written not in Hebrew but in Aramaic.[44]
Moreover, for Roman Catholics, Anglicans, and Eastern Orthodox believers, the Old Testament includes books written in Greek—the Deuterocanonical books, considered Apocrypha by Protestants. The term "Jewish
Scriptures" is inadequate because these books are also sacred to Christians. Conversely, "Christian Scriptures" is not an accurate designation
for the New Testament, since the Old Testament is also part of the Christian Scriptures. Using "First and Second Testament" also has difficulties,
in that it can imply a hierarchy and a value judgment.[45] Jews generally
use the term Tanakh, an acronym for Torah (Pentateuch), Nevi'im
(Prophets), and Ketuvim (Writings).

In Wisdom Commentary, if authors choose to use a designation other
than Tanakh, Old Testament, and New Testament, they will explain how
they mean the term.

Translation

Modern feminist scholars recognize the complexities connected with
biblical translation, as they have delved into questions about philosophy
of language, how meanings are produced, and how they are culturally
situated. Today it is evident that simply translating into gender-neutral
formulations cannot address all the challenges presented by androcentric
texts. Efforts at feminist translation must also deal with issues around
authority and canonicity.[46]

Because of these complexities, the editors of Wisdom Commentary
series have chosen to use an existing translation, the New Revised Standard Version (NRSV), which is provided for easy reference at the top of
each page of commentary. The NRSV was produced by a team of ecumenical and interreligious scholars, is a fairly literal translation, and uses

---

44. Gen 31:47; Jer 10:11; Ezra 4:7–6:18; 7:12-26; Dan 2:4–7:28.
45. See Levine, *The Misunderstood Jew*, 193–99.
46. Elizabeth Castelli, *"Les Belles Infidèles*/Fidelity or Feminism? The Meanings of
Feminist Biblical Translation," in *Searching the Scriptures*, 1:189–204, here 190.

inclusive language for human beings. Brief discussions about problematic translations appear in the inserts labeled "Translation Matters." When more detailed discussions are available, these will be indicated in footnotes. In the commentary, wherever Hebrew or Greek words are used, English translation is provided. In cases where a wordplay is involved, transliteration is provided to enable understanding.

Art and Poetry

Artistic expression in poetry, music, sculpture, painting, and various other modes is very important to feminist interpretation. Where possible, art and poetry is included in the print volumes of the series. In a number of instances, these are original works created for this project. Regrettably, copyright and production costs prohibit the inclusion of color photographs and other artistic work. It is our hope that the web version will allow a greater collection of such resources.

Glossary

Because there are a number of excellent readily-available resources that provide definitions and concise explanations of terms used in feminist theological and biblical studies, this series will not include a glossary. We refer you to works such as *Dictionary of Feminist Theologies*, edited by Letty M. Russell with J. Shannon Clarkson (Louisville: Westminster John Knox, 1996), and volume 1 of *Searching the Scriptures*, edited by Elisabeth Schüssler Fiorenza with the assistance of Shelly Matthews (New York: Crossroad, 1992). Individual authors in the Wisdom Commentary series will define the way they are using terms that may be unfamiliar.

Bibliography

Because bibliographies are quickly outdated and because the space is limited, only a list of Works Cited is included in the print volumes. A comprehensive bibliography for each volume is posted on a dedicated website and is updated regularly.

The link for this volume is: wisdomcommentary.org.

A Concluding Word

In just a few short decades, feminist biblical studies has grown exponentially, both in the methods that have been developed and in the number of scholars who have embraced it. We realize that this series is limited and will soon need to be revised and updated. It is our hope that Wisdom Commentary, by making the best of current feminist biblical scholarship available in an accessible format to ministers, preachers, teachers, scholars, and students, will aid all readers in their advancement toward God's vision of dignity, equality, and justice for all.

Authors' Introduction

Searching for Sophia

In *Searching the Scriptures*, a pioneering feminist commentary on early christian writings, Elisabeth Schüssler Fiorenza classes Hebrews, with other New Testament (NT) epistolary literature, among the "submerged traditions of Sophia."[1] This classification is not necessarily reflected in the commentaries on the letters, but it relates to her metaphor for Scripture as the house of Sophia, divine Wisdom:

> It is the open, cosmic house of divine Wisdom. Her dwelling of cosmic dimensions has no walls; she permeates the whole world. Her inviting table, with the bread of sustenance and the wine of celebration, is set between seven cosmic pillars that allow the spirit of fresh air to blow where it will. This image does not allow for an understanding of canonical authority as exclusive and commanding. Rather, it grasps the original Latin meaning of *augere/auctoritas* as nurturing creativity, flowering growth, and enhancing enrichment. Biblical authority should foster such creativity, strength, and freedom.[2]

Nonetheless, in feminist theological/thealogical discourse, personified Wisdom as a female God-figure is, as Silvia Schroer notes, not "a priori

---

1. Elisabeth Schüssler Fiorenza, ed., *Searching the Scriptures*, vol. 2: *A Feminist Commentary* (New York: Crossroad, 1994), vi–vii.
2. Elisabeth Schüssler Fiorenza, "Transgressing Canonical Boundaries," in *Searching the Scriptures*, 2:11.

. . . a viable theological option."[3] Athalya Brenner observes that the prominence of personified Sophia in the Wisdom corpus (especially Proverbs, Wisdom, and Sirach) can be viewed in two ways: as a manifestation of male constructions of women and femininity, or as "suppressed, submerged or silenced traces of women's traditions."[4] In Christian feminist theology, Elizabeth A. Johnson has shown in her book *She Who Is* that the biblical image of Wisdom, personified as Mother-Sophia, Christ-Sophia, and Spirit-Sophia, provides a rich vein of female God-language for feminist theological reflection, grounded in both Scripture and tradition.[5] The Wisdom literature in particular portrays Sophia as:

- a unique manifestation of the divine image (Wis 7:25-26)
- a preexistent mediator of creation (Prov 8:22-31; Wis 7:22; 8:6)
- the one who orders and sustains creation and good governance among human beings (Wis 8:1; Prov 8:15)
- a redeemer whose saving deeds are apparent throughout history (Wis 10:1–19:17)
- an all-pervading spirit who holds the universe together (Wis 7:22-23) and inspires "friends of God and prophets" (Wis 7:27)
- one who accompanies human beings through hard times (Wis 10:17-18)
- one who imparts the divine gift of life (Prov 8:35; Wis 8:5), who enlightens, nourishes, teaches, and guides (Prov 9:5)
- one who judges wrongdoing (Prov 1:20-33) and triumphs over evil (Wis 7:29-30)
- one who dwells with Israel (Sir 24:8, 10-12) and embodies Torah (Sir 24:23; Bar 3:37)

The NT Scriptures associate the Wisdom tradition with their own experience of Jesus:

- The Pauline tradition calls Jesus the power of God and the Wisdom of God (1 Cor 1:22-24); the mediator of creation (1 Cor 8:6); and the image of the invisible One and the firstborn of creation (Col 1:15).

3. Silvia Schroer, "The Book of Sophia," in *Searching the Scriptures*, 2:19.

4. Athalya Brenner, ed., *A Feminist Companion to Wisdom Literature* FCB 9 (Sheffield: Sheffield Academic Press, 1995), 13.

5. Elizabeth A. Johnson, *She Who Is: The Mystery of God in Feminist Theological Discourse* (New York: Crossroad, 1996).

- Luke portrays Jesus as a child of Sophia who justifies her and is rejected by Jewish authorities (7:35; see also *1 Enoch* 4:1-2).

- Matthew portrays Jesus as an embodiment of Sophia who speaks her words and performs her deeds (11:28-30; see also Sir 6:23-31) and who is rejected in Jerusalem (Matt 23:37-39).

- John, especially, is "suffused with wisdom themes. Seeking and finding, feeding and nourishing, revealing and enlightening, giving life, making people friends of God, shining as light in the darkness, being the way, the truth, and the life: these are but some of the ways Jesus embodies *Sophia's* roles and is interpreted as Wisdom herself."[6]

The above summary of the scriptural portrayal of Sophia is based on an essay by Elizabeth Johnson, but she mentions Hebrews only in passing.[7] One of the major tasks of this commentary will be to excavate the sophialogy of Hebrews by uncovering its foundations in Jewish Wisdom literature and by recovering the implications of this submerged Wisdom discourse for the feminist theological appreciation—and critique—of Hebrews. It will also seek to examine this biblical text from liturgical, postcolonial, and theological perspectives by strengthening interdisciplinary approaches in keeping with the mandate of the Wisdom Commentary Series. It is hoped that such an examination will offer food for thought, promote change in the pastoral and liturgical traditions of the church, and encourage the growth of faith communities.

Hebrews and Wisdom

Hebrews shows an extensive knowledge of the Jewish Scriptures, with many quotations and allusions to books from the Torah, the Prophets, and the Writings.[8] Arguably, however, the Jewish Scripture with which Hebrews has the most affinities is the deuterocanonical book of Wisdom (or Wisdom of Solomon). Scholars often regard both Wisdom and Hebrews as influenced by the Hellenistic Jewish form of scriptural interpretation informed by Greek philosophy and associated with Alexandria and its

---

6. Elizabeth A. Johnson, "Wisdom Was Made Flesh and Pitched Her Tent Among Us," in *Reconstructing the Christ Symbol: Essays in Feminist Christology*, ed. Maryanne Stevens (New York: Paulist Press, 1993; repr. Eugene, OR: Wipf & Stock, 2004), 95–117, at 104.

7. Ibid., 103, on Heb 1:3.

8. See Harold Attridge, *The Epistle to the Hebrews: A Commentary*, Hermeneia (Philadelphia: Fortress Press, 1989), 23–27.

most prolific practitioner, Philo Judaeus. While the Alexandrian origin of Wisdom is a near-consensus view,[9] the connection of Hebrews with the "Alexandrian school" is less certain. However, as James Thompson notes:

> Since the seventeenth century, scholars have noticed the affinities between the argument of Hebrews and the biblical expositions of Philo of Alexandria (ca. 20 BC–AD 40), who consistently employed Platonic categories in his interpretation of the OT, maintaining that the Greek sages were indebted to the Pentateuch for their wisdom.[10]

Martin Luther's frequently cited suggestion that Hebrews was written by Paul's Alexandrian associate Apollos[11] has been favored by some contemporary scholars "because of his Alexandrian background, his connection to the Pauline circle, and his reputation as a powerful preacher whose style could be distinguished from Paul's."[12]

Hebrews never quotes the book of Wisdom, but the words of Wisdom's Sophia aretalogy (7:22–8:1) are paraphrased in the prologue:

> He [Jesus] is the reflection of God's glory and the exact imprint of God's very being, and he sustains all things by his powerful word. (Heb 1:3)

> She [Wisdom] is a reflection of the eternal light, a spotless mirror of the working of God, and an image of his goodness. . . . She reaches mightily from one end of the earth to the other, and she orders all things well. (Wis 7:26; 8:1)

Like Sophia, Christ, the "word" of God, is a mediator of creation (Heb 1:2; Wis 7:22–8:1), enthroned with God (Heb 1:3; 12:2; Wis 9:4, 10), a savior and leader of the people of God (Heb 7:25; 12:2; Wis 10:1–11:14).

In her commentary on the book of Wisdom, Silvia Schroer calls Sophia "a divine agent of salvation and leader of the exodus,"[13] which well describes Jesus in Hebrews, who leads the faithful from the earthly Sinai

---

9. See Schroer, "Book of Sophia," 21.

10. James W. Thompson, *Hebrews*, Paideia Commentaries on the New Testament (Grand Rapids, MI: Baker Academic, 2008), 23–24. The reference is to Ceslas Spicq, *L'Épître aux Hébreux* (Paris: Lecoffre, 1952).

11. See Acts 18:24; 19:1; 1 Cor 1:12; 3:4, 5, 6, 22; 4:6; 16:12; Titus 3:13.

12. Alan C. Mitchell, *Hebrews*, SP 13 (Collegeville, MN: Liturgical Press, 2009), 4; supporters of this view include Paul Ellingworth, *The Epistle to the Hebrews*, NIGTC (Grand Rapids, MI: Eerdmans, 1993), 11; Donald A. Hagner, *Encountering the Book of Hebrews: An Exposition* (Grand Rapids, MI: Eerdmans, 2002), 23; and Victor C. Pfitzner, *Hebrews*, ANTC (Nashville, TN: Abingdon, 1977), 26.

13. Schroer, "Book of Sophia," 33.

to the heavenly Zion (Heb 12:18-24). Other points of resemblance between Hebrews and Wisdom include the following:

- belief in the Greek concept of the immortality of the soul for the righteous (Wis 1:13; 3:4; 5:15; 6:18-19; Heb 5:9; 9:12, 15), combined with the Jewish notion of judgment (Wis 3:18; 4:20–5:8; Heb 6:2; 9:27; 10:27, 29, 30; 12:23; 13:4)

- preference for the permanent and divine over the impermanent and earthly (Wis 5:9-14; Heb 12:25-29)

- notion of the earthly temple as a reflection of the heavenly tabernacle (Wis 9:8; Heb 8:2, 5; 9:8, 11; 13:10)

- emphasis on the exodus narrative (Wis 10–19; Heb 3:1-19; 11:23-27)

- notion of covenants with the ancestors (Wis 12:21; 18:22; Heb 8:6, 10; 10:16)

- catalogue of heroes of sacred history (Wis 10–19; Heb 11)

- use of athletic metaphors (Wis 4:2; Heb 5:13-14;[14] 12:1-4)

- use of nautical images (Wis 5:10; 14:1-7; see also 10:4; Heb 2:1; 6:19)

- use of language of *paideia* (instruction/discipline) with regard to moral and spiritual development (Wis 3:11; 6:17; Heb 5:11-14)

- metaphor of word of God as a sword (Wis 18:15-16; Heb 4:12)

Schroer describes Wisdom as expressing "an internal posture of distance toward current attitudes to life in their cultural environment . . . and a strong orientation toward the divine or heavenly world and order of things that could be experienced in the past and present and was accepted as a certainty for the future."[15] Overall, this view also applies well to the worldview of Hebrews. While these similarities do not prove that the author of Hebrews used Wisdom as a source, they do indicate that the two documents originated within the intellectual milieu of the kind of Hellenistic philosophical Judaism associated with Alexandria in the first centuries BCE (Wisdom) and CE (Hebrews).

Hebrews also has affinities with other Scriptures in the Wisdom tradition, e.g., the portrayal of Jesus-Word/Wisdom as God's firstborn child

14. See Thompson, *Hebrews*, 131.
15. Schroer, "Book of Sophia," 28.

(Heb 1:5, 10; see also Prov 8:22-23; Sir 24:5) and as heavenly priest (Heb 4:14; 5:6, 10; 7:17, 24, 26; 8:1; 9:7, 11; 10:21; see also Sir 24:10). As Cynthia Briggs Kittredge notes, Hebrews shares with the Wisdom tradition "the interpretation of human suffering as the discipline of God, characteristic of Proverbs and other wisdom literature,"[16] and, in general, Hebrews has affinities "with both apocalyptic and wisdom perspectives."[17]

Despite the similarities between Hebrews and the book of Wisdom in particular, and the Wisdom tradition in general, the presence of Sophia is indeed, as Schüssler Fiorenza puts it, "submerged" throughout the discourse. The feminine-gendered term "wisdom" (σοφία) is never used; like the Gospel of John, whose Christology is informed by the attributes of divine Wisdom, the author of Hebrews portrays Christ as the grammatically neuter "word" (ῥῆμα; John: λόγος) to express Jesus' relationship to God (Heb 1:3).[18] Adele Reinhartz's remarks about the Johannine prologue's use of *logos* could equally well be applied to Hebrews: "When the ungendered [non-personified] Logos becomes further defined in relation to God, it becomes not female Sophia but the male Son of God."[19] It is notable that although Jesus is sometimes portrayed as possessing wisdom, or as a prophet or even an incarnation of divine Wisdom elsewhere in the NT,[20] neither John nor Hebrews uses the term "wisdom" (σοφία) at all.

Whether or not the absence of the term "wisdom" in Hebrews is due to a deliberate choice on the part of the author to portray Christ in exclusively masculine terms is impossible to say. Despite this, as noted above, from beginning to end Hebrews contains multiple (and often muted) resonances with the book of Wisdom/Sophia, and with the broader Wisdom tradition, that will be brought to the surface throughout the commentary. Thus, like the Wisdom discourse of ancient Israel, He-

16. Cynthia Briggs Kittredge, "Hebrews," in *Searching the Scriptures*, 2:428–54, at 447.

17. Ibid., 430. The only extended treatment of Hebrews and Wisdom from a decidedly non-feminist perspective is Kenneth Schenk, *Understanding the Book of Hebrews: The Story Behind the Sermon* (Louisville, KY: Westminster John Knox, 2005). For further discussion, see Mary Ann Beavis, "Hebrews and Wisdom," in *Mark, Manuscripts, and Monotheism: Essays in Honor of Larry W. Hurtado*, ed. Chris Keith and Dieter T. Roth (London: Bloomsbury, 2014), 201–18.

18. Adele Reinhartz, "The Gospel of John," in *Searching the Scriptures*, 2:564–65.

19. Ibid., 565.

20. E.g., Matt 11:19, 29-30; 12:42; 23:27-28; Mark 6:2; Luke 2:40, 52; 7:35; 11:31, 49; 13:34; 1 Cor 1:24, 30.

brews is "marked by androcentric translation, composition, selection, and projection"[21] and is not intrinsically amenable to the promotion of feminist, or even proto-feminist, interests. The audible, if muted, voice of Sophia in Hebrews attests, however, to the endurance of "an attempt on the part of wisdom circles in the postexilic period to speak to Israel through the image of a woman, and so to relate the image of God to new experiences and to the daily life of Israel in the period of rebuilding after the exile"[22]—an effort analogous to Hebrews' attempt to inspire a discouraged and (from the author's perspective) wavering community.[23]

Feminist Interpretation

To date only a few chapter-length feminist commentaries on Hebrews have been published.[24] Mary Rose D'Angelo sees Hebrews as offering little edification to first-century women readers and even less to modern feminists, with its gender-exclusive language, the emphasis on Christ's suffering, the allegory of the high priesthood of Christ as "the deed of the high priest on the Day of Atonement, a deed reserved not only to men but to a single man," and the arguments for the superiority of Christ's priesthood to the Levitical priesthood, which have often been used to fuel anti-Judaism.[25] She does, however, suggest some ways in which Hebrews serves as a resource for feminist theology and for "the feminist critique of later Christian theology."[26] The heroes list in Heb 11 portrays the witnesses as part of a community of faith that encompasses the reader/audience. Hebrews emphasizes Jesus' humanity (2:11-18; 5:7)

21. Schroer, "Book of Sophia," 19.
22. Ibid.
23. See, for example, Heb 2:1; 6:1-12; 10:25; 12:1-2.
24. Mary Rose D'Angelo, "Hebrews," in *The Women's Bible Commentary*, ed. Carol A. Newsom and Sharon H. Ringe (London: SPCK; Louisville, KY: Westminster John Knox, 1992), 364–67; Kittredge, "Hebrews." Unfortunately, at the time of writing in 2011–12, the third edition of *Women's Bible Commentary*, edited by Carol A. Newsom, Sharon H. Ringe, and Jacqueline E. Lapsley (Louisville, KY: Westminster John Knox, 2012), had not been published. Another relevant contribution in a one-volume feminist commentary that was unavailable at the time of writing is Ulrike Wagener, "Hebrews: Strangers in the World," in *Feminist Biblical Interpretation: A Compendium of Critical Commentary on the Books of the Bible and Related Literature*, ed. Luise Schottroff, Marie-Theres Wacker, and Martin Rumscheidt (Grand Rapids, MI, and Cambridge: Eerdmans, 2012), 857–69.
25. D'Angelo, "Hebrews," 366.
26. Ibid., 367.

as well as grounding its Christology "in philosophical terms that originated as descriptions of Wisdom/Sophia, identifying her as a philosophical creator goddess (Wisd. Sol. 7:22-27)."[27] The image of Christ's
Melchizedekian priesthood and the comparison of Christ to the high
priest provide a model of ministry that transcends criteria of race, class,
and gender and raises questions about the ecclesiastical propagation of
priestly castes.[28] D'Angelo notes the focus of ancient sacrifice on communion with God, as opposed to blood and death, and concludes:

> Hebrews' vision of Christian life as a journey of transformation toward
> communion offers a starting point for rethinking its message. . . . A
> feminist reading must reject the demand for submission to suffering,
> but can look to Jesus' pioneering passage and the "cloud of witnesses"
> (12:1) as an invitation to revere and remember the suffering of the op
> pressed who died without having received the promise and as a call to
> open for all the oppressed a new and living way.[29]

Kittredge makes many of the same points as D'Angelo, e.g., the potential for anti-Jewish interpretation, the communitarian orientation of
the discourse, and the dangers inherent in a theology of suffering.[30] She
gives more attention than D'Angelo does to the hypothesis that Hebrews
was written by Priscilla (first suggested by Adolf von Harnack and revived by Ruth Hoppin; see the section on authorship below),[31] concluding that although the author cannot be identified with certainty, "As an
anonymous work, the Epistle to the Hebrews is one of the early Christian
works for which female authorship is a possibility."[32] She concludes
by noting that Hebrews does not draw attention to the author and that
the author does not claim authority over the addressees, or over anyone at all;[33] from a feminist perspective, this is an appealing lack of
authoritarianism.[34]

---

27. Ibid.
28. Ibid.
29. Ibid.
30. Kittredge, "Hebrews," 438, 439–40, 447–48.
31. Ibid., 431–34; see also D'Angelo, "Hebrews," 365.
32. Kittredge, "Hebrews," 433.
33. Ibid., 450.
34. In addition to these two brief feminist commentaries, the contributions by
Pamela Eisenbaum and Ruth Hoppin to the *Feminist Companion to the Catholic Epistles
and Hebrews*, ed. Amy-Jill Levine, FCNTECW 8 (Cleveland, OH: Pilgrim Press, 2004),
127–46, 147–70, are discussed below.

These contributions to the feminist reception of Hebrews are valuable but few, leaving ample space for further commentary. Since this work is a comprehensive commentary on the entire discourse, no single "feminist method" will suffice. Alice Ogden Bellis defines feminism broadly as "the conviction that women are fully human and thus entitled to equal rights and privileges, and the critique of patriarchy that flows from this conviction."[35] Following from this, feminist biblical interpretation can be defined very simply as a method of interpretation of biblical texts that *presupposes* women's full humanity and equality (the equality of all human beings), *recognizes and celebrates* biblical traditions and interpretations that support these values, and *critiques* biblical traditions and interpretations that imply that women and other marginalized people are inferior socially, intellectually, morally, or spiritually.

The critical aspect of feminist interpretation is often described as a "hermeneutic of suspicion," that is, a perspective that "scrutinizes the presuppositions and interests of interpreters" (i.e., "traditional" understandings of the Bible) as well as "the androcentric [male-centered] strategies of the biblical text itself."[36] In other words, feminist interpreters recognize that the biblical texts were (mostly) written by men and that historically the "authoritative" interpreters of the Bible have been men; therefore it can be assumed that, to some extent, the Bible—and the way it is interpreted—is affected by male/patriarchal bias (it is androcentric). Feminist interpretation is gynocentric ("woman-centered") as opposed to androcentric. Further, Bellis identifies six areas of feminist interpretation of the Bible:[37]

1. investigations of the status and role of women in biblical times

2. the rediscovery and reassessment of overlooked biblical traditions about women

3. the reassessment of well-known biblical texts relating to women

4. the discovery of female images of the divine in the biblical texts

5. the reassessment of translation principles relating to women's concerns

---

35. Alice Ogden Bellis, *Helpmates, Harlots, and Heroes: Women's Stories in the Hebrew Bible* (Louisville, KY: Westminster John Knox, 2007), 229.

36. Ibid., 23.

37. Ibid., 119.

6. explorations of the history of the cultural reception and appropriation of biblical texts about women, e.g., in art, cinema, literature, and music

To this list should be added the critique of biblical passages and interpretations that have been used to limit, dominate, or oppress women and other marginalized people, animals, and nature. In addition to the attempt to hear the muted voice of Sophia in Hebrews through the echoes of the Wisdom tradition throughout the discourse (no. 4 above), the following pages will engage to some extent with the perspectives outlined above, all of which are well-established approaches to feminist exegesis that have not, to date, figured significantly in the interpretation of Hebrews.

Feminism in general, and feminist biblical interpretation in particular, has been critiqued for its white, Eurocentric (and often America–centric) presuppositions, including the assumption that "women" are an undifferentiated class of persons who share common interests, experiences, and forms of oppression and marginalization, irrespective of factors such as race, class, sexual orientation, health, age, and economic status.[38] Further, Schüssler Fiorenza warns that "feminist discourses must also take care not to portray one group of women—for example, lesbians—as a monolithic, essentialist, and undifferentiated group with no competing interests, values, and conflicts."[39] In keeping with the mandate of the Wisdom Commentary Series, this volume engages multiple feminist voices from different social, geographical, and religious locations. Co-authors Mary Ann Beavis and HyeRan Kim-Cragg provide a feminist exegetical voice (Beavis) and a postcolonial feminist critique from a Korean-Canadian perspective (Kim-Cragg), in which Kim-Cragg's expertise in pastoral theology of worship and religious education figures significantly. Contributing authors include the Filipina biblical scholars Ma. Maricel Ibita, a Hebrew Bible scholar, and her sister Ma. Marilou Ibita, a scholar of the Christian Testament. Justin Jaron Lewis is a Jewish studies scholar with a focus on the storytelling imagination. First Nations poet Marie Annharte Baker is an essayist and cultural activist. And Nancy Calvert Koyzis contributes her expertise in proto-feminist historical biblical interpretation. With the exception of the Ibita sisters, the authors are located in Canada. In addition, this commentary has bene-

---

38. See Elizabeth Schüssler Fiorenza, ed., *Searching the Scriptures*, vol. 1: *A Feminist Introduction* (New York: Crossroad, 1993), 16–21.

39. Ibid., 21.

fited from a series of feminist Bible studies on Hebrews, coordinated by the coauthors with a Saskatoon-based interdenominational feminist Christian organization, the Friends of Sophia.

A Multiauthored, Multicultural, Multidisciplinary Approach

Coauthor

The most distinctive contribution that HyeRan Kim-Cragg brings to this commentary is a voice of a practical/pastoral theologian whose main teaching areas are worship and religious education and the interplay between these two disciplines. In order to fully accomplish the goals of this groundbreaking multivolume commentary and accommodate the anticipated audience of this work—which includes preachers, teachers, pastors, ministers, seminarians, and serious students of the Bible—the study of Hebrews must be approached with a view to practical, pastoral, pedagogical, and theological issues rather than solely to biblical scholarship and hermeneutical issues and problems.

Although there are not many liturgical scholars who have explored Hebrews from the perspectives of liturgical studies or liturgical feminist studies, the need and the connection are obvious, given that Hebrews is considered "an anonymous early Christian sermon."[40] Frequent uses of paraenesis from the beginning (1:5-14; 2:1-4) through the end (13:22), with ethical exhortation and encouragement, are sufficient evidence that interpretation of Hebrews requires a pastoral and homiletic approach. It is not hard to find other examples. The liturgical dimensions of the text are exemplified in the description of Jesus as the high priest and in the discussion of the roles of sacrificial rituals. The hymn-like introduction of the text in Heb 1–2 is another example of a liturgical dimension. The reference to an anointing (1:5-7) is a further instance in which a sacramental liturgical theology comes to the fore. In sacramental terms, themes related to sacrificial rituals (6:12-20) can be connected to the practice of baptism as well as to the meaning of *anamnesis* in Eucharist. Finally, Hebrews was the inspiration for an early Christian liturgical prayer that appeals to the earthly and incarnate Christ, who took on human flesh for the sake of the world as mediator and high priest. (See comment on Heb 10:19-20.)

---

40. Kittredge, "Hebrews," 428.

Similarly, there are few religious educators who have explored and employed Hebrews in their teaching or biblical pedagogy. Nevertheless, the concept of vocation, as a crucial topic of pastoral theology, is found in Heb 3:5, where Moses and Jesus are juxtaposed and the meanings of "servant" and "apostle" are delineated. The meaning of the Sabbath as conveyed in Heb 4:4 can also offer some informative teaching material, especially on how the practice of Sabbath is related to ritual, our human act of praise and thanksgiving. While certain passages in Hebrews need to be critically examined in relation to their apparent justification of child abuse and physical punishment of children (11:7; 12:11), there are also instructive references that can be developed in a positive educational way. References to *paideia* regarding the moral education of children (Heb 5:13) and parent-child relationships (Heb 11:23, 24; 12:10) may hold insights for contemporary religious education. At the same time the ancient understanding of *paideia* can be enhanced by scholarship on the history of education. These are only a few examples.

The second methodological perspective employed in this commentary is a postcolonial approach. It is virtually impossible to define what post-colonial biblical criticism is or does in a monolithic manner, yet R. S. Sugirtharajah, one of the most prolific postcolonial biblical scholars to date, proposes a manageable summary: "What postcolonialism does is to enable us to question the totalizing tendencies of European reading practices and interpret the texts on our own terms and read them from our specific locations."[41] Elsewhere he writes: "What post-colonial criticism will do is to bring out to the front . . . marginal elements in the texts, and in the process subvert the traditional meaning."[42] Musa W. Dube, another leading postcolonial scholar, states the goal of postcolonial biblical criticism more bluntly: it is to "know why the biblical text and its Western readers were instruments of imperialism. . . . [G]iven the role of the Bible in facilitating imperialism, how should we read the Bible as postcolonial subjects?"[43] As a feminist scholar from Botswana, Africa, she asks why, according to a traditional story, "when the white man came to our country he had the Bible and we had the land. The white man

41. R. S. Sugirtharajah, ed., *The Postcolonial Bible,* The Bible and Postcolonialism 1 (Sheffield: Sheffield Academic Press, 1998), 16.

42. R. S. Sugirtharajah, "From Orientalist to Post-Colonial: Notes on Reading Practices," *AsJT* 10 (1996): 25.

43. Musa W. Dube, *Postcolonial Feminist Interpretation of the Bible* (St. Louis, MO: Chalice Press, 2000), 4.

said to us, 'let us pray.' After the prayer, the white man had the land and we had the Bible."[44] She presses the issue further by asking how we can work together toward "arresting patriarchy and imperialism" without saving one at the expense of the other, by showing "how the West, the Bible, and imperialism are interconnected."[45]

While postcolonial discourse and scholarship, beginning with Edward Said's *Orientalism* in 1978, became established in other disciplines such as literary criticism and cultural studies, postcolonial biblical criticism only began to make headway in the 1990s. Other theological disciplines have followed. Kwok Pui-lan, a leading postcolonial feminist theologian who has urged other scholars to engage in postcolonial discourse, makes this point: "While biblical and religious scholars have deployed postcolonial theory to scrutinize their respective disciplines, theologians, with a few exceptions, have scarcely paid any attention to this burgeoning field."[46]

In the foreword to Michael N. Jagessar and Stephen Burns's *Christian Worship: Postcolonial Perspectives*, Jione Havea lifts up Kwok's exhortation by commenting: "Christian worship and postcolonial modes of thinking are unlikely companions, so attempting to relate and interweave them would be similar to putting a ceramic bowl with a clay vessel in the same sack."[47] In this regard, the voice of a nonbiblical scholar who attempts to bring postcolonial perspectives into the conversation can be heard as dissenting and strange, standing apart from the dominant place of Western biblical scholarship. Nevertheless, this kind of challenge is rightly encouraged in the present commentary, which affirms "the importance of subject position in the process of interpretation."[48] This unfamiliar voice, speaking to and about Hebrews, is echoed in the multiple voices of postcolonial scholars, in heterogeneous manners, in a way that destabilizes the homogeneous hegemony of Western scholarship and the authority of male-dominated biblical interpretation. The reader may find that this voice is so fused with the others that it is hard to distinguish them. Care and attentiveness on the part of the reader will, however,

---

44. Ibid., 3.

45. Ibid., 42.

46. Kwok Pui-lan, *Postcolonial Imagination and Feminist Theology* (Louisville, KY: Westminster John Knox, 2005), 6.

47. Michael N. Jagessar and Stephen Burns, *Christian Worship: Postcolonial Perspectives* (Sheffield: Equinox, 2001), vi.

48. Barbara E. Reid, "Editor's Introduction to Wisdom Commentary," xviii above.

make it possible to hear the postcolonial voice and discern its insights and limits.

For more than twenty years biblical studies have been informed by and have employed postcolonial approaches. Nevertheless, very few biblical scholars have attempted to interpret Hebrews from postcolonial perspectives. Thus, the attempt here can be regarded as a unique contribution to an evolving interpretive discussion. Readers of this commentary are encouraged to take the conversation between Hebrews and postcolonial points of view further. To employ another metaphor: we might see this commentary and the thoughts and conversations it engenders as the first trimester of a pregnancy, a new life that is starting to form and take shape in the womb but is not yet fully developed. While much growth is required, and labor is also needed to bring it to birth, we are cognizant of how critical this formative stage is for the well-being of the new life. So it is that in this beginning much is at stake, and we will have to dedicate some effort and love to nurture it well.

Jeremy H. Punt from South Africa, one of the very few to embark on the endeavor to apply postcolonial insights to the letter to the Hebrews, provides a rationale for why it is worth pursuing this conversation: "Hebrews is often accorded a marginal status (due to the particular style, imagery and the anonymous nature of the authorship) in the broader canonical context. . . . Such marginality would in itself call for postcolonial investigation."[49] Feminist biblical scholars agree with his view of the marginality of Hebrews due to the distinctive voice found in it.[50]

Another thing that attracts postcolonial thinkers to Hebrews is its unfamiliar language and certain thought patterns that move beyond a polemic or a set interpretation that represents conventional views and instead advance a perspective "that builds on the traditions for those able to move to greater insight."[51] For example, the dualistic notion of purity that is often deployed by patriarchy in a way that designates women's bodies as unclean and inferior can be overturned by using the theology of Hebrews that views purity as sanctification. (For a discussion of this, see the comment on Heb 1:4.)

49. Jeremy H. Punt, "The Letter to the Hebrews," in *A Postcolonial Commentary on the New Testament Writings*, ed. Fernando F. Segovia and R. S. Sugirtharajah, The Bible and Postcolonialism 13 (London: T & T Clark, 2007), 338–68, at 338.

50. Kittredge, "Hebrews," 429.

51. Luke T. Johnson, *The Writings of the New Testament: An Interpretation* (Philadelphia: Fortress Press, 1986), 417.

Picking up on insights in Ronald Williamson's work,[52] Punt argues that some of the content of Hebrews that seems irrelevant to modern readers, such as references to sacrificial practices, actually continues to have value in the twenty-first-century context.[53] They can be used as tools for enhancing a non-Western (even decolonizing) reading of the Bible, lifting up the location of the reader, which is key to a postcolonial biblical criticism.[54]

The postcolonial approach is crucial to feminist biblical and theological interpretation as well. Our feminist lens should be brought to focus on the dynamics in the text, disclosing the binary ways of thinking and imperialist attitudes that are a crucial part of postcolonial approaches. Susanne Scholz puts it this way: "Postcolonial feminist studies also reinforce the early feminist conviction that it is not enough to study the Bible only for academic purposes. They promote biblical exegesis to foster political, economic, and social change in women's lives [and in other marginalized lives]."[55] In fact, our feminist interpretation in the West must include coming to terms with our complacency with respect to the ongoing worldwide effects of the colonial era. Others are calling us to extend the scope of our biblical and theological studies beyond the history of textual traditions or the theological doctrine embedded in the biblical texts to "include issues of domination, Western expansion, and its ideological manifestations, as central forces in defining biblical scholarship."[56]

There have been constructive attempts by several postcolonial feminist scholars to correlate the biblical women who are treated as the "Other" with modern women who are also being "othered" by the history and effects of colonialism. Their work will be introduced in the section on Heb 11, where Rahab is cited as a hero(ine) of faith. Other women, including Hagar in relation to Sarah, and Pharaoh's daughter, will also be discussed in this light. Furthermore, throughout the commentary those women who have been victimized by colonial militarism, including the

---

52. See, e.g., Ronald Williamson, "The Background of the Epistle to the Hebrews," *ExpTim* 87 (1975–76): 232–36.

53. Punt, "Hebrews," 347.

54. HyeRan Kim-Cragg, *Story and Song: A Postcolonial Interplay between Christian Education and Worship* (New York: Peter Lang, 2012), 33–35.

55. Susanne Scholz, *Introducing the Women's Hebrew Bible* (London: T & T Clark, 2007), 101.

56. R. S. Sugirtharajah, *Postcolonial Criticism and Biblical Interpretation* (Cambridge and New York: Cambridge University Press, 2002), 74.

comfort women of Korea and other Asian countries, will be lifted up. One may hear the echoes of these women's voices talking back to the ancient biblical women and vice versa.

Finally, a significant perspective employed here is Asian North American approaches to reading the Bible and ways of doing theology. This is also a valuable contribution to the commentary as a whole and to Hebrews in particular. While the guidelines of the Wisdom Commentary clearly identify the audience as primarily First World readers, the authors are encouraged to give particular attention to imbalances in power, class, and race. Kim-Cragg's multiple identities as a woman, a diaspora Korean married to a Caucasian person living in Canada, a mother of two biracial children, a clergywoman in a liberal denomination that operates within and privileges white Anglo-Eurocentric norms in practices and decision making, to name a few relevant examples, have been key in shaping her perspective on the text. These identities allow her to explore issues connected to being between different cultures while often forcing her to cross many borders and boundaries. Elsewhere she has explored and articulated these particular personal, therefore political, identities to raise the issue of how our identities matter in feminist thinking and feminist praxis.[57] Therefore, she welcomes and appreciates Liturgical Press's willingness to include voices from many parts of the globe while strongly encouraging the authors to incorporate diverse voices and differing interpretations from around the world, showing the importance of social location in the process of interpretation and that there is no one definitive feminist interpretation of a text.

One of the most recent readings of the Bible from Asian North American perspectives is found in the work of Tat-siong Benny Liew.[58] His approach is particularly helpful for achieving the purpose of our commentary in terms of advancing multicultural and postcolonial methodologies. Pondering the importance of Asian American biblical hermeneutics, Liew concludes:

57. HyeRan Kim-Cragg, "Becoming a Feminist Christian: A Korean-Canadian Perspective," in *My Red Couch: And Other Stories on Seeking a Feminist Faith,* ed. Claire Bischoff and Rachel Gaffron (Cleveland, OH: Pilgrim Press, 2005), 183–89; HyeRan Kim-Cragg, "Between and Beyond Asian-ness: A Voice of a Postcolonial Hybrid Korean-Canadian in the Diaspora," in *What Young Asian Theologians Are Thinking,* ed. Leow Theng Huat, The CSCA Christianity in Southeast Asia Series (Singapore: Asian Theological College, 2014).

58. Tat-siong Benny Liew, *What Is Asian American Biblical Hermeneutics? Reading the New Testament* (Honolulu: University of Hawaii Press, 2008), x, xii.

Asian American communities and Bible-reading communities, despite the "race-of-heathens" construction, are not only *not* mutually exclusive but also actively overlapping. . . . Assembling the Bible and Asian America, in other words, is an intentional attempt to appropriate a cultural canon in order to re-create and transform multiple cultures through a form of multicultural critique. . . . The Bible is particularly good for this purpose . . . because it is a collection of texts that was first written by the colonized but then has become instrumental for colonization.[59]

Liew's approach is also compatible with the overall intention of the Wisdom Commentary when it seeks to disclose the intertwined relationships of gender at the center of the analysis of power, authority, ethnicity, race, and class. For example, the reading of an abusive rhetorical pattern in Hebrews (6:9-10; 12:4) overlaps with a culturally conscious and informative critique of the teaching of Confucianism in Korea, "the Way of Three Obediences," which reinforces the subordination of women. Other culturally embedded concepts including *han* and *jeong* will also be examined as a crucial part of an Asian (and particularly Korean) North American biblical hermeneutic. Such intertextual and intercultural readings of the Bible by Asian North Americans can appropriate the intended meanings of the homilist toward re-creating these meanings for the sake of the well-being of women and their respective communities. Such a connection also successfully demonstrates how gender as the center of analysis is closely intertwined with power, authority, culture, and class. (For a further discussion on this matter, see the comment at 10:19-34.)

As far as Asian North American ways of doing theology are concerned, especially liturgical theology, there are abundant resources in the letter to the Hebrews. The practice of ancestral veneration prevalent in East Asian culture, shaped and influenced by Confucianism, sheds light on the ideas of the communion of saints, the pioneers of faith, and the cloud of witnesses (Heb 12:1-2). Here the deep wisdom of another cultural tradition is brought to bear on a Western text. Theological debates around the truth of a syncretistic versus an exclusivist Christian theology can be critically examined in this way. The Jewish traditional experience of the wilderness, articulated in Heb 3, illuminates Jewish women's ritual of communal singing and dancing under the moon and a similar ancient ritual practiced today by Korean women called *Ganggangsullae*, which can be interpreted as a feminist reconstruction. In the same vein of crossing religious and

59. Ibid., x, xii.

cultural boundaries, the symbolic gesture of veiling by Muslim women will be examined in the discussion of the tabernacle and the veil between the outer room and the holy of holies (9:11). Again, one may see how gender intersects with religion, culture, and sexuality.

The other major theme that underlies Asian North American approaches is diaspora identity. Kim-Cragg's own experience of being part of the Korean diaspora in Canada is reflected in and affirmed by the homilist, who explicitly and implicitly (through the journeys of Noah, Abraham, and Moses) paints a picture of life in the diaspora for his audience, "strangers and foreigners on the earth" (11:13). The homilist's emphasis on the ethnic implication of "hospitality," a theme of Heb 13, finds resonances in diaspora identity as well.

Contributing Voices

Ma. Maricel Ibita explores the biblical social value of "group orientation" in Heb 10 from the standpoint of an Asian and a Filipina doctoral researcher of Scriptures in a European university. Because of her experience as a teacher of biblical-theological courses in seminaries and schools in the Philippines and a church-based nongovernmental organization worker, her investigation of "Christ's sacrifice for all" for this Wisdom Commentary leads to four important outcomes, both for her personally and for the interpretation of Hebrews. First, it shows another perspective on Hebrews by investigating a facet of its biblical social background. Second, this entry point from a patriarchal culture leads to a more profound understanding of the need for interpreting the Scriptures from feminist perspectives, especially those theologically revered texts that negatively impact women. Third, it results in a keener perception of how Wisdom is present and incarnated in today's world through the many women we meet, read about, and share our voice with. Finally, it helped Ma. Maricel to integrate in and outside of herself her own passion for studying the Scriptures and today's pressing concerns for women, justice, peace, and integrity of creation.

The contributing voice of Ma. Marilou Ibita expresses her interest in highlighting marginal characters in the biblical text.[60] Since the homily

---

60. See Ma. Marilou S. Ibita, "Fostering Narrative Approaches to Scripture in Asia: The Primary Task of Explicit Recognition," *EAPR* 46 (2009): 124–41, at 130–31, where she discusses the importance of the messages and the challenges that minor characters play in the biblical stories.

speaks scantily of women, she reminds us once again of the women characters evoked by Heb 13:2: "Do not neglect to show hospitality to strangers, for by doing that some have entertained angels without knowing it." Using a narrative approach,[61] particularly characterization, she rereads the roles of the women characters brought to mind by this hospitality command. She explores the characters from a postcolonial and liberationist perspective as she relates the role of the biblical characters to the roles of a particular group of present-day readers: Filipina domestic workers. As a biblical student in Louvain, Belgium, she had the opportunity to accompany a Filipino/a migrant workers' Charismatic prayer group by means of Bible study and Bible sharing. Some of them work as domestic helpers in different parts of Belgium. Her contribution is an attempt to provide an echo of their voices.

As a contributor to this commentary, Justin Jaron Lewis speaks as a Jew. An ordained rabbi and a professor of Jewish Studies, he reads Hebrews in the light of Jewish teachings and sacred texts. Hebrews' faith in Jesus is not his, but its longing for connection with the Shekinah, the Divine Presence, is. His perspective is also that of a feminist man. There is no contradiction here: feminism is liberating for men as well as for women, breaking down oppressive structures that trap those who are assigned power as well as those who are not. And he speaks as a former Christian, having left the church in his late teens and found his way into Judaism in his mid-twenties, that is, in the midpoint of his life so far. His outlook on life and texts remains grounded in that of his parents, Jack Lewis, of blessed memory, a Quaker and scholar of English literature, and feminist Catholic scholar and activist Gertrud Jaron Lewis.

Nancy Calvert-Koyzis explores the proto-feminist writings of women in previous eras as a Christian New Testament scholar and Presbyterian minister who has taught in universities and seminaries both full time and as a sessional for many years. Her educational journey began in Christian communities that used the Bible to keep women in their place and forbade them from having leadership roles in the church and in society. As she furthered her education, she began to realize that she had not been told the whole story: she was not among the first women who questioned traditional male authority. In fact, women had been writing

---

61. See, for example, Kenneth Schenck, "Hebrews as the Re-presentation of a Story: A Narrative Approach to Hebrews," in *Reading the Epistle to the Hebrews: A Resource for Students*, ed. Eric F. Mason and Kevin B. McCruden, RBS 66 (Atlanta, GA: SBL, 2011), 171–88.

about this for centuries, only their voices had not been remembered or heeded. As she learned more about the important contributions of these women she joined Marion Taylor and Heather Weir who endeavored to make the works of these proto-feminist women biblical interpreters known. Proto-feminists' contributions to Hebrews are only the tip of the iceberg, yet they provide an important glimpse into the significant body of literature that exists, offering us the opportunity to see ourselves in a long line of female feminist interpreters.

In a commentary written primarily by Canadian prairie authors (Beavis, Kim-Cragg, Lewis, Annharte) on an authoritative text that is part of a Christian tradition deeply implicated in the colonization, oppression, and cultural genocide of First Nations, it is important to acknowledge that Scripture, and its use as an instrument of imperialism, is subject to postcolonial critique in the local context of "this place": Saskatchewan and Manitoba.[62] Marie Annharte Baker (aka Annharte) is an Anishinabe grandmother and writer. *Indigena Awry* is her most recent poetry book.[63] In 2000, before she became a grandmother, she wrote "Circling Back Grandma-To-Be Writing" predicting her current life:

> Someday, I will be a grandmother. I carefully pick out my grey hairs and lace them on my nearby cactus plant. She is holding them until I am more ready to be a granny. All I do is dress rehearsal. I am just practicing to teach another crop of Indigena. I want to share some of the struggle to be a writer because it is a mysterious process that enfolds before me.
>
> To become middle-aged Anishinabe woman has meant that I have fought most of the way. I wanted to be sure that the next generation is not fed the lies of concocted history of our people. I am Indigenous writer because I am conscious of fighting not only to express my own thoughts but to allow the voices of our ancestors to be heard.
>
> We are at that critical time, as we take back our power as Indigenous women. Cosmetic change or inclusion of culture is not enough. We need a complete return to the healing role of the women's societies. The women's circle is a basic healing group, if the women that take on the responsibility to recognize more than "new age" conventions. I pack a crystal like anyone might do these days.

---

62. See Fernando F. Segovia and Mary Ann Tolbert, eds., *Reading from this Place: Social Location and Biblical Interpretation in Global Perspective* (Minneapolis: Fortress Press, 1995).

63. Marie Annharte Baker, *Indigena Awry* (Vancouver, BC: New Star Books, 2012).

Our reliance on superstition is trendy. Even if I chose to learn about women healing, I'd find it difficult to find a teacher that has not been influenced by the mass-market spirituality industry. I too have magical beliefs. I actually believe in the occasion of our women being honest with each other and themselves. If women across generations share experience, a more true traditional teaching would occur. Most of what is counselling and therapy is an attempt on the part of an individual woman to rid herself of what society has injected into her mind about having an inferior status in life. The woman's power is best known in the circle.[64]

Annharte's contribution to this commentary consists of thirteen pieces, one written for each chapter of Hebrews, with the overall title "Our Stories Are Our Scripture." These do not comment directly on the text of Hebrews, but, as the title of the collection implies, the connection is more conceptual: in response to a Christian Scripture in thirteen chapters, she has written poetic versions of Aboriginal Scriptures, that is, traditional sacred stories, in thirteen poems. Her poems provide a witty and profound counterpoint to the many voices—proto-feminist, feminist, postcolonial, Jewish—that resonate throughout the commentary. Readers are challenged to make their own connections—or disconnects—between the text of Hebrews and the resistant voice of Annharte, which, as Michael J. Gilmour observes of Cree poet Bernice Louise Halfe, implicitly "simultaneously criticizes colonial religion while articulating an entirely different system of belief."[65] The presence of Annharte's poems, based on multiple First Nations traditions, acknowledges the fact that every land is a holy land. On a continent dominated by postcolonial Christianity, the stories counted as sacred by the majority are conveyed by Scriptures grounded in the land of Israel. Most of us living in the Canadian Prairie region of Turtle Island do not know the sacred stories, ceremonies, places, and languages indigenous to this sacred, native land.

In a multiauthored, multicultural commentary such as this one there will inevitably be differences of perspective, style, opinion, and

64. Marie Annharte Baker, *Imprint and Casualties: Poets on Women and Language, Reinventing Memory*, ed. Anne Burke, Readings from the Living Archives of the Feminist Caucus of the League of Canadian Poets, vol. 2 (Fredericton, NB: Broken Jaw Press, 2000), 133–36.

65. See Michael J. Gilmour, "Confronting Colonial Religion and the Anxiety of Influence in Louise Bernice Halfe's *Blue Marrow*," in *Feminist Theology with a Canadian Accent: Canadian Perspectives on Contextual Feminist Theology*, ed. Mary Ann Beavis, Elaine Guillemin, and Barbara Pell (Ottawa: Novalis, 2008), 371–91, at 373.

interpretation—and sometimes even disagreement—among the contributors. The contributions of the various authors appear in different forms and formats: those of the coauthors are mostly interwoven into the main text, while others are highlighted in text boxes, sidebars, and interpretive essays. Although the contributions of the seven authors involved in the project came together in an extraordinarily harmonious process, there will at times be interpretations that are at odds with each other. Rather than attempting to smooth over the (few) disagreements, we have allowed these differing perspectives to remain open for the reader to ponder.

Authorship

Although the author of Hebrews is anonymous, in the Christian canon it has traditionally been classed as one of the letters of Paul. James Thompson notes:

> In Alexandria, where Hebrews was most influential, church leaders attributed the work to Paul and attempted to explain the anonymity of the book. Pantaenus (d. ca. AD 190) suggested that Paul omitted his name because of modesty (Eusebius, *Hist. Eccl.* 6.14.4), while Clement of Alexandria suggested that Paul omitted his name because as the apostle to the Gentiles, he would evoke suspicion among Jewish listeners (Eusebius, *Hist. Eccl.* 6.14.3).[66]

The stylistic and doctrinal differences between Hebrews and the Pauline letters were, however, apparent to some ancient readers. Clement of Alexandria explained the sophisticated Greek style of Hebrews by suggesting that Paul had written the document in Hebrew and Luke had translated it into Greek.[67] Although Origen, also an Alexandrian, sometimes referred to it as a letter of Paul,[68] his famous remark that only God knows who wrote the epistle is frequently cited.[69]

Although the consensus of critical scholarship is that Hebrews was not written by Paul, the book does contain elements reminiscent of the Pauline literature, e.g., the doctrine of Christ as the mediator of creation (Heb 1:1-4; 1 Cor 8:6), the pattern of humiliation-exaltation (Heb 2:9;

---

66. Thompson, *Hebrews*, 4; on Alexandrian affinities with Hebrews, see Craig R. Koester, *Hebrews*, AB 36 (New York: Doubleday, 2001), 20–21.

67. Eusebius, *Hist. Eccl.* 6.14.2.

68. *On First Principles* 1.1; *Commentary on John* 2.72.

69. Eusebius, *Hist. Eccl.* 6.24.11–14.

Rom 8:3, 34; Phil 2:5-11); the image of a new covenant that supplants the Mosaic order (Heb 7:19; 8:6-13; 2 Cor 3:1-18); the personal greetings and admonitions in Heb 13:16-25, including the mention of Timothy (see comment on these verses).[70] These Pauline echoes have prompted scholars to suggest one or another companion of Paul as candidates for authorship: Apollos, the eloquent Alexandrian Jewish-christian[71] and coworker of Paul (Acts 18:24; 1 Cor 3:5-6; 16:12); Barnabas, a Jewish Cypriot of Levitical descent (Acts 4:36), also a companion of Paul (Acts 13:2–15:35); and Silas, a colleague of Timothy and of Paul (Heb 13:23; see also Acts 17:14-15; 18:5; 2 Cor 1:19; 1 Thess 1:1; 2 Thess 1:1).[72] None of these suggestions have received wide acceptance.

From a feminist standpoint the most interesting suggestion regarding the authorship of Hebrews is the Priscilla hypothesis, which, as noted above, was originally formulated by Adolf von Harnack and has been strongly championed more recently by Ruth Hoppin.[73] A missionary colleague of Paul, Priscilla/Prisca, along with her husband Aquila, is said to have instructed the educated Alexandrian Apollos (Acts 18:26). Priscilla and Aquila hosted a house-church in Rome (Rom 16:3-5; see also Heb 13:24) and knew Timothy (2 Tim 4:19); in addition to Rome, they are associated with Ephesus and Corinth (Acts 18–19; Rom 16:3-6, 21; 2 Tim 4:19; see also Heb 13:23). Harnack argues that Hebrews' use of pronouns points to the presence of more than one author, noting that the author's favorite pronoun is "we"; usually the authorial "we" is inclusive of the audience, but there is a distinction between "we" and "you" in passages where the audience is being praised or rebuked.[74] The

70. See also Koester, *Hebrews*, 52–53.

71. Since the term "Christian" was not commonly used in the first century (in the NT it is found only in Acts 11:26: 26:28; and 1 Pet 4:16, referring to followers of Christ, not to devotees of a religion), and "Christianity" did not exist as a religion, the term "christian" will be used henceforth with reference to the earliest members of the kingdom of God movement, including the author and audience of Hebrews. (See also Jane D. Schaberg, "Magdalene christianity," in *On the Cutting Edge: The Study of Women in Biblical Worlds*, ed. Jane D. Schaberg, Alice Bach, and Esther Fuchs [New York: Continuum, 2003], 193–220.) "Christian" and "Christianity" will be used to refer to the world religion that developed in subsequent centuries.

72. See Koester, *Hebrews*, 44.

73. Adolf von Harnack, "The Authorship of the Epistle to the Hebrews," *LCR* 19 (1900): 448–71; Ruth Hoppin, *Priscilla's Letter: Finding the Author of the Epistle to the Hebrews* (Fort Bragg, CA: Lost Coast Press, 1997).

74. Harnack, "Hebrews," 455–56.

authorial "I" is used only in Heb 11:32 and 13:19, 22, 23. The marital relationship between Priscilla and Aquila would explain this use of pronouns, and why their names were eliminated from the document. Although in the NT Priscilla is usually mentioned before her husband because she was probably of higher social standing than Aquila,[75] authorship, or coauthorship, by a prominent female would discredit the writing:

> Paul already was not favorable to the teaching of women [I Cor. 14:34f], but yielded to certain exceptions as his judgment of Prisca further shows [I Cor. 11:5 and Phil. 4:2f]. In the next era probably in consequence of disagreeable experiences they were much more rigoristic. The conflict which was taken up against women teaching in the church—the author of the "Acta Pauli" forms an exception, and which continued until the beginning of the third century, needs not be mentioned here; only recall I Tim. 21: "But I suffer not a woman to teach, nor to usurp authority of the man, but to be in silence. * * * But she shall be saved in child-bearing."[76]

Cynthia Briggs Kittredge offers further evidence for the denigration of women's teaching, even in documents written by women: the female author of the *Letter of Mary the Proselyte to Ignatius* ends with a disclaimer that she does not write to instruct the bishop; Didymus the Blind extends the ban on women's teaching to women's authoritative writing (*On the Trinity* 3.41.3).[77]

In addition to the evidence offered by Harnack, Hoppin detects a "feminine voice" in Hebrews, evidenced by, e.g., the inclusion of women in the list of heroes of faith in Heb 11; the reference to the moral education of children (Heb 5:13); the reference to parent-child relationships (Heb 11:23, 24; 12:10); and the empathetic depiction of the humanity and suffering of Christ (Heb 5:2, 7; 12:2, 3, 18).[78] Hoppin's claims that Hebrews evidences a "feminine psychological profile" and that Priscilla was a Roman from a patrician family who married a Jewish freedman[79] are generally regarded as the least persuasive of her arguments.[80]

---

75. Ibid., 464.
76. Ibid., 468.
77. Kittredge, "Hebrews," 433.
78. Ruth Hoppin, "Priscilla's Letter," in *Catholic Epistles and Hebrews*, 153–59.
79. Ibid., 167–70.
80. E.g., D'Angelo, "Hebrews," 365; Mitchell, *Hebrews*, 5.

Among recent commentators, Kittredge is notable for maintaining that Priscilla, or another educated and prominent woman, is a viable candidate for the authorship of Hebrews.[81] Although most ancient people were illiterate, and more men than women were educated, there is ample evidence that some women were educated and wrote letters, poetry, and philosophy.[82] Among the Therapeutai/Therapeutrides, a Jewish contemplative sect located near Alexandria, both women and men studied Scripture and composed commentaries, hymns, and songs;[83] early Christian works by women include the diary of Perpetua (ca. 203 CE) and the books of oracles of the Montanist prophets Priscilla and Maximilla.[84] Fokkelien van Dijk-Hemmes has adduced extensive evidence of women's texts embedded in the Jewish Scriptures, e.g., songs, wisdom speeches, warning speeches, prophecies, laments, and prayers.[85]

Although female authorship is appealing from a feminist standpoint, and should not be ruled out—as Virginia Woolf famously remarked, throughout history "anonymous" has often been a woman—there is no unequivocal evidence for Hebrews' authorship. Nevertheless, one hint that has not been heeded, except by Harnack and Hoppin, is the homilist's preference for the authorial "we." While the proponents of the Priscilla hypothesis regard this as evidence of Aquila's (secondary) contribution, a more plausible, and eminently feasible, reason for the "we" is that, as is the case with several of Paul's letters, more than one author contributed to the composition,[86] or that a single author was writing on behalf of a community to which she or he belonged. (See also the comment on 13:18-25.) A more collective understanding of authorship incorporating

81. Kittredge, "Hebrews," 433.

82. Ibid., 432, citing Jane McIntosh Snyder, *The Woman and the Lyre: Women Writers in Classical Greece and Rome* (Carbondale: Southern Illinois University Press, 1989). On ancient women's letter-writing, see Roger S. Bagnall and Raffaela Cibiore, with Evie Ahtaridis, *Women's Letters from Ancient Egypt, 300 BC–800 AD* (Ann Arbor: University of Michigan Press, 2006).

83. Philo, *On the Contemplative Life*, 87–89.

84. Kittredge, "Hebrews," 433; for further examples of female authorship of early christian and Jewish writings, see Ross S. Kraemer, *Her Share of the Blessings: Women's Religions among Pagans, Jews, and Christians in the Greco-Roman World* (New York: Oxford University Press, 1993), 221–42.

85. Fokkelien van Dijk-Hemmes, "Traces of Women's Texts in the Hebrew Bible," in *On Gendering Texts: Female and Male Voices in the Hebrew Bible*, ed. Fokkelien van Dijk-Hemmes and Athalya Brenner (Leiden: Brill, 1993), 17–112.

86. See also 2 Cor 1:1; Phil 1:1; Col 1:1; 1 Thess 1:1; 2 Thess 1:1.

both men's and women's voices would be consistent with Kittredge's observation that "this early Christian sermon does not draw attention to its author at all. No claim to authority over the congregation is ever made, and there is no attempt to assert one position above that of the community."[87] Although this commentary favors the hypothesis of collective authorship, for purposes of convenience the term "the homilist" will be used to denote the author(s) throughout (see section on Literary Genre below).

Letter from an Early Christian Woman (ca. 340–350 CE)

This letter, originally written in Greek, was composed in Egypt by a woman called Valeria to the monk Papnouthis to request his prayers for healing:

> To Apa Papnouthis the most honored and Christ-bearing and adorned with every virtue, (from) Valeria, greetings in Christ.
>
> I ask and beg you, most honored father, to ask for me a kindness for Christ that I might obtain healing. I believe that in this way I might obtain healing through your prayers, for revelations of ascetics and worshipers are manifested.

For I am afflicted by a great disease of terrible shortage of breath. I have believed and believe that if you pray on my behalf I will receive healing. I beg of God, I beg also of you, remember me in your holy prayer. Even if in body I have not come to your feet, in spirit I have come to your feet. I greet my daughters, and remember them in your holy prayer, Bassiane and Theokleia. My husband greets you greatly, and pray for him. My whole house also greets you. I pray for your health, most honored father.
(*Source:* Letter 87, quoted in Bagnall and Cibiore, *Women's Letters.*)

Mary Ann Beavis

Date and Place of Composition

The earliest extra-biblical author to quote Hebrews is Clement of Rome, whose letter to the Corinthians (1 Clement) is dated to 96 CE. Craig Koester lists the most prominent similarities between the two documents:[88]

> Jesus is one "who, being the reflection [of] God's majesty is greater than angels to the extent that he has inherited a more excellent name"

---

87. Kittredge, "Hebrews," 450.
88. Koester, *Hebrews*, 22 n. 7.

(*1 Clem.* 36:2/Heb 1:2-4). Jesus is the "high priest of our sufferings" and "helper in our weakness" (*1 Clem.* 36:1; Heb 1:2-4; 4:14-16). There are quotations of Pss 2:7-8; 104:4; 110:1 in *1 Clem.* 36 and Heb 1:5-13. Both authors list examples of Enoch, Noah, Abraham, Rahab, and those who went about "in the skins of sheep and goats" (*1 Clem.* 9:3-10; 12:1-3; 17:1/Heb 11). Both exhort listeners to hasten toward their goal with eyes fixed upon God (*1 Clem.* 19:2/Heb 12:1), caution that God searches people (*1 Clem.* 21:9/Heb 4:12), say that it is impossible for God to lie (*1 Clem.* 27:2/Heb 6:18), recall that Moses was faithful in God's house (*1 Clem.* 43:1/Heb 3:5), quote Prov 3:12 (*1 Clem.* 56:4/Heb 12:6), and identify God as the master or father of spirits (*1 Clem.* 64:1/Heb 12:9).

Although these similarities could be explained with reference to a common source, most scholars maintain that 1 Clement drew from Hebrews.[89] This implies that Hebrews was composed before 96 CE, that it was known both in Rome and in Corinth, and that by Clement's time it had circulated long enough to garner quasi-scriptural status (see also 2 Pet 3:15-16), probably for several decades. The homilist's argument that Christ's high priesthood in the heavenly sanctuary has rendered the Jewish cult obsolete might point to a date after the destruction of Jerusalem (70 CE); however, since Hebrews never refers to the Jerusalem temple, but only to the tabernacle of the wilderness wandering,[90] this connection cannot be made with certainty. Although the homilist refers to the activities of the priesthood in the present tense,[91] as Thompson notes, "writers spoke of the cultic activities in the present tense after the destruction of the temple (Josephus, *Ant.* 3.151-224)."[92]

In addition to the Roman connection with 1 Clement, the epistolary postscript contains a greeting by "those from Italy" relayed by the homilist to the addressees (Heb 13:24), which could mean either that a group of expatriate Italians was greeting their acquaintances back home or that a home community in Italy was addressing compatriots who had settled elsewhere. The former interpretation is generally preferred by commentators.[93] Although in antiquity the term "Italy" referred to the entire Italian peninsula, the only known church community there in the

---

89. Ibid., 22.

90. Heb 8:2, 5; 9:2, 3, 6, 8, 11, 21; 13:10.

91. E.g., Heb 8:4; 13:11.

92. Thompson, *Hebrews*, 7.

93. For examples, see Attridge, *Hebrews*, 410 n. 84; Attridge himself prefers this construal.

first century was in Rome.[94] Even if, as suggested in the commentary on Heb 13:24, the epistolary postscript was added to the body of Hebrews to align it with the Pauline tradition, the mention of Italy may contain a recollection of the original destination of the homily.

Audience and Circumstances of Writing

From its thematic and scriptural content, early interpreters deduced that Hebrews was addressed to believers located in Jerusalem or its environs, thus the appellation *To the Hebrews*.[95] Some modern commentators argue similarly that Hebrews was addressed to Jewish christians who were in danger of rejecting Christ.[96] The "Judaism" of Hebrews is scriptural, however, focused on Moses and the exodus, the wilderness tabernacle, and the rituals associated with it, not on the socio-religious realities of first-century Jewish life. Moreover, Paul and other teachers use Jewish themes, techniques, and Scriptures in their letters to predominantly Gentile communities,[97] and, as Galatians demonstrates, Gentile christians could be attracted to Jewish practices, while a Jew like Paul could vigorously contest them (see also Phil 3:2). The homilist's intent was not to argue for the superiority of "Christianity" over "Judaism" but to interpret the community's experience of salvation history in light of the Jewish Scriptures as mediated through the Septuagint (LXX). Unfortunately, these kinds of arguments have subsequently figured in Christian anti-Judaism, and consequently must be read with caution. (See also the comment on Heb 2:5-18 and the section on Hebrews, Anti-Judaism, and Supersessionism below.)

Another hypothesis is that Hebrews was written in the aftermath of the Roman siege of Jerusalem in order to explain the destruction of the temple and the cessation of the sacrificial cult.[98] This suggestion does not do much to illumine the ethnic identity of the addressees, since both Jewish and

94. Charles H. Miller, "Italy," *Harper's Bible Dictionary*, ed. Paul J. Achtemeier (San Francisco: HarperSanFrancisco, 1985), 438.

95. E.g., Severian of Gabala, *Fragments on the Epistle to the Hebrews Prologue*; Theodore of Mopsuestia, *Fragments on the Epistle to the Hebrews*; both authors attribute the epistle's anonymity to Jewish suspicion of Paul.

96. For examples, see Attridge, *Hebrews*, 11 n. 85; also Iutisone Saleveo, *Legitimation in the Letter to the Hebrews: The Construction and Maintenance of a Symbolic Universe*, JSNTSup 219 (Sheffield: Sheffield Academic Press, 2002), 28–30.

97. E.g., Gal; 1–2 Cor; see also Attridge, *Hebrews*, 12.

98. Marie Isaacs, *Sacred Space: An Approach to the Theology of the Epistle to the Hebrews*, JSNTSup 73 (Sheffield: JSOT Press, 1992), 67.

Gentile christians were no doubt dismayed by the events of the Jewish War (66–70 CE). Further, Hebrews' consistent use of "tabernacle" (σκηνή) rather than "temple" (ἱερόν) militates against this interpretation. The homilist's only reference to Jerusalem is to the heavenly Zion (Heb 12:22), which is contrasted not with the earthly city, as might be expected if its destruction were at issue, but with the earthly Mount Sinai (12:18-21).

Most commentators judiciously opt for a mixed audience of Jewish and Gentile christians, a description that would fit a Roman christian audience or even a group of Romans, like Priscilla and Aquila, expelled from Rome by Claudius in 49 CE (Acts 18:2).[99] The exhortations addressed to the audience refer to a community that in the past had eagerly received spiritual enlightenment (Heb 6:4; see also 10:32) from their leaders (13:7) and had a powerful experience of the age to come (6:5). Subsequently they had suffered imprisonment, seizure of property, and other trials (10:32-34; 12:4-11), although none had actually been martyred (12:4). Some were still in prison (13:3). While in the past the community had retained their solidarity (6:10; 10:32-34), more recently they have lost their fervor (2:1; 3:12; 4:11; 6:11; 10:25, 35), neglecting even to meet together (10:25). In response, the homilist urges them to emulate the endurance of Jesus and the faithful heroes of old (11:1–13:6), since salvation is near (12:22-24).

Several scholars have interpreted the situation of Hebrews in social-scientific terms, e.g., as the experience of a new religious movement undergoing social alienation and public shame,[100] struggling to establish boundaries between the nascent christian confession and Jewish faith,[101] or to create an ideal society in opposition to the Levitical regime of Second Temple Judaism.[102] From a feminist standpoint it should be noted that women are often attracted by the acceptance, promises, and opportunities offered by new religious movements (NRMs)—e.g., gender egalitarianism, leadership, missionary activity, spiritual status—only to be relegated to traditional gender roles as the sect seeks broader social acceptance, or simply to reassert male prestige.[103] If ancient christian

99. Jews were allowed by Nero to return to the city in 54 CE, and the Neronian persecution of christians after the great fire of Rome in 64 CE is well documented.

100. David A. deSilva, *Perseverance in Gratitude: A Socio-Rhetorical Commentary on the Epistle "to the Hebrews"* (Grand Rapids, MI: Eerdmans, 2000).

101. Saleveo, *Legitimation*.

102. Richard W. Johnson, *Going Outside the Camp: The Sociological Function of the Epistle to the Hebrews*, JSNTSup 209 (London and New York: Sheffield Academic Press, 2001).

103. Kraemer, *Her Share of the Blessings*, 146, 154.

communities followed the pattern of some contemporary NRMs, women may have made up a majority of converts,[104] a fact obscured in the NT by the Greek preference for the masculine grammatical form (the audience is characteristically addressed as "brothers") and a cultural predisposition to conceal women's presence. This is especially true in societies where familial honor (in this case, the surrogate family of the *ekklēsia*) depends on the "shame" of its female members by demanding that women adhere to sexually discreet behavior, spatial segregation, and deferral to male authority (see Heb 13:4). For women, a religious system that exhorts its members to eschew public honor and embrace the shame of suffering (see also Heb 10:36-39; 12:7-12) may strategically valorize "feminine" qualities for men, but it does not necessarily liberate women.

Socio-Economic Context

Although Hebrews does not explicitly discuss the socio-economic context and circumstances of writing, David A. deSilva has shown that the discourse contains enough clues for a plausible reconstruction. In contrast to the stereotype that sectarian groups tend to be of lower-class origins, the high literary quality of the homily suggests that both author and audience were not only literate but highly educated, "capable of attending meaningfully to such language and syntax (much freer and independent of word order than other NT texts)." Some members of the community had possessions worth confiscating (Heb 10:34). Moreover, "community members are capable of charitable activity and hospitality (13:2; 10:33b-34a; 13:16) and even appear to need warnings against overambition, both with regard to possessions (13:5) and status (13:14)."[105] That is, at least some of the addressees were people with social status and property to lose, or to renounce voluntarily. Perhaps this is part of the reason why the homilist is so determined to check perceived "denominationalizing tendencies" among the addressees, i.e., the tendency of sectarian groups to adapt to the norms of the broader society in order to avoid conflict: "But we are not among those who shrink back and so are lost, but among those who have faith and so are saved" (10:39). In socio-economic terms, some community members seem to have had much to gain in terms of wealth,

---

104. Elizabeth Puttick, "Women in New Religious Movements," in *New Religious Movements: Challenge and Response*, ed. Bryan Wilson and Jamie Cresswell (New York: Routledge, 1999), 143–45; see also, e.g., Origen, *Against Celsus* 3.10, 44, 49, 55, 56.
    105. DeSilva, "Hebrews," 6.

status, and security if they abandon their faith and return to their former lives:

> Such members have experienced the loss of property and status without yet receiving the promised rewards of the sect and so are growing disillusioned with the sect's promise to provide. . . . The community members have been becoming increasingly interested in regaining a place of honor and prestige in the larger society, of enjoying the fruits of a peaceful and nourishing relationship within the sociocultural environment in place of the hostile relationship which characterized the earlier years of the sectarian movement.

As deSilva notes, the homilist's portrayal of salvation in terms of "inheritance" (Heb 6:12; 9:15) and "property" (10:34) would be particularly relevant to people whose belongings had been, or were in danger of being, confiscated. In contrast, lower-status members might benefit more from sectarian membership in terms of recognition within the community and economic support in times of need.

In gendered terms, loss of "honor and prestige" would be more acutely felt by men than by women, since according to Greco-Roman cultural norms men were associated with the public sphere of "honor" and women with the domestic sphere of "shame," interpreted as sexual propriety and modesty. Female members' vulnerability to external criticism of their sexual behavior in the context of the fictive family offered by the community might, however, make them more inclined to eschew meetings and conform to the expectations of their biological families, or be pressured by relatives to leave the sect in order to restore the family honor. The strong advocacy of marriage and marital faithfulness and the stern warnings against adultery and fornication (Heb 13:4) may be the author's attempt to address women members' reputational concerns in the face of external, or even familial, accusations of immorality.
(*Source*: Quotations are from David A. deSilva, "The Epistle to the Hebrews in Social-Scientific Perspective," *ResQ* 36 [1994]: 1–21.)

Mary Ann Beavis

Genre and Cultural Milieu

As discussed above, Hebrews is literarily and culturally most closely aligned with the form of Hellenistic Judaism associated with Alexandria, particularly with the book of Wisdom and the works of Philo. The similarities between Hebrews and Wisdom have been enumerated above. With respect to Philo, Thompson notes:

> Philo and Hebrews share not only the insistence of the two levels of reality derived from the Platonic tradition; they also cite numerous passages (e.g., Gen 2:2; Exod 25:40; Josh 1:5; Prov 3:11-14) in ways found only in their writings. . . . By far the most remarkable parallel is the way Heb 13:5 splices together Josh 1:5; Deut 31:8; and possibly Gen 28:15 in the same way that Philo does (*Confusion* 66 . . .). Furthermore, as Spicq (1952, 1:39–91) has shown, the two writers share a common vocabulary, mode of exegesis, and major themes. Philo's description of the *logos* employs vocabulary that resembles the christological language of Heb 1:1-4 (see also *Creation* 146; *Cherubim* 127; *Worse* 83). The two writers employ similar arguments to indicate the ineffectiveness of Levitical sacrifices (Heb 9:1-10; 10:1-18; *Moses* 2.107; *Spec. Laws* 1.257–261). Both Philo and the author of Hebrews present lists of examples (Heb 11; Philo, *Virtues* 198–225).[106]

The author's Platonic worldview is best illustrated by the contrast between the heavenly sanctuary and the earthly tabernacle, in which the wilderness tent and its accoutrements were merely "the sketches of the heavenly things" (Heb 9:23). Consistent with Platonic doctrine, the earthly is a transitory reflection of the heavenly ("ideal"), eternal and unchanging. Hebrews also makes extensive use of typological interpretation, however, a sort of historicized Platonism in which persons, places, and events in Scripture are seen as "types" or prefigurations of the new era inaugurated by Christ. For Hebrews, the present reality (antitype) is superior to the type, e.g., Christ is superior to Moses; the priesthood of Christ is better than the Levitical priesthood; the sacrifice of Christ is more effectual than the Levitical sacrifices; the new covenant is better than the old covenant. Thus typological exegesis enables the author to claim both continuity and discontinuity with the sacred history.[107] These features do not necessarily mean that the homilist was from Alexandria, but they do show that she or he was familiar with Alexandrian Jewish modes of exegesis.

Generically, Hebrews is most often identified as having affinities with Hellenistic synagogue homilies because of the reference to the

---

106. Thompson, *Hebrews*, 24.

107. See Mary Ann Beavis, "A Study of the Relation of the Old and New Covenants in the Epistle to the Hebrews, in the Light of Scholarship 1938–1980" (MA thesis, University of Manitoba, 1981).

document as a "word of exhortation" (13:22), a term used in Acts 13:15 to refer to Paul's sermon in the synagogue at Pisidian Antioch.[108] In view of Hebrews' homiletic writing (or speaking) style, which makes extensive use of the Hebrew Scriptures and their distinctively Hellenistic-christian interpretations, one may agree with George Buchanan's generic identification of Hebrews as a "homiletical midrash."[109] Jeremy H. Punt points out that this view of Hebrews would encourage a sense of freedom for modern readers to explore "more adequate ways of doing theology through Jesus Christ."[110]

Hebrews and Gnosticism

In scholarship, "Gnosticism" has become an umbrella term for a variety of forms of early Christian mysticism, dated to the second century and later, that share doctrines of salvation through enlightenment or knowledge (γνῶσις), a disdain for the material over against the spiritual, and cosmological systems in which the task of the enlightened soul after death is to ascend through the heavenly spheres, which are ruled by hostile powers, to the ultimate divine above.

A Homiletical Fragment in the Book of Susanna

Lawrence Wills ("Sermon," 293–94) sees a homiletical application appended to the Old Greek version of the book of Susanna:

> And the whole assembly shouted for the youth, how out of their own mouths he had established them both as false witnesses by their own admission. And as the law states explicitly, they did to them just as they had wickedly intended against their sister. . . . And guiltless blood was saved that day. For this reason youths are beloved by Iakob, because of their simplicity. And as for us, let us watch out for young able sons. For youths will be pious, and a spirit of knowledge and understanding shall be with them forever and ever.
> (*Susanna* 60–61, NETS 1990)

He also identifies the digression on the evils of idolatry in Wis 13–15 as belonging to the homiletical genre.

Mary Ann Beavis

---

108. For other biblical and extra-biblical examples, see Kenneth Wills, "The Form of the Sermon in Hellenistic Judaism and Early Christianity," *HTR* 77 (1984): 277–99.

109. George W. Buchanan, *To the Hebrews: Translation, Comment, and Conclusions* (New York: Doubleday, 1972), xix.

110. Punt, "Hebrews," 349.

Gnosticism has features feminists might find attractive: the notion of the divine spark within; evidence of women as leaders and teachers in some forms of Gnosticism; theological creativity; the prominent role of women in some Gnostic texts; and the presence of female deities in some Gnostic theologies.[111] Other aspects are less appealing: negativity toward the body and matter, birth and death, and biological femaleness; the interpretation of Sophia as a fallen divinity responsible for the generation of the ignorant creator of the material realm; the otherworldly orientation; spiritual elitism; and the tendency to anti-Judaism. The docetic Christology associated with Gnosticism, in which Christ is seen as a heavenly, spiritual being who only appeared to be human, is at odds with Hebrews' emphasis on Jesus' human suffering and compassion for others (e.g., Heb 2:14-18; 4:15; 5:7-8).

The Repentance of Sophia

The Gnostic *Pistis Sophia* ("Faith-Wisdom"; second/third century CE) describes the divine female aeon Sophia as having fallen from the Pleroma (divine fullness) into the material realm. There she repents of her rebellion and is saved by the redeemer Christ. In this excerpt Martha recites and interprets a psalm of repentance uttered by Sophia, and her insight is praised by Jesus:

> Before Jesus had finished speaking, Martha came forward, she prostrated herself at his feet, she kissed them. She cried out, she wept aloud in humility, saying, "My Lord, have mercy on me, and be compassionate towards me, and allow me to say the interpretation of the repentance which the Pistis Sophia said." Jesus gave Martha his hand, he said to her, "Blessed is every man [*sic*] who humbles himself, for to him will mercy be given. Now at this time, Martha, thou art blessed. Nevertheless, give now the interpretation of the thought of the repentance of the Pistis Sophia." Martha answered and said to Jesus in the midst of the disciples: "Concerning the repentance which the Pistis Sophia said, O my Lord Jesus, thy light power which was in David once prophesied in the sixty-ninth Psalm, saying . . .
>
> This now is the interpretation of the third repentance which the Pistis Sophia said, singing praises to the height." When Jesus

111. See Elaine Pagels, *The Gnostic Gospels* (New York: Random House, 1979), 48–49; Karen King, ed., *Images of the Feminine in Gnosticism* (Harrisburg, PA: Trinity Press International, 1988).

heard Martha saying these words, he said, "Excellent, Martha, and well done." (*Pistis Sophia* 1.38-39, trans. Violet MacDermot, *The Fall of Sophia: A Gnostic Text on the Redemption of Universal Consciousness* [Great Barrington, MA: Lindisfarne, 2001].)	The fall of Sophia can be interpreted as an allegory of the descent of the divine spark into matter, and its salvation through enlightenment. (See MacDermot, *Fall of Sophia*, chap. 1.) *Mary Ann Beavis*

The most notable scholar to make a connection between Hebrews and γνῶσις is Ernst Käsemann, who, as an anti-Nazi dissident in a German prison in 1937, wrote the first draft of *The Wandering People of God*. He found inspiration in Hebrews' image of the faithful journey through a hostile world on the way to a better homeland: "By describing the church as the new people of God on its wandering through the wilderness, following the Pioneer and Perfecter of faith, I of course had in mind the radical Confessing Church which resisted the tyranny in Germany, and which had to be summoned to patience so that it could continue its way through endless wastes."[112] Käsemann connected this motif with the "Gnostic myth" of the "redeemed redeemer," interpreting the Jesus of Hebrews as a Gnostic redeemer sent from the immaterial realm to the material world to deliver the souls of the enlightened from bondage and lead them to the ultimate heaven. Käsemann's work was, however, published before the discovery of the Gnostic library of Nag Hammadi (1946) and depended on the subsequently discredited notion of Gnosticism as a pre-christian religion that early christians took over and applied to Christ.[113] The Gnostic hypothesis has not met with much acceptance, but Käsemann's emphasis on the pilgrimage motif in Hebrews is considered to be of abiding exegetical and theological value.

Structure

Hebrews, like other ancient homilies, alternates between scriptural/doctrinal exposition and exhortation, *paraenesis* in Greek. This structure in Hebrews can be outlined as follows:

---

112. Ernst Käsemann, *The Wandering People of God: An Investigation of the Letter to the Hebrews* (Minneapolis: Fortress Press, 1984).

113. See Daniel J. Harrington, *What Are They Saying about the Letter to the Hebrews?* (Mahwah, NJ: Paulist Press, 2005), 68; Koester, *Hebrews*, 60–61.

Prologue: The Divine Word/Wisdom (1:1-4)

Exposition: The Mediation of Christ Is Better Than the Mediation of Angels (1:5-14)

Paraenesis: Ethical Implications (2:1-4)

Exposition (cont.): The Mediation of Christ Is Better Than the Mediation of Angels (2:5-18)

Exposition: The Mediation of Christ Is Better Than the Mediation of Moses (3:1-6)

Paraenesis: Warning against Disobedience (3:7-19)

Exposition: Mediator of a Better Rest (4:1-16)

Exposition: The Basis of Christ's High Priesthood (5:1-10)

Paraenesis: Perfecting Faith (5:11–6:20)

Exposition: The High Priesthood of Christ (7:1-28)

Exposition: The New Covenant Mediated by Jesus (8:1–10:18)

Paraenesis: Persisting in Faith (10:19-39); Heroes of Faith (11:1-40); Ethical Implications of the Pilgrimage of Faith (12:1-29)

Final Exhortations: (1) Teachings on Relationships within the Community (13:1-6); (2) Warnings against False Teachings (13:7-17); (3) Personal Requests from the Author(s) (13:18-21); (4) Epistolary Postscript (13:22-25)

Although Christian interpretation of Scripture has tended to focus on doctrine, for Hebrews the applications of the expository sections to the lives of the audience are of great importance, as illustrated by the lengthy paraenetic sections (especially Heb 5:1–6:20; 10:1–12:29; 13:1-17).

Major Themes

The marginal status of Hebrews, in terms of texts that are relatively unknown to ordinary readers compared to other epistles, has been identified as an entrance point for a postcolonial conversation with Hebrews. This status does not mean that none of the text is well received by modern readers. In fact, Heb 11:1—"Now faith is the assurance of things hoped for, the conviction of things not seen"—is still memorized by many ordinary readers and praised by scholars in liturgical studies.[114]

---

114. Todd Johnson, ed., *The Conviction of Things Not Seen: Worship and Ministry in the 21st Century* (Grand Rapids, MI: Brazos Press, 2002).

Faith, the central theme of the book, can be articulated by the following three subthemes, all beginning with *p*: pilgrimage, persistence, and perfecter of faith. The three themes are interconnected. Before we move on to articulate these *p* themes, it should be noted that the list of eight themes below ought not to be understood as separate entities. In fact, the themes are so interrelated that they may seem redundant. For example, the high priesthood of Christ cannot be fully understood apart from sacrifice, while sacrifice is tied to the new covenant, which is then related to worship as paying respect to God, an activity that is not possible without the covenant with God, who is in relation with the people.

Throughout the commentary we should keep in mind that the separate ideas cannot be analyzed in a totally linear or isolated manner but rather must be approached in "uncentred, pluralistic, and multifarious" ways.[115] Such approaches are integral to postcolonial, multicultural, and multidisciplinary approaches, all of which are employed in this commentary. Attending to the connections and the overlapping aspects within and between the themes will enable us to illuminate new insights into Sophia, our major goal in writing this book.

The Pilgrimage of Faith

As noted above, the motif of the pilgrimage of faith toward the heavenly Jerusalem pervades Hebrews from chapter 3 through chapter 12. The imperfect "rest" of the earthly territory promised in the exodus and conquest is contrasted with the eternal Sabbath of the heavenly realm (Heb 3:7–4:11). The hoped-for destination of the faithful is the celestial city of Jerusalem/Zion (11:10, 16; 12:22; 13:14), contrasted with the earthly Sinai (12:18-24). Although Moses and the institutions of the "old covenant" serve as a negative foil for the new order inaugurated by the "pioneer" Jesus (6:20; 12:2), Moses and other Israelite women and men are regarded as sharing the faith of the christian community, who will be "perfected" together with them (11:1-40). As noted earlier, Hebrews' celebration of past heroes of faith is similar to passages in the Jewish Wisdom literature (Wis 10–19; Sir 44–50), although, unlike Wisdom and Sirach, the homilist includes heroines as well as heroes.

---

115. Bill Ashcroft, Gareth Griffiths, and Helen Tiffin, *The Empire Writes Back: Theory and Practice in Post-Colonial Literature* (London and New York: Routledge, 1989), 12.

This pilgrimage of faith is particularly important in the postcolonial reality in which diaspora identity is becoming a norm for many people. Punt puts it this way: "The centrality of the diaspora theme in Hebrews cannot be underestimated, particularly amid our renewed awareness of liminality of human existence in the globalizing village of a new millennium. . . . In ch. 4 the exodus theme is developed with the image of the people of God in diaspora, in the desert and underway with a *pistei* (in faith) attitude to the promised land (*katapausis*)."[116] (For a further discussion of liminality in the context of Asian North American scholarship, see the comment on Heb 11:1-40 below.)

In light of cultic practices, the fact that the homilist prefers the tabernacle to the temple as the locus of God's dwelling in Israel is significant. The detailed description of the tabernacle's structure and contents, in which it is termed "the Holy of Holies" (Heb 9:4), containing "the golden altar of incense" (see also Exod 30:1-16), affirms the pilgrim identity of the people of the new covenant. For the homilist it is in the liminal places between earthly and heavenly sanctuaries that christians are called to a life of faith. God, who made the new covenant with this people, is thus the guiding Wisdom, the Spirit who accompanies them on their pilgrimage journey. (For further discussion of this, see the comment on Heb 8–10 below.)

The Persistence of Faith

Along with the pilgrimage of faith, which orients believers toward the future, persistence of faith is a theme that brings to mind the present, the realities the audience of Hebrews faced in their daily lives. As noted above, it is obvious that the audience for this homiletic epistle was dealing with hardships, including imprisonment (Heb 10:34) and martyrdom for their faith, as many early Christians did; thus pastoral advice encouraged them to meet together (10:25) and to work in solidarity with others (6:10). Along with the exhortations to remember Jesus' suffering and to continue in the way of faith, this may seem helpful. The rhetoric of endurance in faith can, however, serve to perpetuate unjust practices imposed on those who already suffer enough and can romanticize suffering and discrimination. For example, the view of Jesus as model and exemplar who endured pain and persecution is closely related to the view of God as parent (father) who disciplines his children. "The interpretation

---

116. Punt, "Hebrews," 353–54.

of human suffering as the discipline of God . . . has had pastoral and theological effects that feminists find unacceptable," as Cynthia Briggs Kittredge observes.[117] Both Abraham's sacrifice of Isaac, interpreted as divinely sanctioned child abuse, and the example of Rahab, which seems to justify the conquest of Canaan, call for attention and proper theological discussion from a pastoral-theological as well as a postcolonial feminist standpoint, a challenge to which this commentary attempts to respond in the following chapters.

The Perfecter of Faith

Jesus Christ as the ultimate example, the perfecter of faith to be imitated by the whole community, is found throughout Hebrews from the beginning, as God made "the pioneer of their salvation perfect" (2:10), to the end, with "Jesus the pioneer and perfecter of our faith" (12:2). Here the term "perfecter" (τελειότής) is not used to claim his supremacy, a sole authority, but to point to his quality of "being helper, and as *perfecter*, making perfection possible . . . for human beings through his death."[118] To put this in another way, the homilist paints a picture of the humanness of Jesus as the one who became "like his brothers and sisters in every respect" (2:17); the focus is not so much on the "perfect" Jesus but on his example for the community. (For a further discussion on this, especially with regard to disability, see the comment on Heb 5–7.) This Christology of humility and the pastoral sensitivity of the homilist are strongly revealed within the context of persecution and hardship with which the audience of Hebrews was living.

Pedagogically speaking, the idea of "perfecter" is closely related to the understanding of Jesus as a model of faith who teaches by example. A discussion of *paideia* (Heb 5:12; 12:5-11), therefore, involves an understanding that education is not a simple acquisition of knowledge or technique but a lifelong practice for the formation of the whole person that is to be cultivated and taught by example in and through the community.

The High Priesthood of Christ

Hebrews' distinctive christological contribution is the doctrine of the high priesthood of Christ. As noted earlier, Sir 24:9-10 comes close to

117. Kittredge, "Hebrews," 447.
118. Punt, "Hebrews," 353.

Hebrews' portrayal of Christ's priesthood: "In the holy tent I [Wisdom] ministered before him, and so I was established in Zion. Thus in the beloved city he gave me a resting place, and in Jerusalem was my domain." While for Sirach heavenly Wisdom ministers through the priesthood in Jerusalem, for Hebrews Christ-Sophia entered the heavenly tent/tabernacle once to offer the definitive sacrifice of his own blood (Heb 7:27; 9:12, 26; 10:1), contrasted with the animals offered yearly by the high priest on the Day of Atonement (9:7-8; 10:2). In Hebrews' typological interpretation the Levitical priesthood is a negative foil for Christ, whose priesthood is positively correlated with the obscure biblical figure of Melchizedek, king of Salem (traditionally identified with Jerusalem), whose priestly "order" Jesus fulfills.[119] For the homilist, Jesus' non-Levitical lineage—he is "descended from Judah" (7:14)—implies that he must belong to a priestly genealogy; he is "a priest forever, according to the order of Melchizedek" (7:17), as prophesied by his ancestor David, also of the "house of Judah" (Ps 110:4; see also Heb 8:8). (On the feminist implications of the priesthood motif, see the comments on Heb 5–7.)

The Earthly Servant Christ

No one would argue against the statement that Hebrews has a high Christology. Influenced by the popular Platonist thought of the day and, perhaps, by proto-Gnosticism, the homilist sees Christ as a heavenly, spiritual being, and this vision is obvious and explicit in the text. One may also find, however, a juxtaposed vision of Jesus as an earthly and material being who is in the long line of prophets, priests, and kings, especially Melchizedek, an unconventional figure whose family origin is in question. This seems, on the one hand, to detach him from the material world in order to foreshadow Jesus' eternal and spiritual priesthood. On the other hand, it may be viewed as the homilist's intention to proclaim a paradoxical message that a new world (not an otherworldly realm or a place beyond this world) has come into existence through Jesus.

The following narrative can be found in Hebrews: Christ the earthly servant, whose power lies in a subversive ability to disrupt the traditional order or a conventional sense of power, has come to break down a patriarchal priestly regime that serves the privileged chosen class (e.g., the

---

119. Gen 14:18; Ps 110:4; Heb 5:6, 10; 6:20; 7:1, 10, 11, 15, 17.

Levitical priesthood). Punt asks: "Can the priesthood of Jesus function as a liberating symbol, breaking through privileged and hegemonic systems insisted upon by religious orthodoxies?"[120] The earthly Christ is a priest who has compassion for others (Heb 2:14-18; 4:15), offers prayers and supplications for the sake of the community (5:7-8), and shows his solidarity with the community (1:11-12). The emphasis on the earthly nature of Jesus Christ gives the concept of perfection (τελειωθείς), a political, perhaps revolutionary aspect. This fullness (being complete), though, includes vulnerability and disability as well as strength and capability. In fact, the consensus that Hebrews expresses a "high Christology" in which the "divinity of Christ" is emphasized may result from the over-literalization of the highly allusive and metaphorical language of the discourse. From the homilist's perspective, what Christ does "for us" (the audience) through his life and death is more important than ontological formulations regarding Jesus' relationship to the divine nature; doctrine is always subordinate to paraenesis. For a further discussion of this Christology in light of διδαχή ("teaching") and τελειωθείς ("perfection"), see the comment on Heb 5–7 below.

Sacrifice and Atonement

Due to its focus on priesthood, tabernacle, and sacrifice, Hebrews is particularly implicated in the Christian doctrine of atonement, a theological model that interprets the death of Jesus as a sacrifice offered in order to atone for the sins of others.[121] Some contemporary Christians, and especially feminist theologians, are highly critical of atonement theology for several reasons: it suggests that God is a sadistic deity who requires blood and death in order to be satisfied; it requires slaughter and so is inherently violent; it pictures God as a harsh patriarch who demands the death of his son so that others might live; and the concept of vicarious atonement, in which an innocent victim suffers and dies for the salvation of others, is incomprehensible in the postmodern world. For specifically feminist critiques of atonement theology, see the comment on Heb 5:8.[122]

120. Punt, "Hebrews," 352.
121. See Christian Eberhart, *The Sacrifice of Jesus: Understanding Atonement Biblically* (Minneapolis: Fortress Press, 2011), 1–11, 111–13.
122. Eberhart, *Sacrifice*, 5–7.

> ### Hildegard of Bingen
>
> Kristin De Troyer cites the medieval mystic Hildegard of Bingen's song, "Voice of the Blood," as integrating the culturally fabricated oppositions between God and creation, holiness and everyday life:
>
> > O redness of blood,
> > who have flowed down
> > from that height
> > which divinely touched:
> > you are the flower
> > that the winter of the ser-
> > pent's breath
> > never withered.
>
> De Troyer explains: "In this text, heaven and earth seem connected through the blood. The text can be read as transcendence touching upon immanence. I, however, also read the text as referring purely to female blood that gives life. Female blood flows down and is the flower out of which life comes forth. When blood is giving life, death cannot touch. Blood is 'divinely touched.' It is intimately connected with holiness." De Troyer hypothesizes that in ancient Israelite religion women were marginal to the sacrificial cult because women's blood loss in childbirth—by participating in the giving of life, a divine prerogative—was perceived as impinging on the power of God. (*Source*: Kristin De Troyer, "Preface," *Wholly Woman, Holy Blood: A Feminist Critique of Purity and Impurity*, ed. Kristin De Troyer, Judith A. Herbert, Judith Ann Johnson, and Anne-Marie Korte [Harrisburg, PA: Trinity Press International, 2003], ix–x; Kristin De Troyer, "Blood: A Threat to Holiness or [Another] Holiness?," in *Wholly Woman, Holy Blood*, 45–64, at 56–57.)
>
> Mary Ann Beavis

Christian Eberhart has shown that distaste for atonement theology is often grounded in misconceptions about the ancient Jewish sacrificial system, which is understood as inherently violent because it involved slaughter and supposedly required divine appeasement through bloodshed and the suffering of innocent animals.[123] In response to such critiques, he offers the following observations:

1. Although the slaughter of animals was part of some Israelite/Judean sacrificial rituals, the *killing* of the animals had no special or constitutive significance for sacrifice: "Cultic *blood application rituals do not enact vicarious death but consecrate through the animal's life*,

---

123. Eberhart, *Sacrifice*, 5–6.

which is in its blood."[124] Moreover, the cereal offering ritual, which operated without an animal victim, illustrates that neither suffering nor death was intrinsic to the functionality of sacrifice.[125]

2. Sacrifice was not concerned with divine appeasement, but the various rituals were conceived "as ways of *approaching the sanctuary* with the goal of *encountering and communicating with God*. In addition, sacrifices are means of *cultic purification and consecration* (expiation)."[126] Here purification/expiation does not refer to moral or physical cleansing but to the worshiper's fitness to approach the divine (see also Heb 12:22-24).

The ancient Israelite/Jewish understanding of sacrifice (from the Latin *sacrificio*, "to make holy") is very much at variance with the modern understandings of the term that connect sacrifice with suffering, loss, and violence.[127] While it cannot be denied that the sacrificial cult of ancient Israel—like the sacrificial rituals of other Ancient Near Eastern/ Mediterranean cultures—involved killing, modern industrialized forms of animal slaughter are much less humane.

The sacrifice/atonement model of salvation is one metaphor among many used by Christians to explicate the meaning of the killing of God's son through crucifixion. In its historical reality, crucifixion was not an atoning sacrifice or any other kind of religious ritual but a brutal and painful form of execution reserved for lower-class and political criminals. Other Christian soteriological metaphors, borrowed from secular life, include such notions as martyrdom, redemption from slavery, ransom from sin, penal substitution, and the satisfaction of divine honor, which tend to be collapsed with the atonement model in popular theology.[128] It is understandable that generations of theologians, including the homilist, have used metaphors from their various religious, historical, and cultural contexts to explicate the meaning of the death of Jesus. Considering the violent and painful nature of crucifixion, it would have been natural for the homilist to associate suffering with Jesus' death (Heb 2:9). Hebrews does not, however, interpret Jesus' suffering as salvific in itself; for the homilist, that suffering enabled Jesus to sympathize in solidarity

124. Ibid., 132. Italics in the original.
125. Ibid.
126. Ibid. Italics in the original.
127. Ibid., 13–14.
128. See also ibid., 123–30, 133.

with other human beings (2:18) and, less appealingly in feminist terms (but consistent with ancient pedagogical theory), to learn obedience and self-discipline (2:10; 5:8), qualities commended to the audience (10:32, 34; 13:17). In relation to Jesus as comforter and advocate for those who suffer, the Johannine concept of the Paraclete can be helpful in understanding the homilist's exhortation to the community to "provoke one another to love and good deeds" (Heb 10:24), receiving the "spirit of grace" (10:29) that is at work in community. For further discussion, see the comment on Heb 10:19-34.

From another perspective, Punt observes, "A Christological appropriation of the Yom Kippur [as a day of repentance] ritual allows one, for example, to de-emphasize Christ's death as 'atoning sacrifice' in favour of viewing it as 'a covenant inaugurating event.'"[129] A call for true worship and the abolition of the hegemony of the institutionalized priesthood along with the end of the sacrificial system can be understood as an argument against the apostolic *kerygma* of the sacrificial death of Christ.[130] In feminist terms, rather than attempting to rehabilitate atonement theology, it is preferable to focus on Jesus' living proclamation of the reign of God instead of fixating on his suffering and death.

Sacrifice, Priesthood, and Patriarchy

A much-quoted anthropological theory that connects blood sacrifice, priesthood, and patriarchy is Nancy Jay's *Throughout Your Generations Forever: Sacrifice, Religion, and Patriarchy*. Jay found a commonality in various religions in which blood sacrifice features prominently: the priests who perform such sacrifices are overwhelmingly male, and fertile women are barred from direct participation in sacrificial rituals due to the ritual impurity conferred on them by patriarchal views of menstruation and childbirth, occasions of women's loss of blood. Jay theorizes that such sacrificial systems are designed to legitimize patrilineal descent by creating a form of fatherly lineage that is sealed by ritual and not by biology alone. Unlike the bloodshed of menstruation and birth, which is natural and uncontrollable, killing can be regulated:

> The only action that is as serious as giving birth, which can act as a counterbalance to it, is killing. This

129. Punt, "Hebrews," 358.
130. Barnabas Lindars, "The Rhetorical Structure of Hebrews," *NTS* 35 (1989): 405–6.

is one way to interpret the common sacrificial metaphors of birth and rebirth, or birth done better, on purpose and on a more spiritual, more exalted level than mothers do it. . . . Unlike childbirth, sacrificial killing is deliberate, purposeful, "rational" action, under perfect control. Both birth and killing are acts of power, but sacrificial ideology commonly construes childbirth as the quintessence of vulnerability, passivity, and powerless suffering.

Pamela Eisenbaum reads Hebrews through the lens of Jay's theory that sacrifice is a means of establishing patriarchal bloodlines; thus the themes of sonship, high priesthood, and sacrifice are essential to Hebrews' argument:

Ritual sacrifices enable participants to be part of a "ritually defined social order, enduring continuously through time, that birth and death (continually changing the membership of the 'eternal' lineage) and all other threats of social chaos may be overcome." . . . . The establishment of a ritually defined social order is the overarching purpose of Christ's sacrifice in Hebrews. . . . Just as Jesus once humbled himself to commune in human form

with his "brothers" (2.10-18), his followers can now join in his exalted, divine, eternal lineage and the promised inheritance that goes with it.

That is, the son's sacrificial death has enabled believers to become "brothers" with Christ in the divine patrilineage, to transcend the contingency of having been "born of woman" (see also Job 14:1). In this view, however, it could be argued that the women of the homilist's audience would become honorary "sons" and heirs, and thus grafted onto the priestly lineage of Christ. (*Source:* Nancy Jay, *Throughout Your Generations Forever: Sacrifice, Religion, and Paternity* [Chicago and London: University of Chicago Press, 1992]; Nancy Jay, "Sacrifice as Remedy for Having Been Born of a Woman," in *Immaculate and Powerful: The Female in Social Image and Social Reality*, ed. Clarissa W. Atkinson, et al. [Boston: Beacon, 1985]; repr. in *Women, Gender, Religion: A Reader*, ed. Elizabeth A. Castelli, et al. [New York: Palgrave, 2001], 174–94, at 182; Pamela Eisenbaum, "Father and Son: The Christology of Hebrews in Patrilineal Perspective," in *Feminist Companion to the Catholic Epistles and Hebrews*, 127–46, at 146, citing Jay, *Generations*, 31.)

Mary Ann Beavis

Covenant

Although other NT documents speak of the new order initiated by Christ as a "new covenant,"[131] Hebrews' treatment of the prophecy of Jer 31:31-34 (Heb 8:8-13; 10:16-17) is unique. Arguably, although the term "covenant" is not explicitly mentioned until Heb 7:22, the theme undergirds the entire argument of the homily. The term "covenant" (διαθήκη) that dominates Heb 8:1–10:18 is used seventeen times in Hebrews, roughly half of the NT occurrences of the term. The frequent use of this concept does not imply that certain groups of people are barred from participation in the new covenant but rather that they are free to embrace any community committed to it. Punt argues, however, that the covenant metaphor for the people of God, like the appeal to the household (οἶκος) of Christ or the gospel symbolism of the church as a boat or ship,[132] can conjure up dangerous images of colonialism in which those in the "houseboat" (or covenant) claim to be the legitimate people of God who can, therefore, sail off to conquer (to civilize) "lesser" humans.[133] For a further discussion of the concept of covenant in the light of insights from Korean and Chinese culture and linguistics, as well as Hebrew concepts ("blessing," ברכה and "firstborn," בכור), see the comment on Heb 8–10 below.

Whereas the "old covenant" was mediated through angels by God's servant Moses (Heb 1–3), the "new covenant" is mediated by the messiah Jesus, son of God (Heb 3:1-6; 2 Sam 7:1-17; 1 Chr 17:1-15), and made with the "house of Judah" (Heb 8:8; Jer 31:31), to which Jesus belongs (Heb 7:14). The Mosaic covenant was ratified with animal blood, but the new covenant has been ratified by the blood/death of Christ (9:12, 13, 19). While the priests of the old covenant share Levitical ancestry (7:5, 9, 11), the priesthood of Jesus belongs to the everlasting "order of Melchizedek."[134] The Mosaic covenant is conditional on the righteousness of Israel,[135] but the new covenant is promissory and eternal (Heb 8:6; 13:20). Under the old covenant the Levitical sacrifices take place continually in the earthly tabernacle/temple (9:6), but the sacrifice of Christ took place "once for all" in the heavenly sanctuary (7:27; 8:2; 9:11,

---

131. Luke 22:20; 1 Cor 11:25; 2 Cor 3:6; see also Gal 4:24.

132. See George Ferguson, *Signs & Symbols in Christian Art* (London: Oxford University Press, 1961), 180–81.

133. Punt, "Hebrews," 354.

134. Heb 5:6, 10; 6:20; 7:1, 15, 17; Ps 110:4.

135. Exod 34:6-9; Jer 31:31-33; 34:18-22; Ezek 16:59-63.

12; 10:10). The Mosaic covenant is associated with the earthly Sinai, but the new covenant is associated with the heavenly Zion (12:18-24).

As noted above, in general the conception of salvation history in terms of covenants with the ancestors is shared by Hebrews and the Wisdom tradition.[136] More specifically, the terms in which Hebrews describes the "new covenant" resemble the characteristics of the covenant with David and his descendants, which is based on Judean lineage, is promissory rather than conditional, and, like the Davidic covenant, is eternal.[137] For further discussion of the continuity between the Davidic covenant and the new covenant of Hebrews, see the comment on 8:1–10:18 below.

True Worship: A Call for Practice

While Hebrews is charged with the offense of supersessionism, and rightly so, the homilist puts a strong emphasis on the renewal of the religious cult, the practice of worship. It is clear that Jewish worship practice and priestly hierarchy, as understood by the homilist, were resistant to openness or change. The homilist's emphasis on obedience rather than sacrifice (Heb 10:1-18),[138] seemingly unnecessary in light of Jesus' "once for all" sacrifice (7:27; 8:2; 9:11), should be read over against this conservative religious context. The central point is found in Heb 7, where Jesus is praised as belonging to the high priesthood "according to the order of Melchizedek," a theme that can be regarded as a main focus of the letter. This unique order of priesthood is used to argue for a new covenant based on the faithfulness and commitment of a community called to practice true worship as they "consider how to provoke one another to love and good deeds" by "meet[ing] together" (10:24-25), a basic and primary act of worship. Also, the emphasis on the close relationship between faith and life, which almost echoes the message of James, should be understood in light of worship, as they practice this "new and living way" by developing a kind of muscle memory, a habit (Heb 10:25). For a further discussion of these themes, see the comment on Heb 5–7 below. As mentioned earlier, faith is one of the most important themes in Hebrews. For the homilist, however, faith is neither a doctrinal matter nor a speculative abstract one. It is, rather, a matter of

---

136. Wis 12:21; 18:22; Sir 17:12; Heb 8:6, 10; 10:16.

137. Heb 13:20; 2 Chr 21:7; 23:3; Ps 89:3; Isa 55:3; Jer 33:21; Sir 45:31; 47:11; see also 1 Kgs 8:25; 9:5; 2 Kgs 8:19; 2 Chr 1:9; 6:16; 1 Macc 2:57.

138. Punt, "Hebrews," 358.

reality and of sanctification. The themes of perfecter of faith, elaborated further in the examples of faith (12:1-12) and of Christ the earthly servant, point to the theme of sanctification, where the homilist advises believers to cultivate and nurture a mature faith in God through Jesus Christ (5:11–6:8).

Hebrews, Supersessionism, and Anti-Judaism

Daniel J. Harrington observes that an open question with respect to Hebrews is "the significance of Hebrews for Christian-Jewish relations (supersessionist or not?)."[139] Indeed, the homilist's contrasts between Christ and Moses, the earthly tabernacle and the heavenly tabernacle, Levitical priesthood and priesthood of Christ, old covenant and new covenant, earthly Sinai and heavenly Zion have led some scholars to regard Hebrews as supersessionist, i.e., as teaching that Christianity supersedes and abolishes Judaism.[140] Conversely, as Richard B. Hayes observes, "Hebrews nowhere speaks of Jews and gentiles, nowhere gives evidence of controversies over circumcision or food laws, criticizes nothing in the Mosaic Torah except for the Levitical sacrificial cult, and contains no polemic against Jews or Jewish leaders. . . . Nowhere does Hebrews suggest that the Jewish people have been replaced by a new and different people of God."[141] Thus to call Hebrews "supersessionist" may be an anachronistic imposition of later Christian doctrines onto the text.

Nonetheless, although there was no such thing as "Christianity" as a religion separate from "Judaism" in Hebrews' time,[142] the charge of supersessionism is warranted to the extent that Hebrews sees the new covenant as superseding and replacing the cultic institutions of the Mosaic order. Within its historical context, however, the homilist worships the Jewish God, makes extensive use of Jewish Scriptures and methods

---

139. Harrington, *Hebrews*, 88.

140. Terence L. Donaldson, *Jews and Anti-Judaism in the New Testament* (London: SPCK, 2010), 143; see also 20; Pamela Eisenbaum, "Hebrews," *The Jewish Annotated New Testament* (New York: Oxford University Press, 2011), 406–26; see also the essays in Richard Bauckham, et al., eds., *The Epistle to the Hebrews and Christian Theology* (Grand Rapids, MI, and Cambridge: Eerdmans, 2009), esp. 151–228.

141. Richard B. Hayes, "'Here We Have No Lasting City': New Covenantalism in Hebrews," in Bauckham, *Hebrews and Christian Theology*, 151–73, at 154.

142. See Pamela Eisenbaum, *Paul Was Not a Christian: The Original Message of a Misunderstood Apostle* (San Francisco: HarperOne, 2009), 5–9.

of interpretation, and shares an eschatological orientation and messianic hope with other "Judaisms" of the first century.[143] In fact, Eisenbaum's observations regarding the essential Jewishness of Paul could equally well be applied to Hebrews:

> Paul's letters would have been regarded as Jewish by other Jews of the time, including Pharisees. . . . In the context of the first century . . . Paul's belief in Jesus did not make him less Jewish. Belief in a messianic savior figure is a very Jewish idea, as can be demonstrated by a historical analogy. Only a half century after Paul wrote his letters, R. Akiba, one of the most revered of all rabbis of antiquity, believed that the Messiah had come in his day, only his name was not Jesus, it was Bar Kokhba. Not all Jews thought Bar Kokhba was the Messiah at the time, and after Bar Kokhba failed in his revolt against the Romans and died, it became clear that R. Akiba had been wrong. But R. Akiba has never been judged a heretic, and his teachings continue to this day to be authoritative because they are preserved in the Mishnah and the Talmud. Thus, Paul's belief in Jesus would not have branded him a heretic—a pain in the neck perhaps, but not a heretic.[144]

Like Paul, the homilist regarded the messiah, Jesus, and his salvific acts as the fulfillment or "perfecting" of the history of Israel. Similarly, the homilist's critique of the Levitical priesthood and tabernacle fits within the range of ancient Jewish criticisms of, and alternatives to, the temple regime in Jerusalem and with Philo of Alexandria's preference for spiritual offerings over literal sacrifice.[145] In fact, as Shaye J. D. Cohen notes, "a common feature of Jewish sectarianism is the polemic against the Temple of Jerusalem: its precincts are impure, its cult profane, and its priests illegitimate."[146] As noted above, however, to the extent that Hebrews as Christian Scripture has figured in the history of Christian anti-Judaism[147] it must be interpreted with care, and anti-Jewish interpretations of Hebrews must be vigorously repudiated.

143. See also ibid., 67–115.

144. Ibid., 8.

145. Timothy Scott Wardle, "Continuity and Discontinuity: The Temple and Early Christian Identity" (PhD diss., Duke University, 2008); Eisenbaum, *Paul*, 71–72; James W. Thompson, *The Beginnings of Christian Philosophy: The Epistle to the Hebrews*, CBQMS 13 (Washington, DC: Catholic Biblical Association of America, 1982), 113–15.

146. Shaye J. D. Cohen, "The Significance of Yavneh: Pharisees, Rabbis, and the End of Jewish Sectarianism," *HUCA* 55 (1984): 27–53, at 43.

147. See also Hayes, "No Lasting City," 154–55.

Philo of Alexandria on Temple and Sacrifice

Although Philo respected the sacrificial regime of the Jerusalem temple, he regarded material sacrifices with some reservations.[148] Philo explains the allegorical meaning of the whole burnt offering in terms of his gendered—and sexist—anthropology (or more accurately, zoology):

> "And then let the whole victim be given to the fire of the altar of God, having become many things instead of one, and one instead of many." These things, then, are comprehended in express words of command. But there is another meaning figuratively concealed under the enigmatical expressions. And the words employed are visible symbols of what is invisible and uncertain. Now the victim which is to be sacrificed as a whole burnt offering must be a male, because a male is both more akin to domination than a female and more nearly related to the efficient cause; for the female is imperfect, subject, seen more as the passive than as the active partner. And since the elements of which our soul consists are two in number, the rational and the irrational part, the rational part belongs to the male sex, being the inheritance of intellect and reason; but the irrational part belongs to the sex of woman, which is the lot also of the outward senses. And the mind is in every respect superior to the outward sense, as the man is to the woman; who, when he is without blemish and purified with the proper purifications, namely, the perfect virtues, is himself the most holy sacrifice, being wholly and in all respects pleasing to God. (*On the Special Laws* XXXVII.199–201)

Philo's view of the Jerusalem temple as a reflection of the heavenly sanctuary is reminiscent of Hebrews:

> We ought to look upon the universal world as the highest and truest temple of God, having for its most holy place that most sacred part of the essence of all existing things, namely, the heaven; and for ornaments, the stars; and for priests, the subordinate ministers of his power, namely, the angels, incorporeal souls, not beings compounded of irrational and rational natures, such as our bodies are, but such as have the irrational parts wholly cut out, being absolutely and

---

148. Thompson, *Beginnings*, 113.

wholly intellectual, pure reasonings, resembling the unit. But the other temple is made with hands; for it was desirable not to cut short the impulses of men who were eager to bring in contributions for the objects of piety, and desirous either to show their gratitude by sacrifices for such good fortune as had befallen them, or else to implore pardon and forgiveness for whatever errors they might have committed. He moreover foresaw that there could not be any great number of temples built either in many different places, or in the same place, thinking it fitting that as God is one, his temple also should be one. (*On the Special Laws* I, XII.66-67)

Similarly, the book of Wisdom describes the temple as a "copy of the holy tent" that God prepared "from the beginning" (9:8), in accordance with the Sophia who sits by the divine throne (9:4).
(*Source: The Works of Philo, Complete and Unabridged*, trans. C.D. Yonge, new ed. [Peabody, MA: Hendrickson, 1993], 540.)

Mary Ann Beavis

Interpretive Essay: Proto-feminist Interpretations of Hebrews

While many scholars see feminist biblical scholarship as a movement that began in the mid-to-late twentieth century, approaches to biblical texts that can be labeled as "proto-feminist" certainly occurred much earlier. For example, in mid-nineteenth-century America, Antoinette Brown Blackwell argued against oppressive interpretations of 1 Tim 2:11-12 ("Let a woman learn in silence with full submission. I permit no woman to teach or to have authority over a man; she is to keep silent") and 1 Cor 14:34-35 ("Let a woman learn in silence with full submission. I permit no woman to teach or to have authority over a man; she is to keep silent") in an article published in *Oberlin Quarterly Review*.[149] Exegetical arguments similar to Brown Blackwell's are found in feminist interpretations one hundred years later, but no one referenced Brown

---

149. Beth Bidlack, "Antoinette Brown Blackwell: Pioneering Exegete and Congregational Minister," in *Strangely Familiar: Protofeminist Interpretations of Patriarchal Biblical Texts*, ed. Nancy Calvert-Koyzis and Heather Weir (Atlanta, GA: SBL, 2009), 151–70; Antoinette L. Brown, "Exegesis of 1 Corinthians, XIV., 34, 35; and 1 Timothy II., 11,12," *OQR* 4 (1849): 358–73.

Blackwell's work.[150] My intention here is not to recount and analyze
Brown Blackwell's arguments but to provide an example of how proto-
feminist voices have been lost through the centuries. Gerda Lerner summarizes it well when she states, "Over and over again, individual women
criticized and re-interpreted the core biblical texts not knowing that other
women before them had already done so. In fact, present day feminist
Bible criticism is going over the same territory and using the very same
arguments used for centuries by other women engaged in the same
endeavor."[151]

In the case of Hebrews, proto-feminist voices are not easy to find.
Nevertheless, we may have to look no further than the author of the
epistle who, as is argued above, could be a collection of individuals including women, perhaps including Priscilla. Whatever the case, the
homilist of Hebrews may be called "proto-feminist" by virtue of the
inclusion of women in the list of heroes of the faith in Heb 11. For example, the homilist names Rahab (11:31) as one who "by faith" was a
heroine. Another possible example of a heroine of faith is found in Heb
11:11. The Greek text states, Πίστει καὶ αὐτῇ Σάρρᾳ στεῖρα δύναμιν εἰς
καταβολὴν σπέρματος ἔλαβεν καὶ παρὰ καιρὸν ἡλικίας, ἐπεὶ πιστὸν ἡγήσατο
τὸν ἐπαγγειλάμενον. This can be translated as "by faith Sarah herself,
though barren, received power to conceive, even when she was too old,
because she considered him faithful who had promised," as in the footnote for the verse in the NRSV. In the main text, the NRSV translates the
verse as referring to Abraham as the subject, thus downgrading Sarah's
role: "By faith he received the power of procreation, even though he was
too old—and Sarah herself was barren—because he considered him
faithful who had promised." Ruth Hoppin argues that the proper translation is in the footnote. When the phrase "received power to conceive"
(δύναμιν εἰς καταβολὴν σπέρματος ἔλαβεν) is translated in the NRSV as
"received power of procreation," it enables Abraham to be made the
subject of the verse. She also notes that the phrase παρὰ καιρὸν ἡλικίας or
"past the age of fertility" is rendered "too old," although several manu-

150. Elisabeth Schüssler Fiorenza, *In Memory of Her, A Feminist Theological Recon-
struction of Christian Origins*, 10th ann. Ed. (New York: Crossroad, 1988; 1998), 230–31;
Craig Keener, *Paul, Women and Wives: Marriage and Women's Ministry in the Letters of
Paul* (Peabody, MA: Hendrickson Publishers, 1992).

151. Gerda Lerner, "One Thousand Years of Feminist Biblical Criticism," in *The
Creation of Feminist Consciousness: From the Middle Ages to Eighteen Seventy* (New York:
Oxford University Press, 1993), 166.

scripts include "for childbearing" and others have the phrase "she gave birth."[152] On the other hand, the editorial committee of the United Bible Societes' Greek New Testament recognized that δύναμιν εἰς καταβολὴν σπέρματος ἔλαβεν as "regularly used of the male, not the female in conceiving" in Greek and so understood the words καὶ αὐτῇ Σάρρᾳ στεῖρα as being a gloss that "somehow got in to the text."[153]

Even the mention of Rahab and Sarah renders the Hebrews' homilist's list of heroes of the faith as a kind of proto-feminist; as Hoppin states, "the author was familiar with the roll call of heroes of faith in Ecclesasticus in the Septuagint, following right along with the mention of Enoch, Noah, Abraham and Moses. However, while Sirach names Abraham he does not name Sarah; he extols Joshua but does not name Rahab [Sir 44:1–50:24]. By contrast the author of Hebrews alludes to Joshua without naming him, then names Rahab instead."[154]

Other examples of heroines of the faith in Heb 11 may include Judith who "won strength out of weakness, became mighty in war" and "put foreign armies to flight."[155] Clement of Rome identified Judith with the "valiant ones of Heb. 11:34" (1 Clem. 55.3-5).[156] Clement also identifies Esther as a valiant model of faith, perhaps as the one who "escaped the edge of the sword" (Heb 11:34; Esth 4:11; 5:1-2).[157] The "women who received their dead by resurrection" (Heb 11:35), presumably referring either to the widow of Zeraphath (1 Kgs 17:17-24) or the Shunammite woman (2 Kgs 4:25-37). The woman described as "tortured, refusing to accept release, on order to obtain a better resurrection" may refer to the mother of the seven sons in 2 Macc 5:27 and 6:12–7:42 whose sons were tortured but proclaimed a better resurrection to come. Thus the homilist of Hebrews interweaves salvation history with women as examples of the faith, and as Hoppin states, "through the eyes of the writer we see women in the world, as agents of salvation, worthy of emulation."[158]

152. Ruth Hoppin, "Priscilla's Letter," 154–55.

153. See the reasons for the NRSV translation in Bruce M. Metzger, *A Textual Commentary on the Greek New Testament* (New York: United Bible Societies, 1994), 602.

154. Hoppin, "Priscilla's Letter," 155.

155. Ibid.

156. Ibid., 155–56; see James Rendel Harris, "Sidelights on the Authorship of the Epistle to the Hebrews," in *Sidelights on New Testament Research Lecture V* (London: The Kingsgate Press, James Clarke & Co., 1908), 169–71.

157. Hoppin, "Priscilla's Letter," 156.

158. Ibid.

Another voice worth listening to is English commentator Gracilla Boddington (1801–87) who published under her initials, G.B. She was born March 27, 1801, to Benjamin Boddington (1773–1853) and his wife, Grace (d. Feb. 10, 1812). Her brother, Thomas, became an Anglican priest, which suggests that the family was well educated. She lived primarily Titley, Herefordshire, and never married. During a career of over forty years, Boddington published multiple volumes on every book in the New Testament in addition to four other books. Her purpose was to write for the common person, using "simple and familiar language."[159]

Although her viewpoint on a woman's place was traditional, including the belief that a wife must be subject to husband, writing and publishing commentaries "was not socially acceptable for a woman of this period. Nevertheless her work was well received, as evidenced by the reprinting of a number of her works during her own lifetime."[160] In her volume, *St. Paul's Epistle to the Hebrews Explained in Simple and Familiar Language*, Boddington also writes of Sarah, much like Ruth Hoppin does. She includes Sarah among the "patriarchs and prophets" who "had faith in God's word, and because of it, He gave her strength to become a mother, when otherwise she was too old. She considered that He, who had made the promise, would certainly be faithful to his word."[161] In Boddington's work Sarah remains the subject who, through her faith, gives birth despite her advancing years.

Later proto-feminist voices included that of Englishwoman Elizabeth Rundle Charles (1828–96). Rundle Charles, born in Devon, was the only child of John Rundle, a Member of Parliament, and his wife, Barbara Gill. Educated at home, Rundle Charles eventually authored dozens of books and was known throughout England for her literary works and her talents as a linguist, poet, painter, and musician.[162]

In her book *Within the Veil: Studies in the Epistle to the Hebrews*, we find some glimmerings of proto-feminist ideas.[163] For example, when discuss-

159. Agnes Choi, "Gracilla Boddington (1801–1887)," *Handbook of Women Biblical Interpreters: A Historical and Biographical Guide*, ed. Marion Taylor and Agnes Choi (Grand Rapids, MI: Baker Academic, 2012), 164–65, at 164.

160. Ibid., 164–65.

161. G.B. (Gracilla Bodington), *St. Paul's Epistle to the Hebrews: Explained in Simple and Familiar Language* (London: James Nisbet, 1846), 148.

162. Marion Ann Taylor and Heather E. Weir, eds., *Let Her Speak for Herself: Nineteenth-Century Women Writing on Women in Genesis* (Waco, TX: Baylor University Press, 2006), 77–78.

163. Elizabeth Rundle Charles, *Within the Veil: Studies in the Epistle to the Hebrews* (London: SPCK, 1891).

ing Jewish temple ritual, she describes the "barriers" between Gentiles, women, men, and priests. About the women she states, "Next, the court of the women: where so many of the gracious words of the Saviour were spoken, where He observed the widow putting in her two mites. Beyond that no woman might pass, not even the Blessed mother of Jesus, except when she came with her humble offering of the two turtle doves for the infant Christ, her 'firstborn son.'"[164] For Rundle Charles, these barriers were based on the "fact of sin." The ritual of the temple and its environment proclaimed the wall of separation between humanity and God and the evil that separated humanity and God: "The ritual made no attempt to remove the barriers or rend the veils. The barriers and veils represented a reality, and the ritual was a shadow and could not annul realities; nor could its sacrifices, which were its dispensation of grace, really cleanse from sin."[165] For Rundle Charles, the remedy for the barriers was in "God Himself" and the barriers were in "man." This remedy was the sacrifice of God's son, who, when he cried out "It is finished . . . the barriers had no existence; they were shadows vanished away. They existed no longer."[166]

For Rundle Charles, the death of Jesus on the cross rent the veil of the Holy of Holies, which meant that religious barriers between class, humanity, and nations vanished, becoming "mere obsolete walls meaning nothing." She continues: "Religious barriers between Jew and Gentile, 'there is neither Jew nor Greek'; religious barriers between man and woman, 'there is neither male nor female'; barriers between class and class, 'there is neither bond nor free'; 'all are one in Christ Jesus.'"

Rundle Charles, then, uses her theological arguments to show that in her view men and women are equal before God; the old barriers have been broken down. She also combines a concern for the equality of women with a concern for barriers between nations and classes. In these ways she provides the beginnings of a proto-feminist template in which she is concerned not only with the equality of women but with the disparities between classes as well.[167]

One other element of Rundle Charles's work might be considered as proto-feminist, at least in her context and milieu. Unlike many of her female compatriots, Rundle Charles had been given an excellent educa-

164. Ibid., 49.
165. Ibid., 48.
166. Ibid., 51.
167. For example, see Leslie McCall, "The Complexity of Intersectionality," *Signs: Journal of Women in Culture and Society* 30 (Spring 2005): 1771–1800.

tion. Generally, nineteenth-century women thought of themselves as the "angel in the house" and were prepared for a life of service to others. Among middle-class women, of which Rundle Charles was a member, the "image of being delicate, of not being able to handle difficult decisions and of having an inferior intellect was cultivated."[168] Yet women were seen as responsible for the education and moral formation of children.[169] This was different from the late eighteenth and early nineteenth centuries, when men were entrusted with shaping the character of children along with providing moral and religious guidance.

As a member of this new generation of women charged with educating her children, Rundle Charles was interested in how Hebrews could be used for moral and religious instruction for the young. In *Within the Veil*, Rundle Charles interprets Heb 12:3-11, which addresses the children of God who are trained and chastened after the example of Christ, as referring to the training of Christians. For her, the passage speaks of the Christian life as a life of "education and of sacrifice." She continues, "The word tendered 'chastening,' extends, no doubt, in other directions, meaning the whole of education, the bringing out of capacities and training of faculties, with the culture which is the result."[170] As she writes about this education, it is clear that it is not only for men but also for women, herself included:

> For the education is home-education. The Master is the Father, which assures us that the highest end of the training will never be lost sight of, that the mere learning of a certain number of lessons, acquiring of a certain amount of knowledge, or achieving a certain amount of successes, will never be substituted for the developing and perfecting, correcting and competing of the whole being, the education of the son.[171]

It is clear from the rest of the chapter that Rundle Charles's use of the term "son" refers to both men and women who, here, should have equal access to knowledge and success.

Although they lived in a different time and were only beginning to address overwhelmingly patriarchal interpretations of the Bible, these women incrementally deconstructed those interpretations and replaced

---

168. Christiana de Groot and Marino Ann Taylor, eds., *Recovering Nineteenth-Century Women Interpreters of the Bible*, SemeiaSt 38 (Atlanta, GA: SBL, 2007), 4.

169. Ibid., 5.

170. Rundle Charles, *Within the Veil*, 89.

171. Ibid., 95.

them with interpretations in which women were granted power and opportunity. While it is unfortunate that most members of the academy were not familiar with their contributions in previous decades, through an understanding of their contributions today we can understand ourselves as joining a long, historical line of female interpreters and draw strength from them and their proto-feminist interpretations.

Nancy Calvert Koyzis

Hebrews 1–2

Discovering Wisdom

Prologue (Heb 1:1-4)

The Hebrews prologue or exordium (Heb 1:1-4) is actually one complex, hymn-like sentence (see also Col 1:15-20; John 1:1-4), beginning with a series of alliterations featuring the letter *pi* (πολυμερῶς, πολυτρόπως, πάλαι, πατράσιν, προφήταις), whose effect is lost in most English translations. (The wordplay would be better captured by something like: "In the past, polyphonically and polymorphically God spoke to the progenitors through the prophets.") There are many hymn-like texts in the Bible. Some, especially in the Hebrew Bible, were sung before they were written down for liturgical use. For example, the creation story in the first chapter of Genesis could have been sung, with "and there was evening and there was morning" functioning like a refrain.[1] Miriam's song in Exod 15:20-21 is another example; it is regarded as one of the earliest songs in Scripture (see also Judg 5:1-31; Jdt 16:1-17).[2] This sung narrative has captivated the imagination of generations, not to mention the interest of scholarship in many different fields, including women's performance genre and feminist ethnomusicology.[3] There are also hymnic

---

1. John L. Bell, *The Singing Thing: A Case for Congregational Song* (Chicago: GIA Publications, 2000), 49–52.

2. Hans-Ruedi Weber, *Experiments with Bible Study* (Geneva: WCC, 1981), 33–34.

3. Carol Meyers, "Of Drums and Damsels: Women's Performance in Ancient Israel," *BA* 54 (1991): 16–27.

Heb 1:1-4

¹Long ago God spoke to our ancestors in many and various ways by the prophets, ²but in these last days he has spoken to us by a Son whom he appointed heir of all things, through whom he also created the worlds. ³He is the reflection of God's glory and the exact imprint of God's very being, and he sustains all things by his powerful word. When he had made purification for sins, he sat down at the right hand of the Majesty on high, ⁴having become as much superior to angels as the name he has inherited is more excellent than theirs.

passages in the New Testament, e.g., Col 1:15-20 and Phil 2:6-11. The purpose of such a carefully written and constructed opening was to capture the attention of the audience and to emphasize the importance of the theme of the homily, which is spelled out here: the contrast between the past, partial prophetic message and the present perfection embodied in the son. The author does not self-identify here or elsewhere in the letter, relying on the rhetorical quality of the discourse to persuade the audience rather than on personal authority or reputation.

Charles L. Bartow advocates this rhetorical approach to preaching to contemporary church leaders, seeing the homily as "*actio divina*," a flesh-and-blood, oral-aural, face-to-face speech event.[4] What is important is not so much the position or the ecclesial authority of the preacher but her or his physicality embodied in the performative character and aural nature of the event. Bartow goes on to say that "the stance of the lector (or preacher or priest as lector) . . . is, or ought to be, a stance of humility." When homily as "living speech" is "undertaken as an act of sacred attentiveness," the preacher is called to be humbly attentive to the written texts and the hearers.[5] In this regard, the author of Hebrews seems to fulfill this role in taking a stance of humility and attentiveness. The author is writing "against the grain" of a culture in which antiquity was respected and novelty, especially in religion, was suspect. Thus the new, definitive revelation "spoken" in "a son" is portrayed as the eschatological completion of manifold divine revelations to "the fathers" (translated in the NRSV inclusively as "the ancestors") through the prophets—in the context of Hebrews, a category encompassing the Jewish Scriptures as a whole.

4. Charles Bartow, *God's Human Speech: A Practical Theology of Proclamation* (Grand Rapids, MI: Eerdmans, 1997), 3, 36–37.

5. Charles Bartow, "Performance Study in Service to the Spoken Word in Worship," in *Performance in Preaching: Bringing the Sermon to Life*, ed. Jana Childers and Clayton J. Schmit (Grand Rapids, MI: Baker Academic, 2008), 211–23, at 221.

From a feminist standpoint the centrality of sonship, with the son portrayed as the male "heir of all things," is problematic in that it functions within a patrilineal legal system in which sons inherit the paternal estate.[6] The only explicit stipulation in Torah referring to inheritance rights, however, speaks of a case in which daughters, not sons, are at issue. This is the story of the daughters of Zelophehad. During the wilderness wanderings of the children of Israel, the father dies, leaving five daughters and no sons to inherit his legacy:

> Moses brought their case before the LORD. And the LORD spoke to Moses, saying: "The daughters of Zelophehad are right in what they are saying; you shall indeed let them possess an inheritance among their father's brothers and pass the inheritance of their father on to them. You shall also say to the Israelites, 'If a man dies, and has no son, then you shall pass his inheritance on to his daughter. If he has no daughter, then you shall give his inheritance to his brothers. If he has no brothers, then you shall give his inheritance to his father's brothers. And if his father has no brothers, then you shall give his inheritance to the nearest kinsman of his clan, and he shall possess it. It shall be for the Israelites a statute and ordinance, as the LORD commanded Moses.'" (Num 27:5-11)

Daughters and Inheritance in Judaism

The interpretation of the law with regard to women's inheritance has changed over time, as illustrated by the story of the daughters of Zelophehad:

Jewish law originally excluded daughters from inheritance rights when sons survived. The Sages modified these laws by providing for the maintenance of the widow and daughters of the deceased. In the 16th century, Moses Isserles permitted fathers to give their daughters a gift of half of their sons' share in their estate. . . . According to a *takkanah* (enactment) of the chief rabbinate of Palestine in 1943, in Israel daughters inherit on an equal footing with sons.

(*Source*: The Rabbinical Assembly, the United Synagogue of Conservative Judaism, *Etz Hayim: Torah and Commentary* [New York: JPS, 2001], 926, note on Num 27:1.)

Mary Ann Beavis

---

6. Pamela Eisenbaum, "Father and Son: The Christology of Hebrews in Patrilineal Perspective," in *A Feminist Companion to the Catholic Epistles and Hebrews*, ed. Amy-Jill Levine with Maria Mayo Robbins, FCNTECW 8 (Cleveland, OH: Pilgrim Press, 2004), 127–47.

While this legislation shows a clear preference for sons and brothers, daughters of sonless families are preferred as heirs over their uncles and male cousins. In Hebrews, the son's inheritance of "all things" is presented as highly desirable and appropriate, but women are included (11:11, 31, 35; see also 13:4)—albeit sparingly—among ancient heroes of faith perfected together with "us" (11:39-40).

From a postcolonial perspective it is not only the preference for the male heir that poses a problem; Jesus, the Son of God as "heir of all things," is also problematic. The Christian universal standard has been to convert "inferior" and "uncivilized" others to Christianity by Western imperial and "civilizing" missions and even to conquer and colonize them. An intertextual reading is helpful here. One such is found in the Gospel of Matthew: "All authority in heaven and on earth has been given to me. Go therefore and make disciples of all nations" (Matt 28:18b-19a). It is a well-researched claim that this text was not written by the original author (evangelist) but was added by a scribe in a later century. We could contend, therefore, that we can discount this verse. We cannot afford to do so, however, because it has played such a huge role in the history of Christianity and was used incessantly as propaganda in "civilizing" evangelism and converting others to Christianity throughout the millennia, particularly in recent centuries. If Matthew was written among colonized Jews within the Roman Empire, such an authoritative claim might have provided confidence and courage for those colonized to fight for their right to worship and maintain their religious and cultural identity. This kind of universal, totalizing power over "all authority and all nations," however, also sets forth an agenda that justifies the imposition of a single perspective on other nations and other religions.[7]

The wording of Heb 1:3a is generally regarded as a paraphrase of Wis 7:26: "For she is a reflection [ἀπαύγασμα] of eternal light, a spotless mirror of the working of God, and an image of his goodness." Similarly for Hebrews, the son, like Wisdom/Sophia, is a "reflection" (ἀπαύγασμα) of God's radiance and the imprint of the divine essence/reality, who "sustains all things" (Heb 1:3).[8] Jesus was often interpreted as a prophet or

---

7. Musa W. Dube, "Go Therefore and Make Disciples of All Nations (Matt. 28:19a): A Postcolonial Perspective on Biblical Criticism and Pedagogy," in *Teaching the Bible: The Discourse and Politics of Biblical Pedagogy*, ed. Fernando F. Segovia and Mary Ann Tolbert (Maryknoll, NY: Orbis Books, 1998), 224–46, at 230.

8. See also Wis 7:24, where Sophia "because of her pureness pervades and penetrates *all things*"; 8:27, where "she renews *all things*"; and 8:1b, where "she orders *all things* well."

embodiment of Sophia by early christians.[9] But Hebrews submerges the origins of this christological language in the Wisdom tradition by never explicitly referring to Woman Wisdom/Sophia.

The statement that the son is the "reflection" of the divine radiance (δόξης) and the "imprint" (χαρακτὴρ) of God's essence is also reminiscent of God's creation of humanity—male and female—in the divine image (κατ᾽ εἰκόνα) and likeness (καθ᾽ ὁμοίωσιν) (Gen 1:27 LXX). The term translated as "word" (ῥῆμα) is used similarly to John's λόγος, which figures in another famous prologue where the masculine Word substitutes for the feminine Wisdom (John 1:1-5). In Hebrews the noun ῥῆμα is neuter and refers to "God's mighty creative word."[10] See also Wis 8:1: "She reaches mightily from one end of the earth to the other, and she orders all things well." The son, the divine utterance spoken in "these last days," differs from Wisdom in that the status of the son is not grounded in creation but is inherited through his having "made purification of sins" and his enthronement by God. That is, the son's participation in the prerogatives of Wisdom is eschatological, not ontological, and imparted by virtue of his saving activity. The son thus can be interpreted as one of the "holy souls," "friends of God and prophets" imbued with Wisdom in every generation: "for God loves nothing so much as the person who lives with Wisdom" (Wis 7:27b-28). The Alexandrian theologian Clement (ca. 150–215) recognizes the Sophia Christology inherent in Heb 1:1 when he writes:

> Christ is called Wisdom by all the prophets. This is he who is the teacher of all created beings, the fellow counselor of God who foreknew all things; and he from above, from the first foundation of the world, "in many and various ways" trains and perfects; hence it is rightly said, "Call no one your teacher on earth." . . . With reason, therefore, the apostle has called the wisdom of God "manifold," and it has manifested its power "in many and various ways"—by art, by knowledge, by faith, by prophecy—for our benefit. "All wisdom is from the Lord and is with him for ever, as says the Wisdom of Jesus (*Stromateis* 1.4).[11]

The notice in Heb 1:4 that the son has inherited a name better (κρείττων) than the angels is developed in the first main section of the homily,

---

9. E.g., 1 Cor 1:22-24; 8:6; Col 1:15; Luke 7:35; Matt 11:2, 5, 19, 25-27, 28-30; 23:37-39. See Elizabeth A. Johnson, *She Who Is: The Mystery of God in Feminist Theological Discourse* (New York: Crossroad, 1996).

10. BDAG 905.

11. Unless otherwise indicated, translations of ancient commentaries on Hebrews are from Erik M. Heen and Philip D. W. Krey, eds., *Ancient Christian Commentary on Scripture, New Testament X* (Downers Grove, IL: InterVarsity, 2005), here at 6.

Katherine Bushnell on Heb 1:3

The American Katherine M. Bushnell was a medical doctor, activist, missionary, and self-taught scholar of Hebrew and Greek. One of her many accomplishments was the writing of *God's Word to Women: One Hundred Bible Studies on Woman's Place in the Divine Economy*, published in the early 1920s. Although it reflects some of the biases and prejudices of her time, this book is a precursor of the feminist biblical scholarship that emerged later in the twentieth century. In her commentary on 1 Tim 1:15 she uses Heb 1:3 to develop her argument for women's full participation in ministry: "Poor, fallen sinful man does not bear God's image and likeness simply because he is *male*! God is not male or female, so that one *sex* bears His image more than the other. It is the glorified Jesus Christ who bears that image and manifests his glory (Heb. 1:3)." (*Source*: Katherine M. Bushnell, *God's Word to Women: One Hundred Bible Studies on Woman's Place in the Divine Economy* [Mossville, IL: God's Word to Women Publishers, n.d.], 114).

Mary Ann Beavis

A Jewish Perspective (Heb 1:1-2)

Hebrews 1:1-3 praises Jesus as the revelation of God and the one through whom all has been created. In later Jewish tradition, these roles are fulfilled by the Torah. The rabbis understand the divine Wisdom (Sophia) who speaks of her role in creation (e.g., Prov 8:22-36) as the Torah, often personified in powerful female terms. "God consulted with the Torah and created the world, as it is written, 'I have good advice and sound wisdom; I have insight, I have strength'" (*Midrash Tanḥuma, Bereshith* 1, citing Prov 8:14).

Actively engaging with the Torah—that is, studying and interpreting the Pentateuch, the rest of Scripture, and the developing oral and written traditions of the rabbis—thus becomes a Jewish way of experiencing divine revelation. Reading holy texts with close attention and discovering new insights in them, individuals and communities come "to know the One who spoke the world into being" (*Sifre Deuteronomy, Ekev* 49).

The homilist of Hebrews engages in this kind of study constantly, quoting and

1:5–2:18. The notion that Sophia and her ways are "better than" or "superior to" foolishness, lack of understanding (Sir 41:8), human strength (Wis 6:1; Eccl 9:16), precious objects (Prov 8:11; 16:16), weapons of war (Eccl 9:18), etc., is a rhetorical topic ubiquitous in the Wisdom literature. This feature of Wisdom discourse informs the many uses of "better" in Hebrews, the first of which is the assertion of the son's superiority to the angels in 1:4; see also Wis 7:29: "She is more beautiful than

A Jewish Perspective—cont'd

creatively interpreting verse after verse of Scripture. Paradoxically, however, this is done with the purpose of arguing for Jesus, not Torah, as the way to know God. But how does one actively engage with Jesus? I see no answer to this question in Hebrews, only an exhortation to faith. As a Jewish reader I am more seduced by the energy and playfulness of the Torah study in Hebrews than by the passive allegiance to Jesus that the homilist apparently wants it to lead to.

Justin Jaron Lewis

Our Stories Are Our Scripture
For Hebrews 1

Wabang[16]

Jaguar purry growl jungle sun
  spears foliage spots fur

Sister mother auntie jaguar
  waits in shade liminal souls

Father and son hunt in parallel
  alignments it is safe to say

Unison presents possibilities no
  differences same as exist

Stars on rosette back night
  traveller shimmers in
  darkness

Next day Indigenous
  Shamanism emerges now
  prophetic

Annharte

the sun, and excels every constellation of the stars. Compared with the light she is superior."[12]

The mention of "purification for sins" (v. 3) draws attention to how liturgy is "interpreter of the texts."[13] Cleansing from sins is one of the most powerful meanings of baptism. Cleansing in the baptismal sense involves both outward washing and inward cleansing (10:22). Along with the practice of anointing with oil (1:9), the act of washing in baptism is closely related to forgiveness of sins. The inward cleansing signified in this rite addresses consciousness of injustice resulting from conversion and leading to sanctification. Feminist liturgical scholar Heather Elkins writes, "Purification in this sense means getting our hands dirty as we assist in God's act."[14] Such a blurring of the line of cleanness and uncleanness is a helpful

12. See also Heb 6:9; 7:7, 19, 22; 8:6; 9:23; 10:34; 11:16, 35, 40; 12:24.

13. Marjorie Procter-Smith, "Feminist Interpretation and Liturgical Proclamation," in *Searching the Scriptures*, vol. 1: *A Feminist Introduction*, ed. Elisabeth Schüssler Fiorenza (New York: Crossroad, 1993), 313–25, at 319.

14. Heather Murray Elkins, *Worshipping Women: Re-Forming God's People for Praise* (Nashville, TN: Abingdon, 1994), 44.

16. "Tomorrow" (Ojibwe).

feminist approach when women's bodies and experiences are associated with uncleanness while purity becomes a domain of male hierarchy that seeks to justify the oppression of women and devalue women's ordinary work.

Exposition: The Mediation of Christ Is Better Than the Mediation of Angels (Heb 1:5–2:18)

The argument of Hebrews is based on a series of comparisons of the son (identified for the first time as Jesus in Heb 2:9) and his significance in salvation history, based on scriptural exposition and intercalated with relatively brief, but significant, subsections of related paraenesis (ethical exhortation and encouragement). The first main section of the homily begins with a series of seven scriptural quotations demonstrating the son's superiority to angels (1:5-14), followed by ethical implications for the addressees (2:1-4), after which the exposition of the topic resumes (2:5-18). Hebrews' insistence that the son is better than angels seems odd to contemporary readers; why would such a comparison be so important to the homilist? In the Second Temple Judaism of the time, speculation about angels played a significant role, especially in apocalyptic prophecy.[16] The law of Moses (in the terminology of Hebrews, the "old covenant"; see also Heb 8:8-13) contains legislation stipulating that the sacrificial worship of Israel is to be carried out by the Levitical priesthood, which, for Hebrews, is less effectual than the perfected heavenly high priesthood of Christ (7:15–9:14). Thus the homilist lays the foundation for the argument that Jesus the son is superior to Moses the servant, that the high priesthood of Christ is superior to the Levitical priesthood, and that the new covenant is better than the old. The homilist argues that the Israelite institutions are grounded in a law mediated by angels through a servant of God, whereas the new revelation is mediated by the son and heir of God.

The catena ("chain") of seven scriptural quotations in Heb 1:5-14 begins and ends with rhetorical questions premised on the conclusion that the son is superior to the angels: "For to which of the angels did God ever say . . . ? Are not all angels spirits in the divine service, sent to serve for the sake of those who are to inherit salvation?" (1:5a, 14). The choice of seven proof texts (inserted between vv. 5a and 14) reflects the Jewish

---

17. James H. Charlesworth, ed., *The Old Testament Pseudepigrapha* (New York: Doubleday, 1985), 2:925–27.

⁵For to which of the angels did
God ever say,
"You are my Son;
today I have begotten you"?
Or again,
"I will be his Father,
and he will be my Son"?
⁶And again, when he brings the
firstborn into the world, he
says,
"Let all God's angels worship
him."
⁷Of the angels he says,
"He makes his angels winds,
and his servants flames
of fire."

⁸But of the Son he says,
"Your throne, O God, is forever
and ever,
and the righteous scepter is
the scepter of your
kingdom.
⁹You have loved righteousness
and hated wickedness;
therefore God, your God,
has anointed you
with the oil of gladness
beyond your
companions."
¹⁰And,
"In the beginning, Lord, you
founded the earth,

notion of seven as the number of perfection or completion.[17] Apart from 2 Sam 7:14, a messianic oracle, all the proofs in the catena are from the Psalms, associated with the ancestor of the messiah, David, interpreted to support the exalted status of the messiah, Jesus. Brief quotations from scriptural sources are marshaled to make the author's case.

In Heb 1:5a, to establish the sonship of the messiah Jesus, the homilist uses Ps 2:7, "You are my son, today I have begotten/given birth to you," an Israelite enthronement hymn portraying the Davidic king of Israel as the adopted son of Yhwh. The verb usually translated "begotten" (γεγέννηκά) can mean either to beget when used of men or to give birth to when used of women (see also Heb 11:23). In one Korean translation of the word "begotten," God is clearly a mother who is "giving birth to" her son (Korean Revised Version, 1961). But God is paradoxically presented as a father in the next part of the verse: "I will be his Father, and he will be my Son" (v. 5b). We could argue that God is mother and father at the same time; thus God is the parent of all people in the world. We can even go on to claim that God is beyond humanly constructed binary gender. Clement of Alexandria acknowledges the gender ambiguity of this language of "begetting" when he observes: "God himself is love.

17. E.g., Gen 1:1–2:4; 29:15-30; Lev 25:2-7; Ps 12:6; Matt 18:21-22; Acts 6:1-6; Rev 2–3.

and the heavens are the
work of your hands;
[11]they will perish, but you
remain;
they will all wear out like
clothing;
[12]like a cloak you will roll them
up,
and like clothing they will
be changed.
But you are the same,
and your years will never
end."
[13]But to which of the angels has he
ever said,

"Sit at my right hand
until I make your enemies a
footstool for your feet"?
[14]Are not all angels spirits in the divine
service, sent to serve for the sake of
those who are to inherit salvation?
[2:1]Therefore we must pay greater
attention to what we have heard, so
that we do not drift away from it. [2]For if
the message declared through angels
was valid, and every transgression or
disobedience received a just penalty,
[3]how can we escape if we neglect so
great a salvation? It was declared at
first through the Lord, and it was at-

And out of love for us became feminine. In his ineffable essence he is
Father. In his compassion to us he became Mother. The father by loving
became feminine, and the great proof of this is whom he begot of himself.
And the fruit brought forth by love is love."[18]

The homilist turns to the dominant metaphor of God as father and the
anointed king/messiah as son in this second quotation: "I will be his
Father, and he will be my Son" (Heb 1:5b//2 Sam 7:14), from an oracle
in which God promises an eternal covenant with David and his descendants (2 Sam 7:4-17), a promise that Jesus, as Davidic messiah (Heb 7:14),
fulfills. The gender blurring returns in Heb 1:6a, however, when the
homilist introduces the quotation of Ps 96:7 (LXX; 97:7 MT; see also Deut
32:43 LXX)—"and let all God's angels worship him"—with the gloss:
"And again, when he brings his firstborn into the world," imaging God
in the role of mother or midwife in the context of the royal adoption. The
Scriptures often invoke the image of God as midwife who assists in the
birth of people[19] and at the birth of the cosmos.[20] In particular, Heb 1:6a

18. *Who Is the Rich Man That Shall Be Saved*, 37. Quoted in April De Conick, *Holy
Misogyny: Why the Sex and Gender Conflicts in the Early Church Still Matter* (New York:
Continuum, 2001), 32.

19. E.g., Pss 22:9-10a; 71:6; Isa 66:9; Job 10:18; Gal 1:15.

20. E.g., Job 38:7-9. See Don C. Benjamin, "Israel's God: Mother and Midwife," *BTB*
19 (1989): 115–20; Juliana M. Claassens, "Rupturing God-Language: The Metaphor

tested to us by those who heard him, [4]while God added his testimony by signs and wonders and various miracles, and by gifts of the Holy Spirit, distributed according to his will.

[5]Now God did not subject the coming world, about which we are speaking, to angels. [6]But someone has testified somewhere,

"What are human beings that you are mindful of them,
or mortals, that you care for them?
[7]You have made them for a little while lower than the angels;

you have crowned them with glory and honor,
[8]subjecting all things under their feet."

Now in subjecting all things to them, God left nothing outside their control. As it is, we do not yet see everything in subjection to them, [9]but we do see Jesus, who for a little while was made lower than the angels, now crowned with glory and honor because of the suffering of death, so that by the grace of God he might taste death for everyone.

[10]It was fitting that God, for whom and through whom all things exist, in

and Job 10:18 use similar language (εἰσαγάγῃ; ἐξήγαγες) to refer to God's "bringing forth" the newborn from the womb. The homilist continues with a quotation from Ps 97:7 LXX (Heb 1:6b), which alters the Hebrew wording "all the gods bow down before him" to "let all God's angels worship him," imaging the homage due to the newly born/adopted royal child. Next, Ps 104:4 (Heb 1:7) is marshaled to demonstrate that the angels—demoted from deities (אלוהים) to messengers (ἄγγελοι) by the LXX—are simply "winds" (πνεύματα; usually translated, as in the NRSV, as "spirits") and "servants flames of fire," like the created elements, as opposed to the divinely begotten/born son.

The first part of this catena in Heb 1:5-7 evokes the baptism of Jesus. The scene of "Let all God's angels worship him" (1:6) can resonate with or can easily be seen as a dramatic stage for the story in the Gospel of Mark of "the heaven torn apart and the Spirit descending like a dove on him" (Mark 1:10). The reference to angels as spirits, messengers, or winds, and flames of fire in Hebrews is further illuminated in the descriptions of the baptizing Spirit as water and a dove in all four gospels.

---

of God as Midwife in Psalm 22," http://home.nwciowa.edu/wacome/Claassens Bakhtin2005.pdf, accessed July 15, 2015; Juliana M. Claassens, "Praying from the Depths of the Deep: Remembering the Image of God as Midwife in Psalm 71," *RevExp* 104 (2007): 761–75.

bringing many children to glory, should make the pioneer of their salvation perfect through sufferings. ¹¹For the one who sanctifies and those who are sanctified all have one Father. For this reason Jesus is not ashamed to call them brothers and sisters, ¹²saying,

"I will proclaim your name to my
brothers and sisters,
in the midst of the congregation I will praise you."
¹³And again,
"I will put my trust in him."
And again,
"Here am I and the children whom
God has given me."

¹⁴Since, therefore, the children share flesh and blood, he himself likewise shared the same things, so that through death he might destroy the one who has the power of death, that is, the devil, ¹⁵and free those who all their lives were held in slavery by the fear of death. ¹⁶For it is clear that he did not come to help angels, but the descendants of Abraham. ¹⁷Therefore he had to become like his brothers and sisters in every respect, so that he might be a merciful and faithful high priest in the service of God, to make a sacrifice of atonement for the sins of the people. ¹⁸Because he himself was tested by what he suffered, he is able to help those who are being tested.

Though the "likening of the spirit to a dove is notoriously obscure," the linkage between this particular text in Mark and the text of Ps 2:7, cited in Heb 1:5, is well supported by the Ancient Near Eastern legend that features the descent of a dove on an elect person.[21] Such biblical cross-references strengthen the liturgical theology of baptism. This includes five meanings rooted in the NT: union with Jesus Christ, incorporation into the church, new birth, forgiveness of sin, and reception of the Holy Spirit.[22] At least two themes resonate with the hymnic catena here: purification from sin (1:3) and the reception of the Spirit (1:7).

We could even suggest that the most obvious intertextual reading lies in the trinitarian baptismal formula—the Father, the Son, and the Holy Spirit—in Heb 1:5-7, though some argue that this passage does not contain any trinitarian formulas.[23] The gender exclusivity of the baptismal formula is challenged not only in biblical scholarship but also in pastoral and liturgical studies. If one of the central meanings of baptism is the conversion to new life, a masculine formula of baptism contradicts itself

21. Mary Ann Beavis, *Mark* (Grand Rapids, MI: Baker Academic, 2011), 37.

22. James F. White, *Introduction to Christian Worship*, 3rd ed. (Nashville, TN: Abingdon, 2000), 218.

23. Fred B. Craddock, "The Letter to the Hebrews," *The New Interpreter's Bible* (Nashville, TN: Abingdon, 1998), 12:1–173, at 12.

and is inadequate because it reflects and reinforces "old ways of patriarchy."[24] A suggested solution to the problem of the androcentric liturgical language of baptism includes creating a nonsexist, inclusive, and emancipatory language so that the vision of baptism as the *birthright* of radical social equality can be lived out. Aidan Kavanagh well sums up the blurring of gender and social boundaries that is deeply rooted and embedded in the theology of baptism:

> Baptism in its fullness is the primary liminal experience during which the Church is shaped each paschal season into a *communitas* of equals in one Body of neither Jew nor Greek, master nor slave, male nor female, and is prepared to receive fresh and new God's grace in Jesus the Anointed One now become life-giving Spirit.[25]

More recently, other feminists and queer theologians have explored baptism as a gender-blurring act in light of Gal 3:27-28. Marcella Althaus-Reid and Lisa Isherwood invite us to the following thought:

> Galatians 3:27-28, a text which suggested to [such women as Thecla, Prisca, and Maximilla] that once the distinctions and divisions of class, race and gender were overcome they were free to embrace their divine natures. . . . In taking seriously the message of equality of the Christian gospel, they queered gender-performance in order to find a way of living the radical equality they professed to believe. . . . Women who break out from the norm in any age face the threat of physical violence . . . and their way of remaining safe was to keep transgressing the norm. . . . These women were not all transsexual but they did push the gender boundaries very hard in order to create space in which to flourish.[26]

In Heb 1:8-13 the homilist turns from proof texts demonstrating the inferiority of the angels to the son and quotes psalms interpreted as addressed directly to the son. Hebrews 1:8-9 quotes Ps 45:6-7 (LXX), in its original context a hymn praising the enthronement of the Davidic king who will rule righteously and in accordance with Torah. The king is addressed in highly exalted terms as "god" (ὁ θεός) in his role as adopted

---

24. Ruth Duck, *Gender and the Name of God: The Trinitarian Baptismal Formula* (New York: Pilgrim Press, 1991), 4.

25. Marjorie Procter-Smith, *In Her Own Rite: Constructing Feminist Liturgical Tradition* (Nashville, TN: Abingdon, 1990), 146, quoting Aidan Kavanagh, *The Shape of Baptism: The Rite of Christian Initiation* (New York: Pueblo, 1978), 200. Emphasis in original.

26. Marcella Althaus-Reid and Lisa Isherwood, *Controversies in Feminist Theology* (London: SCM Press, 2007), 21.

son of the deity, and as God's anointed (ἔχρισεν) "with the oil of gladness beyond your companions." For Hebrews, God's son the messiah ("anointed"), as heir of the eternal covenant with David (2 Sam 7:4-17; see also Heb 1:5b), inherits the divine title from his royal ancestors.[27] Again, these verses demonstrate Hebrews' Jewishness, as well as tensions with modern Jewish practices. On the one hand, Jesus as the anointed one is in line with the anointing of David; on the other hand, he inaugurates the new covenant that supersedes the faulty old one (Heb 8:7). This tension between continuity and discontinuity is kept alive throughout Hebrews. The tension is critical insofar as Christian tradition has either demonized Judaism as bad or patronized it as a wounded religion. In modern terms, it is important to recognize Christianity as in solidarity with Judaism and yet to acknowledge that the two religions are different and distinctive.

The next three verses (Heb 1:10-12) quote Ps 102:25-27, which contrasts the eternity of God with the transitoriness of God's creation, the earth and its inhabitants ("they will perish, but you remain"). Unlike Ps 45:6-7, which uses a divine title to address the human king/messiah, the quotation from Ps 102 is directly addressed to God (κύριε or "lord"), in the Bible a title that can be applied to a high-status human being or to God. But again the homilist applies the language of divinity to the son ("In the beginning, Lord, you founded the earth, and the heavens are the work of your hands"), whose sovereignty extends from the creation to its dissolution ("like a cloak you will roll them up, and like clothing they will be changed"). Again the powers of divine Sophia, "the fashioner of all things" (Wis 7:22; 8:6), created at the beginning (Prov 8:22), renewing all things (Wis 7:27), and ultimately prevailing (Wis 7:29-30), are attributed to the messianic son, addressed as Lord. As the patron of Israelite kingship and the source of messianic rule, Sophia is the source of upright and lawful governance: "By me kings reign, and rulers decree what is just" (Prov 8:15).

In the final two verses of the catena (Heb 1:13-14) the homilist returns to the theme of the superiority of the son to the angels with a rhetorical question that parallels the one that introduces it: "To which of the angels has he [God] ever said . . . ?" (1:13; see also 1:5). Here, the proof text is from Ps 110:1, a coronation psalm alluded to elsewhere in the NT (Matt

---

27. For other biblical examples of human beings designated "god," see Exod 7:1; Ps 82:6; John 10:34-35; see also Mary Rose D'Angelo, *Moses in the Letter to the Hebrews*, SBLDS 42 (Missoula, MT: Scholars Press, 1979), 10.

22:43-44; Mark 12:36; Luke 20:42-43; Acts 2:34-35)[28] and in Hebrews (5:6; 7:17; 10:13). Here the sonship of the messiah is portrayed in terms of his divine co-regency ("sit at my right hand") and eschatological victory ("until I make your enemies a footstool for your feet"), a warlike sentiment that can be translated into more peaceable sophialogical terms, "against wisdom evil does not prevail" (Wis 7:30b). The author concludes Heb 1 with a reminder of the lesser status of the angels ("ministering πνεύματα") relative not to the son but to humanity, "for the sake of those who are to inherit salvation" (Heb 1:14). Throughout Hebrews the solidarity of the son with other human beings is emphasized; like the son, all believers are "heirs to the promise" (6:17; 11:9) of the God who brings "many children" to glory (2:10; 12:5, 7).

A Jewish Perspective (Heb 1:5-14)

Hebrews 1:5-14 is the first of many passages in this book that are in the vein of Jewish midrash, a genre in which verses of Scripture are quoted, interwoven, and interpreted with imaginative freedom. While midrash often cites scriptural verses as "proof texts," the proofs have a tendency to be unconvincing to anyone who does not already accept the desired conclusion.[30] This is my issue as a Jewish reader of this midrashic passage: why would I understand these verses as referring to Jesus?

The explanation in this commentary is helpful: verses about David or David's descendants are understood as applying to the Messiah, "son of David." Therefore, if the reader has already accepted Jesus as the Messiah, many of these citations become convincing.

Even so, the verses from Ps 97 about angels worshiping God and from Ps 102 about God creating the world seem out of place. They are not about David or his descendants but unambiguously about the Creator. This would be no objection for a reader who already accepts Jesus as God; but why would a reader holding

---

28. See Herbert W. Bateman IV, "Psalm 110:1 and the New Testament," *BSac* 149, no. 596 (1992): 438–53.

30. See Tirzah Meacham's critique of rabbinic legal midrash in "Legal-Religious Status of the Jewish Female," *Jewish Women: A Comprehensive Historical Encyclopedia*, ed. Paula Hyman and Dalia Ofer (March 1, 2009), Jewish Women's Archive, http://jwa.org/encyclopedia/article/legal-religious-status-of-jewish-female, accessed July 15, 2015.

that belief need to be convinced that Jesus is greater than the angels? I am left puzzled.

If the text is identifying Jesus, a male human being, with the Creator, this is of course problematic from Jewish and feminist perspectives. While the preponderance of biblical and Jewish imagery for God is male, there are exceptions, including some of the "Sophia" passages mentioned in this commentary. The exceptions gave medieval Jewish theologians resources with which to imagine God as abstract and ungendered, as did Maimonides, or as manifested in vividly masculine, feminine, and genderqueer ways, as did the Kabbalists. Today, Jews of all genders and sexualities are drawing on, and expanding, these insights. This would be more difficult if Jewish tradition had accepted the man Jesus as a uniquely true embodiment of the divine.

Justin Jaron Lewis

Paraenesis: Ethical Implications (Heb 2:1-4)

As a skilled preacher, the homilist shifts from exposition to exhortation, drawing out the implications of scriptural interpretation in the previous verses for the lives of the audience, who, as argued in our introduction, the author sees as in danger of losing their faith in the face of hardship, persecution, and the delay of the parousia.[30] This crisis of loss of faith is coming not only from an external force but also from internal factors. The delay of the second coming of Christ exposed people to demoralizing chaos (10:25, 35-39). The author's attention to liturgical life should be viewed from the perspective of this internal crisis. An urge to repent through confession (3:1; 4:14; 10:23) is well grounded in this sense. The external force of the crisis in this community may include Jewish christians returning to Judaism.[31] The argument of the superiority of the son over the law (Torah) indirectly alluded to in Heb 2:2, discussed below, would be persuasive for those who are tempted to go back to their previous religion. It should be noted, however, that the perceived connection between the son and the law lends weight to the exhortation not to neglect the Jewish heritage (2:3).

The thin line between maintaining and denouncing Jewish tradition is crossed and recrossed many times in this letter and is a theme woven

---

30. E.g., Heb 6:4-6; 10:19-39; 12:3-12.
31. Craddock, "Letter to the Hebrews," 9.

through the text. Throughout the exhortation the homilist uses the inclusive first-person plural rather than accusing the audience ("you," plural) of straying: "therefore we must pay greater attention to what we have heard, so that we do not drift away from it . . . how can we escape if we neglect . . . it was attested to us . . ." (Heb 2:1-4). The term "drift away" (παραρυῶμεν) suggests the sea voyage metaphor often used in early christian literature to describe the life of faith (see also Heb 6:19), e.g., in Origen's writing:

> For as many as are in the little ship of faith are sailing with the Lord; as many as are in the bark of the holy church will voyage with the Lord across this wavetossed life; though the Lord himself may sleep in holy quiet, he is but watching your patience and endurance: looking forward to the repentance, and to the conversion of those who have sinned.[32]

Such multisensory metaphors can be further explored as "feminist amplification of liturgical proclamation,"[33] in which the text does not simply and solely function as the word of God but fully embodies human experience and agency of repentance, renewal, and transformation.

Hebrews 2:2 alludes to a tradition according to which Torah ("the word declared through angels") was not revealed directly to Moses but was mediated to him by angels, a belief taken for granted by other NT authors (see also Gal 3:19; Acts 7:53).[34] In Jewish literature the angels' role at Sinai does not vitiate the status of Torah; in Acts the delivery of the law by angels marks its exalted status. In contrast, here the homilist uses a typical Jewish argument from lesser to greater to establish the superiority of the salvation mediated by the son to the law mediated by angels: the involvement of the angels points to the law's lesser status relative to the new revelation mediated by the son, who has entered the heavenly sanctuary to appear before God (Heb 9:15, 24). Although the "salvation" (σωτηρία) offered through the son is greater than that of the law, the former was legally "valid" (βέβαιος) in that it stipulated just penalties for "every transgression or disobedience" (2:2). Although the homilist implies that even greater punishment will ensue if believers are neglectful of their heritage, the emphasis is on the promise of salvation (2:3a), defined by

---

32. Origen, *Fr. Matt.* 3.3; see also Hippolytus, *Antichr.* 59. Quoted in Thomas C. Oden and Christopher A. Hall, eds., *Ancient Christian Commentary on Scripture, Mark II* (Downers Grove, IL: InterVarsity, 1998), 60.

33. Procter-Smith, "Feminist Interpretation," 323.

34. For Jewish examples, see Harold Attridge, *The Epistle to the Hebrews: A Commentary*, Hermeneia (Philadelphia: Fortress Press, 1989), 65 n. 28.

Gail Paterson Corrington as "safety, security, and well-being, procured by the agency of a deity who can overcome the hostile cosmic forces that produce in individuals feelings of helplessness and powerlessness."[35] This salvation (similar to the biblical concept of *shalōm*) is established and confirmed not by events in the sacred past of Israel but by recent events: "It was declared at first by the Lord [Jesus], . . . while God added his testimony by signs and wonders and various miracles, and by gifts of the Holy Spirit, distributed according to his will" (2:3b-4). Despite the high status attributed to the son by the homilist, the origin in God of the signs, wonders, and miracles, here probably referring to the wondrous deeds done by Jesus and his disciples,[36] points to the theocentric (God-centered) focus of Hebrews; the source of the son's power, as also that of all the faithful, is "the gifts of the Holy Spirit" (Heb 2:4).[37]

Exposition: The Mediation of Christ Is Better Than the Mediation of Angels (Heb 2:5-18)

In the remainder of this section of the homily the author works out the implications of the scriptural proofs presented in Heb 1:5-14 and prepares the ground for the subsequent arguments that the son is superior to Moses (3:1–4:13), that the high priesthood of the messiah ("Christ") is better than the Levitical priesthood (5:1–7:28), and that the new covenant surpasses the old (8:1–10:18). Throughout, the pattern of good (law delivered through angels) to better (salvation wrought by the son) holds; as James W. Thompson notes: "Comparison (Greek *synkresis*) was . . . a common rhetorical device designed, not for polemical purposes, but to demonstrate the greatness of the speaker's subject (Aristotle, *Rhetoric* 1.9.39). Exercises in *synkresis* were a common feature in rhetorical education. Thus the author's comparisons reflect not a polemic against Judaism but his desire to demonstrate the greatness of the Christian revelation."[38]

The author's intent was not to demonstrate the superiority of Christianity to Judaism but to interpret the ongoing process of revelation grounded in the Jewish Scriptures, in the events of Jesus' life, and in the

---

35. Gail Patterson Corrington, "The Milk of Salvation: Redemption by the Mother in Late Antiquity and Early Christianity," *HTR* 4 (1989): 393–420, at 397.

36. E.g., Mark 6:2; Matt 11:20-23; 13:54, 58; Luke 10:13; Acts 4:30; 5:12; 14:3; 15:12.

37. See also Heb 6:4; 1 Cor 12:28-29; Gal 3:5.

38. James W. Thompson, *Hebrews*, Paideia Commentaries on the New Testament (Grand Rapids, MI: Baker Academic, 2008), 36.

experience of the community. This does not obviate Christian responsibility for the anti-Judaism that Hebrews may subsequently have been used to foster. Insofar as the homilist portrays the old covenant (the law of Moses) as obsolete and the new covenant (salvation through Christ) as replacing it, Hebrews is supersessionist, i.e., it maintains that the church has superseded Israel. As Terence Donaldson notes, "To the extent that the intended readership of the epistle included or consisted of Gentiles, its supersessionism could easily slide over into anti-Judaism."[39] Similarly, the christian community represented in the letter might have struggled with establishing their identity as Gentile christian, both seeking to preserve their Jewish inheritance and, on the other hand, relegating parts of this tradition to the past (Heb 8:8-13). One can understand that in this precarious context such an authoritative Christ-centered vision might be necessary for such minority groups as a survival strategy. This view has been used, however, to justify anti-Semitism in that Christ replaces a Judaism that is consumed in the fire of God (12:29).[40] This becomes clear when the homily speaks of "the imperfect copies of the instruments and procedures for approaching God and gaining right relationship with him in historical Israel."[41] Such anti-Jewish attitudes as a springboard for the formation of Christianity might be unavoidably inherent in Hebrews. What is argued here is not that the text of Hebrews itself is false or written to attack Judaism but that its use by subsequent generations of readers and interpreters inevitably contributed to solidifying and sustaining Western Christian imperialism against Jewish and non-Western Christian people.

In Heb 2:5-9 the author picks up the thread of the exposition by answering the rhetorical questions of 1:13-14: God did not subordinate the age to come—a commonplace Jewish expression for the messianic era[42]—to angels but, as attested by Scripture, to humanity. The passage from Ps 8:4-6 quoted in Heb 2:6-8 uses the terms "human being" (ἄνθρωπος)

---

39. Terence L. Donaldson, *Jews and Anti-Judaism in the New Testament* (London: SPCK, 2010), 143.

40. Mary Rose D'Angelo, "Hebrews," in *The Women's Bible Commentary*, ed. Carol A. Newsom and Sharon H. Ringe (Louisville, KY: Westminster John Knox, 1992), 364–67, at 366.

41. Howard Clark Kee, "The Formation of Christian Communities," *The Cambridge Companion to the Bible*, ed. Bruce Chilton, 2nd ed. (Cambridge: Cambridge University Press, 1997), 481–682, at 596–98.

42. E.g., Dan 7:18, 27; 1 En. 71:15; 2 Esd 7:50; 8:1; Sib. Or. 3:608-23; As. Mos. 7–9.

and "son of man" (υἱὸς ἀνθρώπου[43]) as synonymous, a nuance captured by the NRSV: "What are human beings that you are mindful of them, or mortals, that you care for them?" The son, a human being, is portrayed in solidarity with humanity, who have been made "a little" or "for a little while" (βραχύ) lower than the angels, although humanity is destined, collectively with the son, to be "crowned . . . with glory and honor, subjecting all things under their feet" (2:7-8a; see also 1:13). The homilist admits that "we" (inclusive of both author and addressees) do not yet see the fulfillment of this promise of human exaltation over creation (v. 8b) But Jesus, mentioned by name for the first time in v. 9, was briefly made lower than the angels in fulfillment of the Scripture but now is exalted, paradoxically through his undergoing death, the common lot of humanity. Commentators differ as to whether the wording of v. 9b should be rendered "so that by the grace of God he might taste death for everyone" (NRSV) or "apart from God he might taste death for everyone," due to a minority textual variant that substitutes χωρὶς ("apart from") for χάριτι ("by the grace of"). Most translations follow the majority reading χάριτι, perhaps best rendered by the biblical term "lovingkindness" (Hebrew, חסד). Jesus, the human son, in solidarity with other human beings, partook in death, an act the author presents as in accordance with God's care for humanity. This part of Hebrews reveals its beauty and complexity in the way it maintains a tension between an angelic otherworldly eschatological Christology and a human down-to-earth incarnational Christology, speaking of the one who was "made lower than angels" and "became as we are."

> *Our Stories Are Our Scripture*
> *For Hebrews 2*
>
> **Original Bear Upon**
>
> Bears counsel with Earthmaker
>   as eldest admits not being
>
> Worthy of first choice so it is
>   told each decline to youngest
>
> Brother who will bear out or
>   bear witness very bearable
>
> He would bear out or bear
>   witness to bear tough challenge
>
> Clan destiny is to soldier protect
>   then gather healing roots
>
> Upon walk through village
>   during optimum hibernation
>   stage
>
> *Annharte*

---

43. See, e.g., NIV, ASV, AV, NLT, NASB.

TRANSLATION MATTERS

Hebrews 2:6-7 quotes Ps 8:4-8, a hymn extolling God's creation and the human role as caretakers of the earth (see also Gen 1:28). The Authorized (King James) Version famously translates Heb 2:6 as "What is man that thou art mindful of him, or the son of man, that thou visitest him?" In the NRSV the verse reads: "What are human beings, that you are mindful of them, or mortals, that you care for them?" In Greek the words rendered "man" (AV)/"human beings" (NRSV) and "son of man" (AV)/"mortals" (NRSV) are ἄνθρωπος and υἱὸς ἀνθρώπου. While the Greek terms are both singular, their meanings are collective in both Greek and Hebrew, referring to all humankind.[44] The traditional (AV) translation interprets ἄνθρωπος and υἱὸς ἀνθρώπου christologically, as referring to Jesus the human son of man ("child of humanity" or "human one"), a meaning no doubt given to the terms by the homilist because of their frequent use in the gospels to refer to Jesus. The collective interpretation of the terms in the NRSV highlights the solidarity between Jesus the "human one" and all of humankind.

Mary Ann Beavis

TRANSLATION MATTERS: ANOTHER PERSPECTIVE

Hebrews 2:6-9 quotes Scripture with a strikingly cheeky introductory phrase, "someone has testified somewhere." Since the verses quoted are from a well-known psalm ascribed to David, it is not as if there would be any doubt as to whom or where they are from. I do not recall encountering such a phrase in Jewish texts, although the spirit of playful mystification is familiar.

The quotation from Ps 8 this leads into, and the midrashic interpretation that follows, is obscured by the NRSV translation (and here I disagree with the present commentary as well). Following a laudable agenda of removing masculine bias, the NRSV has "human beings" and "mortals" in the plural. But the KJV "man" and "son of man," in the singular, better reflect the Greek text and the original Hebrew language of the psalm, as well as what Hebrews does with it. A common technique of midrash is to ignore contextual meaning in favor of a hyperliteral reading, and this is what Hebrews is doing. In the psalm itself the singular words אֱנוֹשׁ and בֶּן אָדָם certainly refer to humanity as a whole, but Hebrews takes them "literally," in the singular, and reads them as pointing to Jesus, "the Son of Man." So every "them" in the NRSV translation of Heb 2:7-8 should actually be a "him." The psalmist exalted humanity as a whole; the homilist, only Jesus.

Continuing the midrashic approach, the homilist reimagines the psalmist's notion that human beings are, spatially or hierarchically, "a little lower than the angels," as a temporal claim that "Jesus . . . *for a little while* was made lower than the angels."

Justin Jaron Lewis

---

44. See also Pamela Eisenbaum, "Hebrews," in *The Jewish Annotated New Testament* (New York: Oxford University Press, 2011), 406–26, at 408.

The exaltation of humanity promised in the Scriptures is elaborated upon in Heb 2:10-18, bolstered by proof texts from Ps 22:22 and Isa 8:17-18. As a human being, Jesus, who as "pioneer [forerunner] of salvation" appointed by the God "for whom and through whom all things exist," leads many children to glory (Heb 2:10), "for the one who sanctifies and those who are sanctified all have one source" (2:11a). The NRSV renders the term here translated "from one source" as "from one Father," but the Greek term is simply ἐξ ἑνός, "from one," most likely referring to the divine source of all creation but possibly to the common ancestor, Abraham (see also 2:16), or to the primal human, Adam.[45] Again, the Psalmist's words are placed on the lips of Jesus: "I will proclaim your name to my brothers and sisters; in the midst of the congregation I will praise you" (Heb 2:12; Ps 22:22), underscoring the kinship between Jesus and his human family, the ἐκκλησία, often translated as "church" (NRSV: "congregation"). The homilist marshals brief excerpts from Isaiah—"I will put my trust in him [God]" (Isa 8:17b) and "Here I am and the children God has given me" (Isa 8:18a)—to broaden the familial language from brother-sister to parent-children (τὰ παιδία; Heb 2:13).

As a human child of God, Jesus shared in the "blood and flesh" of the human family to overcome the "power" (κράτος) of death by sharing in death (Heb 2:14) to liberate humanity from the fear of death (2:15). The reference in v. 14 to "the devil" (τὸν διάβολον) as the one with the power of death is usually explained as a biblical convention,[46] but it is rather jarring in a document in which the devil (or Satan) is not referred to elsewhere. Perhaps in the context of this section, where the "testing" (πειρασθείς) of Jesus enables him to help those who are

---

Katherine Bushnell on Heb 1:13

In her christological reading of Gen 3:15, Katherine Bushnell describes the kinship of believers as "children of the kingdom": "the children of God are, by faith in Jesus Christ, also called the *children* of Christ,—Heb. 2:13: and *the seed* of Christ in Isa. 53:10. But since Christ is the Seed of the woman . . . all believers are, through Christ, the seed of the woman also." Here the evangelical Bushnell is not referring to Jesus as a child of Mary, but as the offspring of Eve who redeems humankind. (*Source*: Bushnell, *God's Word to Women*, 353.)

Mary Ann Beavis

---

45. See Alan C. Mitchell, *Hebrews*, SP 13 (Collegeville, MN: Liturgical Press, 2009), 74.

46. E.g., Attridge, *Hebrews*, 92; Thompson, *Hebrews*, 75; see also Wis 2:24a: "through the devil's envy death entered the world."

"tested" (πειραζομένοις) (2:18), the synoptic "temptation narratives" are in view.[47] Jesus' kinship is thus not with angels but with the offspring of Abraham (2:16). Here Abraham is probably conceived as the ancestor of Israel, but with his wives Sarah, Hagar, and Keturah he is ancestor of many nations (Gen 25:1-6, 12-18). The next verse (Heb 2:17) announces the unique christological theme highlighted in the central section of the homily (4:14–5:10; 6:20–7:28; 9:1–10:18), the high priesthood of the messiah, the one whose suffering enables him to identify with the sufferings of "those who are being tested" (2:18), the homilist and the addressees.

Although they are not directly cited, the argument of this section is grounded in the biblical creation accounts, especially as filtered through the Wisdom tradition. The homilist reassures the community that, like their brother Jesus, they reflect the image of God (Heb 1:3; see also Gen 1:27) and will share in Jesus' destiny, which includes death (Heb 2:14-18; see also Gen 3:19), glorification (Heb 2:6-9), and even immortality (Heb 1:8-12; see also Wis 2:23: "for God created us for incorruption ['immortality'], and made us in the image of his own eternity"). In the world to come (Heb 2:5) the primal relationship between humanity and the new creation will be restored.[48]

There is a parallel here between the community addressed by the homilist and the audience of the Priestly (P) creation account (Gen 1:1–2:4a) as reconstructed by Alice Laffey.[49] Laffey suggests that P was composed for the returning exiles of Judah, who felt out of control and abandoned by God due to the hardships they faced in their devastated homeland. In this situation, the Judean settlers needed to be reassured: "Those whose consciousness is pervaded by their powerlessness as a conquered people do have power, a God-given power to use what they need of creation, a power they have in common with, to the same extent as, their conquerors. They are okay—they share in relationship with creation, similar to their conquerors; they are okay—animals are not their superiors."[50]

47. See also Mark 1:12-13; Matt 4:1-11; Luke 4:1-13; see also Heb 5:7.

48. See also Gen 1:26, 28, where humanity is given "rule" (LXX: ἀρχέτωσαν, ἄρχετε) over creation, and the reference to the "subjection" of "all things" to humanity in Heb 2:8.

49. Alice Laffey, "The Priestly Creation Narrative: Goodness and Interdependence," in *Earth, Wind, and Fire: Biblical and Theological Perspectives on Creation*, ed. Carol J. Dempsey and Mary Margaret Pazdan (Collegeville, MN: Liturgical Press, 2004), 24–34.

50. Ibid., 29.

Laffey further proposes that "the dominion directed in Genesis 1:26, 28 of human beings over other elements of creation was not originally meant to be interpreted as humans over other living things, but rather as human beings on an equal footing with all of creation."[51] Like the Priestly author, the homilist assures the wavering community that they, like Jesus, are made in the divine image, positively related to the whole of creation: "despite their recent history and current situation, *really* good." In parallel with the language of the "subjection" of creation (Heb 2:8; see also Ps 8:6), the homilist, like P, "does not necessarily intend to imply that humankind, made in the image of God and possessing dominion over other living things, is consequently superior."[52]

While Laffey makes a convincing argument for the author's intention to empower the intended hearers, Christians in the West, shaped by European civilization, cannot afford to ignore the dangerous implications of the wording of this text, in particular the assertion that humans are given the authority to "rule" over creation. Among the figures who played a role in the beginnings of modern civilization, Francis Bacon clearly found the domination of nature and women by men a logical implication of scientific civilization and Enlightenment. For Bacon, reason, the noble and autonomous virtue humans seek to achieve, belongs only to men. Men, he said, must unlock the secrets of nature and gain control over "her" in order to attain the goal of becoming "Men of Reason." The rationale behind such control is that the Man of Reason is strong, forceful, potent, and masculine as God intended him to be and therefore cannot be subordinated to nature, which is supposed to be weak, docile, impotent, and feminine. The exploitation of nature is endorsed by God, the omnipotent and omnipresent ruler of all. Bacon writes: "For you [European noblemen] have but to follow and as it were hound nature in her wanderings, and you will be able, when you like, to lead and drive her afterwards to the same place again. . . . Neither ought a man to make scruple of entering and penetrating into these holes and corners, when the inquisition of truth is his sole object."[53]

Mary Grey makes the brilliant point that in the quotation above the language of discovering nature's secrets is similar to the religious lan-

---

51. Ibid., 29–30.
52. Ibid., 31.
53. Francis Bacon, "De Dignitate et Augmentis Scientiarum," in *The Philosophical Works of Francis Bacon*, ed. John M. Robertson (London: Routledge; New York: Dutton, 1905), 413–638, at 428.

guage used during the inquisition's witch hunts.[54] Not only were nature and women linked, but verbal and visual images of the inquisition were put into use for the exploitation of nature and oppression of women in Bacon's discourse. Violence (even torture) was encouraged in the name of discovering nature's secrets and saving people from the wicked witches. Subordination of anything weak and feminine was also justified for the sake of attaining to the status of Man of Reason.

By fully and faithfully exposing the Western colonial European and anthropocentric theology influenced by the biblical text and its patriarchal interpretation, one may begin to fully appreciate the insight from the Wisdom tradition in which domination is the least of Sophia's desires. The human mandate for creation, especially as presented in the image of divine Sophia (Prov 8:27-31; Wis 7:17-22), implies responsibility rather than domination. As Elizabeth A. Johnson puts it, the interest of Wisdom discourse

> lies in the right order of creation and it focuses often and intensely on human life in the context of an interrelated natural world, both ideally forming a harmonious whole. . . . Interpreting the ministry, death and resurrection of Jesus by means of the wisdom tradition orients Christology beyond the human world, to the ecology of the earth and, indeed, to the universe, a vital move in this era of planetary crisis.[55]

The implicit Wisdom Christology of Hebrews intensifies the identification of God, Jesus, humanity, and creation: "reaching out to the world, forming the beloved community, forever drawing near and passing by."[56]

Interpretive Essay: Jesus as High Priest and Sacrifice: A Jewish Perspective

Hebrews 2:17 introduces the image of Jesus as both high priest and sacrifice. As noted in the introduction to this commentary, it is not clear whether Hebrews was written before or after the Roman destruction of the temple and occupation of Jerusalem in 70 CE, which brought the

---

54. Mary Grey, *Sacred Longings: The Ecological Spirit and Global Culture* (Minneapolis: Fortress Press, 2004), 14–15.

55. Elizabeth A. Johnson, "Wisdom Was Made Flesh and Pitched Her Tent Among Us," in *Reconstructing the Christ Symbol: Essays in Feminist Christology*, ed. Maryanne Stevens (New York: Paulist Press, 1993; repr. Eugene, OR: Wipf & Stock, 2004), 95–117, at 113.

56. Ibid., 102.

sacrificial service of the Jewish priests to an end. Hebrews itself seems to point in different directions—sometimes it refers to the high priests in the past tense, sometimes in the present; sometimes it refers to the tent-like sanctuary described in the book of Exodus, as if the Jerusalem temple of wood and stone were irrelevant, at other times to a changing succession of high priests, as in the actual temple.

It is easiest for me to imagine Hebrews as written post-destruction. If so, it can be seen as responding to a question that likely preoccupied the Jews of the time and certainly exercised the rabbis of the next several centuries: in the absence of the temple, the home of the Shekinah (Divine Presence), and the קורבנות (*qorbanot*, "sacrifices," from a Hebrew root connoting "drawing near"): how can we draw near to the Divine?

In later Jewish tradition, quite a number of ritual and ethical actions are seen as acceptable equivalents of the *qorbanot*: study of the scriptural instructions for sacrifices; liturgical prayers conducted at the times of the temple service; eating accompanied by appropriate blessings (echoing the eating of sacrificed meat by priests and their families); fasting (which diminishes one's own blood and fat as if it were being sacrificed); acts of love and kindness (praised by the prophets of Israel as superior to sacrifices). Poignantly, the liturgy for the circumcision of a baby boy equates that ancient blood ritual too with a sacrifice.

For Jewish women, there have traditionally been three commandments that were their particular responsibility. Each of these "women's commandments" can be seen as linked to the temple and its sacrificial service. *Niddah* (נידה), the set of rules surrounding menstruation, is the only area of traditional Jewish life in which ritual purity remains a major concern: after her menstrual period and a count of several additional days, a married woman immerses in a מקוה, a ritual pool, and returns to a state of purity. When the temple was standing, however, ritual purity was required of anyone entering it, and a pilgrim would immerse in a מקוה before entering the temple precincts; many of these pools can be seen in the archaeological excavations around the Temple Mount. Women are also commanded to remove חלה, a portion of dough, when baking bread; this is "a donation to the Lord," commanded in Num 15:18-21. In ancient times this portion of dough would be given to a כהן (priest) but since the destruction of the temple it is simply burned. A popular women's prayer in the Yiddish vernacular of Eastern European Jewry, written by Sarah bas Tovim in the eighteenth century and often reprinted, asks God that "my *ḥallah* be accepted like a sacrifice [קורבן *qorban*] on the altar."[57] The third "women's commandment" is to kindle lights at the beginning of the Sabbath and holy days. The same Yiddish prayer asks that the fulfillment of this commandment "be accepted like the commandment fulfilled by the High Priest when he kindled the lights in the dear Temple . . . and as the light of the olive oil which burned in the Temple and never went out"[58] (Exod 27:20-21; Lev 24:1-4). Thus Jewish tradition offers men and women many equivalents of the missing temple and *qorbanot*. Yet the fact that there are so many of these "equivalents" perhaps suggests an enduring anxiety that none of them quite satisfies.

On the other hand, in our own time few Jews are preoccupied by the absence of the temple with its sacrifices. The radical view of Maimonides (1135–1204) that God, who is properly approached through prayer or intellectual contemplation, only commanded sacrifices because that was the accepted mode of worship in ancient times has come to seem self-evident to many. While the Temple Mount in Jerusalem has been claimed by Israel since 1967, successive Israeli governments have left it in the hands of the Muslim custodians of the mosques located there. Only a fringe minority among Israeli Jews have advocated that steps be taken to rebuild the temple on its ancient site; most seek a sense of nearness to the Shekinah in other ways.

The bold argument of Hebrews, then, that Jesus takes the place of the entire sacrificial system is unlikely to have much purchase among Jews today, just as it probably has little resonance for today's Christians. Yet, it points back to a time of unity between believers in the God of Israel, whether "Jews" or "Christians": a time of shared desire for nearness to the Divine Presence, and shared anxiety over how this could be possible in the aftermath of destruction.

Justin Jaron Lewis

57. Tracy Guren Klirs et al., *The Merit of Our Mothers: A Bilingual Anthology of Jewish Women's Prayers* (Cincinnati, OH: Hebrew Union College Press, 1992), 19. On Sarah bas Tovim and her prayers, see Chava Weissler, *Voices of the Matriarchs: Listening to the Prayers of Early Modern Jewish Women* (Boston: Beacon Press, 1998), 126–46.

58. Klirs, *Merit of Our Mothers*, 21.

Hebrews 3–4

Mediating Wisdom

Hebrews 3–4 is structured similarly to 1:5–2:18, alternating between scriptural exposition (3:1-6; 4:1-16) and exhortation (3:7-19). Commentators usually identify the theme of the section, which begins and ends with the catchwords "Jesus," "high priest," and "confession" (3:1; 4:14), as the superiority of Jesus to Moses, not in the sense that Moses, and the revelation he mediated, is without value and dignity, but that "Jesus is worthy of more glory than Moses" (3:3a). The length of the paraenetic section suggests, however, that the main focus of the argument falls not on the figure of Moses but on the testing of the children of Israel in the wilderness and the "rest" (κατάπαυσις) in the promised land pledged to them by God.

Exposition: The Mediation of Christ Is Better Than the Mediation of Moses (Heb 3:1-6)

As noted above, although the theme of this section is often considered to be the greatness of Jesus relative to Moses, the latter is mentioned explicitly only four times (3:2, 3, 5, 16). More germane to the homilist's purpose is the argument that, based on the exposition of Ps 95:7b-11 (quoted in 3:7-11), Jesus leads his people to a better "rest" than the one to which Moses and his successor Joshua led the children of Israel (3:11,

29

¹Therefore, brothers and sisters, holy partners in a heavenly calling, consider that Jesus, the apostle and high priest of our confession, ²was faithful to the one who appointed him, just as Moses also "was faithful in all God's house." ³Yet Jesus is worthy of more glory than Moses, just as the builder of a house has more honor than the house itself. ⁴(For every house is built by someone, but the builder of all things is God.) ⁵Now Moses was faithful in all God's house as a servant, to testify to the things that would be spoken later. ⁶Christ, however, was faithful over God's house as a son, and we are his house if we hold firm the confidence and the pride that belong to hope.

18; 4:1-11). Here the author offers Jesus' sonship as evidence of his superiority: "Jesus, the apostle and high priest of our confession, was faithful to the one who appointed him, just as Moses also 'was faithful in all God's house.' Yet Jesus is worthy of more glory than Moses, just as the builder of a house has more honor than the house itself" (3:1b-3). Here the term "apostle" (ἀπόστολος)—meaning "one who is sent"—is synonymous with "pioneer" or "forerunner" (2:10), referring to Jesus' role as leader of God's people; the theme of Jesus as "high priest" is developed later in the sermon (7:15–9:14) and distinguishes him from Moses, whose brother, Aaron, was the archetypal high priest of Israel. The homilist supports his assertion that Moses was a "servant" (θεράπων) with an allusion to Num 12:7 (Moses was "faithful in all God's house"; Heb 3:5), a divine speech affirming the exalted prophetic status of Moses, in which God identifies his trusted "servant" Moses as one with whom he speaks "mouth to mouth," in clear speech, rather than in obscure dreams and visions (Num 12:6, 8).

The juxtaposition of Moses and Christ can also be viewed in light of a "calling." The homilist's grand opening address—"brothers and sisters, holy partners in a heavenly calling"—is more than a rhetorical declaration when it is followed in the next line with the naming of Jesus as "the apostle." It is significant that the title "the apostle" applied to Jesus appears only here and is found nowhere else in the entire New Testament, though the idea of Jesus as "the one who is sent" is found in other texts.[1] Along with 1 Peter, Hebrews is concerned to lift up the role of the high

---

1. See Matt 10:40; Mark 9:37; Luke 10:16; John 3:17. Fred B. Craddock, "The Letter to the Hebrews," *The New Interpreter's Bible* (Nashville, TN: Abingdon, 1998), 12:1–173, at 45.

priest as a communal identity. Such identity formation is closely related to vocation, *vocare* in Latin, meaning "to call." Jesus is "the apostle" because he has been sent to call us to be God's people and "partners of Christ" (3:14). Vocation, which is epistemologically connected to the word "voice," evokes the notion of a voice internal to oneself, often hidden, and thus to be discovered by discerning the voices external to oneself. Parker Palmer calls this "a strange birthright gift of self."[2] Vocation is something each person is born with, yet it is never fully disclosed unless one seeks it. It is always found through communal relationships. One's personal vocation is determined by one's community. In the case of Moses, his personal vocation as "servant" becomes clear when he speaks to his community. Moses' identity and vocation as servant and prophet are found in communal relationships, the relationship with his brother Aaron and that with his people.

Contemporary Christian readers may not be attuned to the audacity of the claim that Jesus could surpass Moses, who, according to Deuteronomy, is the greatest of all prophets: "Never since has there arisen a prophet in Israel like Moses, whom the LORD knew face to face" (Deut 34:10). In Jewish tradition he is "Moses our teacher [*Mosheh Rabbenu*]. The cognomen combines affection and awe: he is Israel's own teacher par excellence. . . . The revelation at Sinai encompassed the totality of the divine law and was called Torah in its wider sense. It revealed what God wanted of His people, and this will was made known to Moses, His servant and our teacher."[3]

The Wisdom literature extols Moses as the "holy prophet" whom Sophia inspired to lead God's people out of bondage (Wis 10:15-16; 11:1; see Sir 45:1-5) and identifies the law he mediated with Wisdom herself (Sir 24:23; Bar 4:1). The juxtaposition of Christ and Moses as "high priest" and "holy prophet" seems stark, but the Torah's vision of worship, according to Samuel Balentine, is that priestly identity has to be met with prophetic vision. "Priestly rituals," he explains, "do not simply reinforce existing assumptions about order and structure. . . . [They are] . . . a means of enacting, maintaining, and where necessary recreating the

---

2. Parker Palmer, *Let Your Life Speak: Listening for the Voice of Vocation* (San Francisco: Jossey-Bass, 2000), 10.

3. W. Gunther Plaut, ed., *The Torah: A Modern Commentary* (New York: Union of American Hebrew Congregations, 1981), 1584; see George Wesley Buchanan, *To the Hebrews*, AB 36 (Garden City, NY: Doubleday, 1972), 56–57.

world of God's design."[4] Wisdom literature describes Wisdom as a mediator who blurs the line between prophet and priest. Wisdom is the one who enacts the rites of passage between the world as lived and the world as imagined, the world here and now and the world to come. In this vein, the homilist's juxtaposition does not seem to aim to dismiss Moses and replace him with Christ but to demonstrate the tension between their two roles, a tension that also resides in these two distinct but equally important roles for the christian community in the formation of its identity. Such tension is necessary, just as the coexistence of priest and prophet is necessary, for human life is shaped by the boundaries between order and disorder, between control and resistance, between security and chaos, between life and death. The "faithfulness" or trustworthiness (πιστός) of Moses over his "house"—the household (οἶκος) of Israel—prefigures the faithfulness of Jesus to the God who appointed him son (Heb 3:2) in the family of "brothers and sisters, holy partners in a heavenly calling" (3:1-2).

In addition to the allusion to Num 12:7 in v. 3, some interpreters see influence from the oracle of Nathan (2 Sam 7:1-17; 1 Chr 17:1-15),[5] quoted explicitly in Heb 1:5b. In this famous passage the prophet reveals to David God's plan to build a "house" (temple) in which to dwell; it will be built by David's "son," through whom a royal "household" (in the sense of "dynasty") will be raised up for all eternity: "Your house and your kingdom shall be made sure forever before me; your throne shall be established forever" (2 Sam 7:16; see also 1 Chr 17:14). In the context of the Deuteronomistic History (as well as the Chronicler's History), the prophesied "son" is Solomon, who both builds the temple in Jerusalem and is the son through whom the kingly lineage of David is perpetuated. The promise of an heir to David with a divinely established and eternal throne is, however, amenable to messianic interpretation: "He shall build a house for my name, and I will establish the throne of his kingdom forever. I will be a father to him, and he shall be a son to me" (2 Sam 7:13-14a; 1 Chr 17:13a). In David's prayerful response to the oracle, God's pledge of eternal rule for David's dynasty is called a "promise" (2 Sam 7:21, 25, 28; 1 Chr 17:26), but elsewhere in the Scriptures it is referred to

---

4. Samuel Balentine, *The Torah's Vision of Worship* (Minneapolis: Fortress Press, 1999), 75.

5. E.g., Mary Rose D'Angelo, *Moses in the Letter to the Hebrews*, SBLDS 42 (Missoula, MT: Scholars Press, 1979), 92; Susanne Lehne, *The New Covenant in Hebrews*, JSNTSup 44 (Sheffield: JSOT Press, 1990), 29.

as a "covenant" (2 Chr 13:5; 21:7; 23:3; Ps 89:3; Isa 55:3; Jer 33:21; Sir 47:11), reminiscent of the new, eternal covenant that is a major theme of Hebrews (Heb 8:1–10:18). For Hebrews, Christ is the prophesied heir who is "faithful over God's house as a son," and his faithful followers belong to this household/family "if we hold firm the confidence and the pride that belong to hope" (Heb 3:6). The notion of Jesus, but not Moses, as a builder of God's "house" (οἶκος) relies on the sense of house as "household" or "dynasty" (see 2 Sam 7:1-29; 1 Chr 17:1-27); a son has a role in the propagation of a dynasty in a way that a servant does not. The parenthetical comment in Heb 3:4 reminds the reader/audience that although Jesus is the "builder" of the household of faith as messianic heir, "the builder of all things is God."

Paraenesis: Warning against Disobedience (Heb 3:7-19)

The scriptural text that holds Heb 3–4 together is Ps 95:7b-11, quoted in full in 3:7-11. The Scripture is introduced with the formula "as the Holy Spirit says" (Heb 3:7a), evoking the life-giving spirit of prophetic inspiration that speaks to the community not simply of the past but in the present tense (λέγει).

Holy Spirit Mother

Hebrews refers to the holy spirit as the speaker of Scripture (3:7; 9:8; 10:15), which contains deeper significance pertaining to the meaning of the Christ revelation. Although the Greek of the New Testament speaks of the spirit with the neuter πνεῦμα, early Aramaic-speaking christians related to the spirit as maternal, since the Aramaic term for spirit is *rucha* (רוחא), a feminine noun like the Hebrew *ruach* (רוח). As late as the fourth century the Persian Aphraates, a convert from Judaism, teaches that the true parents of a man about to be married are "God his Father and the Holy Spirit his Mother" (Aphraates, *Demonstrations* 18). Similarly, the monk Macarius speaks of the spirit as "the good kind mother" (Macarius, *Homily* 28.4). The biblical tradition frequently identifies the spirit with Wisdom (e.g., Exod 28:3; 31:3; 35:31; Deut 34:9; Isa 11:2; Wis 1:6; 7:7; 9:17; Sir 15:5; 17:6; Acts 6:10; Rom 8:6; 1 Cor 12:8; Eph 1:17). (*Source*: April De Conick, *Holy Misogyny: Why the Sex and Gender Conflicts in the Early Church Still Matter* [New York: Continuum, 2001], 22.)

Mary Ann Beavis

Heb 3:7-19

[7]Therefore, as the Holy Spirit says,
"Today, if you hear his voice,
[8]do not harden your hearts as in
the rebellion,
as on the day of testing in the
wilderness,
[9]where your ancestors put me to
the test,
though they had seen my
works [10]for forty years.
Therefore I was angry with that
generation,
and I said, 'They always go astray
in their hearts,
and they have not known my
ways.'
[11]As in my anger I swore,
'They will not enter my rest.'"
[12]Take care, brothers and sisters,
that none of you may have an evil, unbelieving heart that turns away from
the living God. [13]But exhort one another every day, as long as it is called
"today," so that none of you may be
hardened by the deceitfulness of sin.
[14]For we have become partners of
Christ, if only we hold our first confidence firm to the end. [15]As it is said,
"Today, if you hear his voice,
do not harden your hearts as in
the rebellion."
[16]Now who were they who heard
and yet were rebellious? Was it not all
those who left Egypt under the leadership of Moses? [17]But with whom was
he angry forty years? Was it not those
who sinned, whose bodies fell in the
wilderness? [18]And to whom did he
swear that they would not enter his
rest, if not to those who were disobedient? [19]So we see that they were unable
to enter because of unbelief.

This psalm is one of many that evokes the exodus experience of Israel,[6] where the wilderness wandering is used as a warning to the nation against resisting the call of God in the present day: *"Today,* if you hear his voice, do not harden your hearts as in the rebellion [Hebrew: מסה], as on the day of testing [Hebrew: מריבה] in the wilderness" (Heb 3:7b-8; Ps 95:8). Again, hearing God's voice and finding one's vocation is not easy. Temptations disguised in the form of the expectations and pressures of social norms can lead one to wander. The people of the exodus are portrayed as the "ancestors" of the "brothers and sisters" of the community (οἱ πατέρες ὑμῶν); the latter are warned through the prophetic words of the Psalmist not to emulate their forebears: "where your ances-tors put me to the test, though they had seen my works for forty years" (Heb 3:9-10a). Here there is an implicit comparison with Jesus, who "was tested by what he suffered" (Heb 2:18) but who proved faithful and can

6. See John Bright, *A History of Israel*, 4th ed. (Louisville, KY: Westminster John Knox, 2000), 107–43.

help those who are currently undergoing trials. The psalm recalls the divine anger at the exodus generation for their disobedience, and God's pledge that because of their unfaithfulness the generation that left Egypt—even the leaders Moses, Aaron, and Miriam (Mic 6:4)—would not enter the land of promise: "As in my anger I swore, 'They will not enter my rest'" (Heb 3:11; see Num 14:1-35). In biblical terms the description of the promised land as God's "rest" refers both to the promise that Israel would enjoy respite from its tribulations in the wilderness and that the people would find a permanent home in the land of Israel (Deut 12:10; 25:19; Josh 22:4), and to the resting of God on the seventh day of creation (Gen 2:2-3; Exod 20:8-11). Thus the land of promise is presented as a second creation, the Sabbath: "The crowning glory . . . that completes God's life-giving work and provides ultimate coherence for the cosmos" (see Heb 4:3-5).[7]

In the context of Torah, the story of the wilderness testing can be interpreted positively, as Michael Kolarcik explains: "The fact that the people doubted during the wanderings and tested God as at the waters of Meribah (Ex 17:1-8, 13:17-18, 16:9-19) points to the central motif of the wanderings in the wilderness as a time for learning the ways of the Lord and learning to trust in God."[8] Similarly, for Parker Palmer the "journey into darkness," the time in the wilderness, is a "transformative passage" leading to the discovery of the trajectory of one's vocation.[9] Elsewhere in Hebrews the Israelites "who passed through the Red Sea"

> *Our Stories Are Our Scripture*
> *For Hebrews 3*
>
> **Starts with a Bit of Mud**
>
> So it was Turtle and Muskrat got together near end cycle
>
> What turned out to be actual beginning or so they found
>
> Out because the Earth Diver made it all the way down
>
> Touched bottom under waterworld pressure to push paw
>
> Scratch sediment so successful nearly drowned doing it
>
> So small a donation to turtle's back where it grew wild
>
> *Annharte*

---

7. Barbara E. Reid, "Sabbath, the Crown of Creation," in *Earth, Wind, and Fire: Biblical and Theological Perspectives on Creation*, ed. Carol J. Dempsey and Mary Margaret Pazdan (Collegeville, MN: Liturgical Press, 2004), 67–76, at 70.

8. Michael Kolarcik, "The Exodus Motif in the Psalms," in *The Psalms* (Toronto: Regis College, 2003), 33. See Pss 77:20; 78:52; 107:4, 33-37; Wis 11:9-14; 12:2.

9. Palmer, *Let Your Life Speak*, 17, 23.

are held up as examples of faith (11:29). Here, however, the homilist chooses to interpret the wilderness wandering in purely negative terms: as punishment for their straying "in their hearts" and their deviance from God's ways, God angrily swore, "They will not enter my rest" (Heb 3:11; Ps 95:11). The audience is exhorted to ensure that their hearts are not "evil" and "unbelieving" like those of the wilderness generation and to encourage each other in the here-and-now ("today") not to succumb to "the deceitfulness of sin" (Heb 3:13). The homilist emphasizes the necessity of the community's maintaining its "first confidence firm to the end" (3:14), unlike those who escaped from Egypt under the leadership of Moses but were not allowed to enter the land of promise "because of unbelief" (3:19). For the homilist, Ps 95:7b, quoted twice in Heb 3 (vv. 7, 15), refers to the present-day situation of the audience: "Today, if you hear his voice, do not harden your hearts as in the rebellion." A series of rhetorical questions cites the rebelliousness of the wilderness generation, in implicit contrast to the desired behavior of the reader/audience. Unlike "those who left Egypt under the leadership of Moses," the audience must remain faithful, or they will share in the harsh consequences that befell the children of Israel: God was angry with them for forty years, and the bodies of those who sinned fell in the desert (3:18; see Num 14:32). Because of their disobedience and unbelief, the disobedient children of Israel were barred from entering God's promised rest (3:18-19). Politically, the homilist is writing this letter in difficult circumstances. On the one hand, the delay of Jesus' return has some in the community impatient for something to happen. On the other hand, some Jewish christians who have grown tired of waiting may have returned to their Jewish communities.[10] It is understandable that, caught between these pressures, the homilist focuses the demands for faithfulness on the present life rather than the past or the future.

Exposition: Mediator of a Better Rest (Heb 4:1-16)

So far the homilist's argument corresponds to the exodus traditions of the Hebrew Bible, where the first generation who fled Egypt under the leadership of Moses, Aaron, and Miriam were punished for their disobedience by being prevented from entering the promised land: "none of the people who have seen my glory and the signs that I did in Egypt and in the wilderness, and yet have tested me these ten times and have

---

10. Craddock, "Hebrews," 9.

Heb 4:1-16

¹Therefore, while the promise of entering his rest is still open, let us take care that none of you should seem to have failed to reach it. ²For indeed the good news came to us just as to them; but the message they heard did not benefit them, because they were not united by faith with those who listened. ³For we who have believed enter that rest, just as God has said,

"As in my anger I swore,
'They shall not enter my rest,'"

though his works were finished at the foundation of the world. ⁴For in one place it speaks about the seventh day as follows, "And God rested on the seventh day from all his works." ⁵And again in this place it says, "They shall not enter my rest." ⁶Since therefore it remains open for some to enter it, and those who formerly received the good news failed to enter because of disobedience, ⁷again he sets a certain day—"today"—saying through David much later, in the words already quoted,

"Today, if you hear his voice,
do not harden your hearts."

⁸For if Joshua had given them rest, God would not speak later about another day. ⁹So then, a sabbath rest still

not obeyed my voice, shall see the land that I swore to give to their ancestors; none of those who despised me shall see it" (Num 14:22-23). Only the faithful Israelite spies, Joshua and Caleb, and the second generation would realize God's promise: "your little ones . . . I will bring in, and they shall know the land that you have despised" (Num 14:31). The homilist, however, argues that since it was long after the time of the exodus when the Psalmist ("David") spoke of God's pledge that Israel would not enter the promised land (Heb 4:7), the divine promise of κατάπαυσις still remains to be fulfilled: "For if Joshua had given them rest, God would not speak later about another day. So then, a sabbath rest still remains for the people of God" (Heb 4:8-9).

In its original context the psalm warns Israelites of monarchical times not to resist God as their ancestors had. Hebrews' argument is similar but goes much further, seeming to defy the literal sense of the exodus story, which includes God's assurance that the second wilderness generation would "know the land" (Num 14:31), and culminates in the stories of conquest and occupation in Joshua and Judges. The homilist's argument, however, is not that Joshua did not lead the people of God into the land of Canaan but that Israel never achieved true, eternal rest there, an assertion borne out by the subsequent history of Israel as attested in the Hebrew Scriptures. The ultimate destination of the people of God is not the earthly promised land but the Sabbath rest divinely ordained at the time of creation: "For in one place it speaks about the

remains for the people of God; [10]for those who enter God's rest also cease from their labors as God did from his. [11]Let us therefore make every effort to enter that rest, so that no one may fall through such disobedience as theirs.

[12]Indeed, the word of God is living and active, sharper than any two-edged sword, piercing until it divides soul from spirit, joints from marrow; it is able to judge the thoughts and intentions of the heart. [13]And before him no creature is hidden, but all are naked and laid bare to the eyes of the one to whom we must render an account.

[14]Since, then, we have a great high priest who has passed through the heavens, Jesus, the Son of God, let us hold fast to our confession. [15]For we do not have a high priest who is unable to sympathize with our weaknesses, but we have one who in every respect has been tested as we are, yet without sin. [16]Let us therefore approach the throne of grace with boldness, so that we may receive mercy and find grace to help in time of need.

seventh day as follows, 'And God rested on the seventh day from all his works.' . . . So then, a sabbath rest still remains for the people of God; for those who enter God's rest also cease from their labors as God did from his" (Heb 4:4, 9). The vision of Sabbath in the cycle of creation in Gen 1–2 affirms this claim of the homilist: God, the world as God's creation, and the people in it are in a constant dance. When the seventh day comes around (Gen 2:1-3) it embraces them in ultimate peace, *shalōm*, *right relationship*. Samuel Balentine calls Sabbath "the liturgy of creation" in that it proclaims *an orderly world* (creation), *a ritual world* (God's covenant with humans and human response to it), *a relational world* (God's invitation to share the responsibility of restoring the creation).[11] The "rest" Israel never achieved in history is eschatological and heavenly, and thus still open to the people of God; if they persist in their faithfulness to the gospel (4:1-2) they will attain the eternal Sabbath created by God at the foundation of the universe (4:3-4). For Hebrews, the real rest promised by God is the preexistent Sabbath of the "world to come," ordained in heaven before it was established on earth. Abraham Joshua Heschel's recollection of a famous legend resonates with these ideas:

> At the time when God was giving the Torah to Israel, He said to them: "My children! If you accept the Torah and observe my *mitzvot*, I will give you for all eternity a thing most precious that I have in my possession." "And what," asked Israel, "is that precious thing which Thou

11. Balentine, *Torah's Vision*, 81.

wilt give us if we obey Thy Torah?" "The world to come." "Show us in this world an example of the world to come." "The Sabbath is an example of the world to come."[12]

The exalted status of the Sabbath in early Judaism is illustrated by the words of the *Book of Jubilees* (second century BCE): "On this day we kept the sabbath in heaven before it was made known to any human to keep the sabbath thereon upon the earth. The Creator of all blessed it, but he did not sanctify any people or nations to keep the sabbath thereon with the sole exception of Israel. . . . And the Creator of all, who created this day for a blessing and sanctification and glory, blessed it more than all days."[13] In Jürgen Moltmann's exposition, "In creation, God went out of God's self. In God's rest, God returns to God's self. In creation, God engaged creatures. In God's rest, God gives them space."[14]

The homilist's argument that God's promise of rest was not decisively fulfilled by the generation that entered the land of Canaan under Joshua (Heb 4:8) reflects the latitude and creativity of ancient Jewish forms of interpretation. For example, a rabbinic tradition about the wilderness generation (*Pirke R. El.* 45) teaches that the Israelite women were more faithful than the men; when Aaron commanded the people to remove their earrings so he could fashion the golden calf, the women refused, stating that a graven image would have no power to deliver them, as indicated by the Hebrew text of Exod 32:3: "In Hebrew, 'their' is in the masculine gender, indicating that the women did not

---

Lecha Dodi

The prayer *Lecha Dodi*, "Come, My Beloved," welcoming the Sabbath as a bride, is sung at the beginning of Sabbath evening service:

> Come my beloved
> to meet the bride,
> Let us welcome the
>   Sabbath.
> A Sabbath of peace,
> Blessed Sabbath.

(*Source*: http://www.hebrew songs.com/song-lechadodi.htm, accessed July 15, 2015.)

Mary Ann Beavis

---

12. Abraham Joshua Heschel, *The Sabbath: Its Meaning for Modern Man* (New York: Farrar, Strauss, 1948), 73.

13. *Jub* 2:30b, 31a, 32a, in James H. Charlesworth, *The Old Testament Pseudepigrapha* (New York: Doubleday, 1985), 2:58.

14. Jürgen Moltmann, "Sabbath: Finishing and Beginning," *LP* 7 (April–June 1998): 4–5, at 4.

cooperate. They preserved their piety."[15] For this they were rewarded by God in this world by being privileged to observe the New Moon festival more stringently than the men (by being excused from work), and in the world to come "to be renewed like the New Moons, as it is said, 'Who satisfieth thy years with good things so that thy youth is renewed like the eagle' (Ps. ciii.5)."[16] According to this tradition the Israelite women enjoyed a quality of "rest"—from work during the monthly New Moon festivals and even in the coming age—denied to the men. The New Moon (Rosh Hodesh) is a monthly celebration involving sacrifice, rest, and feasting,[17] whose special association with women fell out of use in Judaism over the centuries, but it has recently been revived as a women's festival[18] "through storytelling, singing, dancing and eating the special foods associated with our 'text,' i.e., the month we are marking. . . . As Barbara Myerhoff, noted Jewish anthropologist, said of her grandmother, 'Sofie knew and taught me that everyone had some story. . . . Stories told to oneself or others could transform the world.'"[19]

The famous words of Heb 4:12-13, comparing the word of God to a "two-edged sword,"[21] seem loosely related to the previous argument, but they relate back to the divine utterance quoted in Heb 3:7-11 (Ps 95:7b-11)—"Today, if you hear God's voice, do not harden your hearts"—and more generally to the homilist's conviction that "the history of salvation can be

> *Our Stories Are Our Scripture*
> *For Hebrews 4*
>
> ### Meanwhile Back on the Prairie
>
> White Buffalo Calf Woman brings a gift so people won't
>
> Hunger for bison hunt until Fat Takers attack the spirit
>
> Perform ecocide toward natural providence of blessing
>
> White Buffalo Calf Woman taught *tiyopaye*[20] ceremonies
>
> Giving with the Sacred Pipe the way of Sundance Rite
>
> Today this promise to keep trueheart beliefs stands
>
> *Annharte*

15. Plaut, *Torah*, 652.

16. Gerald Friedlander, *Pirke de-Rabbi Eliezer* (Skokie, IL: Varda Books, 2012), 406.

17. Num 29:6; 1 Sam 20:5, 18, 24; Ezra 3:5; Neh 10:33; Ps 81:3.

18. Penina V. Adelman, *Miriam's Well: Rituals for Jewish Women around the Year* (Fresh Meadows, NY: Biblio Press, 1986), 4–5, 28–29.

19. Ibid., 8, citing Barbara Myerhoff, *Number Our Days* (New York: Dutton, 1978), 8.

20. "Extended family/clan" (Lakota).

21. See Rev 1:16; 19:15, 21; Wis 18:15-16.

A Korean Women's Ritual

The ancient tradition of the Jewish women's ritual of communal singing and dancing under the new moon is similar to an ancient Korean women's ritual called *Ganggangsullae*, which was recognized in 2009 as one of UNESCO's intangible cultural heritages of humanity. This ritual, which originated in South Korea, has an oral legend embedded in it. During the Japanese invasion of Korea in the sixteenth century, women were gathered and dressed in men's military uniforms to trick the Japanese into believing the Korean forces were much stronger and larger in numbers than they actually were. The plot was successful, and this eventually led to Korean victory. *Ganggangsullae*, involving dance, song, and movement, has been passed down through several thousand years of history and continues to be performed by a group of women to this day. It is usually done in early fall, in the season of the harvest *Chuseok* celebration, under the full moon (usually the fullest moon of the year, in the eighth month according to the lunar calendar). The openness and creativity of the song and dance form a key characteristic of the ritual, in which anyone may participate. It also enables women to release their pain and suffering by experiencing dynamic energy, playfulness, and freedom. Such a social and public gathering and its effect can only be fully appreciated, however, when viewed from the context of the historic patriarchal, Confucian culture of Korea in which women were prohibited from going out on their own most of the time. The summary of *Ganggangsullae* by UNESCO captures this well: "Once a rare break from restrictive rules governing the behavior of rural young women who were not allowed to sing aloud or go out at night, except during the *Chuseok* Thanksgiving celebration (August 15th according to lunar calendar), the ritual is mostly preserved today by middle-aged women in cities and taught as part of the music curriculum of elementary schools. Now practiced as a performing art throughout Korea, it can be seen as a representative Korean folk art."

Both these ancient traditions of Jewish and Korean women may lead contemporary readers to ponder whether such subversive, creative, and energy-filled rituals can be captured in modern-day liturgical acts. Can we find Sophia, the spirit of wisdom, today in our communal worship? If the homilist attempts to argue that the conquest of Canaan is a sign of God's unfulfilled promise, it may be possible to imagine a postcolonial scene in which the original inhabitants of Canaan and the Hebrews who were coming into contact with them might have enacted a ritual in dreaming of a new world to transform the current world. Musa Dube, using "the doubly colonized decolonizing method," attempts to imagine this transformed reality by creating "the Rahabs' reading prism." The imagined Rahabs are heterogeneous in that the patriarchally oppressed and race-privileged colonializing subjects are working together, transgressing the boundaries of race, gender, class, sexuality, ethnicity, and religion. In this transgressing act, be it a gathering under the new moon, or dressing in male clothing to stop an invasion, or rediscovering the meaning of Sabbath in a women's ritual, a new world based on postcolonial interdependence can be envisioned. In a world defined by conquest and oppression, violence and killing, a new world fueled by the energy of singing, dancing, gathering, protesting is also birthed. Indeed, the ritual of "enchantment" is a daring act, living "as if" real change can occur, "from the world of creation to the creation of the world."

(*Sources*: http://www.unesco.org/culture/ich/RL/00188, accessed July 15, 2015; see also YouTube (www.youtube.com) for Ganggangsullae. Published sources: I-hwa Yi, *Korea's Pastimes and Customs: A Social History*, trans. Ju-Hee Park (Paramus, NJ: Homa Sekey Books, 2006), 170–72; Musa Dube, "The Doubly Colonized Decolonizing Method," in *Postcolonial Feminist Interpretation of the Bible* [St. Louis, MO: Chalice Press, 2000], 111–26, at 122; Jacob Neusner, *The Enchantment of Judaism: Rites of Transformation from Birth Through Death* [New York: Basic Books, 1987], 95.)

HyeRan Kim-Cragg

described in terms of God's speech and the human response."[22] Here the divine word, written and unwritten, is extolled in terms reminiscent of the Wisdom poem that underlies Heb 1:3:

Hebrews 4:12-13

Indeed, the word of God is living and active [ἐνεργὴς], sharper than any two-edged sword, piercing until it divides soul from spirit [ἄχρι μερισμοῦ

22. James W. Thompson, *Hebrews*, Paideia Commentaries on the New Testament (Grand Rapids, MI: Baker Academic, 2008), 96. See 1:1-2, 5-13; 2:2, 3, 12-13; 3:7; 12:19, 26; 13:22.

ψυχῆς καὶ πνεύματος], joints from marrow; it is able to judge the thought and intentions of the heart. And before him no creature is hidden, but all are naked and laid bare to the eyes of the one to whom we must render an account.

Wisdom 7:22-26, 30

There is in her a spirit that is intelligent, holy, unique, manifold, subtle, mobile, clear, unpolluted, distinct, invulnerable, loving the good, keen . . . and penetrating through all spirits [διὰ πάντων χωροῦν πνευμάτων]. . . . For wisdom is more mobile than any motion; because of her pureness she pervades and penetrates all things. For she is a reflection of eternal light, a spotless mirror of the working of God [τοῦ θεοῦ ἐνεργείας] . . . therefore nothing defiled gains entrance into her . . . against wisdom evil does not prevail.

Although the Wisdom imagery is masculinized and militarized, the qualities of Sophia—dynamism, clarity, and incisiveness—underlie the homilist's portrayal of Jesus, through whom God "in these last days has spoken to us" (Heb 1:2). The book of Wisdom also portrays the divine word as a sword in a poetic account of the plague of the death of the firstborn: "your all-powerful word leaped from heaven, from the royal throne, into the midst of the land that was doomed, a stern warrior, carrying the sharp sword of your authentic command, and stood and filled all things with death, and touched heaven while standing on earth" (Wis 18:15-16). Like the "two-edged sword" of Hebrews, the warrior-word of God is a judge of the disobedient (Heb 4:11) that sees into the hearts of all creatures (4:12-13).

The early Christian theologian Basil of Caesarea related the metaphor of the word as sword to Simeon's prophecy that Mary's child was destined as a sign to Israel that would be opposed: "so that the inner thoughts of many will be revealed—and a sword will pierce your own soul too" (Luke 2:35). Basil explains to his fourth-century Cappadocian audience: "Therefore, some doubt will touch even you yourself who have been taught from above concerning the Lord. That is the sword. 'That the thoughts of many hearts may be revealed,' meaning that, after the scandal which happened at the cross of Christ to both the disciples and Mary herself, some swift healing will follow from the Lord, confirming their hearts in their faith in him."[23]

23. *Letter* 260.

Commentators often see Heb 4:14-16 as the beginning of a new section; however, in view of its parallelism with Heb 3:1 it is better to regard these verses as transitional to the next main phase of the argument on the theme of the high priesthood of Christ (5:1–7:28). The high priestly status of Jesus, who "has passed through the heavens" is cited as the reason for both homilist and audience to remain faithful to their commitment to the gospel ("our confession," 4:14). It is an undeniable fact that the presence of women in Hebrews is marginal.[24] It should be remembered that this text has been used to justify the exclusion of women from the ministry, especially where the issue of ordination is concerned. Also, when the text speaks of atonement and priesthood, authority is attributed only to Christ, which can easily lead to the exclusion of others.

Balentine, however, offers a different view, regarding 4:14–5:10 as significant in light of the ministry of Jesus. Interpreting this section as endorsing the ecclesial hierarchy, lifting up the vocation of the male priesthood to the highest position, is actually contested, he argues, by the position of Jesus as the "high priest," which allows him to perform "an act of boundary-crossing" in order to "re-establish contact between God and humankind." It is the "flesh-ness" and "blood-ness" of his redemptive incarnation out of earthly human nature that purifies what is tainted, transforming it into "heavenly things" (9:23).[25] According to Catherine Keller, this earthly nature is beyond an androcentric understanding, instead located within the interstices of creation: "It is precisely its embodiment that renders love Christian. This incarnation, this *incarnality*, does not transcend the radical immanence of the infinitely expansive postmodern space."[26] From this point of view it seems to make sense to read Heb 2:18 in terms of Jesus' human compassion (συμπαθῆσαι) for the weaknesses of his brothers and sisters: "we have one who in every respect has been tested as we are, yet without sin" (4:15). To contemporary readers steeped in a Christian worldview dominated by the Augustinian doctrine of original sin, the notion of Jesus' sinlessness might seem to deny his full

---

24. Mary Rose D'Angelo, "Hebrews," in *The Women's Bible Commentary*, ed. Carol A. Newsom and Sharon H. Ringe (Louisville, KY: Westminster John Knox, 1992), 364–67, at 366.

25. Balentine, *Torah's Vision*, 252–53.

26. Catherine Keller, "The Love of Postcolonialism," in *Postcolonial Theologies: Divinity and Empire*, ed. Catherine Keller et al. (St. Louis, MO: Chalice Press, 2004), 221–42, at 242; repr. in Catherine Keller, *God and Power: Counter-Apocalyptic Journeys* (Minneapolis: Augsburg Fortress, 2005), 133.

humanity. In an ancient Jewish context, however, the idea that a human being could be perfectly righteous according to the law is more plausible. For example, the book of Job, which is part of the Wisdom literature, portrays the protagonist as a blameless man whose faithfulness is brutally tested, who endures the temptation to renounce God and is richly rewarded after all his trials.[27] Thus there is a Jewish context for the idea that Jesus could be "without sin," also found elsewhere in the NT.[28]

Jesus' approach to God—passing through the heavens and thus attaining the heavenly rest denied to the Israelites (Heb 4:14)—is visualized as a celestial journey, a common way of portraying a visionary's ascent to the divine in Jewish apocalyptic literature.[29] In the pseudepigraphal *Testament of Job* (first century BCE to first century CE), the three daughters of Job, Hemera, Kasia, and Amaltheia, are granted the power to speak in the dialect of the angels (chaps. 48–50), and when their father dies they watch as his soul is borne up to heaven in a chariot invisible to those without spiritual insight (chap. 52).

Since the brothers and sisters of Jesus have been adopted into the family of their "great high priest" (Heb 4:14; 2:10-11), they are enabled to "approach the throne of grace with boldness" (4:16). Here the expression "the throne of grace" is a circumlocution for God, with the characteristic of "grace" or "lovingkindness" substituting for the divine name. The "mercy" and "grace" that characterize God are thus accessible to the children of God who seek them in times of need. Daniel Harrington notes that elsewhere in the LXX the only other pairing of the terms grace (χάρις) and mercy (ἔλεος) occurs in the book of Wisdom:[30]

> Those who trust in him will understand truth, and the faithful will abide with him in love, because grace and mercy are upon his holy ones. (Wis 3:9)

> Yet the peoples saw and did not understand, or take such a thing to heart, that God's grace and mercy are with his elect, and that he watches over his holy ones. (Wis 4:15)

27. See Jas 5:11; see also Ezek 14:14, 20, where Noah and Daniel are mentioned together with Job as paragons of righteousness.

28. 2 Cor 5:21; 1 Pet 2:22; 1 John 3:5; see also John 8:46.

29. E.g., Apocalypse of Zephaniah, 2 Enoch, Martyrdom and Ascension of Isaiah. Cited in Daniel J. Harrington, *What Are They Saying about the Letter to the Hebrews* (Mahwah, NJ: Paulist Press, 2005), 105.

30. Ibid., 107.

In Wisdom, the divine qualities of grace and mercy are mentioned in the context of the hope of immortality for the faithful (Wis 3:4; 4:1), a hope that is shared by Hebrews (2:9, 14-15; 9:15). The trio of "grace, mercy, and peace" is often found in the greetings of late NT letters (1 Tim 1:2; 2 Tim 1:2; Titus 1:4; 2 John 1:3).

A Jewish Perspective (Heb 4:1-16)

Hebrews 4:1-16, about the promise of rest, depends on a midrashic technique called by the rabbis *gezerah shavah* (גזרה שוה), meaning something like "a rule of likeness." Looked at through the lens of this technique, every word of Scripture is "hyperlinked" to every other occurrence of the same word, and this vast array of links is understood to shape not only Scripture but reality itself. Thus the classic Torah commentary of Rashi (1040–1105) links the word "beginning" in Gen 1:1 to other verses in which (at least in midrashic understanding) the same word alludes to the Torah or to the Jewish people. Therefore, "in the beginning . . ." means that God created the heavens and the earth "for the sake of the Torah and for the sake of the Jewish people."

Here in Heb 4:4-5 the homilist notes, "For in one place it speaks about the seventh day as follows, 'And God *rested* on the seventh day from all his works.' And again in this place it says, 'They shall not enter my *rest*.'" This verbal connection means that the latter verse must be read in light of the earlier one: we are speaking not merely of a physical resting place but about a divine Sabbath rest.

I find it heartwarming to see this and other midrashic techniques at work in the first century, predating any of the canonical works of Rabbinic literature (Mishnah, Midrash, Talmud) from which I know them best. In rabbinic Judaism, however, *gezerah shavah* only works with the original words of Scripture. Here it is applied to a word that recurs in the Greek translation of Scripture but not in the Hebrew original. In the Hebrew, when God "rested" the word is *vayishbot* (וישבות), from the same root as the word "Sabbath"(שבת) while "my rest" is *menuḥati* (מנוחתי), an unrelated word. These two distinct words would not have registered as linked to one another in the "search engine" of a rabbinic mind, wedded to the Hebrew text.

Here, the fact that the homilist works this way with the Greek text underlines how authoritative and holy the Septuagint was considered to be—much as the King James Version was, for many years, simply *the* Bible to many English-speaking Christians. At the same time, the homilist clearly knows Hebrew, as shown later by his interpretations of the names "Melchizedek" (*malki tzedek* [מלכי צדק], "king of righteousness") and "Salem" (related to *shalōm* [שלום], "peace") (7:2). Even among the rabbis of the Talmud there is an opinion that a holy scroll of the Torah may be written either in Hebrew or in Greek (Megillah 9a). This subverts the mainstream Jewish notion of Hebrew as the language of God and tradition, opening up the possibility that the eternal word of God can manifest itself in a kaleidoscope of human languages. This is a particularly liberating possibility for Jewish women and their allies, since women historically have had far less access than men to the Hebrew of sacred texts and have studied and expressed themselves in Yiddish, Judeo-Spanish, and other vernaculars.

Justin Jaron Lewis

Hebrews 5–7

The Priesthood of Wisdom

These chapters develop the high-priestly Christology distinctive to Hebrews. This theme is so important to the homilist's argument that it is announced at the beginning and end of the previous section, where Jesus is called "the apostle and high priest of our confession" (3:1) and "a great high priest who has passed through the heavens . . . who is [able] to sympathize with our weaknesses" (4:14-15). Similar to the previous sections, which argue that the son is superior to the angels and that the "rest" offered by Jesus is better than the promised land held out to the wilderness generations, the argument is that the high priesthood of Christ is better than the Levitical priesthood. The section lays the final layer in the groundwork for the doctrinal centerpiece of the homily: the contrast between the old and new covenants in Heb 8:1–10:18.

Exposition: The Basis of Christ's High Priesthood (5:1-10)

After introducing the theme of Jesus' high priesthood in Heb 4:14-16, the homilist goes on to explain the basis of this doctrine, unique to the NT. The first four verses (5:1-4) remind the audience of the ministry of the high priests of the Jewish sacrificial service: they are chosen by God "to offer gifts and sacrifices for sins" (5:1), and, like all Levitical priests,

49

Heb 5:1-10

¹Every high priest chosen from among mortals is put in charge of things pertaining to God on their behalf, to offer gifts and sacrifices for sins. ²He is able to deal gently with the ignorant and wayward, since he himself is subject to weakness; ³and because of this he must offer sacrifice for his own sins as well as for those of the people. ⁴And one does not presume to take this honor, but takes it only when called by God, just as Aaron was.

⁵So also Christ did not glorify himself in becoming a high priest, but was appointed by the one who said to him,

"You are my Son,
today I have begotten you";

⁶as he says also in another place,

they belong to the lineage of Moses' brother, Aaron (5:4). Like Jesus, the Aaronid high priests are able to treat worshipers kindly since they share their human weaknesses (5:2), but unlike Jesus—who, as the author has already noted, is "without sin" (4:15)—Jewish high priests are sinful like everyone else, so they must sacrifice for their own transgressions as well as on behalf of the congregation of Israel (5:3).

The debate around the sinfulness or sinlessness of the priest as presider over sacraments was heated in the early church. "Ever since New Testament times," James F. White explains, "the church has found certain sign-acts essential for expressing the encounter between God and humans. . . . Practices of sacrifice of food and drink became ways of establishing and maintaining relationships with God. Without this Jewish mentality and these practices, the sacramental life of Christianity would never have been born."[1] This very role of priest as the mediator between God and humans has, however, created certain difficulties and even heresies, in the opinions of ancient theologians. Augustine, in an attempt to define what a sacrament is, wrestled with the challenge put forth by the Donatists, who believed that only good people could perform good sacraments. In response to this challenge, Augustine made one of his most famous doctrinal statements, that sacraments are effective *ex opere operato*, meaning that God operates simply through the work being done independently of the human agent, rather than *ex opere operantis*, God operating through the work done through the human agent.[2] The hom-

---

1. James F. White, *Introduction to Christian Worship* (Nashville, TN: Abingdon, 2000), 175–76. It should be noted, however, that sacrifice was not a uniquely Jewish practice; it was ubiquitous in ancient religion.

2. Augustine, *Contra Cresconium* 4.19, cited in ibid., 183.

"You are a priest forever,
according to the order of
Melchizedek."
[7]In the days of his flesh, Jesus offered up prayers and supplications, with loud cries and tears, to the one who was able to save him from death, and he was heard because of his reverent submission. [8]Although he was a Son, he learned obedience through what he suffered; [9]and having been made perfect, he became the source of eternal salvation for all who obey him, [10]having been designated by God a high priest according to the order of Melchizedek.

ilist's view that priests are as sinful as everyone else, thus needing their own sacrifices, seems to be in line with Augustine's opinion. Both claim that the power of the sacrament (or sacrificial ritual) is independent of the leadership of the privileged male priesthood. This claim that divine rituals have power "independent of the human agent" opens up possibilities for feminist reconstructions of liturgical practices and for "a preferential option for liturgical historiography 'from below.'"[3] After all, the power of sacrament and that of grace are up to God alone and not dependent on human ability or moral excellence. One should not jump to the conclusion that such a theology of sacrament makes humans completely passive. In fact, the opposite reality is possible. God is so active in disclosing God's self-giving nature that we who abide in God are and must be active as well in giving ourselves in loving and serving our neighbors.

The reference to the offering of sacrifices for sins (5:1) indicates that the homilist is referring to the ritual of the Day of Atonement (*Yom Kippur*), described in detail in Lev 16 (see also Lev 23:27-32). This ritual was so holy that it was performed only once a year (Lev 23:27) and could only be performed by one person, the high priest, who entered the innermost sanctuary of the temple (the "Holy of Holies") and performed animal sacrifices, first on behalf of his own sins and those of his household (Lev 16:6, 11), and then on behalf of the people of Israel, including the other priests (Lev 16:7-10, 15-19, 33). In addition to the sacrifices of a bull and a goat, the observance included the ritual expulsion of the scapegoat, when the sins of the people were symbolically transferred through the high priest to a second goat that was driven out into the

3. Teresa Berger, *Women's Ways of Worship: Gender Analysis and Liturgical History* (Collegeville, MN: Liturgical Press, 1999), 8.

desert (Lev 16:10, 20-22). As John E. Alsup notes, "Covenant renewal and restoration were connected to the Day of Atonement."[4] Margaret Barker connects the atonement rituals with "the covenant of peace, the covenant of the priesthood of eternity, elsewhere called the covenant of eternity or, more recently, the Cosmic Covenant."[5] In this interpretation atonement did not merely cover sin or hide it from God's sight but repaired the fabric of creation damaged by sin.[6] The book of Wisdom captures the cosmic dimension of high priestly atonement as enacted by Aaron in the wilderness:

> For a blameless man was quick to act as their champion; he brought forward the shield of his ministry, prayer and propitiation by incense . . . by his word he subdued the avenger, appealing to the oaths and covenants given to our ancestors. . . . For on his long robe the whole world was depicted, and the glories of the ancestors were engraved on the four rows of stones, and your majesty was on the diadem upon his head. To these the destroyer yielded, these he [or they] feared; for merely to test the wrath was enough. (Wis 18:21-25; see also Num 16:41-50)

A Jewish Perspective (Heb 5:1-4)

Hebrews 5:1-4 offers a strikingly sympathetic description of the Jewish high priests, whose awe-filled responsibilities are carried out in a spirit of gentleness and humility. I am particularly struck by the emphasis on the advantage of the high priest's human frailty: "He is able to deal gently with the ignorant and wayward, since he himself is subject to weakness" and himself commits sins which he must expiate through sacrifices. This is a sane view that can be contrasted with the common religious temptation to invest authority figures with an aura of sinless perfection, denying the sins they do commit and exposing the vulnerable people they come in contact with to great danger.

---

4. John E. Alsup, "Atonement," *Harper's Bible Dictionary*, ed. Paul J. Achtemeier (San Francisco: HarperSanFrancisco, 1985), 80.

5. See also Gen 9:16; Lev 26:5-6, 9, 12; Isa 54:9-10; Jer 31:31-37; 33:20-26; Ezek 34:25; Hos 2:18-20; and Heb 13:20. Margaret Barker, "Atonement: The Rite of Healing," paper presented at the Society for Old Testament Study, Edinburgh, 1994; available at http://www.marquette.edu/maqom/atonement.html, accessed July 15, 2015, citing Robert Murray, *The Cosmic Covenant: Biblical Themes of Justice, Peace and the Integrity of Creation* (Piscataway, NY: Gorgias Press, 1992).

6. Barker, "Atonement," 8; see also Mary Douglas, "Atonement in Leviticus," *JSQ* 1 (1993–94): 109–30, at 117.

There is no longer a Jewish high priest, though our close cousins the Samaritans still have one, just as they have maintained the annual Passover sacrifice at their holy place, Mount Gerizim. Although no individual fills that exalted role in traditionalist Jewish communities, the hereditary priesthood of temple times continues nonetheless. In the absence of sacrifices, the major role of Jewish priests (כהנים) today—including, in a few congregations, women as well as men—is to bless the community, chanting the priestly blessing (Num 6:24-26) in a dramatic ritual. Before giving this blessing, the *kohanim* thank God "for sanctifying us with the sanctity of Aaron [the first high priest] and commanding us to bless Your people Israel with love." Thus the emphasis on the priest's gentle care for the people, emphasized here in Hebrews, continues in Judaism today.

I cannot see how to reconcile the homilist's humane insight that the priest's gentle dealing with the people is rooted in his own sinful weakness with the notion that Jesus is both a superior high priest and a perfect being "without sin" (4:15, see also 7:26-28). While Hebrews insists that in Jesus "we do not have a high priest who is unable to sympathize with our weaknesses," the logic of the text itself does not bear this out.

Justin Jaron Lewis

Evidence from the Second Temple period indicates that the high priest, who wore the sacred name on his forehead when officiating in the temple (Wis 18:25; Philo, *Mos.* 2.114; *Abr.* 103; *Let. Aris.* 93), corresponded to YHWH, the heavenly high priest who sustained the universe.[7]

Verses 5-10 introduce the scriptural focus of chapters 5–7, Ps 110:4, which is combined with Ps 2:7 (see also Heb 1:5). The homilist reminds the reader/audience of Christ's exaltation to divine sonship (5:5) and introduces the motif of his appointment as high priest "forever, according to the order of Melchizedek" (5:6; see also 5:9; 7:17, 21). Like Ps 2:7 ("you are my Son, today I have begotten/given birth to you"), Ps 110:1, already quoted in Heb 1:13 (see also 10:13), is frequently alluded to in the NT,[8] but the reference to the priesthood of Melchizedek is found only in Hebrews. The christological significance of Melchizedek is explicated in chapter 7; here Jesus' priestly status is connected to his human suffering, to which he responded by reaching out to God: "In the days of his

7. Barker, "Atonement," 10.
8. Matt 22:43-44; Mark 12:36; Luke 20:42-43; Acts 2:34-35.

flesh, he offered up [προσενέγκας] prayers and supplications, with loud cries and tears" (5:7a),[9] implicitly contrasting Jesus with the Levitical priests who "offer" (προσφέρη) material gifts and sacrifices (5:1), as opposed to Jesus' spiritual offerings. As James Thompson notes, the homilist "is also signifying that Jesus has joined the vulnerable community in crying out to God. The 'prayers and supplications' indicate that Jesus sympathizes with the community's helplessness as it calls on God in prayer."[10] The solidarity of Jesus with the community implies that his sisters and brothers (Heb 2:11-12) share in his priesthood and that their prayers and spiritual lives are likewise pleasing (metaphorical) sacrifices (see also 13:15-16).

The distinctive view of Jesus as high priest presented here is not incompatible with his role as prophet and/or pastor vis à vis his advocacy for and solidarity with the poor, an understanding that profoundly influenced the early church's teachings. The *Didachē*, in speaking of apostles and prophets, emphasizes the moral transparency of the priests, their integrity in speaking the truth for the service of the community: "Select for yourselves bishops and deacons: men who are worthy of the Lord, humble, not greedy for money, honest, and well tested, because these too carry out for you the service of the prophets and teachers."[11] One should also note, however, that it does not go just one way. The community, being made up of ordinary people, should also show its respect for its leaders and share what it has. "So," the *Didachē* continues, "take the first fruits of the vine and the harvest, of cattle and sheep, and present these first fruits to the prophets because they are, to you, the *high priests*. But if you have no prophet [settled in your community], then give the first fruit to *the poor*."[12] This kind of offering is clearly connected to the tithe, which appears later in chapter 7 when Jesus is shown to be in the priestly line of Melchizedek. As the homilist identifies the high priesthood of Jesus with the vulnerable community, the writer of the *Didachē* also identifies the prophets (playing the role of high priests) with the poor. The conventional sense of "high" from a hierarchical point of view is turned on its head by this radical teaching of healthy leadership. One may even hear

9. See also Mark 14:32-42; Matt 26:36-46; Luke 22:39-46; Pss 22:1-24; 31:23; 39:13.

10. James W. Thompson, *Hebrews*, Paideia Commentaries on the New Testament (Grand Rapids, MI: Baker Academic, 2008), 115.

11. Thomas O'Loughlin, *The Didachē: A Window on the Earliest Christians* (Grand Rapids, MI: Baker Academic, 2010), 170.

12. Ibid., 169. Emphasis supplied.

the echoes of the voice of Mary in the *Magnificat* in this bit of instruction found in the *Didachē*, "He has brought down the powerful from their thrones, and lifted up the lowly; he has filled the hungry with good things, and sent the rich away empty" (Luke 1:52-53).

Our Stories Are Our Scripture
For Hebrews 5

Honoring Wiyaka Sinte Win[13]

Tail Feather Woman ran to lake
hid under lily pads escaping
from Blue Coats after loss

Of four sons in massacre but in a
vision Great Spirit tells her
when she returns to what

Is left of her people they are to
make a Drum and she learns
rituals songs to share with
them

Teaching "It will be the only
way you are going to stop the
soldiers from killing your
people"

Especially now the Drum shows
that Indians had power so
much which they kept
secret so

Ceremonial powwow drum
celebrates gratitude for
survival and everyone likes
powwow

Annharte

From a feminist standpoint the emphasis on Jesus' suffering (5:8) in Christian theology has been criticized in that it may glorify or trivialize suffering, value suffering as an end in itself, fetishize self-sacrifice, or lead to the deification of violence, ultimately portraying God as a stern patriarch who sentences his son to death in order to "save" humanity.[14] In this passage, however, it is not Jesus' suffering that is the offering commended by the homilist; rather, it is his reaching out to God in prayer. The "perfection" (τελειωθεὶς) he achieves through heeding God is accessible to everyone who follows his example (5:9). Similarly, the homilist's apparent emphasis on Jesus' obedience (5:8, 9) is problematic from a feminist perspective. Barbara E. Reid, for example, notes that "myths that God tests faith or that one learns obedience through suffering (Heb 5:8)" need to be dismantled insofar as they justify oppression or

---

13. "Eagle Tail Feather Woman" (Lakota name).

14. Joanne Carlson Brown and Carole R. Bohn, eds., *Christianity, Patriarchy, and Abuse: A Feminist Critique* (Cleveland, OH: Pilgrim Press, 1989), 26–27.

abuse.[15] She also observes that obedience can have either deadly or liberating consequences, depending on context:

> As many women are discovering, the greater good is not served when any of God's beloved sons or daughters are sacrificed for a supposed greater good. When anyone is subjected to unjust pain or death, whether in abusive relationships or in war, all suffer. True obedience requires hard, analytical work, a discerning heart, and a freeing of the imagination to discover the ways to break cycles of violence through creative acts of self-gift that result in wellbeing for all.[16]

From this standpoint Jesus' suffering can be interpreted in terms of the arduous labor of discernment that enables him to live out his prophetic mission to announce salvation/*shalōm* to his brothers and sisters in the family of the God who has begotten/given birth to them.[17] Like his brothers and sisters, Jesus is portrayed as a child of God in need of salvation (he "offered prayers and supplications, with loud cries and tears, to the one who was able to save him from death"), whose pleas were heard by God (5:7). The NRSV, which translates εὐλαβείας ("piety" or "reverence") as "reverent submission," adds an element of subservience to this verse that is not there in the Greek text.[18] Similarly, the words translated in the NRSV in terms of "obedience" (ὑπακοήν; ὑπακούουσιν) in verses 8 and 9 imply "listening." An alternative translation follows from the description of God as "listening" (εἰσακουσθείς) to Jesus' prayers (5:7):

> [8]despite being a son, he learned to listen [ὑπακοήν] through suffering,
> [9]and being perfected he became to all who listen to him [ὑπακούουσιν] the source of eternal salvation/*shalōm*

Ruth Hoppin on Jesus' Suffering in Hebrews

Ruth Hoppin notes that Hebrews interprets Jesus' suffering differently from Paul, and she sees this distinctive Christology as relevant to the issue of gender equality in the church:

The crucifixion was, for Paul, a salvational event directly impacting the

---

15. Barbara E. Reid, *Taking Up the Cross: New Testament Interpretations through Latina and Feminist Eyes* (Minneapolis: Fortress Press, 2007), 71.

16. Ibid., 69.

17. See also Heb 1:5; 5:5; on prophetic rejection/suffering, see 2 Chr 24:19-22; 36:16; Neh 9:26, 30; Isa 53:3; Jer 35:15; Ezek 2:5; Hos 9:7; Dan 9:6, 10.

18. See also NCV: "because he trusted God"; NLV: "because he honored God"; NLT: "because of his deep reverence for God"; CEB: "because of his godly devotion"; RSV: "because of his godly fear"; Inclusive Version: "because of his reverence."

believer, encompassing mystical union with Christ.

For Paul, the crucifixion changes the believer, atoning for sin, facilitating a right relationship with God:

> "We know that our old self was crucified with him, so that the body of sin might be destroyed, and we might no longer be enslaved to sin (Rom. 6:6)";

> "I have been crucified with Christ: . . . it is Christ who lives in me . . . (Gal. 2:20)";

> "May I never boast of anything except the cross of our Lord Jesus Christ, by which the world has been crucified to me, and I to the world (Gal. 6:14)."

For the Hebrews author, the crucifixion was essential to salvation because it changed Jesus. Through the experience of suffering and death he was enabled to completely empathize with humanity (Heb. 5:7-10; 2:9-18):

> "Although he was a Son, he learned obedience through what he suffered (Heb. 5:8)."

> "and having been made perfect, he became the source of eternal salvation for all who obey him (Heb. 5:9)."

> "crowned with honor and glory because of the suffering of death that he might taste death for everyone (Heb. 2:9)."

> "He had to become like his brothers and sisters in every respect, so that he might be a merciful and faithful high priest, . . . to make a sacrifice of atonement for the sins of the people (Heb. 2:17)."

> "Because he himself was tested by what he suffered, he is able to help those who are tested (Heb. 2:18)."

Only by having undergone this transformation through suffering could Jesus offer himself, a perfect offering for sin, in the capacity of High Priest (Heb. 10:12).

So for Paul, the crucifixion is sanctification, offering holiness through mystic union with Christ. For the writer of Hebrews, the crucifixion is redemption (Heb. 10:19-22), restoring the believer to a right relationship with God and a rightful place in the religious and spiritual life of the community. This is possible through the perfection of Jesus through suffering, refining his qualities of tenderness and empathy to the highest possible level.

The author of Hebrews does not claim that tenderness, sympathy and empathy are exclusively feminine traits; on the contrary, they are considered human traits, for Jesus' development of these traits [is] the pathway by which he fully identifies with humankind. The path began with incarnation in human form and ended with the experience of death as mortals experience death. Nonetheless, whether rightly or wrongly, the traits in question are traditionally perceived as feminine. By making these stereotypical feminine qualities perquisite to the salvational activity of Christ, they are elevated in value.

The theology of Hebrews thus has subtle but profound implications for gender equality. In such a theological milieu, both men and women are subliminally and overtly enjoined to value "feminine" traits through recognizing them as decisive in God's plan of salvation. The per-

ception of women is ultimately elevated. Since women are encouraged to value more highly the traits imputed to them their own self-perception is sure to be elevated.

(*Source*: Ruth Hoppin, "The Book of the Hebrews Revisited: Implications of the Theology of Hebrews for Gender Equality," http://www.womenpriests.org/scriptur/hoppin2.asp, accessed July 15, 2015.)

Hoppin's suggestions regarding the implications of Hebrews for feminist theology are part of her argument for female authorship, but they are valid regardless of the gender of the homilist. On this interpretation suffering is regarded not as an intrinsically "Christian" or "feminine" virtue, or as something to be sought after, but as an inevitable part of the spectrum of human experience through which Jesus, like other people of faith, struggled to understand his relationship with God.

Mary Ann Beavis

Paraenesis: Perfecting Faith (5:11–6:20)

The exposition of Ps 110:4 is interrupted by a lengthy paraenetic section (5:11–6:20), which relates back to the theme of Jesus' reliance on God in the context of suffering (5:7-9). The author's warnings against deviating from commitment to the path of perfection exemplified by Jesus expand on the admonition in Heb 2:1-4 not to "drift away" from "what we have heard" (see also 3:7-19). The argument alternates between re-

[11]About this we have much to say that is hard to explain, since you have become dull in understanding. [12]For though by this time you ought to be teachers, you need someone to teach you again the basic elements of the oracles of God. You need milk, not solid food; [13]for everyone who lives on milk, being still an infant, is unskilled in the word of righteousness. [14]But solid food is for the mature, for those whose faculties have been trained by practice to distinguish good from evil.

[6:1]Therefore let us go on toward perfection, leaving behind the basic teaching about Christ, and not laying again the foundation: repentance from dead works and faith toward God, [2]instruction about baptisms, laying on of hands, resurrection of the dead, and eternal judgment. [3]And we will do this, if God permits. [4]For it is impossible to restore again to repentance those who have once been enlightened, and have tasted the heavenly gift, and have shared in the Holy Spirit, [5]and have tasted the

proaching the audience for their straying from previous teaching (5:11-14), warning of the dire consequences of straying (6:1-8), and encouragement to stay the course (6:9-12). Although the manipulative sermonizing, in which the homilist alternately belittles and flatters the audience in order to get them back in line, is problematic from a feminist standpoint, it is typical rhetorical technique.[19] As I have noted elsewhere, such coercive rhetoric places the author in a dominant position over the audience; rhetorical belittling is a strategy that has often been used to quash dissent.[20] The alternation between insults, threats, and flattery is disturbingly reminiscent of the dynamics of abusive relationships.

After tantalizing the audience with another enigmatic reference to the Melchizedekian high priesthood of Christ (5:10), the homilist scolds them for not being ready to receive such advanced teaching: they have become "dull" or "sluggish" in understanding (5:11). They should by now have attained what is presumably the author's status as teacher (διδάσκαλος);[21] instead, they need to be retaught the basics or elementary principles (στοιχεῖα) of divine revelation (5:12). The homilist uses the commonplace metaphor of elementary education (παιδεία) as the activity of a mother

19. Thompson, *Hebrews*, 135.

20. Mary Ann Beavis, "2 Thessalonians," in *Searching the Scriptures*, vol. 2: *A Feminist Commentary*, ed. Elisabeth Schüssler Fiorenza (New York: Crossroad, 1994), 263–71, at 270.

21. On the status of teachers in early Christianity, see 1 Cor 12:28-29; Eph 4:11; 1 Tim 2:7; 2 Tim 1:11; 4:3; on women teachers, see Titus 2:3; see also Acts 18:25-28.

goodness of the word of God and the powers of the age to come, [6]and then have fallen away, since on their own they are crucifying again the Son of God and are holding him up to contempt. [7]Ground that drinks up the rain falling on it repeatedly, and that produces a crop useful to those for whom it is cultivated, receives a blessing from God. [8]But if it produces thorns and thistles, it is worthless and on the verge of being cursed; its end is to be burned over.

[9]Even though we speak in this way, beloved, we are confident of better things in your case, things that belong to salvation. [10]For God is not unjust; he will not overlook your work and the love that you showed for his sake in serving the saints, as you still do. [11]And we want each one of you to show the same diligence so as to realize the full assurance of hope to the very end, [12]so that you may not become sluggish, but imitators of those who through faith and patience inherit the promises.

[13]When God made a promise to Abraham, because he had no one greater by whom to swear, he swore

or nurse: "You need milk, not solid food; for everyone who lives on milk, being still an infant, is unskilled in the word of righteousness" (Heb 5:12c-13; see also 1 Cor 3:1-3; Rom 2:20).[22] In 1 Thess 2:7, Paul uses the nursing metaphor more positively: "we were gentle among you, like a nurse tenderly caring for her own children," an image famously applied to Christ by the medieval mystic Julian of Norwich:

> A mother can give her child milk to suck, but our precious mother, Jesus, can feed us with himself. He does so most courteously and most tenderly, with the Blessed Sacrament, which is the precious food of true life. With all the sweet sacraments he sustains us most mercifully and graciously. That is what he meant in these blessed words, where he said, "I am that which holy Church preaches and teaches you."[23]

Ruth Hoppin offers the maternal imagery of this passage as evidence of female authorship.[24] Here, however, the "milk" of basic doctrine is a foil for the "solid food" of the mature ("perfect," τελείων), and the homilist shifts from maternal imagery to the male-oriented language of ath-

22. For Greco-Roman examples, see Thompson, *Hebrews*, 120–21.

23. *Revelations of Divine Love of Julian of Norwich*, trans. M. L. Del Maestro (New York: Doubleday, 1977), 191–92.

24. Ruth Hoppin, *Priscilla's Letter: Finding the Author of the Epistle to the Hebrews* (Fort Bragg, CA: Lost Coast Press, 1997), 28.

by himself, [14]saying, "I will surely bless you and multiply you." [15]And thus Abraham, having patiently endured, obtained the promise. [16]Human beings, of course, swear by someone greater than themselves, and an oath given as confirmation puts an end to all dispute. [17]In the same way, when God desired to show even more clearly to the heirs of the promise the unchangeable character of his purpose, he guaranteed it by an oath, [18]so that through two unchangeable things, in which it is impossible that God would prove false, we who have taken refuge might be strongly encouraged to seize the hope set before us. [19]We have this hope, a sure and steadfast anchor of the soul, a hope that enters the inner shrine behind the curtain, [20]where Jesus, a forerunner on our behalf, has entered, having become a high priest forever according to the order of Melchizedek.

letics: "for those whose faculties have been trained by practice to distinguish good from evil" (5:14). The term translated by the NRSV as "trained" is a form of γυμνάζω, literally "to do gymnastic exercises in the nude," applied figuratively to the development of spiritual and mental abilities.[25]

Here the homilist seems to take a theological stance from a very concrete and ordinary life situation, referring to Jesus as the "high" priest. From the caring and tender feminine characteristics of Jesus one can draw insights for the practice of Christian faith. The ancient concept of φρόνησις is helpful here. This word can be translated as "pastoral wisdom" or "theological know-how." Such knowledge is more than the acquisition of theoretical and historical data on theological matters; it refers to embodying practices for "full, conscious, and active" participation in "real-life issues facing real people."[26] The homilist's concrete examples, by elaborating on faith, and hope in particular, can be understood as φρόνησις as they provide the community a way to discern good from evil (v. 14).

25. BDAG 208.

26. Bonnie J. Miller-McLemore, "Practical Theology and Pedagogy: Embodying Theological Know-How," in *For Life Abundant: Practical Theology, Theological Education, and Christian Ministry*, ed. Dorothy C. Bass and Craig Dykstra (Grand Rapids, MI: Eerdmans, 2008), 170–90, at 171, 174.

Our Stories Are Our Scripture
For Hebrews 6

Wolf Girl wonder

Left to own device wonder what
to do what next why it reoccurs
often

Enough to accept everyday wolf
anxiety exception makes
wonderment

Probable question whether wolf
mother entrance feeds plenty
wonder

Gives lost deserted girl child
and also wounded little brother
hope for

Healing marrow from bone
works while they are safe warm
inside den

With family cubs until eventual
human rescue the kids walk out
of bush

Annharte

Next the homilist turns from scolding the audience for its failure to develop in faith to dire warnings of the consequences of spiritual stagnation (6:4-8), beginning with a hint that the audience may be too obtuse to pay attention: "And we will do this, if God permits" (6:3). The use of the first-person plural ("we"), which up to this point has been inclusive of author (or authors) and audience, now refers only to the "we" of the homilist and his or her associates—a possible indication of multiple authorship[27]—and these are portrayed as more spiritually advanced than the audience. After a hint that it may be futile to try to bring to repentance "those who have once been enlightened," the metaphor of advanced doctrine as nourishment resumes in vv. 4-5: those who have "*tasted* the heavenly gift, and have *shared* in the Holy Spirit, and have *tasted* the goodness of the word of God and the powers of the age to come" are in danger not only of failing to thrive spiritually but of near-blasphemy: "crucifying again the Son of God and . . . holding him up to contempt" (v. 6). The rhetorical manipulation escalates to an implicit threat of accursedness, with an agricultural parable: "Ground that drinks up the rain falling on it repeatedly, and that produces a crop useful to those from whom it is cultivated, receives a blessing from God. But if it produces thorns and thistles, it is worthless and on the verge of being cursed; its end is to be burned over" (vv. 7-8).

27. See also 1 Thess 1:1; Phil 1:1; 1 Cor 1:1; 2 Cor 1:1.

The imagery of the parable has scriptural,[28] Greco-Roman,[29] and rabbinic analogues,[30] as well as similarities to the teaching of Jesus.[31] The vehemence of the threat is particularly reminiscent of NT warnings against false teaching: "They are waterless clouds carried along by the winds; autumn trees without fruit, twice dead, uprooted" (Jude 12; see also 2 Pet 2:1-22; 3:7, 12). Here, however, the issue does not seem to be unapproved doctrine but simply lack of spiritual development despite the availability of advanced teaching.

The escalating rhetoric of the previous verses is tempered in 6:9-12, where the homilist changes tone, addressing the audience as "beloved" (ἀγαπητοί) and reassuring them that despite the harsh criticism of 5:1–6:8 "we are confident of better things in your case, things that belong to salvation" (6:9). The first-person plural continues to refer to the author (or authors) over against the audience (see also 6:3), in contrast to earlier usages that include them. In good rhetorical style the homilist compliments their work and love in the name of God in service of the saints ("holy ones"), i.e., members of the community (6:10). While conceding that God will righteously acknowledge their continuing service, v. 11 implies that their diligence in service is not being matched by their commitment to "the full assurance of hope to the very end," that is, they are in danger of falling away, like the apostates described in 6:4-8, and of sharing their dismal fate. The final verse of the paraenetic section reiterates the veiled accusation that the audience suffers from "sluggish" or "dull" (νωθροί) spiritual faculties (6:12; see also 5:11) and introduces the example of "faith and patience" elaborated in vv. 12-20.

As noted above, the alternation of accusations, threats, and expressions of approval in 5:11–6:12 is in keeping with ancient rhetorical technique:

> The warning in 6:4-8 was designed to awaken fear of divine judgement, but in order to prevent fear from debilitating the listeners, the author now expresses his confidence of their salvation (6:9). Rhetorically, "confidence is the opposite of fear" (Aristotle, *Rhetoric* 2.5.16 . . .), and it was understood that listeners were more likely to persevere (6:12) when

28. E.g., Gen 3:17-18; Isa 5:1-6; 28:23-29; Ezek 19:10-14.

29. E.g., Euripides, *Hecuba* 592; Quintilian, *Institutio Oratoria* 5.11.24.

30. See Albert Vanhoye, "Heb 6,7-8 et le mashal rabbinique," in *The New Testament Age: Essays in Honor of Bo Reicke*, vol. 2, ed. William C. Weinrich (Macon, GA: Mercer University Press, 1984), 527–32.

31. Mark 4:3-9; Matt 3:10; 7:18-20; 12:33; 13:1-9, 24-30; Luke 8:4-8; see also Luke 6:43-44; 13:6-9.

convinced that the speaker himself is confident. The tone reinforces the message.[32]

From a feminist standpoint, however, the homilist's argumentation bears a disturbing resemblance to that of an abuser who insults and intimidates his or her victim and then uses flattery and reassurances of love and approval (note the use of "love" language in 6:9-10) to convince the victim to remain in the relationship and to assert the power of the abuser over the abused. Such coercive and manipulative techniques should have no place in contemporary homiletics.

The Dangerous Rhetoric of Service and Korean Women

Alarming historical lessons bring into sharp relief the consequences of the use of the idea of "serving" as articulated in Heb 6:10. The Korean women who were made sexual slaves of the Japanese army throughout the Asian Pacific during the Second World War are an extreme example of what can be justified by using such distorted language. Korean women under Japanese colonization were "recruited" (most of them were actually kidnapped) to give their bodies to "serve" the sexual desires of Japanese soldiers. This program of "recruitment" was endorsed and encouraged by the Korean government, which used propaganda to express the sentiment that these women were patriots (lovers of the nation) who "served" their nation by playing this role in the war.[33] The history of the "comfort women," as they were euphemistically called, heightens awareness of the transnational migration of sex workers from all over the world to North America in our present-day context. When the language of service dominates in the context of women's relationships to men, to their families, or to their nation, a great deal is at stake.

The issue of women's labor in the twenty-first century is another example of the problematic nature of the language of service when it comes to women. The intersection between gender and race at the threshold of globalized labor markets finds many racialized women in service, living far from their families in the homes of wealthy, often white families and caring for children and the elderly. The globalized labor markets also put racialized women to work sewing jeans they are unable to buy or selling their bodies to the

32. Craig R. Koester, *Hebrews*, AB 36 (New York: Doubleday, 2001), 324.
33. Elaine H. Kim and Chungmoo Choi, *Dangerous Women: Gender and Korean Nationalism* (New York: Routledge, 1998).

people of other nations to raise money for their families. These glimpses of complicated problems reveal classist, sexist, colonialist, and racist practices.[34] For such women it may be too late, or scarcely any comfort (let alone help) to hear a sermon that

proclaims: "For God is not unjust; he will not overlook your work and the love that you showed for his sake in serving the saints, as you will do" (6:10).

HyeRan Kim-Cragg

The final part of the paraenetic section (6:12-20) continues the more positive tone of vv. 9-11, introducing the figure of Abraham as an example of the quality of faithfulness and patience expected of the audience (see also v. 11). Rhetorically, like 4:14-16, these verses are also transitional to the main exposition of Christ's high priesthood in 7:1-28, where the meeting between Abraham and Melchizedek in Gen 14:17-20 figures prominently. In contrast to the wilderness generation's alleged failure to attain the rest promised by God (Heb 3:7-19), the homilist portrays Abraham positively, as one who attends to God's promise. Since, for the homilist, the "rest" of the promised land—which is very much part of the promises to Abraham in Genesis (Gen 12:1, 7)—is eschatological, the focus is on the divine pledge of offspring: "I will surely bless you and multiply you" (Heb 6:14; see also Gen 22:16-17). The homilist portrays Abraham as a paragon of confidence in God's self-sworn oath (ὀμόσαι in 6:13) of offspring: "And thus Abraham, having patiently endured, obtained the promise" (6:15). Elsewhere in the Scriptures the divine promise/oath to Abraham is called a covenant,[35] which has in common with the "new covenant" of Heb 8:1–10:18 an eternal character: "I will establish my covenant between me and you, and your offspring after you throughout their generations, for an everlasting covenant, to be God to you and to your offspring after you" (Gen 17:7; see also 17:13, 19). The homilist recommends that the audience emulate Abraham's faith in God's unchangeable promise (Heb 6:18), returning to the inclusive use of "we": "*we* who have taken refuge might be strongly encouraged to seize the hope set before *us*" (v. 18b). The homilist also returns to the sea

34. Nami Kim, "My/Our Comfort *Not* At the Expense of 'Somebody Else's,'" *JFSR* 21 (2005): 75–94.

35. E.g., Gen 15:18; 17:9; Exod 2:24; Lev 26:42; 2 Kgs 13:23; 1 Chr 16:16; Ps 105:9; Sir 44:20; Acts 3:25; 7:8.

voyage metaphor (see comment on Heb 2:1): "*We* have this hope, a sure and steadfast anchor of the soul" (v. 19a). John Chrysostom vividly elaborates on the homilist's meaning:

> For through hope we are already in heaven. . . . As the anchor, dropped from the vessel, does not allow it to be carried about even if ten thousand winds agitate it but, being depended upon, makes it steady, so also does hope. . . . For the surge and the great storm toss the boat, but hope does not permit it to be carried back and forth, although winds innumerable agitate it, so that, unless we had this hope we would long ago have been sunk.[36]

In vv. 19b-20 the homilist segues into the exposition of the high priesthood of Christ; the hope shared by the community is one "that enters the inner shrine behind the curtain," where the forerunner Jesus has entered, "having become a high priest forever according to the order of Melchizedek."

The homilist's portrayal of Abraham as a model of faith resembles Paul's teaching,[37] although for Paul the object of faith is Christ, whereas for the homilist faith relates to the divine promise of heavenly rest. The biblical Wisdom tradition, in contrast, emphasizes Abraham's obedience to the divine command: "He kept the law of the Most High, and entered into a covenant with him; he certified the covenant with his flesh, and when he was tested he proved faithful" (Sir 44:20; see also Wis 10:5), a perspective echoed in the NT in Jas 2:21-23:

> Was not our ancestor Abraham justified by works when he offered his son Isaac on the altar? You see that faith was active along with his works, and faith was brought to completion by works. Thus the scripture was fulfilled, "Abraham believed God, and it was reckoned to him as righteousness," and he was called the friend of God.

Abraham's high repute in the Jewish and Christian tradition is belied by the many stories in Genesis that portray him in a less than flattering light. Rather than displaying unswerving confidence in God's promise of offspring through Sarah, he follows her advice to take Hagar as a concubine (Gen 16:1-4). The mother of his firstborn is treated so abusively in his household that she flees temporarily during her pregnancy (Gen 16:5-14); subsequently she and their son are permanently expelled by the patriarch (Gen 21:1-20). Abraham's cowardice leads him twice to

---

36. *On the Epistle to the Hebrews* 11.3.
37. Rom 4:1-25; Gal 3:1-18; see also Heb 11:8-12, 17-19.

deliver Sarah, his principal wife and mother of his promised heir, into the harems of foreign kings (Gen 12:10-20; 20:1-18). Despite the divine promise and covenant, he falls on his face laughing when God tells him that Sarah will bear a son in her old age (Gen 17:9, 17); unlike her husband, Sarah is later criticized for her laughter on hearing the unlikely tidings (Gen 18:9-15). His most impressive act of obedience—the near-sacrifice of Isaac (Gen 22:1-19)—is so horrific that Jewish tradition speculates that Sarah's death, reported shortly afterward (Gen 23:2), was the result of her grief or shock over the incident.[38] From a feminist standpoint, then, Abraham is a deeply flawed figure who seems unworthy of his prominence in Jewish and Christian tradition.

Sacrifice and Eucharist

The idea of the offering of human sacrifice is first introduced in the Bible with the story of Abraham. Although human sacrifice (or more precisely, child sacrifice) is reviled elsewhere in the Hebrew Scriptures (e.g., Deut 12:31; 18:9-12; 2 Kgs 16:3; Ps 106:38; Jer 19:4-5), Abraham's willingness to provide a human offering to God is portrayed in Heb 11:17 as proof of his faith. This provokes an examination of the idea of sacrificial rites and their implications for faith (see also the comment on Heb 12 below). According to James White, a well-known historian of Christian worship, Jewish sacrificial worship dates back to the seventh century BCE: The whole sacrificial cultus had developed as a communal means of relating to God as a nation and of achieving communion with God as individuals."[39] From this emerged the meaning of Christian Eucharist as a sacrificial offering, God's self-giving, which is received with "Eucharist (thanksgiving)." Sacrifice in this sense is highly relational and mutual rather than a unilateral imposition by one person on another.

Sacrificial rituals are also a way of commemorating and remembering. This is more than a simple mental exercise of calling to mind what happened in the past. Instead, it is about the whole community participating in a ritual in anticipation of a community to come. The Greek term ἀνάμνησις encompasses the meanings of

---

38. B'reishit Rabbah 58:5; Pirkei D'Rabbi Eliezer 32; Tanchuma on Vayera 23; Midrash HaGadol. Cited in Tamara Cohn Eskenazi and Andrea L. Weiss, eds., *The Torah: A Women's Commentary* (New York: Women of Reformed Judaism, 2008), 106.

39. White, *Introduction to Christian Worship*, 230.

"remembrance, recalling, representation," all of which are enacted in the recital during the eucharistic prayer of the saving work of God revealed in Jesus. In ritualizing this self-giving, the community is to gain insights into and experience "nuances of sacrifice and presence" as they are able to remember the past, taste the present, and behold the future.[40] One might say that the ritualization of faith is "the assurance of things hoped for, the conviction of things not seen" (11:1), as the homilist so eloquently puts it.

HyeRan Kim-Cragg

The authors of *The Torah: A Women's Commentary* offer another insight on the faith of Abraham, as they observe that the "warts-and-all" portrayal of Abraham and his family can be used by contemporary people of faith:

> This Torah portion makes clear that our ancestors are by no means always models of ethical behavior that edify and inspire us. On the contrary, often the Torah holds up a mirror to the ugliest aspects of human nature and human society. It provides us with opportunities to look honestly at ourselves and the world we have created, to reflect on destructive patterns of human relating, and to ask how we might address and change them.[41]

Doctrine: The High Priesthood of Christ (7:1-28)

Daniel J. Harrington observes that this chapter is sometimes regarded as the main focus of Hebrews, since it develops the distinctive theme of Christ's high priesthood "according to the order of Melchizedek."[42] Melchizedek is not mentioned elsewhere in the NT, although there is considerable speculation in early Samaritan, Jewish, and Christian (including Gnostic) literature about this obscure biblical figure (Gen 14:17-20; Ps 110:4),[43] most famously in the Qumran scroll 11Q13 (ca.

40. Ibid., 233.

41. Eskenazi and Weiss, *Torah: A Women's Commentary*, 107.

42. Daniel J. Harrington, *What Are They Saying about the Letter to the Hebrews* (Mahwah, NJ: Paulist Press, 2005), 46.

43. See Harold Attridge, *The Epistle to the Hebrews: A Commentary*, Hermeneia (Philadelphia: Fortress Press, 1989), 192.

Heb 7:1-28

¹This "King Melchizedek of Salem, priest of the Most High God, met Abraham as he was returning from defeating the kings and blessed him"; ²and to him Abraham apportioned "one-tenth of everything." His name, in the first place, means "king of righteousness"; next he is also king of Salem, that is, "king of peace." ³Without father, without mother, without genealogy, having neither beginning of days nor end of life, but resembling the Son of God, he remains a priest forever. ⁴See how great he is! Even Abraham the patriarch gave him a tenth of the spoils. ⁵And those descendants of Levi who receive the priestly office have a commandment in the law to collect tithes from the people, that is, from their kindred, though these also are descended from Abraham. ⁶But this man, who does not belong to their ancestry, collected tithes from Abraham and blessed him who had received the promises. ⁷It is beyond dispute that the inferior is blessed by the superior. ⁸In the one case, tithes are received by those who are mortal; in the other, by one of whom it is testified that he lives. ⁹One might even say that Levi himself, who receives tithes, paid tithes through Abraham, ¹⁰for he was still in the loins of his ancestor when Melchizedek met him.

¹¹Now if perfection had been attainable through the levitical priesthood—for the people received the law under this priesthood—what further need

first century BCE), where Melchizedek is portrayed as an eschatological judge. Harold Attridge affirms that Hebrews' Melchizedek chapter is probably related to the milieu of Jewish speculation "that saw Melchizedek as an angelic defender of Israel (Qumran) or as an exalted, possibly angelic, heavenly priest (Philo?, *2 Enoch, 3 Enoch*, Nag Hammadi)."[44] Although the Melchizedek passage constitutes part of the advanced teaching hinted at in 6:1-2, it is preparatory to the "main point" of the discourse—the fulfillment of Jeremiah's "new covenant" prophecy—exegeted in 8:1–10:18.

The doctrinal (5:1-10; 7:1-28) and paraenetic (5:11–6:20) parts of this section are connected by the figure of Abraham (6:13-16). The homilist uses the Jewish method of *gezera shawa*, bringing together two scriptural passages that share the same word, in this case the name Melchizedek (Hebrew: "righteous king"): (1) the citation of Ps 110:4 introduced in Heb 5:6, "You are a priest forever, according to the order of Melchizedek" (repeated in 7:17; see also 7:21); and (2) an allusion to Gen 14:17-20, the only other scriptural reference to Melchizedek. In the latter, Abram/

---

44. Ibid., 194.

would there have been to speak of another priest arising according to the order of Melchizedek, rather than one according to the order of Aaron? [12] For when there is a change in the priesthood, there is necessarily a change in the law as well. [13] Now the one of whom these things are spoken belonged to another tribe, from which no one has ever served at the altar. [14] For it is evident that our Lord was descended from Judah, and in connection with that tribe Moses said nothing about priests.

[15] It is even more obvious when another priest arises, resembling Melchizedek, [16] one who has become a priest, not through a legal requirement concerning physical descent, but through the power of an indestructible life. [17] For it is attested of him,

"You are a priest forever,
    according to the order of
        Melchizedek."

[18] There is, on the one hand, the abrogation of an earlier commandment because it was weak and ineffectual [19] (for the law made nothing perfect); there is, on the other hand, the introduction of a better hope, through which we approach God.

[20] This was confirmed with an oath; for others who became priests took

Abraham, returning from a triumph in battle, meets the king of Salem, "priest of God Most High" (Gen 14:18), who offers him bread and wine. Not surprisingly, early Christian authors often interpreted this shared meal as prefiguring the Eucharist,[45] although the homilist makes no such

---

Our Stories Are Our Scripture
For Hebrews 7

Down with Big Stink

Fight takes Giant Skunk down
Wolverine held squirter but tail
still up

Pressurized spray got right in
his face dirty job somebody
would do

Suspicious vibrations why Great
Skunk followed animals escape
after

They cross his path broke rule so
they made a stand special bear
song

Ask help to take out big bully
after all Wolverine washed his
face at

Hudson Bay explains why salty
dirty water why Winnipeg so
named

Annharte

---

45. E.g., Augustine, *Homilies on the Gospels* 2.19; *Letter* 62.4; Eusebius of Caesarea, *Proof of the Gospel* 5.3. See Erik M. Heen and Philip D. Krey, *Ancient Christian Commentary on Scripture, New Testament X* (Downers Grove, IL: InterVarsity, 2006), 96–98.

their office without an oath, [21]but this one became a priest with an oath, because of the one who said to him,

"The Lord has sworn
and will not change his mind,
'You are a priest forever'"— [22]accordingly Jesus has also become the guarantee of a better covenant.

[23]Furthermore, the former priests were many in number, because they were prevented by death from continuing in office; [24]but he holds his priesthood permanently, because he continues forever. [25]Consequently he is able for all time to save those who approach God through him, since he always lives to make intercession for them.

[26]For it was fitting that we should have such a high priest, holy, blameless, undefiled, separated from sinners, and exalted above the heavens. [27]Unlike the other high priests, he has no need to offer sacrifices day after day, first for his own sins, and then for those of the people; this he did once for all when he offered himself. [28]For the law appoints as high priests those who are subject to weakness, but the word of the oath, which came later than the law, appoints a Son who has been made perfect forever.

connection. Melchizedek blesses Abraham for his success, and Abraham in turn gives him one-tenth of the spoils of the battle. Ps 110, in contrast, is a coronation hymn in which the Davidic king is accorded priestly status by divine oath:

The LORD has sworn and will not change his mind,
"You are a priest forever according to the order of Melchizedek."

Although Torah stipulates that the priesthood belongs only to Israelites of Levitical descent (see also Heb 7:14), the psalm seems to acknowledge that sometimes kings engaged in sacerdotal roles (see also 2 Sam 6:13, 17; 8:18; 1 Kgs 3:4) and legitimizes this by the precedent of the priest-king Melchizedek, who, like the Davidic kings, served "God Most High" (*El Elyon*).

The homilist interprets the psalm, and its relation to the Genesis passage, quite differently by arguing for the superiority of Melchizedek to Abraham and his descendants. His titles are "king of righteousness" and "king of Salem, that is 'king of peace'" (v. 2); since in Jewish tradition Salem is often identified with Jerusalem, the place name may subtly associate the ancient priest-king with the Davidic capital. Although there is no hint in the Genesis account that Melchizedek was anything but a human being, the author uses the lack of scriptural references to his lineage as indicative of near-divine qualities: he is "without father, without mother, without genealogy," with "neither beginning of days nor end of life," thus resembling the son of God, "a priest forever" (v. 3).

The suggestion that Jesus, like Melchizedek, is without parents or lineage is puzzling in view of the homilist's acknowledgment that he belongs to the royal tribe of Judah (v. 14). The early Christian writer Epiphanius of Salamis (ca. 315–403) refutes the theory that Melchizedek's parents are not mentioned because his mother was a prostitute with the example of Rahab, a prostitute mentioned in Scripture:[46] "For the Saviour receives harlots, if only they repent."[47] James Thompson explains:

> The divine predicates, ἀπάτωρ and ἀμήτωρ [*apatōr, amētōr*, "fatherless," "motherless"], are well known in the Hellenistic world. One may compare Philo's description of Sarah as ἀμήτωρ (*Ebr.* 14). She, as ἀμήτωρ, had no connection with the senses. Philo implies also that Melchizedek was "without parents," for he contrasts Melchizedek to the Moabites and Ammonites whose parents are νοῦς and ἀσθένεια [*nous, astheneia*, "consciousness," "weakness"] (*Leg. All.* 3.79-82). Thus for both Hebrews and Philo, Melchizedek is a heavenly being, not a part of the world of sense perception (see also 7:16). Similarly, Plotinus claims that Aphrodite, who has her home in the intelligible world, is ἀμήτωρα; and because she has no contact with matter, she is immutable. . . . In the Pistis Sophia ἀπάτωρες is frequently used for heavenly beings.[48]

Since Philo would have been aware that Sarah's parents are mentioned in Genesis (20:12), it is unlikely that he meant that she literally had no mother; likewise, Hebrews' attribution of parentlessness to Melchizedek and Jesus refers to their spiritual status: "not to have a genealogy is characteristic of the man [or woman] of God,"[49] i.e., such a one is detached from the material world.

The homilist's unique argument that Jesus' priestly lineage follows the line of Melchizedek, and that Melchizedek's family origin is in question, suggests an intriguing possibility for breaking down the patriarchal priestly tradition. The homilist seems to proclaim a paradoxical message that a new world is to come through the eternal priest whose power lies in the subversive ability to disrupt the traditional order through an authority not derived from the conventional places. Unlike the author of Malachi, who calls for the restoration of the "pure offering" of the Levitical priests (1:11), the homilist seems to blur lines of purity and

46. Josh 2:1, 3; 6:17; 23, 25; Matt 1:5; Jas 2:25; Heb 11:31.
47. *Panarion 4, Against Melchizedekians* 7.1-2.
48. James W. Thompson, *The Beginnings of Christian Philosophy: The Epistle to the Hebrews*, CBQMS 13 (Washington, DC: Catholic Biblical Association of America, 1982), 119.
49. Ibid.

authority in order to behold a new vision, of a "priest forever" (Heb 7:3) who does not come from a prestigious pure class, born of a well-protected womb of an obedient mother. Rather, the "priest forever" may well have come from a prostitute, the womb of a socially tainted, "dirty" sex worker, from a vulnerable and exploited womb. According to the gospels this new, eternal, and perfect priest is born as an illegitimate child, who is favorably identified with Jesus, the messiah, conceived by a poor, unmarried young woman, thus also illegitimate.[50] Just as Jesus asserts that "no one puts new wine into old wineskins" (Mark 2:22), the Levitical system of priestly authority is destabilized by the "new covenant" fulfilled in Jesus, the theme of the next section (8:1–10:18). This at least is one possible way to interpret the homilist's view of Jesus as a priest in the order of Melchizedek. Some early Christian interpreters, however, used this passage to disassociate Jesus as Logos from human maternity altogether.[51] Presumably they were uncomfortable exploring the possibilities of this text for challenging the patriarchal notions of the place of women and other marginalized persons in the story of salvation.

For the homilist, the significance of Melchizedek is illustrated by Abraham's gift of one-tenth of the spoils of his military victory (Heb 7:4); this points to the superiority of the priest-king not only to the patriarch but to his descendants, including the priestly tribe of Levi, who collect tithes from other Israelites: "But this man, who does not belong to their ancestry, collected tithes from Abraham and blessed him who had received the promises. . . . One might even say that Levi himself, who receives tithes, paid tithes through Abraham, for he was still in the loins of his ancestor when Melchizedek met him" (7:6, 9).

For the homilist, Melchizedek's blessing of Abraham further indicates his greater status, since it is indisputable that "the inferior is blessed by the superior" (7:7). Moreover, the psalm's oracle of "a priest forever" implies that Melchizedek's priesthood is eternal, unlike that of the mortal Israelite priests (7:8), and since the Psalmist spoke of a kingly priesthood distinct from the Aaronid order, it must refer to a figure, like Jesus, who is from Judah, the tribe of David and, ultimately, of the messiah (7:14). Jesus resembles Melchizedek as the messiah who has "become a priest" not through physical descent "but through the power of an indestructible

---

50. See Jane D. Schaberg, *The Illegitimacy of Jesus* (Sheffield: Sheffield Academic Press, 1995).

51. E.g., Theodore of Mopsuestia, *Treatises against Apollinaris* 3.1; Nestorius, *First Sermon against the Theotokos*; Theodoret of Cyr, *Interpretation of Hebrews* 7.

Tithing, Trust, and Christian Community

The fact that the biblical origin of the concept of the tithe began with Abraham to Melchizedek seems to point to the value of trust in building up an interdependent community. The practice of tithing is deeply rooted in sharing what one has in order to satisfy the needs of others, as much as it has to do with respecting the leader who is committed to serve the community. In this give-and-take practice, the danger of corruption is balanced with the need for accountability. Tithing requires an "ethic of hospitality" as much as the recognition of "mutually assured vulnerability."[52]

HyeRan Kim-Cragg

life" (7:15-16), i.e., through the resurrection (6:2). Thus the prophecy of "a priest forever" refers to Jesus, of whom Melchizedek is the antitype (7:17). Jesus' messianic priesthood is better than the Levitical priesthood, corresponding to the superiority of the son to the angels and of the heavenly "rest" to the promised land. For the homilist, the revelation of Christ's superior priesthood, authenticated by divine oath (7:20-21), amounts to the abrogation of the Levitical law (which "made nothing perfect") (7:18-19), and the offer of a "better hope" guaranteed by Jesus (7:19, 21-22). In 7:22, for the first time, the author connects the eternal priesthood to the "better covenant" fulfilled in Jesus, the theme of the next section (8:1–10:18).

Although Melchizedek is never called a "high priest" in the Hebrew Scriptures, the homilist repeatedly refers to Jesus by this title (ἀρχιερεύς) rather than simply as "priest" (ἱερεύς), since only a high priest was divinely authorized to enter the holy of holies on the Day of Atonement (see also Heb 6:19; 9:25); this argument is elaborated in the next section on the nature of the new covenant. Once the homilist has established Christ's high-priestly credentials, the argument elaborates on the theme of the superiority of his priesthood to that of the Levitical line: whereas the Aaronid priests were many and subject to death, Jesus' priesthood is permanent and eternal (7:23-24); this empowers Christ to offer salvation "for all time" to those who approach God through him and for whom he intercedes (7:25); as "holy, blameless, undefiled, separated from sinners," the high-priestly Christ is not obligated to sacrifice on behalf

52. Catherine Keller, "The Love of Postcolonialism," in *Postcolonial Theologies: Divinity and Empire*, ed. Catherine Keller, Michael Nausner, and Mayra Rivera (St. Louis, MO: Chalice Press, 2004), 221–42, at 226, 225.

of his own sins or to offer daily sacrifices on behalf of the people, because of his self-offering "once for all" (7:27). The superiority of Jesus' priesthood does not reside in its power to establish the exclusive privilege of christian identity but to embrace all who believe his message for the sake of the salvation of all. The human weakness of the Levitical priests is contrasted with the "word of the oath"—"The LORD [YHWH] has sworn, and will not change his mind" (Ps 110:4a; Heb 7:21)—which is the basis of the appointment of "the Son" to the perfect, eternal priesthood. The author bases this argument on chronology; since God's oath guaranteeing the eternity of the kingly priesthood was sworn "later than the law" (i.e., Torah), the latter abrogates the stipulations of the former regarding the nature of priesthood (7:28).

Mary Rose D'Angelo suggests that the priestly Christology of Hebrews "may draw on the image of Wisdom/Sophia as priest":[53] "Before the ages, in the beginning, he created me, and for all the ages I shall not cease to be. In the holy tent I ministered before him, and so I was established in Zion" (Sir 24:9-10). She further notes that from a feminist standpoint "the metaphor of priesthood, especially high priesthood, has long been used to bar women from Christian ministry."[54] Following the logic of Hebrews, however, Jesus' "brothers and sisters"—the Christian community—can be interpreted as sharing in his priestly vocation.[55] For Hebrews, the material sacrifices of the Levitical priests are no longer necessary due to the definitive sacrifice of Christ, but as heavenly high priest, his ministry is eternal (7:25). Later the homilist encourages the audience in priestly terms, exhorting them to "continually offer a sacrifice of praise to God" and to "do good and to share what you have, for such sacrifices are pleasing to God" (13:15-16). The nature of Christ's "sacrifice" according to Hebrews will be discussed in the next section.

53. Mary Rose D'Angelo, "Hebrews," in *The Women's Bible Commentary*, ed. Carol A. Newsom and Sharon H. Ringe (Louisville, KY: Westminster John Knox, 1992), 364–67, at 367.

54. Ibid., 366.

55. See also Rev 1:6, where, echoing Exod 19:6, the members of the Asian churches are addressed as "a kingdom, priests."

Hebrews 8:1–10:18

Wisdom and Covenant

In contrast to the previous sections, where doctrinal passages are interspersed with related paraenesis, the entirety of Heb 8:1–10:18 is concerned with developing the theme of the "new covenant" mediated by Jesus, an extended midrash on Jer 31:31-34, quoted at the beginning and, in part, at the end of the exposition (8:8-12; 10:16-17; see also Jer 31:33). The central theme of the section, previously announced in 7:22— "Jesus has also become the guarantee of a better covenant"—amounts to the "main point" (κεφάλαιον) of the entire homily: Jesus, the heavenly high priest, "has now obtained a more excellent ministry, and to that degree he is the mediator of a better covenant, which has been enacted through better promises" (8:6). Although interpreters often assert that the focus of the argument is christological—Jesus is the high priest seated at the right hand of the divine throne (8:1)—the account of Christ's ministry in the heavenly tabernacle is part of the larger argument that he mediates a new and better covenant than that of Moses (8:6b). The concept of "covenant" (διαθήκη) dominates this section (8:6, 7, 9, 10, 13; 9:1, 4, 15, 18, 20; 10:16) and is used to undergird the ethical teaching in the remainder of the discourse (10:29; 12:24; 13:20). For the homilist the new covenant heralds a new quality of relationship between God and God's people.

In the Hebrew Bible the term "covenant" (ברית) is used in both secular and sacred contexts to refer to "a relationship based on commitment, which includes both promises and obligations, and which has the quality of

[1]Now the main point in what we are saying is this: we have such a high priest, one who is seated at the right hand of the throne of the Majesty in the heavens, [2]a minister in the sanctuary and the true tent that the Lord, and not any mortal, has set up. [3]For every high priest is appointed to offer gifts and sacrifices; hence it is necessary for this priest also to have something to offer. [4]Now if he were on earth, he would not be a priest at all, since there are priests who offer gifts according to the law. [5]They offer worship in a sanctuary that is a sketch and shadow of the heavenly one; for Moses, when he was about to erect the tent, was warned, "See that you make everything according to the pattern that was shown you on the mountain." [6]But Jesus has now obtained a more excellent ministry, and to that degree he is the mediator of a better covenant, which has been enacted through better promises. [7]For if

reliability and durability. The relationship is usually sealed by a rite—for example, an oath, sacred meal, blood sacrifice, invocation of blessings and curses—which makes it binding."[1] While the term is often used to describe secular treaties between individuals, communities, and nations,[2] in theological terms covenant refers to undertakings between God and God's people that "express God's gracious commitment and faithfulness and thus establish a continuing relationship."[3] Thus, not surprisingly, marriage is sometimes described in covenantal language (see Mal 2:14), and the covenant metaphor is applied to God's often troubled "marriage" with Israel (e.g., Hos 2:18; Jer 31:32 MT), echoing an earlier time when the divine consorts "YHWH and his Asherah" ruled the land.[4] The most prominent of the covenantal traditions are as follows: the covenant with Noah (Gen 9:1-17), God's promise to human beings and other creatures never again to destroy the earth by a flood; the covenant between God and the descendants of Abraham and Sarah (Gen 15:1-21; 17:1-22; in Gen 17:18 also associated with Hagar's son, Ishmael); the covenant mediated by Moses between God and Israel at Sinai (e.g., Exod 24:1-8; 34:10; Deut 4:13; 5:2); and the covenant between God and David, founded on the promise that

---

1. Bernhard W. Anderson, "Covenant," in *Oxford Companion to the Bible*, ed. Bruce M. Metzger and Michael D. Coogan (New York and Oxford: Oxford University Press, 1993), 138.

2. E.g., Gen 21:25-31; 1 Kgs 20:34; 1 Chr 11:3; 2 Kgs 11:4; Ezek 17:13-19.

3. Anderson, "Covenant," 138.

4. See William G. Dever, *Did God Have a Wife? Archaeology and Folk Religion in Ancient Israel* (Grand Rapids, MI: Eerdmans, 2005).

that first covenant had been faultless, there would have been no need to look for a second one. [8]God finds fault with them when he says:

"The days are surely coming, says the Lord, when I will establish a new covenant with the house of Israel and with the house of Judah;

[9]not like the covenant that I made with their ancestors, on the day when I took them by the hand to lead them out of the land of Egypt; for they did not continue in my covenant, and so I had no concern for them, says the Lord. [10]This is the covenant that I will make with the house of Israel after those days, says the Lord:

an anointed Davidic king would always rule in Jerusalem (e.g., 2 Sam 23:5; 2 Chr 13:5; see also 2 Sam 7:1-29; Ps 78:67-72). A distinction often made between the covenant with the ancestors Abraham and Sarah and the covenant with David, on the one hand, and the Mosaic covenant, on the other, is that the former are "everlasting covenants" guaranteed by God alone, not dependent on human behavior. The Mosaic covenant, in contrast, is conditional on Israel's obedience to the commandments of Torah. As Bernhard Anderson notes, "Carried to the extreme, this covenant could even be annulled, so that no longer would Yahweh be their God and no longer would Israel be God's people (Hos. 1.9). The renewal of the covenant, in this view, would be based solely on God's forgiving grace (Exod. 34.6-9; Jer. 31.31-33; Ezek. 16.59-63)."[5]

Our Stories Are Our Scripture
For Hebrews 8

One Who Loved Ravens

All started laughing hard even
Anishinabe found funny what

Older Raven did to the one too
different to understand good

The Raven People accepted him
anyway as one of them to play

To fight back they liked an
Anishinabe as is though One
couldn't

Fly sit on branches pull tricks
instead the One had learned
their

Language so what dropping on
his head he just said Good One

Annharte

5. Anderson, "Covenant," 139.

I will put my laws in their minds,
  and write them on their hearts,
and I will be their God,
  and they shall be my people.
[11]And they shall not teach one another
  or say to each other, 'Know the
    Lord,'
for they shall all know me,
  from the least of them to the
    greatest.
[12]For I will be merciful toward their
  iniquities,

and I will remember their sins
  no more."
[13]In speaking of "a new covenant," he
has made the first one obsolete. And
what is obsolete and growing old will
soon disappear.

[9:1]Now even the first covenant had
regulations for worship and an earthly
sanctuary. [2]For a tent was constructed,
the first one, in which were the lampstand, the table, and the bread of the
Presence; this is called the Holy Place.
[3]Behind the second curtain was a tent

In the NT the eternal and promissory Abrahamic and Davidic covenants are emphasized (Gal 3:6-18; Eph 2:12) over against the Mosaic
covenant, founded on Torah observance; it will be shown below that the
"everlasting covenant" with David[6] and its messianic promise[7] undergird
Hebrews' portrayal of the "new" and "better" covenant mediated by
Jesus, "enacted by better promises" (8:6)[8] This new and everlasting covenant resonates with the depiction of the Davidic covenant as a "covenant
of salt" by the Chronicler (2 Chr 13:5; 21:7), conceived as the "source of
life, law, and liturgy for Israel."[9] The image of the eternal covenant im-
bues the stories of Noah, Abraham, Israel, and David with the purpose
of blessing the world. Here the blessing (ברכה) is related to the covenant,
which is also related to the identity of Israel as a people "set apart" to
be God's firstborn among the peoples of the world. The blessing is passed
down to the firstborn of Israel with whom God made a covenant. The
homilist's understanding of Jesus as the mediator of a new covenant
culminates in a messianic Jesus, God's beloved son, sent to love and bless
people. This divine sonship has a twofold nature: one conferring a
priestly blessing on the world and the other fulfilling God's promises.
Hebrews' references to Christ's offering and self-sacrifice mainly focus
on the theme of his service to and blessing of the world.

6. 2 Chr 21:7; 23:3; Ps 89:3; Isa 55:3; Jer 33:21; Sir 45:31; 47:11.
7. 1 Kgs 8:25; 9:5; 2 Kgs 8:19; 2 Chr 1:9; 6:16; 21:7; 1 Macc 2:57; Sir 45:31.
8. See also 4:1; 6:12, 13, 15, 17; 7:6; 9:15; 10:23; 10:36; 11:9, 13, 17, 33, 39; 12:26.
9. Scott W. Hahn, *The Kingdom of God as Liturgical Empire: A Theological Commentary
on 1–2 Chronicles* (Grand Rapids, MI: Baker, 2012), 20.

called the Holy of Holies. ⁴In it stood the golden altar of incense and the ark of the covenant overlaid on all sides with gold, in which there were a golden urn holding the manna, and Aaron's rod that budded, and the tablets of the covenant; ⁵above it were the cherubim of glory overshadowing the mercy seat. Of these things we cannot speak now in detail.

⁶Such preparations having been made, the priests go continually into the first tent to carry out their ritual duties; ⁷but only the high priest goes into the second, and he but once a year, and not without taking the blood that he offers for himself and for the sins committed unintentionally by the people. ⁸By this the Holy Spirit indicates that the way into the sanctuary has not yet been disclosed as long as the first tent is still standing. ⁹This is a symbol of the present time, during which gifts and sacrifices are offered that cannot perfect the conscience of the worshiper, ¹⁰but deal only with food

Covenant in Korean Cross-Cultural Perspective

In Korean, the term "covenant" can be translated as *"geyak"* (契約) or *"oenyak"* (言約). Both terms share a common character, *yak*, whose meaning is promise and agreement between the two parties or more. While both words are used interchangeably in secular settings, the former has been used to emphasize mutual agreement under certain conditions. In this sense, *geyak* has a sense tilted toward "contract." In such a case, without conditions there is no agreement and when the conditions change the agreement becomes void. Though the latter term is often used in marriage vows, as noted below, *oenyak* has been distinctively used in the Korean Bible for two theological reasons: In the term *oenyak* the combination of *oen*, meaning "spoken word," with *yak*, meaning "promise," presumes an initiative by God, who first makes a promise to Abraham, a blessing (Gen 12:2; Gal 3:8). This covenant, unlike *geyak*, is unconditional and unilateral in that it is God who spoke to Abraham first without any conditions or mutuality. Even though the other party (the people of Israel in this case) does not keep the agreement, the covenant is still in effect. The other difference between *oenyak* and *geyak* is its continuity, its everlasting nature. There is no end term for this promise and agreement. There is no expiration date. Though the covenant has been renewed and restated (Jer 31:31-34), because the people of Israel broke it, it continues in effect from God's

and drink and various baptisms, regulations for the body imposed until the time comes to set things right. ¹¹But when Christ came as a high priest of the good things that have come, then through the greater and perfect tent (not made with hands, that is, not of this creation), ¹²he entered once for all into the Holy Place, not with the blood of goats and calves, but with his own blood, thus obtaining eternal redemption. ¹³For if the blood of goats and bulls, with the sprinkling of the ashes of a heifer, sanctifies those who have been defiled so that their flesh is purified, ¹⁴how much more will the blood of Christ, who through the eternal Spirit offered himself without blemish to God, purify our conscience from dead works to worship the living God!

¹⁵For this reason he is the mediator of a new covenant, so that those who are called may receive the promised eternal inheritance, because a death has occurred that redeems them from the transgressions under the first cove-

point of view; God invites and calls the other party, the believing community, to respond to its commitment. This particular cultural and linguistic understanding sheds more light on the use of the term "new covenant" in this section of Hebrews. God's unconditional love and unilateral blessing is incarnate in the ministry of Jesus as high priest who lives up to the quality of this relationship between God and God's people.

HyeRan Kim-Cragg

As noted earlier, the nature of Christ's high-priestly self-sacrifice is developed in this section in relation to the founding of the new covenant. As heavenly high priest, Christ is both "seated at the right hand of the throne of the Majesty in the heavens"—a typically Jewish circumlocution for the divine name—and "a minister in the sanctuary and the true tent that the Lord, and not any mortal, has set up" (8:1-2). The homilist observes that, like other high priests, Jesus must have something to offer (8:3) but does not reveal the nature of his offering until 9:11-14. Rather, the audience is reminded of Jesus' familial disqualification for the earthly high priesthood, or for Jewish priesthood at all: "if he were on earth, he would not be a priest at all, since there are priests who offer gifts according to the law" (8:4). Jesus' lack of tribal suitability for priestly service has already been dealt with in the previous section, where Jesus' eternal, messianic priesthood "according to the order of Melchizedek" is explicated (6:20–

nant. [16]Where a will is involved, the death of the one who made it must be established. [17]For a will takes effect only at death, since it is not in force as long as the one who made it is alive. [18]Hence not even the first covenant was inaugurated without blood. [19]For when every commandment had been told to all the people by Moses in accordance with the law, he took the blood of calves and goats, with water and scarlet wool and hyssop, and sprinkled both the scroll itself and all the people, [20]saying, "This is the blood of the covenant that God has ordained for you." [21]And in the same way he sprinkled with the blood both the tent and all the vessels used in worship. [22]Indeed, under the law almost everything is purified with blood, and without the shedding of blood there is no forgiveness of sins.

[23]Thus it was necessary for the sketches of the heavenly things to be purified with these rites, but the heavenly things themselves need better

7:22), an implicit rejection of the privileged purity line of the priesthood in relation to the new covenant. Moreover, his heavenly priesthood is decisively different from the priesthood "according to the law" in that the Levitical priests offer gifts in an inferior sanctuary that is only "a sketch and shadow of the heavenly one," as indicated by Exod 25:40, where God instructs Moses to build the tabernacle (σκηνή; translated "tent" in the NRSV) according to the pattern revealed on Mount Sinai (Heb 8:5).

Some knowledge of what exactly the tabernacle in the Hebrew Bible was enhances understanding of the overall theme of this section. While the gradual sophistication and restriction around the temple edifice in Jerusalem led to restrictions concerning access (e.g., the prohibition against women entering the inner courts of the temple), the tabernacle enabled Israel to encounter their God, who dwelled with them as they traveled (Exod 40:34-38). The tabernacle's portability as a tent that could be easily dismantled and erected as the people moved through the wilderness reflects the nomadic nature and pilgrim life of Israel at that time.[10] This may suggest a connection in the homilist's mind with the faith of Abraham, who is introduced as an example of the faithful pilgrim in the following section (Heb 11:8-12). It is clear, however, that the homilist intends to portray the earthly sanctuary, Moses' tabernacle, in negative terms, because the heavenly archetype of the earthly sanctuary is

10. Christian Eberhart, *The Sacrifice of Jesus: Understanding Atonement Biblically* (Minneapolis: Fortress Press, 2011), 35.

sacrifices than these. ²⁴For Christ did not enter a sanctuary made by human hands, a mere copy of the true one, but he entered into heaven itself, now to appear in the presence of God on our behalf. ²⁵Nor was it to offer himself again and again, as the high priest enters the Holy Place year after year with blood that is not his own; ²⁶for then he would have had to suffer again and again since the foundation of the world. But as it is, he has appeared once for all at the end of the age to remove sin by the sacrifice of himself. ²⁷And just as it is appointed for mortals to die once, and after that the judgment, ²⁸so Christ, having been offered once to bear the sins of many, will appear a second time, not to deal with sin, but to save those who are eagerly waiting for him.

¹⁰:¹Since the law has only a shadow of the good things to come and not the true form of these realities, it can never, by the same sacrifices that are continually offered year after year,

used to demonstrate the inferiority of the latter; it is simply a reflection of the eternal sanctuary above.

The notion that the Jerusalem temple, and its forerunner, the wilderness tabernacle, had a heavenly counterpart is ubiquitous in early Jewish literature.[11] In Solomon's prayer for wisdom (Wis 9:8) the king extols God, and God's partner Sophia, for commanding him to build a temple, "a copy of the holy tent that you prepared from the beginning" (see also 2 Macc 2:9). Rabbinic sources emphasize the correspondence between the heavenly and earthly sanctuaries to underline the dignity of the latter.[12] In Greek thought, however, earthly temples could be contrasted with the true temple, the cosmos,[13] to the detriment of traditional cults; the identification of the heavenly tabernacle with the cosmos is also found in early Christian authors.[14] As Harold Attridge notes, Hebrews shows affinities with the kind of Hellenistic Jewish tradition represented

11. E.g., 1 En. 14:9-23; T. Levi 3:2-4; Bar 4:5; Philo, *Heir* 112; see also Rev 3:12; 11:19; 15:5.

12. See Aelred Cody, *Heavenly Sanctuary and Liturgy in the Epistle to the Hebrews: The Achievement of Salvation in the Epistle's Perspectives* (St. Meinrad, IN: Grail, 1960), 18.

13. Harold Attridge, *The Epistle to the Hebrews: A Commentary*, Hermeneia (Philadelphia: Fortress Press, 1989), 22.

14. E.g., Gregory of Nazianzus, *On the Doctrine of God, Theological Oration* 2.31; Theodoret of Cyr, *Interpretation of Hebrews* 9. Quoted in Erik M. Heen and Philip D. Krey, *Ancient Christian Commentary on Scripture, New Testament X* (Downers Grove, IL: InterVarsity, 2006), 132.

make perfect those who approach. [2]Otherwise, would they not have ceased being offered, since the worshipers, cleansed once for all, would no longer have any consciousness of sin? [3]But in these sacrifices there is a reminder of sin year after year. [4]For it is impossible for the blood of bulls and goats to take away sins. [5]Consequently, when Christ came into the world, he said,

"Sacrifices and offerings you have not desired,

but a body you have prepared for me;

[6]in burnt offerings and sin offerings you have taken no pleasure.

[7]Then I said, 'See, God, I have come to do your will, O God'

(in the scroll of the book it is written of me)."

[8]When he said above, "You have neither desired nor taken pleasure in sacrifices and offerings and burnt offerings and sin offerings" (these are offered

by Philo of Alexandria, who, in his various works, expresses the notion that the true temple is the cosmos,[15] but more often he interprets the Jewish concept of corresponding heavenly and earthly sanctuaries[16] through the lens of Platonic philosophy, where incorporeal, heavenly archetypes are reflected by earthly counterparts that are "a reflection and copy" (see also Heb 8:5).[17] For Philo, "the ultimately real counterpart of the earthly temple is seen to be a variety of spiritual and ethical realities, the human soul, virtue, wisdom, or the 'powers' of God."[18] Although the homilist's portrayal of the heavenly and earthly sanctuaries is different from Philo's, it has affinities with the Hellenistic Jewish milieu he represents. The argument that the earthly sanctuary is inferior because it was revealed in the context of an "obsolete" covenant (Heb 8:13) is, however, unique to Hebrews. Pamela Eisenbaum goes so far as to call the homilist's argument a "supersessionist theology": "Not only is Jesus the *mediator of a better covenant*, but the first covenant was faulty because it failed to create the perfect relationship between humans and God."[19]

The quotation of Jer 31:31-34 (Jer 38 LXX) in Heb 8:8-12 is certainly supersessionist to the extent that it construes the prophecy to mean that

15. *Spec. Leg.* 1.66.
16. E.g., *Cherubim* 23–26; *Mos.* 2.88, 98, 102–3, 117–26.
17. Attridge, *Hebrews*, 223.
18. Ibid.
19. Pamela Eisenbaum, "Hebrews," in *The Jewish Annotated New Testament*, (New York: Oxford University Press, 2011), 406–26, at 416, on Heb 8:6-7.

according to the law), [9]then he added, "See, I have come to do your will." He abolishes the first in order to establish the second. [10]And it is by God's will that we have been sanctified through the offering of the body of Jesus Christ once for all.

[11]And every priest stands day after day at his service, offering again and again the same sacrifices that can never take away sins. [12]But when Christ had offered for all time a single sacrifice for sins, "he sat down at the right hand of God," [13]and since then has been waiting "until his enemies would be made a footstool for his feet."

[14]For by a single offering he has perfected for all time those who are sanctified. [15]And the Holy Spirit also testifies to us, for after saying,

[16]"This is the covenant that I will
      make with them
after those days, says the
      Lord:
I will put my laws in their hearts,
   and I will write them on their
      minds,"
[17]he also adds,
   "I will remember their sins and their
      lawless deeds no more."
[18]Where there is forgiveness of these, there is no longer any offering for sin.

the Mosaic covenant "is obsolete and growing old [and] will soon disappear" (8:13), to be replaced by a new covenant. The homilist introduces the divine promise with the notice that God "finds fault with them" (8:8). As Eisenbaum observes: "In its original context, Jeremiah was suggesting that the Torah would be renewed after the Babylonian exile by being implanted in people's hearts or minds, so that they could instinctively observe it; therefore they would not any longer sin, and so there would not be another exile."[20] That is, Jeremiah's prophecy envisioned a renewal and internalization of the Mosaic covenant, when Israel would consistently obey Torah, rather than neglecting and defying it as their predecessors had done: "not like the covenant that I made with their ancestors . . . for they did not continue in my covenant" (Heb 8:9; Jer 31:32). The LXX translation of Jer 31:32, which replaces the Hebrew "I was their husband" with "I had no concern for them" (Heb 8:9), undermines the poignancy of the original prophecy, which portrays God as an abandoned and grieving spouse, with a note of divine dismissal that is supportive of the homilist's radical exegesis. For Hebrews, the new covenant is not conceptualized as a renewal of the Mosaic covenant in which Torah would be joyously observed and the temple would be restored in Jeru-

20. Ibid.

salem but as its replacement and abolition. The argument is supersessionist to the extent that the new covenant supersedes and replaces the Mosaic covenant rather than renewing and deepening it (see also Exod 34:6-9; Ezek 16:59-63). The homilist is not arguing, however, that "Christianity" has replaced "Judaism"; from Hebrews' perspective the first covenant was good, but the new is better because it fulfills and perfects the divine promises to Israel transmitted through the prophets, including the promise of an "everlasting covenant" with David and his descendants, culminating in the appearance of the messiah, Jesus.[21] Nevertheless, insofar as this text has been used in the service of anti-Jewish theologizing, it should be repudiated, following the precedent of Pope John Paul II, who in 1980 forthrightly spoke of the Jewish people as "the people of God of the old covenant never revoked by God."[22]

Hebrews 9:1-28 develops a detailed contrast between worship in the earthly tabernacle and its heavenly archetype. In the biblical tradition the wilderness tabernacle is extolled as the locus of God's dwelling in Israel (Ezek 37:27; see also Ps 78:60), identified with the temple in Jerusalem (e.g., Isa 4:5-6; 16:5; 33:20; Lam 2:6; Amos 9:11; Pss 15:1; 43:3; 76:2; Tob 13:12), a place of joy and celebration (Pss 27:6; 46:4; 84:1; 132:7) and of shelter (Pss 27:5; 61:4). By referring to the tabernacle instead of the temple the homilist seems to emphasize the less structured and formalized, more movable and moving nature of the faith. It is in this more fluid context that Jesus becomes identified with the new covenant, the mediator, and the dwelling place of God. Christ's incarnation as the Word become flesh sits better with the notion of Jesus who "tented among us" (John 1:14) than of Jesus "the temple of God" (1 Cor 3:16-17; 6:19; Eph 2:21).[23] No wonder, then, that Hebrews' elaborate explanations of the earthly sanctuary (9:1-10) do not sound like architectural measurements but rather seem to describe or even extol how God as Spirit, guiding Wisdom, can accompany and achieve a new covenant between God and humanity through Jesus.

---

21. 2 Sam 23:5; 2 Chr 13:5; 21:7; 23:3; Ps 89:3; Isa 55:3; Jer 33:21; Sir 47:11; see also 1 Kgs 2:24; 8:20, 24, 25; 9:5; 2 Kgs 8:19; 2 Chr 1:9; 6:10; 6:15, 16; 1 Macc 2:57; Sir 45:25.

22. Quoted by Hans Herman Henrix, "The Covenant Has Never Been Revoked: Basis of the Christian-Jewish Relationship" (2010), www.jcrelations.net/The _covenant_has_never_been_revoked.2250.0.html#; accessed July 15, 2015.

23. Eberhart, *Sacrifice*, 59.

The tabernacle as sign of God's presence is closely associated with the "pillar of cloud by day" and the "pillar of fire by night" that guided the Israelites in the wilderness (Num 9:15-23), identified with Sophia in the book of Wisdom:

> A holy people and blameless race
> Wisdom delivered from a nation of oppressors.
> She entered the soul of a servant of the Lord,
> and withstood dread kings with wonders and signs.
> She gave to holy people the reward of their labors;
> she guided them along a marvelous way,
> and became a shelter to them by day,
> and a starry flame through the night. (Wis 10:15-17)

Our Stories Are Our Scriptures
For Hebrews 9

Rolls with the Time

She becomes dangerous each time it happens she loses her head takes back

Power balance that is how she rolls past all that is thrown at her by precious

Children when they try to escape new wisdom by running away believing only

How mide[24] say she became wetigo[25] had to have her head removed by an axe

So with only her head grown much bigger quite scary still she cried in pursuit

To listen to her now they will get free to love the mother she is always to be

Annharte

According to Exod 31:3 the tabernacle was constructed through Wisdom: "ability, intelligence, and knowledge." Women figured significantly in the construction of the tabernacle, contributing jewelry (Exod 35:22) and other offerings (Exod 35:29). In particular, "every woman [with] wisdom of heart" contributed colored yarns and fine linen to the project (Exod 35:25),[26] and "all the women whose hearts moved them [or who excelled] to use their skill spun the goats' hair" (Exod 35:26). The women who served at the entrance to the tent of meeting contributed their mirrors for the laver of copper constructed by Bezalel (Exod 38:8). In Sir 24:10-12, divine Sophia describes herself as offering priestly service in the tabernacle:

---

24. "Spiritual leaders" (Ojibwe).

25. "Deviant" (Ojibwe).

26. See Tamara Cohn Eskenazi and Andrea L. Weiss, eds., *The Torah: A Women's Commentary* (New York: Women of Reformed Judaism, 2008), 527.

In the holy tent I ministered before him,
and so I was established in Zion.
Thus in the beloved city he gave me a resting place,
and in Jerusalem was my domain.
I took root in an honored people,
in the portion of the Lord, his heritage.

Medieval Kabbalah conceptualizes God's presence in Israel as the Shekinah, "the preeminent feminine aspect of God," a loving mother figure who suffers along with her exiled children and, like the tabernacle, dwells with them and protects them.[27] The Hebrew words for "tabernacle" (משכן) and "Shekinah" (שכנה) are both formed from the root שכן, "to dwell." Alisa Fineman captures the meaning of Shekinah as an abiding Presence for contemporary Jewish feminists:

> When I can glimpse or locate a piece of the divine in me, it is a sense of Divine Love whose quality is the Mother of All Life. In singing in the sacred, I direct my energy toward her. Our gratitude is Her nourishment. Sing in her arrival, A Holy Guest, the Shechinah who is always waiting for us to come home.
>
> The Sacred Feminine for me is the Shechinah—the one who dwells in the harmonious exchanges and places of kindness and beauty—this is the place where all transformation is possible. It is an open and vulnerable energy where sensitivity IS strength and where our heart's passion, wisdom and direction is affirmed.[28]

Women and the Tabernacle

The accounts of the women's contributions to the tabernacle construction are elaborated in Jewish tradition. The reference to women's "wise-hearted" skill in spinning (Exod 35:25) prompted Rabbi Eliezer's misogynistic statement that "A woman's wisdom is only in the spindle" (b. Yoma 66b); this is the same rabbi who ruled that women were not fit to study Torah. A contrary view was offered by the sage Ben Azzai, who opined that a man was obligated to teach his daughter Torah (b. Sotah 20a)—unfortunately, a minority view among the rabbis.

27. Sharon Koren, "Contemporary Reflection on *Parashat Va-eira*," in *The Torah: A Women's Commentary*, 351–52.

28. Alisa Fineman, "U'vachein, And Then," in *Talking to Goddess: Powerful Voices from Many Traditions*, ed. D'vorah J. Grenn (Napa, CA: Lilith Institute, 2009), 211–12. Italics in the original. Reprinted by permission of D'vorah J. Grenn (dvorahgrenn@me.com).

Several rabbis agree that the women who contributed their mirrors for the copper lavers had cast aside their jewelry to devote themselves to God: "They came to the Tent of Meeting to pray and hear either 'the words of the living God' (Sforno), the praises of God pronounced by the priests (Chizz'kuni), or words of *mitzvoth* (commandments) (Ibn Ezra)." By donating their mirrors they also renounced personal vanity. According to Ibn Ezra, these women constituted a large group.

Another tradition, transmitted by the renowned medieval scholar Rashi, holds that Moses initially rejected the offering of the mirrors as objects associated with vanity, unfit for holy usage. God corrected Moses by explaining that the women had employed the mirrors for a holy purpose by using them to flirt with their husbands as they labored in Egypt, thus awakening the men's desire for them and ensuring future generations of Israelites. In b. Sotah 11b this midrash is cited, along with other instances of women's righteousness during the enslavement in Egypt, as the reason for Israel's liberation. (*Source*: Ruth H. Sohn, "Post-biblical Interpretations on *Parashat Vayahk'heil*," in *The Torah: A Women's Commentary*, 538–39.)

Mary Ann Beavis

Shekinah *Prayer*

Blessed be G'd, Shekhinah
In this world of Her
  Creation
May Her will be fulfilled
And her vision and wisdom
  be revealed
So that our own purpose
  may become ever clearer

In the days of our lifetime
Speedily and soon
And let us say Amen.

(Excerpted from D'vorah J. Grenn, "A Celebration of Her, and of Life: A Reinterpretation of the Traditional Jewish Kaddish Memorial Prayer," *Talking to Goddess*, 229.)

In contrast to the reverence for the tabernacle expressed in the Jewish tradition, the homilist sketches its magnificent contents (Heb 9:1-5) and the priestly service that took place there (9:6-10) under the "first covenant" as a foil for the superior service of Christ (9:11-14). Jesus, who replaces the tabernacle in the view of the homilist, is a breathing, living, and embodied place of salvation dwelling among humanity, rather than a human construction. Strangely, although according to the scriptural account the wilderness tabernacle ceased being the primary Israelite worship center after the erection of the temple of Solomon (1 Kgs 8:1-13;

2 Chr 5:2-14), the homilist speaks as if the "first tabernacle" were still standing at the "present time" (Heb 9:8-9). Thus the description of the tabernacle's structure and contents is mostly based on the Hebrew Scriptures: the holy place ("the first tabernacle") contained "the lampstand, the table, and the bread of the Presence."[29] The inner shrine, curtained off from the holy place, was "a tent called the Holy of Holies" (Heb 9:4), containing "the golden altar of incense" (see also Exod 30:1-6) and, for the homilist, the most important object, the gold-coated ark of the covenant and the "mercy seat" that covered it. Hebrews' account of the ancient holy places deviates in some details from its scriptural sources;[30] most notably, while the Hebrew Bible stipulates that the ark contained only the two stone tablets associated with Moses (1 Kgs 8:9), the homilist mentions two other sacred artifacts: "a golden urn holding the manna, and Aaron's rod that budded" (Heb 9:4; see also Exod 16:33-34; Num 17:2-5). The "cherubim of glory" overshadowing the "mercy seat" (Heb 9:5) would have resembled the kinds of hybrid supernatural beings typical of Ancient Near Eastern iconography: "The usual image is that of a huge eagle-winged, human-faced bull-lion, iconographic features familiar in Assyrian and Canaanite sources."[31] The enigmatic term "mercy seat" (ἱλαστήριον) can also be translated as "place of propitiation," from the Hebrew כפרת, "cover" (Num 7:89). As with the tabernacle, the homilist speaks of the ark and its contents as if they were a present reality (Heb 9:8-9); historically, the ark is thought to have been carried off by the Babylonians when Jerusalem fell in 587/586 BCE, although its later history is uncertain. According to Jewish legend the prophet Jeremiah rescued it and hid it on Mount Nebo (2 Macc 2:4-8), despite Jeremiah's prophecy that the ark would disappear utterly from Israel (Jer 3:16). The description of the tabernacle's contents ends with the mysterious note that "of these things we cannot speak now in detail" (Heb 9:5b), perhaps indicating that the author, like other Hellenistic Jewish interpreters,[32] sees deeper spiritual symbolism in the sacred objects that is not directly relevant to the argument of the homily (see also Heb 9:8-9).

29. Exod 25:31-35; 26:35; 25:30; see also 1 Chr 28:16.

30. See James W. Thompson, *Hebrews*, Paideia Commentaries on the New Testament (Grand Rapids, MI: Baker Academic, 2008), 178.

31. David G. Burke, "Cherub, Cherubim," in Metzger and Coogan, *Oxford Companion to the Bible*, 107–8.

32. E.g., Philo, *Mos.* 2.74–160; Josephus, *Ant.* 3.123; *B.J.* 5.213–18.

> **The Lampstand and the Tree of Life**
>
> The lampstand (λυχνία; Heb 9:2) of the wilderness tabernacle, later of the Jerusalem temple, is better known by its Hebrew name, the menorah (מנרה), described in detail in Exod 25:31-40; 37:17-24. Due to the botanical elements in its design—almond blossoms, buds, and branches—it is often related to the tree of life, a common motif in the Ancient Near East shared by the Bible (Gen 2:9; 3:22, 24; Prov 11:30; 13:12; 15:4; Rev 2:7; 22:2, 14).[33] Prov 3:18 describes Wisdom as "a tree of life to those who lay hold of her; those who hold her fast are called happy," and she is often extolled as a source of divine light (Wis 6:12; 7:10, 29; Bar 3:14; see also Eccl 2:13). Sir 26:17 compares the face of a good wife to "the shining lamp on the holy lampstand."
>
> *Mary Ann Beavis*

In Heb 9:6-10, having described the contents of the tabernacle, the homilist expands on the theme of the ineffectualness of the repeated sacrifices performed by the Levitical priesthood (see also 7:27; 9:25; 10:11). The priests go "continually" (διὰ παντὸς) into the holy place ("the first tent") to perform sacrifices; the high priest enters the holy of holies ("the second [tent]") once a year to make the atoning sacrifice for his own sins and the sins of Israel (9:6; see also 7:27-28) on the Day of Atonement (see also Lev 16). For the homilist, these rituals have no value in and of themselves, but rather they are "a symbol" (literally, "a parable") of their own inadequacy; while the "first tabernacle" stands, the conscience (συνείδησις) of the worshiper cannot be "perfected," i.e., permanently cleansed of sin (9:8-9). The homilist assumes that the ineffectualness of the sacrificial rituals extends to other dietary requirements and ritual washings ("baptisms"). On this spiritual interpretation (9:8), the true meaning of these earthly "regulations for the body imposed until the time comes to set things right" (9:10) points to the need for a better, definitive atonement in the heavenly sanctuary that is the archetype of the earthly tabernacle.[34]

The next four verses describe the "good things that have come" (or "the good things that are to come") through Christ's high priesthood (Heb 9:11-14). Through his death he has entered "the greater and perfect" tabernacle in the heavens, and thus "not made with hands, that is, not of

---

33. See Judith R. Baskin, "Menorah," in Metzger and Coogan, *Oxford Companion to the Bible*, 512.

34. See also Exod 25–31, 35–40, where Moses receives divine instruction on the construction of the earthly holy places.

The Day of Atonement

Sacrificial worship in the temple ended with the fall of Jerusalem in 70 CE. In contemporary Judaism, the Day of Atonement is a time of prayer and repentance. The preface to *Gates of Repentance*, a Reform Jewish prayer book for the "Days of Awe," observes:

> Measuring ourselves against our ideals during this season, we are moved to express regret for past errors and to reaffirm our aspirations for the future. This our tradition calls *cheshbon hanefesh*, "the examined life." This is the season of self-judgment, of struggle, of inward turning, the season when a whole people labors heroically to remake itself. Though year after year that effort meets with little success, still we believe that we will ulti- mately succeed.

This excerpt from the Day of Atonement (Yom Kippur) evening service illustrates the meaning of the observance for Jews today:

> Birth is a beginning
> And death a destination
> And life is a journey
> From childhood to maturity
> And youth to age;
> From innocence to
>   awareness
> And ignorance to knowing;
> From foolishness to
>   discretion
> And then, perhaps, to
>   wisdom . . .

(*Source*: Chaim Stern, ed., *Gates of Repentance: The New Union Prayerbook for the Days of Awe* [New York: Central Conference of American Rabbis, 1996], ix, 283.)

Mary Ann Beavis

The contemporary meaning of the Day of Atonement in Judaism as captured in the prayer above finds a parallel in a Christian Lenten prayer of absence:

> God of presence, help us to
>   bear your mysterious
>   absence.
> Help us through the
>   darkness of the nights
> when we cannot see you,
> the discontent of winter
>   when we cannot feel you,
> the sorrow of seasons when
>   we cannot hear you.
> Attune us to the absence
>   that is generous—
> emptying us of a cherished
>   past
> in preparation for your
>   surprising future.
> Lead us not into despair,
> but toward the hope of
>   your coming.

Though certain meanings cannot be fully conveyed (as the homilist says, "of these things we cannot speak now in detail") a sense of holy wisdom and sacredness of place can be felt. (*Source*: James D. Whitehead and Evelyn Eaton Whitehead, *Holy Eros: Recovering the Passion of God* [Maryknoll, NY: Orbis Books, 2009], 152.)

HyeRan Kim-Cragg

this [earthly] creation" (9:11). Unlike the human high priests, who enter the holy of holies every year, Christ has entered the heavenly sanctuary "once for all" (ἐφάπαξ; see also 7:27; 10:10) with his own blood rather than animal sacrifices (9:12). In view of the heavenly and immaterial locus envisioned for his high priestly service it is unlikely that the homilist regarded Jesus' "blood" literally as a material substance but rather in figurative terms of "Christ's self-giving on the cross. This sacrifice is of such superior quality that it provides 'eternal redemption' in contrast to the levitical δικαιώματα σαρκὸς ['fleshly regulations']."[35] A characteristically Jewish *qal wahomer* argument from minor to major clinches the argument: if the material blood of goats and bulls can sanctify the flesh through the atonement ritual performed by the earthly high priest (9:13), the unblemished spiritual sacrifice of the sinless Jesus must have the power to "purify our conscience from dead works to worship the living God" (9:14). The reference to the burning of the ashes of the red heifer in the author's account of the Day of Atonement ritual is, as Pamela Eisenbaum notes, out of place—it belongs to a separate purification ritual from corpse defilement described in Num 19.[36] John Chrysostom tacitly acknowledges the conflation of the rituals by equating "dead works" with corpses: "If any man touched a dead body, he was polluted. And here also, if any touch a 'dead work,' those ones are defiled through their conscience."[37]

That the homilist does not take the death of Christ as a literal sacrifice is illustrated in Heb 9:15-22, where the atonement ritual is compared not only with purification from corpse defilement but also with a covenant ratification ceremony analogous to the ritual performed by Moses to inaugurate the covenant between God and Israel. Through the offering of his blood—a metonymy for his life and death (see also 9:15, 17)—in the heavenly tabernacle Christ has become the "mediator of a new covenant," enabling believers to receive "the promised eternal inheritance," releasing them from "the transgressions under the first covenant" (9:15). The homilist goes on to present a rather strained argument based on the twofold meaning of the term διαθήκη, "covenant." Whereas in Greek literature the usual word for covenant is συνθήκη, in the LXX and the NT

35. James W. Thompson, *The Beginnings of Christian Philosophy: The Epistle to the Hebrews*, CBQMS 13 (Washington, DC: Catholic Biblical Association of America, 1982), 108.

36. Eisenbaum, "Hebrews," 417, note on Heb 9:13.

37. *On the Epistle to the Hebrews* 15.5. Quoted in Heen and Krey, *Ancient Christian Commentary*, 140.

the preferred term is διαθήκη, which also means "testament" or "will." Since in order for a will/testament to take effect a death must occur, the new covenant/testament required Christ's death before it could be established (9:16-18). Fred B. Craddock notes that the term "covenant" must be understood in terms of a guarantee or "surety," which is different from the role of the mediator: "One who is a 'surety' guarantees the work or commitments of another, even at the risk of property and even life itself. . . . While it is possible to interpret the expression to mean that Christ offers his life as our surety toward God, the context argues for the opposite meaning: God who promises and makes oaths guarantees the covenant with Christ's priestly offering of himself for us."[38] Whichever way we look at it, this concept of διαθήκη affirms that God unconditionally makes a covenant with people and this covenant is not to be terminated but to be fulfilled by Jesus.

The homilist goes on to summarize the covenant ratification ritual recounted in Exodus (24:1-18), with its famous words "This is the blood of the covenant that God has ordained for you" (Heb 9:20; Exod 24:8), and reiterates the principle that blood must be shed in order for sins to be forgiven (9:22; see also 9:14). Scott Hahn delineates a liturgical theology of reconciliation and atonement from Heb 9:22, "without the shedding of blood there is no forgiveness of sins." The threshing floor of Moriah/Mount Zion, the traditional site of the temple, is where Abraham's son was saved to bless all the nations through his offspring (Gen 22:14-18). It was also where David was asked to build an altar to save his people from plague (1 Chr 21:22).[39] In both narratives the ritual of sacrifice in response to the saving of lives is placed in a context in which God's mercy is praised and God's covenant is renewed as it is expressed in the refrain of the liturgy, "his steadfast love endures for ever" (Ps 136; 1 Chr 16:34, 41). Such a liturgical theology is far from penitential and solemn. Rather, it is joyful, filled with thanksgiving to God on the part of humanity and of delight and faithfulness on the part of the divine. The liturgical theology of Hebrews is sacramental as it portrays the body of Christ as the threshold between earth and heaven through which the world is sanctified and the people blessed. In the case of David, however, repentance was a prerequisite for forgiveness. Here the human agency of repentance and recognition of sin are still important. Although it is

---

38. Fred B. Craddock, "The Letter to the Hebrews," in *The New Interpreter's Bible* (Nashville, TN: Abingdon, 1998), 12:1–173, at 92.

39. Hahn, *Kingdom of God as Liturgical Empire*, 92.

not the intention of the homilist or the Chronicler to interpret God as
one who demands sacrifices or as judgmental and condemning—the
portrayal of God that often figures prominently in atonement theology—
it is still critical to emphasize the work of justice and human responsibility. Perhaps God's disgust and displeasure over David's sin in 1 Chr 22:8
can fit nicely with the following verses in Hebrews concerning divine
judgment "at the end of the age" (9:26-28).

These concluding verses of the chapter (9:23-28) recapitulate and amplify
the argument of Heb 9:6-14, contrasting the superior, heavenly sacrifice of
Christ with the earthly rituals that sufficed for the temporary purification
of the earthly shadow of the tabernacle above. The sanctuary Christ entered
is the archetype, not the reflection, and he offered himself as high priest
"once for all," not year after year. His sacrifice took place "at the end of the
age," as a prelude to divine judgment, corresponding to the principle that
mortals are subject to judgment when they die (9:26-27): "so Christ, having
been offered once to bear the sins of many, will appear a second time, not
to deal with sin, but to save those who are eagerly waiting for him" (9:28).
Like the new covenant, which is eternal, the sacrifice that establishes it is
effectual to guarantee salvation for all time.

The homilist goes on to offer scriptural warrant for the argument that
in view of the nearness of divine judgment the appearance of the new
covenant heralds the abolition of the Mosaic covenant and its rituals,
whose inefficacy is indicated by their repetition (see also 10:11). While
the law has value in that it contains "a shadow of the good things to
come," only "the true form of these realities" can offer the perfection of
a permanently clear conscience (10:1-2). A quotation from Ps 40:6-8, attributed to Christ, is offered to demonstrate that God does not honor a
plurality of "sacrifices and offerings . . . burnt offerings and sin offerings," but rather delights in the body of Christ, who does the divine will
(10:5-7). In its original context the psalm is one of many critiques found
throughout the Hebrew Scriptures of sacrifice that is unaccompanied by
righteous conduct and social justice.[40] These are calls for reform of Israel's
religion, not for the abolition of temple and sacrifice; however, for Hebrews the words of the psalm indicate that God "abolishes the first [cove-
nant] in order to establish the second [new covenant]" (10:9). The homilist
interprets "body" in the psalm as "the offering of the body of Jesus Christ
once for all" (v. 10). Ps 110:1, already quoted twice in the discourse (Heb
1:13; 8:1), is reiterated to demonstrate that Christ's death ("when [he]

---

40. E.g., 1 Sam 15:22-23; Isa 1:11-13, 17; Jer 7:1-11; Hos 6:6; see also Ps 50:10-13.

had offered for all time a single sacrifice for sins") is the moment of his enthronement, where he abides at the right hand of God awaiting the imminent judgment (9:12-13). The section concludes with a reiteration of Jeremiah's new covenant prophecy (Jer 31:33; Heb 9:16-17), this time reworded to replace the phrase "the house of Israel" with "them" (9:16) and adding "and their lawless deeds" (9:17), thus extending the scope of the new covenant beyond Israel, perhaps with an allusion to the former "lawlessness" of Gentile believers.

Priesthood, Sacrifice, and Cosmic Unity in Levitical Perspective

The argument that the sacrificial system associated with the Mosaic covenant was brought to an end by the "once for all" death of Christ assumes that the daily and seasonal rituals that took place in the temple were ineffectual and unsatisfying because they did not achieve permanent purification from sin for Jewish worshipers and because the priests themselves—even the high priest himself—had to offer sacrifices on behalf of their own sins as well as for those of the people. Nehemia Polen notes that the very shortcomings imputed to Jewish ritual by the homilist were valued by the Priestly source (P) of Leviticus that Hebrews critiques:

> The aspects of P highlighted here—the never-ending repetition of the core sacrifices, and the imperfection of the human priests—are indeed basic to the priestly system as a whole. Hebrews evaluates these features negatively, but P enthusiastically affirms these aspects of the ritual system and the theology that hovers behind it. The repetition marks an endless chain of days, linking the singular awe of Sinai with the quotidian rhythms of time's unfolding: sunrise, sunset; breakfast, dinner. What could be simpler, what could more powerfully represent the security, the sense of natural inevitability, that bonds Israel and her God?

Polen goes on to contrast the worldview of Hebrews, which insists on the need for a perfect priest and sacrifice in the heavenly tabernacle "once for all," and Leviticus's delight in

> endless repetition, the day-by day regularity of one lamb in the morning and one in the evening. . . . Precisely for that reason, blessings are always needed, always in order. Human imperfection is anticipated and accounted for, indeed greeted with joy rather than apprehension, for it is the occasion to go deeper, to penetrate into the inner precincts of the holy

domain in search of renewal and restoration, in search of the One who dwells on the Ark-cover, whose Presence is the reminder of Creation and therefore assures an endless succession of new beginnings. (*Source*: Nehemia Polen, "Leviticus, and Hebrews . . . and Leviticus," *The Epistle to the Hebrews and Christian Theology*, 213–28, ed. Richard Bauckham, et al. [Grand Rapids: Eerdmans, 2009], 217, 224–25.)

The British biblical scholar Margaret Barker proposes that the worldviews of Hebrews and P are not as far apart as Polen assumes, since the rituals performed by the high priest in the earthly sanctuary were equated with the activity of Yhwh in the heavenly tabernacle:

The role of the high priest, the Lord, was to remove the damaging effect of sin from the community and the creation, and thus to restore the bonds which held together the community and the creation. . . . The whole point of the argument in the Epistle to the Hebrews is that it was Jesus the high priest who took his own blood into the heavenly sanctuary and thereby became the mediator of a new covenant (Heb.

9.11-15). What I propose would explain the cosmic unity described in Ephesians 1.10: "to unite all things in him, things in heaven and things on earth . . ." and in Colossians 1.17, 20: "In him all things hold together . . . through him to reconcile to himself all things whether on earth or in heaven. . . ." It would explain Matthew's use of the Servant text "he took our infirmities and bore our diseases" in the context of healing miracles (Matt. 8.17). It would explain why a sermon in Acts refers to Jesus as the Righteous One and the Servant but also as the Author of Life (Acts 3.13-15). It would explain all the new life and new creation imagery in the New Testament.

(*Source*: Margaret Barker, "Atonement: The Rite of Healing," *SJT* 49 [1996]: 1–20, at 17, 20.)

In Barker's interpretation the difference between the Priestly understanding of sacrifice and that of Hebrews is that while both see sacrifice as achieving cosmic unity, P values the repetition and cyclicality of the ritual order while Hebrews looks forward to the cosmos being brought to eschatological perfection through Christ's one-time sacrifice.

Mary Ann Beavis

A Jewish Perspective
(Heb 10:11-12)

Hebrews 10:11-12 contrasts the daily sacrifices offered in the Jerusalem temple with the "single sacrifice for sins" offered by Jesus. Nehemia Polen has pointed out that the homilist seems blind to the beauty of the endless cyclical routine of the temple service—or, one could add, of the prayers and other ritual and ethical acts that take its place today.

In Judaism this beautifully endless routine of religious life means, among other things, that as sinning continues, so does forgiveness. Most dramatically in the exalted liturgy of Yom Kippur, the yearly Day of Atonement, but also in the daily prayers and in all our attempts at repair and reconciliation among ourselves, the weary awareness that we keep sinning is balanced by the tearful assurance that we are forgiven again and again.

Hebrews rejects this possibility. Jesus' "single sacrifice" is also "once for all" (10:10). Presumably it is effective for each person at the moment it is accepted in faith—once and for all. But what if one sins again after that? The answer of Hebrews is clear and disturbing: "there no longer remains a sacrifice for sins, but a fearful prospect of judgment, and a fury of fire" (10:26-27). After all, Jesus did not come "to offer himself again and again"; he "appeared once for all at the end of the age to remove sin by the sacrifice of himself" (9:25-26) and there is no room left for another sacrifice or any more sinning.

I am often puzzled by the widely accepted stereotype that the "Old Testament" depicts a God of judgment and wrath, while the New Testament shows us a God of love and forgiveness. For those of us whose human weaknesses keep us failing again and again, the Old Testament God offers ongoing forgiveness, but the God of this book, at least, of the New Testament offers only damnation.

Justin Jaron Lewis

Michael Morrison perceptively suggests that the reason for the homilist's emphasis on the concept of covenant is that it is broad enough to encompass both the priesthood and the rituals that involved all of Israel; "covenant provides the umbrella term by which all the laws could be undercut simultaneously."[41] The following table summarizes the way Hebrews conceptualizes the contrast between the Mosaic and new covenantal regimes:

41. Michael D. Morrison, *Who Needs a New Covenant? Rhetorical Function of the Covenant Motif in the Argument of Hebrews* (Eugene, OR: Pickwick, 2008), 158.

Old Covenant	New Covenant
Mediated by angels to Moses	Mediated by Jesus, messiah, son of God (descendant of David)
Ratified with animal blood	Ratified with blood/death of Christ
Levitical priesthood	Melchizedekian priesthood (Ps 110:4)
Conditional	Promissory
Temporal	Eternal
Earthly tabernacle	Heavenly tabernacle
Yearly atonement	One-time atonement
Associated with earthly Sinai (Heb 12:18-21)	Associated with heavenly Jerusalem (Heb 12:22-24)

None of the three monographs[42] written on the theme of covenant in Hebrews captures the Davidic resonance of the new covenant as it is interpreted by the homilist in relation to Jesus the Messiah, of the tribe of Judah, priest according to the order of Melchizedek (Heb 7:14-15). The dichotomy between the Mosaic covenant and the eternal covenant mediated by Christ, the messianic heir of David (Heb 9:15, 13:20)[43] is implicit in the next section, in the climactic contrast between the earthly Sinai and the heavenly Jerusalem (Heb 12:18-24).

Interpretive Essay:
Blood, Sacrifice, Atonement, and Ritual: Cross-Cultural, Postcolonial, and Ecological Perspectives

The relationships among blood, sacrifice, atonement, and ritual have never been easy or clear in Christian history. In discussing the relationship as articulated in this section of Hebrews it is worth examining the understanding of blood in Judaism that influences the homilist. It may

---

42. Ibid.; John Dunnill, *Covenant and Sacrifice in the Letter to the Hebrews*, SNTSMS 75 (Cambridge: Cambridge University Press, 1993); Susanne Lehne, *The New Covenant in Hebrews*, JSNTSup 44 (Sheffield: JSOT Press, 1990); see also Mary Ann Beavis, "A Study of the Relation of the Old and New Covenants in the Epistle to the Hebrews, in the Light of Scholarship 1938–1980" (MA thesis, University of Manitoba, 1981); Mary Ann Beavis, "The New Covenant and Judaism," *TBT* 22 (1984): 24–30.

43. See also 2 Sam 23:5; 2 Chr 13:5; 21:7; 23:3; Ps 89:3; Isa 55:3; Jer 33:21; Sir 47:11.

also be fruitful to study and compare other religious and cultural understandings of blood. Blood, as a symbol of life, is sacred. Thus it is offered to God, the giver of life, in a sacred place and on sacred occasions. The question of how ritual, blood, and sacrifice are related can be viewed through the connection of the roles of the priest, the mediator, and the performer as laid out by the homilist in 9:11-28. Ironically, however, in order to offer blood to God one has to kill. That is where sacrifice, the act of laying life down, comes in. Paradoxically, religion that requires such sacrifice seems "bent on the annihilation of life," and those who perform such rituals of sacrifice appear to be "butchers" rather than bringers of life. Eberhart argues that "cultic *blood application rituals* [found in ancient Judean cults] do not enact vicarious death but *consecrate through the animal's life*, which is in its blood."[44]

A consecrating ritual that involves the recognition of the animal's generous gift of life given to humanity is common in other traditions, including those of First Nations people in Canada. A Nishnawbe teacher, Arthur Solomon, expresses his people's tradition as follows: "We saw that the animals had a life like our own and that their life was sacred and precious to them. We regarded them as our brothers and we knew that when we killed one of them for food we must give thanks to the Creator, to our Mother Earth and to the Guardian Spirit of that animal. . . . And we offered the sacred tobacco to its spirit . . . [as we are taught to practice] the sacred purifying way of the sweat lodge [for ourselves]."[45]

Andrew Sung Park, a Korean American theologian, suggests that Jesus' atonement should be extended to animals and the entire creation beyond humanity. Using Paul H. Santmire's ecological theology, he contends that there are two motifs in the Bible: the spiritual one, which refers mainly to the redemption of the fallen spirits and the eschatological union of humanity with Jesus Christ, well demonstrated in the Gospel of John and Hebrews, and the ecological one, which signifies the divine restoration of all creation and is seen in most of the Hebrew Bible as well as in the writings of Paul and of the Pauline authors of Colossians and Ephesians.[46] What Park seems to argue is that what belongs to creation, whether it be blood or motionless rock, has a quality of life that requires

44. Eberhart, *Sacrifice*, 132.

45. Michael Posluns, ed., *Songs for the People: Teachings on the Natural Way; Poems and Essays of Arthur Solomon* (Toronto: NC Press Ltd., 1990), 69–70.

46. Andrew Sung Park, *The Wounded Heart of God: The Asian Concept of Han and the Christian Doctrine of Sin* (Nashville, TN: Abingdon, 1993), 97.

respect from us and redemption from God. The life of creation groans with what he calls "nature's *han*" because of human sin, committed to the destruction of the sacredness of nature. Park elsewhere defines and explores this Korean concept of *han* as "the wounded heart," describing the "depths of human suffering, abysmal experience of pain," first developed by Korean contextual theologians in what is called *minjung* theology.[47] In his later work (2009), this concept of *han* is extended to nature beyond humanity as he ponders the atonement theology in trinitarian perspective, in light of the relational and interdependent nature of God, while reflecting the increasingly urgent issue of life in jeopardy under the ecological degradation of the twenty-first century.[48] Perhaps this interconnected view of blood, sacrifice, ritual, and atonement, uniquely positioned in Heb 9, may enhance our understanding and awareness of the interdependence between nature, humanity, and God.

Here it may be useful to consider again a postcolonial goal of "liberated interdependence." Musa W. Dube, a feminist theologian from Botswana, claims that Western interpretation of the Bible, including that of colonialists who used it to justify conquest, has had a direct impact on African realities even after the political independence of the postcolonial era. This apparent international power relation calls us, postcolonial readers, to make the ethical commitment of seeking "liberating ways of reading for interdependence."[49] A deliberate effort to read Heb 9–10 in ways that make connections between blood, sacrifice, ritual, and atonement is integral to this particular postcolonial reading of the Bible because it is our attempt to respect blood as deeply connected to the well-being of animals on which we, as the people of the land, depend.

---

47. Ibid., 15. *Minjung* encompasses ordinary people, the oppressed, and the marginalized in society. Due to their social reality of injustice and oppression, *han* is created internally in people's experience and expressed as anger, despair, and pain. For an extended period of time, as this reality continues, *minjung* feel their hearts blocked and pressed, as if they cannot breathe. Some Korean theologians refer to the *minjung* as *han*-ridden people. For more on *minjung* theology, see Nam-Dong Suh, *Development of Minjung Theology in Korea* (Seoul: Han'gilsa, 1983); Byung-Mu Ahn, *A Story of Minjung Theology* (Seoul: Theological Institute, 1987); Taesoo Yim, *Minjung Theology towards a Second Reformation* (Hong Kong: Christian Conference of Asia, 2006).

48. Andrew Sung Park, *Triune Atonement: Christ's Healing for Sinners, Victims, and the Whole Creation* (Louisville, KY: Westminster John Knox, 2009).

49. Musa W. Dube, *Postcolonial Feminist Interpretation of the Bible* (St. Louis, MO: Chalice Press, 2000), 19.

Moreover, animals are then offered as sacrifices in a human ritual to mark our interdependent relationship with God. Our ethical commitment further involves a critical awareness and an investigation of how we treat animals (and the creation) through a consideration of how the role of priests in rituals can be abused and distorted. It also compels us to articulate an atonement theology that does not lead to the endorsement of violence against the vulnerable. Out of this kind of ethical and inter-dependent reading of the Bible the citation of Ps 40:6-8 in Heb 10:5-7, criticizing the unjust conduct of sacrifice referred to there, makes sense and sheds a new light.

In terms of Jesus as high priest who entered the heavenly sanctuary once for all with his blood (9:12), Asian women connect with this Jesus as shaman, as healer, comforter, and, most of all, mediator between this world and the world beyond this world. Given that most shamans are women, the image of Jesus as the female messiah has also been sug-gested, most vividly expressed in a poem by Gabriele Dietrich, a theo-logian of German origin from India. Her poem is provocative in that she makes a connection between women's menstruation and Jesus' shedding of blood on a cross, while criticizing the hypocrisy of eucharistic practice corrupted by the priests. It is relevant to the theme of Hebrews here in terms of ritual, purity, blood, and the sacrifice of Jesus. Here Jesus' atone-ment is associated with his solidarity with the women and the marginal-ized, while his blood is related to the life-giving bleeding of women:

The Blood of a Woman

I am a woman
and my blood
cries out:
Who are you
to deny life
to the life givers?
Each one of you
has come from the womb
but none of you
can bear woman
when she is strong
and joyful and competent.
You want our tears
to clamour for protection.
Who are you

to protect us
from yourselves?

I am a woman
and my monthly bloodshed
makes me aware
that blood
is meant for life.
It is you
who have invented
those lethal machines
spreading death:
Three kilotonnes of explosives
for every human being
on earth.

I am a woman
and the blood
of my abortions
is crying out.
I had to kill
my child
because of you
who deny work to me
so that i cannot feed it.
I had to kill my child
because i am unmarried
and you would harrass me
to death
if i defy
your norms.

I am a woman
and the blood
of being raped
is crying out.
This is how you keep
your power intact,
how you make me tremble
when i go out at night.
This is how you keep
me in place
in my house where
you rape me again.

I am not taking this
any longer.

I am a woman
and the blood
of my operations
is crying out.
Even if i am a nun
you still use my body
to make money
by giving me historectomy
when i don't need it.
My body is in the clutches
of husbands, policemen,
doctors, pimps,
there is no end
to my alienation.

I am a woman
and the blood
of my struggles
is crying out.
Yes, my comrades,
you want us
in the forefront
because you have learnt
you cannot do without us.
You need us
in the class struggle
as you need us
in bed
and to cook
your grub
to bear
your children
to dress
your wounds.
You will celebrate
women's day
like mother's day
garlands
for our great supporters.
Where would we be
without our women?

I am a woman
and the blood
of my sacrifices
cries out to the sky
which you call heaven.
I am sick of you priests
who have never bled
and yet say:
This is my body
given up for you
and my blood
shed for you
drink it.
Whose blood
has been shed
for life
since eternity?
I am sick of you priests
who rule the garbagriha,[50]
who adore the womb
as a source of life
and keep me shut out
because my blood
is polluting.

I am a woman
and i keep bleeding
from my womb
but also from my heart
because it is difficult
to learn to hate
and it might not help
if i hate you.

I still love
my little son
who bullies his sister
he has learnt it outside,
how do i stop him?
I still love
my children's father

---

50. The innermost sanctum of a Hindu temple. —Ed.

because he was there
when i gave birth.
I still long
for my lovers touch
to break the spell
of perversion
which has grown
like a wall
between women and men.
I still love
my comrades in arms
because they care
for others who suffer
and there is hope
that they give their bodies
in the struggle for life
and not just for power.
But i have learned
to love my sisters.
We have learned
to love one another.
We have learned
even to respect
ourselves.

I am a woman
and my blood
cries out.
We are millions
and strong together.
You better hear us
or you may be doomed.[51]

HyeRan Kim-Cragg

51. Gabriele Dietrich, *One day i shall be like a banyan tree (Poems in Two Languages)* (Belgaum: Dileep S. Kamat, 1985). "The Blood of a Woman," dated "Hiroshima Day, August 1984," appears on pp. 31–35.

Interpretive Essay: "Christ's Sacrifice Once for All": Understanding, Critique, and Reappropriation of the Biblical Social Value "Group Orientation" from a Feminist Perspective

In conversation with the authors on "sacrifice and atonement" and the problem its interpretation has posed for women throughout time, this section will deal with some of the biblical socio-cultural values discernible in Hebrews, especially "group orientation" in light of Christ's "sacrifice once for all" in Heb 10. I shall proceed in three steps. First, some clues to understanding "Christ's sacrifice once for all" will be provided by looking at the biblical social value of "group orientation." Next, I will expose some critical issues in this christo-theological claim that impact women negatively. Last, I will offer concrete examples from Asia of how women may reappropriate this biblical social value in today's world.

Understanding the Biblical Social Value of "Group Orientation"

In the biblical worldview people live corporately as persons embedded in their own community where each finds life's meaning (identity, role and status, duties and rights). This biblical social value of "group orientation" and identification in relation to someone or something (Jesus of Nazareth, Son of God) is called "dyadism."[52] It is discernible in Hebrews in a number of ways. One is the set of in-group appellations describing the boundaries that determine who are the insiders and who the outsiders from the perspective of the homilist and the addressees. Examples are "the children of God" (2:10, 14; 12:5-10), "those who are sanctified" (2:11, 10:14), "brothers and sisters" of Christ and of one another (2:11-12; 3:1; 12; 10:19; 13:22), "descendants of Abraham" (2:16), "holy partners in a heavenly calling" (3:1), "God's house" (3:6), "partners of Christ" (3:14), "we who have believed" (4:3), "the people of God" (4:9), "we who have taken refuge" (6:18), "those who are called" (9:15), and "the saints" (13:24).[53]

Another indication of group orientation signaled by these terms is the thread of kinship that runs through the group. As "brothers and sisters"

---

52. Jerome H. Neyrey, "Group Orientation," in *Biblical Social Values and Their Meaning: A Handbook*, ed. John J. Pilch and Bruce J. Malina (Peabody, MA: Hendrickson, 1993), 88–91, at 88; Jerome H. Neyrey, "Dyadism," 49–52, in ibid.

53. David A. deSilva, "The Epistle to the Hebrews in Social-Scientific Perspective," *ResQ* 36 (1994): 13, 15–16.

of Christ the addressees are "children of God." Through this family-centered bond expressed in the father-son relationship[54] the homilist finds meaning in the suffering of the community: as Jesus the Son of God suffered, was rejected, and died, so they must endure (9:26; 10:29; 12:5-10).[55] This justification of parental discipline through obedience and subordination is attested in the biblical tradition (e.g., Prov 13:24; 23:13).[56] Harsh physical discipline of adolescent boys by the paternal figure was used to train them, since the "authentic male in this culture is one who can endure pain."[57] This is seen in how Jesus died. His voluntary act gained victory over death for him and his followers (2:14-16) and has also become "a sign of divine adoption, an affirmation of the believer's status as an heir of the promise and hence a goad to press on."[58] Through suffering, the believer also reaches perfection, attains communion with Jesus, and forges a deeper bond with the community.[59]

A third sign of group orientation is relationship to authority and peers. Group members imitate and follow their leader(s) and seek the good of others to uphold group honor (10:10, 19-25). The high importance of obedience to authority is exemplified in Jesus' obedience to God's will (3:2-6; 10:7; Ps 40:7-8).[60] Preoccupation with the welfare of the group guarantees the good of each member and the honor of the group.[61] "Honor" and "shame" relate to a person's or group's public claim to worth in the areas of power, sexual status, and religion.[62] "Honor" is public acknowledgment of such status, while "shame" is public denial of such an assertion.[63] In Hebrews the kinship terminology of the group's belonging to God, how Christ's sacrifice is better than the previous ones

---

54. Mark McVann, "Family Centeredness," in Pilch and Malina, *Biblical Social Values*, 70–73.

55. DeSilva, "Hebrews," 18–19.

56. John J. Pilch, "Parenting," in Pilch and Malina, *Biblical Social Values*, 128–31; deSilva, "Hebrews," 19.

57. Pilch, "Parenting," 130.

58. DeSilva, "Hebrews," 19.

59. Ibid.

60. See Neyrey, "Group Orientation," 91.

61. John J. Pilch, "Values and Human Relationships," in his *Introducing the Cultural Context of the New Testament*, Hear the Word, vol. 2 (Eugene, OR: Wipf & Stock, 2007), 129.

62. Bruce J. Malina, *The New Testament World: Insights from Cultural Anthropology* (London: SCM, 1983), 27–50.

63. Joseph Plevnik, "Honor/Shame," in Pilch and Malina, *Biblical Social Values*, 95–104, at 95, 96.

offered according to the Law (10:8-9), the special relationship between Jesus Christ and God (10:11-12), and the appeal to care for each other (10:19-25) are examples of being honorable. Subjection to outside persecution, ridicule, and the threat of defection are shameful (10:33). Thus, in face of a "crisis of commitment"[64] the homilist exhorts the members to choose honor over shame. The appeal includes remembering what the addressees have invested in terms of "work and love" (6:10), as well as what they have endured, such as shame, persecution, and confiscation of property (10:32-34), in light of the proximity of the reward (10:35-36; also 11:24-26).[65]

Feminist Critiques and Responses

While the biblical social background of group orientation and other related values may explain the dynamics within the text, feminists validly critique the implications for women of the christo-theological claims of "Jesus is Son of God" and "Christ's sacrifice once for all," which denote self-abasement, sacrifice, and suffering.

Ulrike Wagener clarifies opposition to the christological model of abasement and exaltation because of its androcentrism, which prioritizes the father-son relationship as a central metaphor for human-divine relations, thus symbolically masculinizing the participation of women in Christ's saving act, and which may promote a kyriocentric theology of domination supportive of patriarchy.[66] She also cites the difficulties arising from a simplistic juxtaposition of Christ's self-sacrifice and suffering with "obedience to God's will" that unnecessarily promotes necrophilia, trivializes violence, and idealizes suffering.[67] As "divine child abuse," it may "[put] a divine sanction behind the abuse of women and abusive child rearing."[68]

---

64. DeSilva, "Hebrews," 10, 11.

65. Ibid., 12.

66. Ulrike Wagener, "Hebrews: Strangers in the World," in *Feminist Biblical Interpretation: A Compendium of Critical Commentary on the Books of the Bible and Related Literature*, ed. Luise Schottroff and Marie-Theres Wacker (Grand Rapids, MI: Eerdmans, 2012), 857–69, at 861.

67. Ibid., 865; Bryan R. Dyer, "'A Great Conflict Full of Suffering': Suffering in the Epistle to the Hebrews in Light of Feminist Concerns," *MJTM* 12 (2010–2011): 179–98.

68. Joanne Carlson Brown, "Divine Child Abuse?," *Daughters of Sarah* 18 (1992): 24–28; Mary Rose D'Angelo, "Hebrews," in *The Women's Bible Commentary*, ed. Carol

In his more detailed study on suffering in Hebrews and feminist scholars' concerns, Bryan Dyer sums up the issues under three headings: understanding how Christ's suffering is redemptive, correcting the notion that Jesus' way of suffering encourages believers to seek suffering, and the idea that Jesus was sent by God to suffer, which equates to divine abuse.[69] On the first concern, Dyer affirms Mary VandenBerg's response to the question of glorifying suffering.[70] Both authors elucidate that the redemptive nature of Jesus' suffering is once for all and unique to Jesus alone because of its accomplishments: "bringing God's children to glory (2:10), becoming the source of eternal salvation (5:9), and making people holy (13:12)."[71] It should make us reject all suffering and impel us to look for ways to lessen or eliminate suffering as we wait for Christ's return.[72] On the claim that Jesus' suffering encourages believers to seek suffering, Dyer clarifies that what Hebrews presents is Jesus' living a life of obedience rather than choosing suffering.[73] Jeanne Stevenson-Moessner regards it as a "call . . . to resist evil, even though resistance, in some cases, may cost our life."[74] This is why Jesus is a "pioneer of faith."[75] On the accusation of "divine child abuse," Dyer supports Reta Halteman Finger's objection that Brown's claim dismisses Jesus' humanity and capacity as an adult to choose freely the suffering consequent to his fight against evil.[76] He also affirms Margo Houts's rejoinder that the problem of God as an abusive and tyrant-like father arises when Jesus is cut off from the Trinity, when Father and Son are not treated as agents of reconciliation and subjects of atonement.[77]

Newsom and Sharon H. Ringe (Louisville, KY: Westminster John Knox, 1998), 364–67, at 366.

69. Dyer, "Great Conflict," 183.

70. Ibid., 184; Mary VandenBerg, "Redemptive Suffering: Christ's Alone," *SJT* 60 (November 2007): 394–411.

71. Dyer, "Great Conflict," 184.

72. VandenBerg, "Redemptive Suffering," 410.

73. Dyer, "Great Conflict," 188.

74. Jeanne Stevenson-Moessner, "The Road to Perfection: An Interpretation of Suffering in Hebrews," *Int* 57 (2003): 280–90, at 289; Dyer, "Great Conflict," 188.

75. Dyer, "Great Conflict," 188.

76. Ibid., 191; Reta Halteman Finger, "Liberation or Abuse," *Daughters of Sarah* 18 (1992): 37–38.

77. Margo Houts, "Atonement and Abuse: An Alternate View," *Daughters of Sarah* 18 (1992): 29–32.

An important aspect of Dyer's investigation for us is Hebrews' focus on the community. He notes that the homilist adjures the addressees that overcoming suffering is a communal effort (10:32, 12:1-13).[78] Dyadism is seen in the exhortations for the community to encourage one another daily (3:13), enter together into the rest God has promised (4:1), rouse each other to love and good works (10:24), and endure suffering as did Jesus the pioneer and perfecter of faith (12:2). Jesus' disregard of the shame of the cross was rewarded with a seat at the right hand God.[79] The homilist cleverly twists the understanding of Jesus' death from society's perception of it as shameful to something honorable in God's eyes.[80]

Reappropriating "Christ's Sacrifice Once for All" in an Asian Context

Our discussion of the biblical-social value of "group orientation" allowed us to understand better the background of "Christ's sacrifice once for all" and the problematic issues arising therefrom for women. Rosemary Radford Ruether and Elizabeth A. Johnson offer insights on how to reconstruct the Christ symbol.[81]

For Ruether, Christians must recognize the particularity of Jesus in terms of gender, ethnicity, and culture as well as accepting the "limitations of any single individual to be universally paradigmatic."[82] She suggests three ways to liberate christology from patriarchy. First, Christians need to understand that "what is paradigmatic about Jesus is not his biological ontology, but rather his person as a lived message and practice."[83] Second, Christ's work should not be isolated from the ongoing Christian community (see Heb 10:19-25; 12:1-2, 12).[84] For her, "if we are clear that the redemption signified by Christ is both carried on and communicated through redemptive community, Christ can take on

78. Dyer, "Great Conflict," 192.

79. Ibid., 192–93.

80. Wagener, "Hebrews," 866.

81. Rosemary Radford Ruether, "Can Christology Be Liberated from Patriarchy?," and Elizabeth A. Johnson, "Wisdom Was Made Flesh and Pitched Her Tent Among Us," in *Reconstructing the Christ Symbol: Essays in Feminist Christology*, ed. Maryanne Stevens (New York and Mahwah, NJ: Paulist Press, 1993), 7–29, 96–116.

82. Ruether, "Christology," 23.

83. Ibid., 24; see also VandenBerg, "Redemptive Suffering," 410; Stevenson-Moessner, "Road to Perfection," 289; Dyer, "Great Conflict," 188.

84. Ruether, "Christology," 24.

the face of every person and group and their diverse liberation struggles. We must be able to encounter Christ as black, as Asian, as Aboriginal, as women." [85] Finally, "Christ need not, and should not, be seen as excluding other ways."[86] This includes welcoming examples from other religious cultures and spiritualities and accepting the limits of the Christ symbol to perceive God's self-revelation today in dialogue with other peoples, cultures, and beliefs.

Another way to address the feminist issue is by regarding Jesus as Sophia, wisdom of God.[87] For Johnson, to conceptualize Jesus as Sophia primarily breaks the "'necessary ontological connection' between the male human being Jesus and the male God" and decentralizes the androcentric focus on Jesus' relationship with God as primarily that of Father-Son.[88] Second, Jesus-Sophia reveals in the male human being Jesus the graciousness of God symbolized as female and manifested in creative transcendence, passion for justice, and quest for truth. These are traits women disciples share equally in the redemptive mission of Jesus.[89] Third, Jesus-Sophia serves as a continuing affirmation of the powers of incarnation and resurrection of the crucified, of the ultimate gift of Wisdom that is life.[90] Finally, Jesus-Sophia furthers women's liberation in a "community of genuine mutuality." The use of Jesus-Sophia language will help inaugurate a new imagination of the world apart from the patriarchal one. It will also liberate christological language from the monopoly of male images and concepts. Moreover, it will allow a vast range of values that women of all cultures hold dear to come to the fore, such as friendship, connectedness, justice, prophecy, ecological care, delight and passion, suffering with, integration, attention to ordinary and not only heroic deeds, the value of both mind and body, and the presence of God coinherent with the world.[91] In this sense "group orientation" becomes inclusivity and seeking out the marginalized. We therefore offer three concrete examples of Asian women who embody the Jesus-Sophia tradition in many ways, spiritualities, and cultures.

85. Ibid.
86. Ibid.
87. Johnson, "Wisdom," 108.
88. Ibid.
89. Ibid.
90. Ibid., 109.
91. Ibid.

"I am Malala"

"How dare the Taliban take away my basic right to education?"[92] This is one of the basic questions expressed by Malala Yousafzai when her father brought her to speak before local press. She is a courageous, outspoken, and intelligent Muslim girl of Pashtun ethnicity who is known for her staunch campaign for girls' education and women's rights in Pakistan. She comes from Mingora, a town in the Swat District of the province of Khyber Pakhtunkhwa. Her name, Malala, recalls the Afghan heroine Malala of Maiwand and the activist Malalai Joya.[93] Her father, Ziauddin Yousafzai, who is himself a school owner and activist, influenced her greatly in this advocacy.

In 2009, Malala started blogging under the pen name "Gul Makai" for BBC Urdu, detailing her life under Taliban rule and promoting girls' rights to education.[94] "I wanted to scream, shout and tell the world what we were going through. But it was not possible. The Taliban would have killed me, my father, my whole family. I would have died without leaving any mark. So I chose to write with a different name. And it worked, as my valley has been freed."[95] *The New York Times* documentary about the Taliban's ban on girls' education in Pakistan features Malala's defiance: "They cannot stop me. I will get my education, if it is in home, school or any place. This is our request to all the world to save our schools, save our world, save our Pakistan. Save our Swat."[96]

Malala became chairperson of the District Child Assembly in Swat in 2010. Spearheaded by the Khpal Kor Foundation and UNICEF, this meeting allows young people to articulate the pressing concerns they face

---

92. Rick Westhead, "Brave Defiance in Pakistan's Swat Valley," *TheStar.com*, October 26, 2009, http://www.thestar.com/news/world/pakistan/article/716131--brave-defiance-in-pakistan-s-swat-valley, accessed July 15, 2015.

93. Owais Tohid, "My Conversations with Malala Yousafzai, the Girl Who Stood Up to the Taliban," *The Christian Science Monitor*, October 11, 2012, http://www.csmonitor.com/World/Global-News/2012/1011/My-conversations-with-Malala-Yousafzai-the-girl-who-stood-up-to-the-Taliban-video, accessed July 15, 2015.

94. "Diary of a Pakistani School Girl," *BBC News*, January 19 2009, http://news.bbc.co.uk/2/hi/south_asia/7834402.stm, accessed July 15, 2015.

95. Tohid, "Conversations."

96. Adam B. Ellick and Irfan Ashraf, "Class Dismissed: The Death of Female Education," *The New York Times*, October 9, 2012, http://www.nytimes.com/video/2012/10/09/world/asia/100000001835296/ class-dismissed.html, accessed July 15, 2015.

and propose solutions.[97] Malala's use of national and international media for her advocacy earned her nomination for the 2011 International Children's Peace Prize. This prestigious award is "presented annually to a child whose courageous or otherwise remarkable acts have made a difference in countering problems which affect children around the world."[98] That year the Pakistani government also awarded her the first National Peace Award, subsequently renamed the National Malala Peace Prize.[99]

Malala's passion for learning and peace angered the Taliban. On October 9, 2012, while she was aboard her school van, Taliban gunmen shot Malala in the head and between the neck and chest in an assassination attempt.[100] Seriously wounded, she was rushed to a district hospital and was eventually airlifted for further treatment to Birmingham in the United Kingdom.[101] While this cowardly attack of the Taliban gained national outrage and international denunciation, support and recognition of Malala's efforts for education and peace in Pakistan became better known.[102] On November 10, 2012, a month after the horrendous attack, United Nations Special Envoy for Global Education and former British Prime Minister Gordon Brown presented to Pakistan's President Asif Ali Zardari the "I am Malala" global petition demanding education for children around the world by the end of 2015.[103] Certainly, as her father

97. Eduardo Cure, "Child Assembly Ensures a Voice for Youth Affected by Crises in Swat, Pakistan," January 28, 2011, https://www.youtube.com/watch?v=5THfRXtOBrc, accessed July 15, 2015.

98. "Desmond Tutu Announces Nominees for Children's Peace Prize 2011," October 25, 2011, http://www.kidsrights.org/News/tabid/121/articleType/ArticleView/articleId/43/Desmond-Tutu-announces-nominees-Childrens-Peace-Prize-2011.aspx, accessed July 15, 2015.

99. "Malala Yousafzai: Portrait of the Girl Blogger," *BBC News Magazine*, October 10, 2012, http://www.bbc.co.uk/news/magazine-19899540, accessed July 15, 2015.

100. Haroon Siraj, "Peace Icon Who Opposed Taliban Shot," *The Nation*, October 10, 2012, http://www.nation.com.pk/pakistan-news-newspaper-daily-english-online/editors-picks/10-Oct-2012/peace-icon-who-opposed-taliban-shot, accessed July 15, 2015.

101. Laura Smith-Park, "Malala's Parents Arrive in Britain," *CNN*, October 28, 2012, http://edition.cnn.com/2012/10/25/world/europe/uk-pakistan-teen-activist/index.html, accessed July 15, 2015.

102. "UNICEF Condemns Shooting of School Girls in Pakistan," http://www.unicef.org/media/media_66146.html, accessed July 15, 2015.

103. Gordon Brown, "Stand with Malala on November 10th," October 22, 2012, http://www.huffingtonpost.com/gordon-brown/malala-yousafzai_b_2000197.html, accessed July 15, 2015.

said: "The person who attacked her wanted to kill her, but she fell temporarily. She will rise again and she can stand now. But when she fell, Pakistan stood and the world rose. This is a turning point."[104] When the world of Malala turns around with help from around the globe, there is also a glimmer of hope that people will meet Malala's mother, Toorpekai,[105] and hear her side of the story, a story that could be one of pride or fear for her daughter's life and future. It could be a narrative of pain because of what they suffered under the Taliban or of joy and hope that her daughter is alive and is fighting for Pakistan's and the world's future through every girl who will be given the gift of knowledge and wisdom, one step at a time. Or it could be a mix of all, for after all, Malala is not only her father's daughter but her mother's as well.

Lucy D'Souza-Krone and "The Feminine Aspect of God"

The painting "Biblical Female Figures: Guide to the Kingdom of God" is the 1990 Misereor Hungertuch.[106] I first saw a copy of it at the main audiovisual room of the Institute of Formation and Religious Studies (IFRS), where I got my master's degree. This institute, a "daughter" of the group of women religious who fought against martial law in the Philippines, for more than forty years has been offering students from Asia, Africa, and the Pacific an integrated, contextual, transformational, and inclusive religious education. This painting, which features Miriam (Exod 15:19-21), Shiphrah and Puah (Exod 1:15-21), Ruth (Ruth 1:4; 2:8; 4:13-17), Mary and Elizabeth (Luke 1:39-56), the Syro-Phoenician woman (Mark 7:25-30; Matt 15:22-28), Mary of Magdala (John 20:11-18), and the woman kneading dough (Luke 13:20-21; John 12:24) has accompanied us through the years. It was, therefore, a pleasure to meet its painter, Lucy D'Souza-Krone, in October 2012. She was visiting Belgium and she dropped by the University Parish International Community (UPIC)

---

104. Rob Crilly (Islamabad) and Lucy Kinder, "Malala Yousafzai: Still Defiant, Girl Shot by Taliban Walking, Talking—and Studying," *The Telegraph,* October 26, 2012, http://www.telegraph.co.uk/news/worldnews/asia/pakistan/9635714/Malala -Yousafzai-Still-defiant-girl-shot-by-Taliban-is-walking-talking-and-studying.html, accessed July 15, 2015.

105. Hasan Suroor, "A Happy Moment for Malala," *The Hindu,* October 27, 2012, http://www.thehindu.com/news/international/a-happy-moment-for-malala /article4035282.ece, accessed July 15, 2015.

106. See "Das Hungertuch, Biblische Frauengestalten—Wegweiser zum Reich Gottes," http://www.misereor.de/fileadmin/redaktion/1990-Das_Hungertuch -Biblische-Frauengestalten.pdf, accessed July 15, 2015.

of the Katholieke Universiteit Leuven to share about her *Kunst fürs Klima*.[107]

Before the meeting I browsed the internet to look for D'Souza-Krone's other works. One of the most interesting pieces is "The Feminine Aspect/ Face of God." The MISSIO website features it as a painting symbolizing the Easter season.[108] As an encounter between Christianity and traditional Indian thought and belief, the painting expresses God's feminine aspects through elements of nature. At its center is the evergreen mango tree, serving as the cross and the tree of life, with a feminine representation of Jesus embraced by four peoples. This image resonates perfectly with the Christ symbols in Hebrews and how women can reappropriate them. Encircling this central image are four female biblical figures symbolizing God's mercy in Ruth, kindness in Mary the mother of Jesus, luminous presence in Hannah, and wisdom in Mary of Bethany. They also represent the four elements of nature: earth, water, fire, and wind.

Mary Grey appreciates this artwork against the backdrop of the diverse contexts of Asian women, woven together by the common experience of oppression and suffering.[109] Grey calls Jesus in this painting "Christa" and the group around her "Christa community." She observes how the whole painting describes a "messianic community [that] collectively gives birth to new creation," with Christa in birth agony and the surrounding figures as co-creators.[110] This artwork offers alternative christo-theological representations: (1) Jesus as a suffering brother in the struggle is a uniting factor and not a stumbling block; (2) Christology is soteriology, in which women mediate the sacred power of healing and redemption; and (3) "christic living" is the continuing life-praxis of the community.[111]

---

107. See http://www.lucy-art.de/klimakunst.htm, accessed July 15, 2015.

108. See "Biblische Themen treffen auf die indische Kultur," http://www.missio .com/spiritualitaet/mit-missio-durch-das-kirchenjahr/ostern-2012/biblische -themen-treffen-auf-die-indische-kultur/d8aab21d-c136-408e-abdc-e60c7d8dbd88 ?mode=detail, accessed July 15, 2015; http://www.lucy-art.de/galerie.htm, accessed July 15, 2015.

109. Mary Grey, "'Who Do You Say That I Am?' Images of Christ in Feminist Liberation Theology," in *Images of Christ: Ancient and Modern*, ed. Stanley E. Porter, Michael A. Hayes, and David Tombs, Roehampton Institute London Papers 2 (London and New York: T & T Clark, 2004), 189–205.

110. Ibid., 197.

111. Ibid.

Lucy D'Souza-Krone, "The Feminine Aspect/Face of God"

Nicola Slee, in her study of Christa theology, points out that while Christa registers positively for some, others only see the dominance of suffering.[112] In her quest for an alternative image she finds D'Souza-Krone's painting a potent expression of a resurrected Christa through the different feminine faces of God.[113] She highlights the brown skin of the image, which is intertwined with and indistinguishable from the tree, the roots of the tree that reach down deeply, and the branches that extend to the corners of the painting. For her, the painting depicts not only human or female suffering but also cosmic travails. Moreover, the interweaving of the branches connects the four corner symbols as if they are the "fruits of its branches, representing compassion, glory, wisdom and nurture—thus suggestive of the biophilic, life orientation of this image."[114] These observations are correct, for as D'Souza-Krone has said, she got the inspiration for this painting from the Chipko (Hindi, "embrace") movement, which started out as a spontaneous campaign of hugging trees in order to protect

112. Nicola Slee, "Visualizing, Conceptualizing, Imagining and Praying the Christa: In Search of Her Risen Forms," *FemT* 21 (2012): 71–90.
113. Ibid., 75.
114. Ibid., 76.

them from being cut down. In 1974 it was particularly associated with a group of women from Chamoli district who protected 2,500 trees from being felled by embracing them.[115] Through this painting D'Souza-Krone not only allows the "suffering of Christ once for all" to represent women, human, and cosmic suffering; her colors, strokes, meditations, and prayers also bring them forth and celebrate their liberation and resurrection.

The "Babaylan" and/in "Dok Susan"

While Malala stands for knowledge through education and D'Souza-Krone expresses wisdom through art, the *babaylans* of the Philippines employ wisdom for community and nation building.

Contrary to objections that Filipina feminism is an imported concept, scholars who have delved into its history opine otherwise.[116] Pre-colonial Philippines is said to have been governed by a triad: the economic czar (*datu*), the technical expert (*panday*), and the supernatural mediator-healer or animist shaman (*babaylan*). The *babaylans* are usually women; "the only men who [became] *babaylans* were those who were more female than male, such as hermaphrodites, homosexuals and old men."[117] Their power is best known in the realm of culture or folk wisdom, specifically healing, religion, and literature.[118] The presence of the *babaylan* in the pre-colonial Philippines is attested by the different terms referring to the *babaylan* found in other linguistic groups.[119]

The *babaylan* thrived in pre-colonial times because of the self-sustaining agricultural communities. The natural resources were owned by all then, with the family as the basic unit of production. Since everyone in the community was involved in producing basic life necessities, marked division of labor among men and women at home or in the fields was unknown.

---

115. Nuzrat Azim, "Chipko Movement Saves Trees; with Love and Hugs," June 30, 2011, http://www.global1.youth-leader.org/2011/06/chipko-movement-saves-trees-with-love-and-hugs, accessed July 15, 2015.

116. Lilia Quindoza-Santiago, "Roots of Feminist Thought in the Philippines," trans. Thelma B. Kintanar, *Review of Women Studies* 6 (1996): 159–72; Ma. Luisa T. Camagay, "Ang Kababaihan at Pambansang Kamalayan," *Philippine Social Sciences Review, Gender Issues in Philippine Society* 50, nos. 1–4 (1995): 1–14.

117. Maria Teresa Martinez-Sicat, "The Filipino Woman and/in *The Filipino Rebel*," *RWS* 6 (1996): 173–74.

118. Quindoza-Santiago, "Feminist Thought," 162.

119. See ibid., 161–62; Luciano P. R. Santiago, "The Development of the Religious Congregations for Women in the Philippines during the Spanish Period (1565–1898)," *The Journal of Sophia Asia Studies* 12 (1994): 49–71, at 51.

This is even seen in the absence of sexual bifurcation in Philippine languages, especially in nouns and pronouns.[120] As there was no concept of private property yet, the notion of women as men's property had no social basis. Thus, aside from access to production, women also had "inheritance rights" to communal property and opportunities for education, divorce before the law, liberty of movement, and positions of leadership.[121]

This situation changed when the Spanish *conquistadores* came.[122] The governor general who represented the Spanish king and the military took over the political leadership of the *datu*. The conquerors introduced new methods of farming technology. Most important, the friars and missionaries subverted the role of the *babaylan* by imposing foreign ways of worship, burning old symbols for worship, and outlawing indigenous rites and rituals. As rivals of the priests, the *babaylans* were also vilified as witches or sorcerers and as bandits, thieves, and criminals. As this denigration of the indigenous political-scientific-cultural order subjugated the women,[123] the subjugation of the Filipino race also began.[124] Reclaiming the role of the *babaylan* or *babaylanism* in contemporary Filipino society therefore means not only being in solidarity with the voices of women all over the world but also "re-discover[ing] and remember[ing] the *babaylan*," and "to *name*, describe and connect Filipina feminism more firmly with the babaylan's *proto*-feminist strategies of resistance" and community/nationbuilding.[125]

As the *babaylans* are well-versed in cultural or folk wisdom, especially in healing and maintaining well-being in sustainable ways, this description came to my mind when I met Dr. Susana "Dok Susan" Balingit. I had to see her during my brief stay in the Philippines in September 2012 to ask for an alternative opinion. It was just a week before I was to return to Belgium to continue my doctoral studies when I suddenly developed swollen lymph nodes. Two doctors prescribed an immediate incision biopsy, but she told me to try modifying my diet first, since the change in environment, food, and activities might have caused this lymphatic reaction. She suggested taking the surgical route only if the condition

---

120. Quindoza-Santiago, "Feminist Thought," 163, 161.
121. Martinez-Sicat, "Filipino Woman," 173.
122. Quindoza-Santiago, "Feminist Thought," 163.
123. Ibid.
124. Martinez-Sicat, "Filipino Woman," 174.
125. Flaudette May V. Datuin, "Reclaiming the Southeast Asian Goddess: Examples from Contemporary Art by Women (Philippines, Thailand and Indonesia)," trans. Izumi Nakajima, *Image and Gender* 6 (2006): 105–19.

should persist. After I had followed her prescription for a week, the lymph node went back to its normal size and has not shown any other abnormal sign. While I am not a specialist who can rule out a possible medical condition, what is revolutionary with the approach of Dok Susan is its implication for nation building and the magnitude of its impact on individual and communal socio-economic sustainability in terms of food security, independence from multinational pharmaceutical companies and unnecessary medical procedures, and recognition of indigenous remedies and folk wisdom for the maintenance of well-being.

Balingit studied medicine in the Philippines and has postdoctoral training abroad. She is executive director of the *Sandiwaan* ("oneness of spirit") Center for Responsible Health Care, a nongovernment organization (NGO) focusing on rediscovering and promoting health traditions and indigenous diet to achieve and maintain health, abundance, and empowerment among the marginalized sectors, especially women, in the Philippines.[126] She also works at the Center for Complementary and Integrative Medicine of the De La Salle Health Sciences Institute in Dasmarinas, Cavite, where she shares her research and advocacy with students. Her partnership with NGOs has helped them transform contemporary mentality on food security/sustainability, health promotion and disease prevention, poverty reduction, cultural preservation, biodiversity conservation, and community building.[127] In my encounter with her she asked me not to draw people to her, for this would deplete her of energy and time; instead, she encouraged me to help her expand her advocacy by spreading her message that "food is medicine" and "you are what you eat."[128] Yes, the *babaylan* urges that "with what we eat, we will build ourselves, our country, and our world."

126. See http://www.althealthfoundation.org/adviser/dr-susana-balingit.html; Carmela G. Lapeña, "Back to Basics with Dok Susan at the Women's Market," *GMA News,* 26 March 2011, http://www.gmanetwork.com/news/story/216251/lifestyle/food/back-to-basics-with-dok-susan-at-the-women-s-market; links accessed July 15, 2015.

127. Charlotte Floors, "Rediscovering Indigenous Food in Quezon, Palawan," *Community and Habitat: Climate Change and Resilience* 13 (2008), http://www.prrm.org/publications/comhab13/rediscovering.htm; Joshua B. Guinto, "Chronicles of PRRM Rooftop Gardening," July 2009, http://www.prrm.org/prrm-rooftop-garden/chronicles-of-prrm-rooftop-gardening.html; links accessed July 15, 2015.

128. Lapeña, "Back to Basics"; Juan Escandor Jr., "Health Advocates Say Indigenous Food Healthy," *Inquirer Mobile,* September 4, 2007, http://services.inquirer.net/mobile/07/09/04/html_output/xmlhtml/20070817-83208-xml.html, accessed July 15, 2015.

To conclude: our understanding of the biblical social value of group orientation and its limitations opens us to reappropriate "Christ's suffering for all." It also allows us to see Christ's continued presence in the suffering community that, through people like Malala, Lucy, and Dok Susan, reaches out toward liberation and resurrection for all creation.

Ma. Maricel Ibita

Hebrews 10:19–12:29

Following Wisdom

The lengthy doctrinal exposition of Heb 8:1–10:18 is followed by a similarly extensive paraenetic section featuring the famous celebration of scriptural "heroes of faith" in 11:1-40. The unifying theme of the section is the faithful persistence of the people of God in the face of difficulty, persecution, and uncertainty. This section completes the exodus metaphor that recurs throughout the sermon—the messiah Jesus is the "pioneer" (6:20) who liberates his brothers and sisters from "slavery" (2:15), the mediator of a new covenant better than the one mediated through angels by Moses, who leads his people to a better "rest" than Joshua (3:11; 4:1-11). The audience is warned not to disobey as their ancestors did in the desert (3:7-11, 16-19) but to follow the example of the faithful men and women of Israel who looked toward the "promise" (11:39), so that they will finally arrive at the heavenly Jerusalem (12:22-24).

The list of heroes and heroines of faith in chapter 11 is regarded by some scholars as a separate source edited into the discourse by the homilist.[1] Whatever its original source, the chapter is smoothly integrated into the larger argument of the section to provide a roster of moral *exempla* from the scriptures for the recipients.

---

1. For examples, see James W. Thompson, *Hebrews*, Paideia Commentaries on the New Testament (Grand Rapids, MI: Baker Academic, 2008), 226.

[19]Therefore, my friends, since we have confidence to enter the sanctuary by the blood of Jesus, [20]by the new and living way that he opened for us through the curtain (that is, through his flesh), [21]and since we have a great priest over the house of God, [22]let us approach with a true heart in full assurance of faith, with our hearts sprinkled clean from an evil conscience and our bodies washed with pure water. [23]Let us hold fast to the confession of our hope without wavering, for he who has promised is faithful. [24]And let us consider how to provoke one another to love and good deeds, [25]not neglecting to meet together, as is the habit of some, but encouraging one another, and all the more as you see the Day approaching.

[26]For if we willfully persist in sin after having received the knowledge of the truth, there no longer remains a sacrifice for sins, [27]but a fearful prospect of judgment, and a fury of fire that will consume the adversaries. [28]Anyone who has violated the law of Moses dies without mercy "on the testimony of two or three witnesses." [29]How much worse punishment do you think will be deserved by those who have spurned the Son of God, profaned the blood of the covenant by which they were sanctified, and outraged the Spirit of grace? [30]For we know the one who said, "Vengeance is mine,

Paraenesis: Persisting in Faith (10:19-39)

As throughout Hebrews, the paraenesis draws out the practical, ethical implications of the doctrinal section that precedes it. The new covenant ratified by the metaphorical "blood" of Jesus, that is, his self-giving life and death, has opened the way not to an earthly promised land but to the "rest" of the heavenly places. The metaphorical, as opposed to literal, meaning of the reference to Jesus' blood is indicated by the apposition that follows: "the new and living way that he opened for us through the curtain (that is, through his flesh)" (10:20); here the crucified body of Jesus is allegorically interpreted in terms of the inner curtain of the tabernacle that veiled the holy of holies (Exod 26:31-37; see also Heb 9:11). The early Christian theologian John Chrysostom's interpretation of the metaphor of the body as heavenly tabernacle veil develops this hermeneutical train of thought:

> See how he calls the body tent and curtain and heaven: "Through the greater and more perfect tent." "Through the curtain, that is, through his flesh." And again, "into the inner shrine behind the curtain." And again, "entering into heaven itself, now to appear in the presence of God." Why then does he say this? In accordance with whether one thing or another is signified. I mean, for instance, the heaven is a curtain, for

I will repay." And again, "The Lord will judge his people." [31]It is a fearful thing to fall into the hands of the living God.

[32]But recall those earlier days when, after you had been enlightened, you endured a hard struggle with sufferings, [33]sometimes being publicly exposed to abuse and persecution, and sometimes being partners with those so treated. [34]For you had compassion for those who were in prison, and you cheerfully accepted the plundering of your possessions, knowing that you yourselves possessed something better and more lasting.

[35]Do not, therefore, abandon that confidence of yours; it brings a great reward. [36]For you need endurance, so that when you have done the will of God, you may receive what was promised. [37]For yet

"in a very little while,
The one who is coming will
come and will not delay;
[38]but my righteous one will live by
faith.
My soul takes no pleasure in
anyone who shrinks
back."

[39]But we are not among those who shrink back and so are lost, but among those who have faith and so are saved.

as a curtain it walls off the Holy of Holies; the flesh is a curtain hiding the Godhead; and the tent likewise holds the Godhead. Again, heaven is a tent, for the priest is there within.[2]

Teresa Berger, a feminist liturgical historian, traces an early Christian liturgical text that is drawn from Heb 10:19-20:

We thank Thee, O Lord our God, that Thou hast given us boldness for the entrance of Thy holy places, which Thou hast renewed to us as a new and living way through the veil of the flesh of Thy Christ. We therefore, being counted worthy to enter into the place of the tabernacle of Thy glory, and to be within the veil, and to behold the Holy of Holies, cast ourselves down before Thy goodness: Lord, have mercy on us: since we are full of fear and trembling, when about to stand at Thy holy altar.[3]

This prayer reflects a theology in Hebrews that is earthly and incarnational. Liturgically speaking, the worshiping assembly is encouraged to enter into God's presence, which is hidden yet revealed, not only through a veil

---

2. *On the Epistle to the Hebrews* 15.4; Erik M. Heen and Philip D. Krey, *Ancient Christian Commentary on Scripture, New Testament X* (Downers Grove, IL: InterVarsity, 2006), 140.

3. Liturgy of St. James, Prayer of the Veil, cited in Teresa Berger, *Gender Differences and the Making of Liturgical History: Lifting a Veil on Liturgy's Past* (Farnham, UK, and Burlington, VT: Ashgate, 2011), 180–81.

The Veil in Postcolonial Perspective

The ambiguity of the veil is not limited to the discussion of Christian liturgical and biblical scholarship. In Islam the issue of the veil has been important for Muslim women. The discussion around the *burqa* (a veil that covers a woman from head to toe), the *hijab* (headscarf), and the *niqab* (a full-face veil) has become even more important since the 9/11 attacks. While we are aware that the meaning of the veil for these women is never monolithic and has always been ambiguous, changing over time, the European Western Christian imperial hand has often painted this religious practice as oppressive, antidemocratic, and barbaric. Under the Western gaze, Muslim women wearing a veil are viewed as people desperately needing to be rescued by liberal, democratic, and civilized white men and feminists. Gayatri Chakravorty Spivak warns against this way of reinscribing the colonial ideology of "white men saving brown women from brown men." In this ideology the brutality of Western colonialism is veiled and the violence of the civilizing mission is masked. Kwok Pui-lan, observing a movement of Muslim women in the United States after 9/11, supports Leila Ahmed's research on the veil. Ahmed's research finding confirms that the veil, traditionally viewed as "an emblem of patriarchy and oppression of women has been reappropriated . . . for their own empowerment." Citing Ahmed's research, Kwok observes that "wearing a veil becomes a means of public display of identity and solidarity against Islamphobia. . . . Some of the women say that the veil is a call for justice, recalling that the veil was an anticolonial symbol in an earlier time." Hebrews' reference to the veil, its early liturgical use, and the contemporary discourse on the veil in religious interfaith dialogue affirm a complex relationship between religion, gender, and liturgical practice in public spaces, always intersecting with socio-political ideologies in complex ways. At the same time, the findings help those of us who are Christians, and who hold power on a global scale, to unveil our own bias and prejudices and to disclose our own shortcomings. "Full of fear and trembling," we are called to keep our eyes on the "inner curtain of the tabernacle" as a new, living way.

(*Sources*: Gayatri Chakravorty Spivak, "Can the Subaltern Speak?," in *Marxism and the Interpretation of Culture*, ed. Cary Nelson and Lawrence Grossberg [Urbana: University of Illinois Press, 1988], 271–313, at 296–97; Kwok Pui-lan, *Globalization, Gender, and Peacebuilding: The Future of Interfaith Dialogue* [New York: Paulist Press, 2012], 39–40.)

HyeRan Kim-Cragg

but also "within the veil." Berger speculates about whether this prayer contains a clue to a liturgical practice of veiling the altar area, the communion elements, and/or the veiling of the baptized at a prebaptismal exorcism.[4] The critical insight from this prayer shaped by Hebrews is not so much the inaccessibility of the veiled altar as it is the ability to encounter God, "the flesh of Christ," however partial and unknowable. The meaning of "veil," whether metaphorical or symbolic, remains ambiguous.

The "way" that Jesus, the one better than Moses and messianic high priest, has opened up is "for us," i.e., for the community of the new covenant to which the homilist and the audience belong, the "household" or "family" (οἶκος) of God (10:21). The World Council of Churches, the world's largest ecumenical Christian organization today, uses the word *oikoumenē*, a word whose root is *oikos*, in its logo. The English word "ecumenical" is formed from the Greek *oikoumenē*, signifying the whole household of faith beyond all races, all nations, and all church divisions.

This "ecumenical" aspect of *oikos* can shed new light on another concept, *ochlos* (ὄχλος, meaning "crowd"). This term is one of the most important concepts in *minjung* theology, especially in the work of Byung-Mu Ahn, one of the founding *minjung* theologians. Examining the Gospel of Mark, he notes that this word for crowd (2:4) does not appear in the Pauline epistles, which were all written before Mark, but is used first in the earliest gospel. In Mark it is used thirty-six times for "the crowd" around Jesus, including the hungry (6:34), tax collectors, and sinners (2:13-17). They are *minjung* from Galilee and are like sheep without a shepherd (6:34). After the narration in 3:34, which says, "and looking at those who sat around him . . ." Jesus declares that they (the crowd) are his mother, brothers, and sisters (3:34). This, according to Ahn, is where the concept of *ochlos* intersects with that of *oikos*, breaking the ties of blood kinship to form the basis for a new community, a new family.[5] *Ochlos*, as the homilist puts it, becomes the new and living way, *oikos* (Heb 10:20-21).

For the homilist, the implication of Christ's achievement is that the community must recognize that "the Day" is approaching (10:25). "The Day" evokes the prophetic phrase "the day of the Lord," usually envi-

---

4. Ibid., 182.

5. Byung-Mu Ahn, "Jesus and Minjung in Mark's Gospel," *Reading Minjung Theology in the Twenty-First Century: Selected Writings by Ahn Byung-Mu and Modern Critical Responses*, ed. Yong Suk Kim and Jin-Ho Kim (Eugene, OR: Pickwick Publications, 2013).

sioned as a time of judgment for disobedient Israel,[6] interpreted in the NT to refer to the return of Christ as eschatological judge and savior.[7] Rather than shrinking from the awesome expectation of the parousia, the addressees are exhorted to draw near the heavenly sanctuary that has been opened up by Jesus, even to the point of entering the holy places (10:19-22). Following the allegorical method illustrated above, the homilist interprets the community's entrance into the heavens in terms of their meeting (or "synagoguing") together (τὴν ἐπισυναγωγὴν ἑαυτῶν),

Oikos and Ekklēsia

Although the word ἐκκλησία ("assembly," "church") is not used in this section, its meaning is implied and well substantiated. Elsewhere this word points to a group of people "called out" from throughout the world to gather and to encounter God through the Spirit and in their neighbors by physically "meeting together" and demonstrating "love and good deeds." The very identity of ἐκκλησία is found in the people offering themselves to God in praise and thanksgiving through the practice of gathering and caring for one another. In doing so they pay respect and attribute worth to God, who has made a loving, life-giving covenant with them. It is a call the homilist reminds the audience of here. In and through worship as a ritual, "the habit" (10:25), the bodily and mental act, and as a primary expression of ἐκκλησία, the Christian assembly responds to

this call. Liturgy, striving for full, active, and conscious participation of the people, is like developing "persistent muscular habits," which includes the awareness of acquired habits, critical appraisal of habits, and openness to change them in order to participate in worship at a deeper level, as John D. Witvliet puts it.

(*Sources*: HyeRan Kim-Cragg, "To Love and Serve (or to Be Loved and Served)," in *Called to be the Church: Intercultural Visions*, ed. Rob Fennell [Toronto: United Church Publishing House, 2012], 23–32, at 24; John D. Witvliet, "Teaching Worship as a Christian Practice," 117–48, in *For Life Abundant: Practical Theology, Theological Education, and Christian Ministry*, ed. Dorothy C. Bass and Craig Dykstra [Grand Rapids, MI: Eerdmans, 2008], 127.)

HyeRan Kim-Cragg

---

6. E.g., Isa 2:2; 13:6, 9; Jer 46:10; Ezek 13:5; 30:3; Joel 1:15; 2:1, 11, 31; 3:14; Amos 5:18, 20; Obad 1:15; Zeph 1:7, 14; Zech 14:1; Mal 4:5.

7. Acts 2:20; 1 Cor 5:5; 2 Cor 1:14; 1 Thess 5:2; 2 Pet 3:10.

where they are exhorted to "consider how to provoke one another to love and good deeds" (10:24), a practice they seem to have been neglecting (10:25).

The reference to the approaching Day of the Lord is an encouragement to faithful persistence and solidarity but also a warning against the consequences of drifting away from the community and sound doctrine, a theme that recurs throughout Hebrews (see 2:1; 3:1; 6:4-6; 12:25). Since Christ's self-offering is "once for all," those who intentionally persist in sinfulness are subject to harsh judgment, vividly described as a consuming "fury of fire" (10:27) and divine vengeance (10:30; see also Deut 32:35-36); to fall into "the hands of the living God" is a "fearful thing" (Heb 10:31). Once again the homilist uses a *qal wahomer* argument (see also 9:13-14) to make the point: if a person who violated the Mosaic law could be put to death on the testimony of two or three witnesses (Deut 17:6; 19:15), those who have profaned the holiness imparted by the ratification of the new covenant will be subject to even worse punishment (10:29). Since the covenant is mutual and reflects a relationship of interdependence, the consequence of wrongdoing and of breaking the covenant is significant. While the threatened Day of the Lord did not arrive as the homilist warned, and the resort to threats and manipulation is unworthy of the spirit of Wisdom, the exhortation to the addressees to encourage one another to loving deeds in community is a message that reflects the "Spirit of grace" (10:29): "a spirit that is intelligent, holy . . . loving the good . . . for God loves nothing so much as the person who lives with wisdom" (Wis 7:22, 28).

True to the verbally abusive rhetorical pattern of alternating threats and compliments (see the comment on 6:1-12), the homilist now reminds the community of their "former days," a perverse "honeymoon period" of endurance through suffering, public shame, solidarity with the persecuted faithful, even prisoners,[8] in the knowledge that "you yourselves possessed something better and more lasting" (10:32-34). The exhortation to uphold the confidence of the past in the expectation of a "great reward" is bolstered by a prophetic quotation that mirrors the combined themes of threat and promise: "in a very little while, the one who is coming will come and will not delay; but my righteous one will live by faith. My soul takes no pleasure in anyone who shrinks back" (Hab 2:3-4). The reference to living "by faith" (ἐκ πίστεως) in the prophecy

---

8. See also Phil 2:25; 4:14-18; 2 Cor 11:23; Acts 5:18; 8:3; 12:1-17; 16:23-40.

introduces the theme of the next chapter, announced in 10:39: "But we are not among those who shrink back and so are lost, but among those who have *faith* and so are saved."

From a feminist standpoint, the homilist's rhetorical bullying of the audience seems to trivialize the community's genuine suffering due to religious persecution, insisting, "you have not yet resisted to the point of shedding your blood" (12:4). As James Thompson observes:

> From the beginning the readers have faced abuse, suffering, and marginalization. The athletic images [see also 12:1-13] suggest that the readers are like runners whose efforts have brought them close to exhaustion. Consequently, Christian experience is a matter of enduring. The need to endure was not unique to this community, for it was the common experience of Christian communities throughout the ancient world until Constantine declared Christianity the established religion in the Edict of Milan in 313.[9]

The likelihood that the audience had endured real maltreatment on account of their faith does not justify the homilist's rhetorical hectoring, which may have compounded, rather than relieved, their exhaustion and distress. Emerson B. Powery observes, "Oftentimes, the emphasis on suffering historically has had damaging effects, as suffering (on behalf of a cause) has often become the rhetoric of the powerful—who tend to 'suffer' little."[10] If we plot this on the global map of power dynamics, we see that the global north benefits from the rhetoric of endurance in suffering. The patience and perseverance of the global south's unnecessary suffering is (unwontedly) rewarded by the self-absorption, greed, and gluttony of the self-proclaimed "First World." Carter Heyward even calls this a kind of narcissistic aggression in which Christian theology, the theology of the suffering Christ in particular, feeds "twisted psychospiritualities that normalize sadistic and masochistic dynamics . . . violence against people and all creatures, and wars justified as holy."[11]

This pattern of thinking can be particularly damaging to women in abusive relationships, who may be socialized to believe that their patient suffering will eventually be rewarded by renewed love. Often this kind

9. Thompson, *Hebrews*, 223; see also 215–17.

10. Emerson B. Powery, "The Gospel of Mark," in *True to Our Native Land: An African American New Testament Commentary*, ed. Brian R. Blount (Minneapolis: Fortress Press, 2007), 121–57, at 142.

11. Carter Heyward, *Saving Jesus from Those Who Are Right: Rethinking What It Means to be Christian* (Minneapolis: Fortress Press, 1999), xiii, 175.

of distorted relationship is tangled in the convergence of sex and violence, or violence perpetrated through sexual assault. Delores S. Williams addresses this convergence from the perspective of African American women whose lives have been violated by white men's sexual desires and pleasures to the point of "shedding of their blood" (12:4). In this violence they become "surrogate" sexual objects, servants, and nursemaids to white men, women, and children. She contests the theology of surrogacy enacted in bloody violence: "Redemption of humans can have nothing to do with any kind of surrogate or substitute role Jesus was reputed to have."[12]

Our Stories Are Our Scripture
For Hebrews 10

Lost Bird of Wounded Knee

Zintkala Nuni found alive as miracle baby Lakota by mother's frozen body shield

Four days after the massacre yet no chance ever found she would live up to her own

Culture as she faced continued rejection exposure to cold racism abuse yet success

Buffalo Bill's Wild West Show gave tragic entertainment exhibit work opportunity

In search for her roots found welcome cool vaudeville act three times she visited

South Dakota fourth time finally came home her remains buried at mass grave site

Annharte

Interpretive Essay: Women and Suffering in Korean Feminist Theology

A prime example of a distorted perspective on women's relationship to suffering is found in neo-Confucian practice in Korea. *SamJongGeeDo* (三從之道), literally meaning "the Way of Three Obediences," about which I have written elsewhere, has been developed and practiced for centuries.[13] This teaching encourages women to resign themselves to a lifelong "endurance of a hard struggle with sufferings" (see also Heb

---

12. Delores S. Williams, *Sisters in the Wilderness: The Challenge of Womanist God-Talk* (Maryknoll, NY: Orbis Books, 1994), 165.

13. HyeRan Kim-Cragg, "Women and Confucianism: A Korean-Canadian Postcolonial Feminist Perspective," in *Introduction to Asian Feminist Perspectives on Religions: Toward Interfaith Dialogue* (Kuala Lumpur, Malaysia: AWRC, 2008), 84–103, at 90–91.

10:32). An unmarried woman must follow her father; a married woman must follow the will of her husband; the widow must follow her son. Such strict rules only work under the hierarchical logic of male superiority in childhood, marriage, and parenthood. In this neo-Confucian ideal it is unimaginable for women to resist (opt out of) marriage or pregnancy. It is virtually impossible to think of women who are lesbians or divorced and seeking to marry again. In Korea, biblical references that exhort "Wives, be subject to your husbands" (Eph 5:22-24) or "be self-controlled, chaste, good managers of the household, kind . . . submissive to [your] husbands" (Titus 2:5) are too often coupled with culturally ingrained neo-Confucian values that reinforce and sanction the suffering of women and encourage them to remain in that suffering.

In a similar vein, another neo-Confucian rule, *NamJonYoBi* (男尊女卑), literally meaning "men are (worthy of) respect, women are worthless," is another sad example of how women are encouraged to view their lives as deserving nothing but suffering. In this male-centered interpretation of gender relations the pressure to bear sons is so harsh that barren women or those who have only given birth to girls can be expelled from their marriages and forbidden to return to their fathers' homes. Similar, though not identical, practices under patriarchy are found in other parts of Asia and are then exported and transplanted to North America. In remnants of such customs as *sati* or widow burning in India, or the abandonment of girl babies in China, or the selective killing of unborn female life through abortion, "an overarching patriarchal ethos still obtains" among many communities in the world today.[14]

Feminists may relate to the homilist's exhortation to courage and persistence in the face of the scorn and harassment they may encounter when upholding women's rights. Hyun-Kyung Chung finds a poetic expression of this courage in a poem, Hiratsuka Raicho's "Struggle to Be the Sun Again." It points to Asian women's yearning for wholeness, claiming that Asian women's communities for resistance and struggle must define the meaning of liberation for themselves. "If a religious teaching or practice provides a life-giving power to Asian women so that we can sustain and liberate our lives, that teaching and practice becomes 'good news'—gospel—for us. If it makes Asian women die both inside

14. Greer Anne Wenh-In Ng, "Pastoral Care in the Context of North American Asian Communities," in *Injustice and the Care of Souls: Taking Oppression Seriously in Pastoral Care*, ed. Sheryl A. Kujawa-Holbrook and Karen B. Montagno (Minneapolis: Fortress Press, 2009), 73–88, at 81.

and outside, it becomes 'bad news.'"[15] Insights from the Korean concept of *han* can be deployed to address the courageous struggle with suffering. There are said to be two modes of *han* (a concept briefly discussed above). *Junghan* is *han* that is accepted. *Wonhan* is *han* that is not accepted, a rejection of the fate of *han*. Chung lifts up the strength and persistence of Korean women who refuse to accept their *han*-ridden lives and instead seek a radical change, as radical as changing from being the moon to becoming the sun.[16] It is worth noting that the word *won* 怨 in *wonhan* resembles Hebrews' concept of "vengeance" (10:30), taken from Deut 32:35. The "vengeance" of God is juxtaposed with the "vindication" of God (Deut 32:36), in the sense of a holding accountable for wrongdoings, a dismissal of wrong accusations, a rightful defense of rightful claims. A sense of justice rather than simple revenge is implied in both Korean feminist theology and the concept in Hebrews drawn from Deuteronomy.

Fifteen years after Chung another Korean theologian, Anne Joh, revisits these two modes of *wonhan* and *junghan* as she explores a Christology of *jeong* 情 in relation to and juxtaposed with *han*. *Jeong* in Chinese characters literally means "heart with vulnerability," and is often understood as "sticky, lasting, and complex relationships," though it is impossible to accurately translate and fully capture the sense in English. For Joh, following the psychology of Jae Hoon Lee, *wonhan* is activated when hate gets the upper hand in a relationship, while *jeonghan* is the reality in relationships in which love becomes the stronger force. By connecting love with *jeong* she frames its operative definition as "the in-between space created by the juxtaposition of *han* and love."[17] While destabilizing patriarchal divinity and the masculine dominance of Logos-centered theology, Joh navigates the discourse of Christology from the realm of the symbolic to that of the semiotic, where *jeong* coexists with *han* as erotic power, the power of heart, of love, and of vulnerability, shown in the life and death of Jesus. This Christology of *jeong* also encompasses persistence that operates "within the terrain of confrontational and oppositional relationships."[18]

---

15. Hyun-Kyung Chung, *Struggle to Be the Sun Again: Introducing Asian Women's Theology* (Maryknoll, NY: Orbis Books, 1991), 6.

16. Ibid., 42–43.

17. Wonhee Anne Joh, *Heart of the Cross: A Postcolonial Christology* (Louisville, KY: Westminster John Knox, 2006), 121.

18. Ibid., 97.

Women heroes of faith, including the pharaoh's daughter (Heb 11:24) and Rahab (Heb 11:31) found in the next chapter of Hebrews, can capture this complex notion of *jeong* as persistence that overcomes the boundaries between nations, cultures, races, and social classes. The women portray a courage "that is able to wedge itself into the smallest cracks/gaps between the oppressed and the oppressor."[19] Pharaoh's daughter, for example, would obviously appear to reside in the camp of the oppressor as far as Moses' family was concerned (Heb 11:23). She surprises them, however, and a crack in the system is opened that enables her to oppose her own father's regime and inhumane order. The homilist's description of the faith involved in saving the life of Moses (11:23-28) can perhaps be fully understood by appreciating this concept of the *jeong* of Christology. Joh continues to explain the concept: "When *Jeong* is present in a relationship, a person might appear as an 'enemy' because of structural impositions, but in one-to-one relationality, the relation between self and that enemy could be fraught with compassion, recognition, and even acceptance."[20] Rahab, though in fear and trembling at the destruction of her city and her country, was able to create a peaceful relationship with her enemy because she recognized and accepted the God of the enemy "by faith" (11:31), an act that resulted in saving her household.

HyeRan Kim-Cragg

Examples of Faith (11:1-40)

Hebrews 11 resembles other Jewish lists of scriptural heroes presented as examples of moral and spiritual qualities for readers to emulate.[21] The list in Hebrews differs from these by including several explicit references to women heroes of faith: Sarah (11:11); Rahab (11:31); and "women who received their dead by resurrection" (11:35). (See Text Box: "Jewish Lists of Heroic Women.") There is also an implicit reference to the mother of Moses in a mention of his "parents" (11:23), and a passing reference to Pharaoh's daughter (11:24). Ruth Hoppin sees the presence of women in this chapter as evidence of female authorship, concluding, rather exaggeratedly, that "the presence of women is pervasive. . . . Their influence is in all cases noble, their deeds essential in God's providential

---

19. Ibid.
20. Ibid.
21. E.g., Sir 44:1–49:16; Wis 10:1-21; 4 Macc 18:6-24; 4 Ezra 7:106–11.

¹ Now faith is the assurance of things hoped for, the conviction of things not seen. ² Indeed, by faith our ancestors received approval. ³ By faith we understand that the worlds were prepared by the word of God, so that what is seen was made from things that are not visible.

⁴ By faith Abel offered to God a more acceptable sacrifice than Cain's. Through this he received approval as righteous, God himself giving approval

A Mother's Discourse on Martyred Heroes (4 Macc 18:7-24)

The mother of seven sons expressed also these principles to her children: "I was a pure virgin and did not go outside my father's house; but I guarded the rib from which woman was made. No seducer corrupted me on a desert plain, nor did the destroyer, the deceitful serpent, defile the purity of my virginity. In the time of my maturity I remained with my husband, and when these sons had grown up their father died. A happy man was he, who lived out his life with good children, and did not have the grief of bereavement. While he was still with you, he taught you the law and the prophets. He read to you about Abel slain by Cain, and Isaac who was offered as a burnt offering, and about Joseph in prison. He told you of the zeal of Phinehas, and he taught you about Hananiah, Azariah, and Mishael in the fire.

"He praised Daniel in the den of the lions and blessed him. He reminded you of the scripture of Isaiah, which says, 'Even though you go through the fire, the flame shall not consume you.' He sang to you songs of the psalmist David, who said, 'Many are the afflictions of the righteous.' He recounted to you Solomon's proverb, 'There is a tree of life for those who do his will.' He confirmed the query of Ezekiel, 'Shall these dry bones live?' For he did not forget to teach you the song that Moses taught, which says, 'I kill and I make alive: this is your life and the length of your days.'"

O bitter was that day—and yet not bitter—when that bitter tyrant of the Greeks quenched fire with fire in his cruel caldrons, and in his burning rage brought those seven sons of the daughter of Abraham to the catapult and back again to more tortures, pierced the pupils of their eyes and cut out their tongues, and put them to death with various tortures. For these crimes divine justice pursued and will pursue the accursed tyrant. But the sons of Abraham with their victorious mother are gathered together into the chorus of the fathers, and have received pure and immortal souls from God, to whom be glory forever and ever. Amen. (NRSV)

to his gifts; he died, but through his faith he still speaks. [5]By faith Enoch was taken so that he did not experience death; and "he was not found, because God had taken him." For it was attested before he was taken away that "he had pleased God." [6]And without faith it is impossible to please God, for whoever would approach him must believe that he exists and that he rewards those who seek him. [7]By faith Noah, warned by God about events as yet unseen, respected the warning and built an ark to save his household; by this he condemned the world and became an heir to the righteousness that is in accordance with faith.

[8]By faith Abraham obeyed when he was called to set out for a place that he was to receive as an inheritance; and

---

Jewish Lists of Heroic Women

In Jewish tradition a list of women prophets and their accomplishments is found in the Talmud (Meg. 14a):

> Our rabbis taught: "Forty-eight prophets and seven prophetesses prophesied to Israel. . . . Seven prophetesses. Who were these?— Sarah, Miriam, Deborah, Hannah, Abigail, Huldah and Esther." . . .
>
> Sarah, as it is written [Gen. xi. 29]: "The father of Milcah and the father of Yiscah." And R. Itz'hak said: By Yiscah is meant Sarah. Why was she called Yiscah? Because that signifies seeing, and she was a seer through the Holy Spirit. Miriam, as it is written [Ex. xv. 26]: "Then took Miriam the prophetess, the sister of Aaron." Aaron's, and not Moses' sister? Said R. Na'aman in the name of Rabh: She had prophesied even when she had been yet but Aaron's sister, before Moses' birth, and she said: In the future my mother will give birth to a child that will deliver the Israelites. Finally, when Moses was born, the whole house was filled with light. And her father rose, and kissed her on her head, and said: Daughter, thy prophecy is fulfilled. Afterward, when he was cast into the river, the father asked: Daughter, what has become of thy prophecy? And this is what is written [ibid. ii. 4]: "And his sister placed herself afar off, to ascertain what would be done to him," i. e., to know what would be the end of her prophecy.
>
> Deborah, as it is written [Judges, iv. 4]: "And Deborah, a prophetess." Hannah, as it is written [I Sam. ii. I]: "And Hannah prayed and said, My heart is glad in the Lord, my horn is exalted through the Lord." My horn is exalted,

he set out, not knowing where he was going. ⁹By faith he stayed for a time in the land he had been promised, as in a foreign land, living in tents, as did Isaac and Jacob, who were heirs with him of the same promise. ¹⁰For he looked forward to the city that has foundations, whose architect and builder is God. ¹¹By faith he received power of procreation, even though he was too old—and Sarah herself was barren—because he considered him faithful who had promised. ¹²Therefore from one person, and this one as good as dead, descendants were born, "as many as the stars of heaven and as the innumerable grains of sand by the seashore."

¹³All of these died in faith without having received the promises, but from a distance they saw and greeted them.

and not my flask. David and Solomon, who were anointed with the horn, their dynasty endured; but Saul and Jehu, who were anointed with a flask, their dynasties did not last. . . .

Abigail, as it is written [I Sam. xxv. 31]: "And when the Lord will do good unto my lord." She prophesied that he would be king.

Huldah, as it is said [II Kings, xxii. 14]: "Huldah the prophetess."
And Esther, because it is written [Esther, v. 1]: "Esther put on royalty." It should be written, "royal apparel"? That means, she clothed herself in the Holy Spirit. . . .

"And it came to pass on the third day that Esther put on royalty" [v. 1]. Said R. Eleazar in the name of R. Ḥanina: From this we infer that she clothed herself in the Holy Spirit, as explained above. . . .

Another rabbinic text, *Midrash Eshet Chayil*, lists twenty biblical women who illustrate the qualities of the "woman of valor" of Prov 31:10-31: (1) the wife of Noah; (2) Sarah; (3) Rebekah; (4) Leah; (5) Rachel; (6) the daughter of Pharaoh; (7) Jochebed; (8) Miriam; (9) Hannah; (10) Jael; (11) the widow of Zarephath; (12) Rahab; (13) Bathsheba; (14) Michal; (15) the mother of Samson; (16) Elisheva, wife of Aaron; (17) the wise woman of 2 Sam 20:16; (18) the wife of Obadiah; (19) the Shunamite; (20) Ruth. Three of these—Sarah, Pharaoh's daughter, and Rahab—appear in Heb 11. (*Sources: Babylonian Talmud, Book 4: Tracts Pecharim, Yomah and Hagiga*, trans. Michael L. Rodkinson [New York: Talmud Society, 1918], 37–38; Shulamit Valler, "Who is ēšet ḥayil in Rabbinic Literature?" in *A Feminist Companion to Wisdom Literature*, ed. Athalya Brenner, FCB 9 [Sheffield: Sheffield Academic Press, 1995] 85–99.)

Mary Ann Beavis

They confessed that they were strangers and foreigners on the earth, [14]for people who speak in this way make it clear that they are seeking a homeland. [15]If they had been thinking of the land that they had left behind, they would have had opportunity to return. [16]But as it is, they desire a better country, that is, a heavenly one. Therefore God is not ashamed to be called their God; indeed, he has prepared a city for them.

[17]By faith Abraham, when put to the test, offered up Isaac. He who had received the promises was ready to offer up his only son, [18]of whom he had been told, "It is through Isaac that descendants shall be named for you." [19]He considered the fact that God is able even to raise someone from the dead—and figuratively speaking, he did receive him back. [20]By faith Isaac invoked blessings for the future on Jacob and Esau. [21]By faith Jacob, when dying, blessed each of the sons of Joseph, "bowing in worship over the top of his staff." [22]By faith Joseph, at

activity, their faith a touchstone."[22] Although the other scriptural catalogues of heroes do not include women, it should be noted that the account of heroic martyrs in 4 Maccabees is narrated by the mother of seven martyred sons, who herself dies upholding Torah.

In Wis 10:1–11:1, divine Sophia is portrayed as the salvific driving force behind the sacred history from Adam to the exodus;[23] the repetition of the pronoun "she" (αὐτή) emphasizes *her* heroic role in strengthening, guiding, and rescuing the righteous: "*She* entered the soul of a servant of the Lord. . . . *She* gave to holy people the reward of their labors. . . . *She* brought them over the Red Sea" (Wis 10:16a, 17, 18). As Thompson notes, the repetition of "she" in Wis 10 is similar to the use of the introductory formula "by faith" in almost every verse of Heb 11 (vv. 3, 4, 5, 7, 8, 9, 11, 17, 20, 21, 22, 23, 24, 27, 29, 30, 31).[24] The formula "by faith," borrowed from the prophetic quotation in 10:38 ("but my righteous one will live *by faith*"; Hab 2:3), precedes the announcement of the theme of the chapter in 10:39: "But we are not among those who shrink back and so are lost, but among those who have *faith* and so are saved." The homilist cites the heroes and heroines of chapter 11 as examples of these

22. Ruth Hoppin, *Priscilla's Letter: Finding the Author of the Epistle to the Hebrew* (Fort Bragg, CA: Lost Coast Press, 1997), 48.

23. Following from the reference to those who were "saved by wisdom" in Wis 9:18; see also 10:4, 9, 15, 21.

24. Thompson, *Hebrews*, 227.

the end of his life, made mention of the exodus of the Israelites and gave instructions about his burial.

²³By faith Moses was hidden by his parents for three months after his birth, because they saw that the child was beautiful; and they were not afraid of the king's edict. ²⁴By faith Moses, when he was grown up, refused to be called a son of Pharaoh's daughter, ²⁵choosing rather to share ill-treatment with the people of God than to enjoy the fleeting pleasures of sin. ²⁶He considered abuse suffered for the Christ to be greater wealth than the treasures of Egypt, for he was looking ahead to the reward. ²⁷By faith he left Egypt, unafraid of the king's anger; for he persevered as though he saw him who is invisible. ²⁸By faith he kept the Passover and the sprinkling of blood, so that the destroyer of the firstborn would not touch the firstborn of Israel.

²⁹By faith the people passed through the Red Sea as if it were dry land, but when the Egyptians attempted to do so

qualities of courage and faith for the addressees to follow on their journey to salvation (see also 12:22-24).

Apart from their utility as exemplars of these virtues, it is difficult to discern the reasons why the homilist included—or omitted—the specific figures cited in the chapter. Pamela Eisenbaum opines that they share three general characteristics:

> (1) Near-death experience: Noah would have perished in the flood; Moses would have died as an infant; (2) Ability to see the future and act faithfully in light of that knowledge: Noah receives an oracle about the flood and builds the ark; Abraham receives a promise about Isaac, and very late in his life that promise is realized; (3) Alienation: The heroes are portrayed as alienated from the people of their generation: Abraham lives in the land "as if in a foreign land," and Moses was not really one of his people, because he was raised by Pharaoh's daughter.²⁵

She further notes that this chapter lays the groundwork for later Christian interpretation of the Hebrew Scriptures, since the heroes are portrayed as alienated from Israel, either because they are depicted as outsiders in some way or because they are actually non-Israelites.²⁶

Eisenbaum is right insofar as these figures are treated as "honorary Christians" by virtue of their status as spiritual ancestors of followers of

25. Pamela Eisenbaum, *The Jewish Heroes of Christian History: Hebrews 11 in Literary Context* (Atlanta, GA: Scholars Press, 1997), 420.

26. Ibid.

they were drowned. [30]By faith the walls of Jericho fell after they had been encircled for seven days. [31]By faith Rahab the prostitute did not perish with those who were disobedient, because she had received the spies in peace.

[32]And what more should I say? For time would fail me to tell of Gideon, Barak, Samson, Jephthah, of David and Samuel and the prophets—[33]who through faith conquered kingdoms, administered justice, obtained promises, shut the mouths of lions, [34]quenched raging fire, escaped the edge of the sword, won strength out of weakness, became mighty in war, put foreign armies to flight. [35]Women received their dead by resurrection. Others were tor-

Jesus, whether Jewish or non-Jewish, but in fact most of them are alienated not from Israel but from the unrighteous people of their times: the pre-Israelite Noah from the "condemned" nations of the world (11:7); Abraham from the Canaanite nations of the promised land (11:9). Moses is alienated not from the "people of God," with whom he chooses to suffer, but from the Egyptians, represented by his foster mother, Pharaoh's daughter (11:24-37). All of them, Israelite and non-Israelite, are "strangers and foreigners on the earth" (11:13) who faithfully yearned for the promised heavenly inheritance and acted courageously (see also 11:32-38). Significantly, forms of the word "witness" or "martyr" (μάρτυς) recur at the beginning and end of the chapter (Heb 11:2, 4, 5, 39; see also 12:1).

As discussed in the introduction to this commentary, the claim of christian identity—not as determined or predestined as the chosen race or belonging to a certain group in a certain location, but as belonging to those whose faith witnesses beyond their Jewishness or Gentile-ness—is one of the most crucial themes throughout Hebrews. Interestingly, such a claim is integral to the notion of pilgrims and a sense of diaspora in which Noah, Abraham, and Moses are listed by the homilist as examples of faith. All of them have lived out the life of diaspora, a life of being forced (by flood or slavery or divine call) to leave their homeland, make their homes in foreign lands, and never return to their original homes. In a world in which migration is a constant and ever-increasing reality, the intention of the homilist to emphasize the examples of diaspora faith here seems appealing and can bear relevant insights for contemporary readers. Many Asian North American theologians conjure up theologies of journey, pilgrimage, and diaspora that capture their experiences of being "strangers and foreigners on the earth" (Heb 11:13). Jung-Young

tured, refusing to accept release, in order to obtain a better resurrection. [36]Others suffered mocking and flogging, and even chains and imprisonment. [37]They were stoned to death, they were sawn in two, they were killed by the sword; they went about in skins of sheep and goats, destitute, persecuted, tormented—[38]of whom the world was not worthy. They wandered in deserts and mountains, and in caves and holes in the ground.

[39]Yet all these, though they were commended for their faith, did not receive what was promised, [40]since God had provided something better so that they would not, apart from us, be made perfect.

Lee writes: "I was a stranger in the land where I now hold my citizenship. . . . People still ask, 'When will you go back to your homeland?'"[27] Paul M. Nagano shares a similar experience, "An American citizen, I was stripped of my rights . . . uprooted from my home . . . treated as an 'enemy alien' . . . being interned in America's concentration camps during World War II."[28] Their diaspora and alienating experiences are indeed part of being marginalized, which, nonetheless, constitutes a vantage point. Peter C. Phan articulates this experience: "Belonging to both worlds and cultures, marginal(ized) persons have the opportunity to fuse them together . . . so that persons at the margins stand not only between these two worlds and cultures but also *beyond* them." He calls it a "theology betwixt and between," a theology that enables people to do the thinking religiously from both sides of the boundaries while not falling into the trap of imagining one has a monopoly on the search for truth.[29] Elsewhere he elaborates this experience as "the experience of migration as source of intercultural theology."[30] The following generations of young Asian North American scholars further articulate this kind of theology with concepts such as "diasporic hybridity in this land

27. Jung-Young Lee, "A Life In-Between: A Korean-American Journey," in *Journeys at the Margin: Toward an Autobiographical Theology in American-Asian Perspective*, ed. Peter C. Phan and Jung Young Lee (Collegeville, MN: Liturgical Press, 1999), 23–39, at 39.

28. Paul M. Nagano, "A Japanese-American Pilgrimage: Theological Reflections," in Phan and Lee, *Journeys at the Margin*, 76, 79.

29. Peter C. Phan, "Betwixt and Between: Doing Theology with Memory and Imagination," in Phan and Lee, *Journeys at the Margin*, 113–34, at 113–14.

30. Peter C. Phan, *Christianity with an Asian Face: Asian American Theology in the Making* (Maryknoll, NY: Orbis Books, 2003), 3–25.

of exile,"[31] "enchanting diasporas,"[32] and "revealing the Sacred in Asian and Pacific America."[33]

Although relatively few women heroes are celebrated in this chapter, in keeping with the feminist mandate of this commentary they will be highlighted and their roles amplified in the comments that follow. The discourse begins with the famous line, "Now faith is the substance of things hoped for, the evidence of things not seen" (Heb 11:1, AV); the term translated "our ancestors" by the NRSV in 11:2 is οἱ πρεσβύτεροι, "our elders," who received divine approval through their faith. The term "elders" has the implication of trusted authorities responsible for the transmission of sacred tradition;[34] in this case "faith" (πίστις) refers not only to an attitude of trust but also to a quality of steadfastness (or faithfulness) in the face of difficulty and a mode of insight into the invisible, spiritual realm (11:3). The reference to the divine preparation of the worlds by the "word of God" (ῥήματι θεοῦ) prepares for the homilist's review of sacred history by alluding to the Priestly creation account (Gen 1:1–2:4a; see also Heb 1:2-3; Wis 7:25-26).

The first three exemplars of faith are the primordial figures of Abel (Gen 4:1-16), Enoch (Gen 5:21-24), and Noah (Gen 6:9–9:28). Perhaps not surprisingly, Abel's parents, Adam and Eve, are left off the list, since their disobedience is the theme of Gen 2–3. Abel, their second son, is murdered by his elder brother Cain, due to the superior quality of the younger brother's sacrifice. The homilist does not actually mention the fratricide but emphasizes God's "witness" to Abel's righteousness, and God's "witness" of Abel's offerings. The reference to Abel's faith, still speaking despite his death (11:4; see also 12:24), alludes to Gen 4:10, where God hears the slain brother's blood crying out to him from his grandmother the earth (see also Gen 2:7). Matthew 23:35 (see also Luke 11:51) cites Abel as the first in a long line of Israelite martyrs.[35] The book of Wisdom attributes the murder of Abel to Cain's departure from the ways of Sophia (10:3). Enoch, who according to Genesis "walked with God; then he was no more, because God took him" (Gen 5:14), was popularly believed

---

31. Julius-Kei Kato, *How Immigrant Christians Living in Mixed Cultures Interpret Their Religion: Asian-American Diasporic Hybridity and Its Implications for Hermeneutics* (Lewiston, NY: Edwin Mellen Press, 2012), 177.

32. David Kyuman Kim, "Enchanting Diasporas, Asian Americans, and Passionate Attachment of Race," in *Revealing the Sacred in Asian and Pacific America*, ed. Jane Naomi Iwamura and Paul Spickard (New York: Routledge, 2003), 327–40.

33. Iwamuri and Spickard, *Revealing the Sacred*.

34. See BDAG 862.

35. See also T. Ab. 11.

never to have died but to have been exalted directly to heaven because of his righteousness; according to Sir 44:16: "Enoch pleased the Lord and was taken up, an example of repentance to all generations" (see also Sir 48:12). Again, the homilist uses the language of martyrdom or "witness" to describe him: "For it was attested [μεμαρτύρηται] before he was taken away that 'he had pleased God'" (Heb 11:5). To the homilist the reference to Enoch pleasing God implies that he had faith, meaning belief in God's existence and confidence that God "rewards those who seek him" (11:6). Noah is also an example of faith in the unseen: in this case the divine warning of cosmic destruction through the flood; true to the values espoused by the homilist, Noah thereby "condemned the world" and inherited righteousness (11:7). Like Enoch, Noah is a figure admired in the Wisdom tradition: "When the earth was flooded because of him [Cain], wisdom again saved it, steering the righteous man by a paltry piece of wood" (Wis 10:4; see also Wis 14:6-7; Sir 44:17-18).

From a feminist standpoint the next figure in the homilist's list of heroes of faith, Abraham, is a severely flawed character due to his many deficiencies as a husband and father: he passes his wife off to foreign kings as his sister (which, in fact, she is, according to Gen 20:12) because he fears they will kill him so they can add her to their harems (Gen 12:10-20; 20:1-18); he allows his concubine Hagar to be driven out of his household twice, once when she is pregnant with their son, the second time permanently, along with the child (Gen 16:1-14; 21:1-20); without protest, he is willing to sacrifice his younger son, Isaac (Gen 22:1-19; see also Heb 11:17-20). Although he is cited as an example of faith here and elsewhere in the NT,[36] he has little confidence in God's promise of a son through Sarah (Gen 17:19). As the vaunted common ancestor of the so-called Abrahamic religions of Judaism, Christianity, and Islam, he falls far short. For Hebrews, however, he is paradigmatic because of his willingness to live as a stranger in the hope of a promised inheritance, which is not a geographical territory, "for he looked forward to the city that has foundations, whose architect and builder is God" (Heb 11:10). With Abel, Enoch, and Noah, Abraham and Sarah (see below) and their faithful progeny (11:9) were foreigners on earth who sought a homeland in "a better country, that is, a heavenly one" (11:16), content to die "in faith" without achieving the celestial city (11:13, 16).

The reference to Sarah appears near the end of the homilist's paean to the faith of Abraham, in Heb 11:11. The NRSV, rather awkwardly, makes

---

36. See also Rom 4:3, 9, 16; Gal 3:8, 9, 14; Jas 2:23; for Abraham as a paragon of wisdom, see Sir 44:19-21; the hero list in Wis 10:6-10 skips from Lot to Jacob.

A Jewish Perspective
(Heb 11:8-10, 17-19)

Hebrews 11:8-10, 17-19 praises Abraham, the father of the Jewish people. This commentary is rather harsh with him because of his alleged moral failings; so, indeed, are many Jewish thinkers and teachers in our time. At the same time, it is a commonplace of Jewish Torah study today that Scripture does not present us with flawless individuals but with human beings like ourselves. The same consideration applies to the men listed in 11:32, including the beloved King David, summarily dismissed by this commentary.

I am particularly taken aback at this commentary's choice to blame Abraham for allowing his concubine Hagar to be driven from his house, without mentioning that the impetus for driving her out comes from Sarah—who had insisted on Abraham's taking Hagar as his concubine in the first place (Gen 16:1-3). Further, God backs up Sarah's demand to drive out Hagar and her son, telling the distressed Abraham, "whatever Sarah says to you, do as she tells you" (Gen 21:12). The commentary likewise faults Abraham for doubting God's promise of a son to Sarah, though Sarah herself is so skeptical of this promise as to laugh at it (Gen 18:10-15). The women and men of the Torah are not one-dimensional models of virtue but believable human beings coping with the complex challenges of life and the unpredictable ways of a loving but terrifyingly inscrutable God.

In terms of the logic of Hebrews itself, it would make little sense if the heroes of faith, models for the Christian reader, were plaster saints. It makes sense for them to be human beings with both strengths and weaknesses, who persevered in faith in spite of their own imperfection.

Justin Jaron Lewis

Abraham the subject of the sentence, so that *he* is the faithful recipient of the "power of procreation," relegating his wife to a parenthetical remark that "Sarah herself was barren." As the NRSV translators indicate in a footnote, the verse can also be translated in a way that emphasizes the matriarch's faith: "By faith Sarah herself, though barren, received the power to conceive, even when she was too old, because she considered him faithful who had promised." The reason for the choice to render Abraham, rather than Sarah, as the subject of the sentence is that the phrase translated "power of procreation" refers literally to the power to "deposit seed" (δύναμιν εἰς καταβολὴν σπέρματος ἔλαβεν). This translation presupposes the ancient view that only the male plays an active role in procreation by "depositing" seed in the incubator of the womb. The belief that women as well as men possessed fertile seed is, however, also well attested in antiquity (see "Translation Matters").

TRANSLATION MATTERS: HEB 11:11

The NRSV (like the popular NAB) prefers a translation of this verse that makes Abraham the subject:

By faith he [Abraham] received power of procreation, even though he was too old—and Sarah herself was barren—because he considered him faithful who had promised.

Many other English translations, however, make Sarah the model of faith, e.g.:

Sara herself received strength to conceive seed, and was delivered of a child when she was past age, because she judged him faithful who had promised. (AV)

And by faith even Sarah, who was past childbearing age, was enabled to bear children because she considered him faithful who had made the promise. (NIV)

By faith even Sarah herself received power to conceive seed when she was past age, since she counted him faithful who had promised. (ASV)

Sarah herself received ability to conceive, even beyond the proper time of life, since she considered Him faithful who had promised. (NASB)

It was equally by faith that Sarah, in spite of being past the age, was made able to conceive, because she believed that he who had made the promise was faithful to it. (NJB)

An early Christian example of this interpretation is Ephrem the Syrian:

"By faith Sarah herself received the power to conceive, even when she was past the age." She who was barren gave birth—that is, received the powers and youth that were necessary to conception and bearing—even though her old age was unable to cope with these things. And all this happened to her because, in the midst of the pagan Canaanites, she "considered him faithful who had promised" to give her these things.[37]

The NRSV/NAB translation presupposes the Aristotelian notion that only men produced "seed" (σπέρμα), the active principle in procreation, and that women simply provided the "ground" for its planting. Many ancient physicians, however, held that procreation was achieved by the mingling of female and male seed;[38] early Christian writers who shared this view included John Chrysostom, Pseudo-Oecumenius, Theophylact, and Augustine.[39]

---

37. *Commentary on the Epistle to the Hebrews.* See Heen and Krey, *Ancient Christian Commentary*, 185.

38. Moisés Mayordomo Marin, "Construction of Masculinity in Antiquity and Early Christianity," *Lectio Difficilior* 2 (2006); http://www.lectio.unibe.ch/06_2/marin_construction.htm, accessed July 15, 2015.

39. For references, see Harold Attridge, *The Epistle to the Hebrews: A Commentary*, Hermeneia (Philadelphia: Fortress Press, 1989), 324 n. 53.

The hero list is interrupted by an exposition of the meaning of the ancestors' faith, which emphasizes the themes of promise, alienation from the earth, and the heavenly homeland of the celestial city (11:13-16). The homilist then returns to an incident in the story of Abraham that has been both extolled and deplored by subsequent interpreters:[40] the near-sacrifice of Isaac, known by Jews as the Aqedah ("binding"; Gen 22:1-19), interpreted in Torah as a "test" or "trial" of the patriarch (Gen 22:1). Hebrews' use of the story as an example of faith (11:17-19) is distinctive in that no similar interpretation appears in extra-biblical Jewish literature until the third century CE,[41] when Isaac's assent to the sacrifice (an element not found in Genesis) begins to be invoked as a model for Jewish martyrdom.[42] The Jewish New Year liturgy represents Abraham's willingness to sacrifice Isaac as meritorious.[43] Nevertheless, some contemporary Jewish literature is much more critical of the story, interpreting it as an "ugly metaphor" of intergenerational abuse.[44] Carol Delaney sees the Aqedah as the founding myth of patriarchy, in which the father's authority to sacrifice his child is presupposed and interpreted as a noble act; she invites readers to imagine how society would have evolved if protection of children rather than the willingness to sacrifice them had been the model of faith.[45] Like some later Jewish interpreters, the homilist softens the impact of the story by imagining that Abraham believed in God's power to resurrect his son: "and, figuratively speaking, he did receive him back" (Heb 11:19; see also 11:35a). Several feminist poets have reimagined the story from Sarah's perspective,[46] a move anticipated by the midrashic legend that Sarah died of grief when she heard about it (*Midrash Mishle* 31).[47]

40. See, e.g., W. Gunther Plaut, *The Torah: A Modern Commentary* (New York: Union of American Hebrew Congregations, 1981), 145, 152–54; Mary Ann Beavis, "The Aqedah, Jephtha's Daughter, and the Theme of Child Sacrifice in the Work of Canadian Women Authors," in *Feminist Theology with a Canadian Accent: Canadian Perspectives on Contextual Feminist Theology*, ed. Mary Ann Beavis, with Elaine Guillemin and Barbara Pell (Ottawa: Novalis, 2007), 353–70, at 354–55.

41. See Philip R. Davies and Bruce D. Chilton, "The Aqedah: A Revised Tradition History," *CBQ* 40 (1978): 514–46.

42. Ibid., 536.

43. Ibid., 533.

44. Michael Brown, "Biblical Myth and Contemporary Experience: The *Akedah* in Modern Jewish Literature," *Judaism* 31 (1982): 99–111.

45. Carol Delaney, *Abraham on Trial: The Social Legacy of Biblical Myth* (Princeton, NJ: Princeton University Press, 1998), 253.

46. See, e.g., Tamara Cohn Eskenazi and Andrea L. Weiss, eds., *The Torah: A Women's Commentary* (New York: Women of Reformed Judaism, 2008), 110.

47. Cited by Plaut, *Torah*, 159, 1699.

Hagar as Model of Faith

It is instructive to reconsider the Aqedah (Heb 11:17-19) from the perspective of the slave-concubine Hagar, a figure whose life was even more dramatic and painful than Sarah's. An archetype of womanist theology, as developed by Katie Cannon, Jacquelyn Grant, and Delores Williams, Hagar has been the most prominent figure identified with African American women's communities from the nineteenth century until today.[48] The faithful persistence of the people of God in the face of difficulty, persecution, and uncertainty, an underlying theme in this section, can perhaps not be spoken more truthfully of any biblical figure than of Hagar. Ishmael, the son of Hagar, is Abraham's firstborn, בכור, worthy of God's blessings, ברכות, so the story of Hagar and Ishmael belongs as intrinsically to the grand narrative of God's salvation as the binding of Isaac. Although her narrative, or the lack thereof, in Hebrews and elsewhere makes the history of salvation complicated, it is still one of great value.[49]

HyeRan Kim-Cragg

The next three verses (Heb 11:20-22; see also 11:9) present a highly selective list of Abraham's faithful male descendants through Isaac, focusing on Isaac's younger son Jacob and Jacob's son by Rachel, Joseph. Isaac's blessing on his twin sons, Jacob and Esau, is mentioned with reference to "the future" (11:20), but Esau's faith is not mentioned; in the next chapter Esau is dismissed as "an immoral and godless person, who sold his birthright for a single meal" (12:16). Jacob's deathbed blessing of Joseph's two sons "by faith" is mentioned (see also Gen 48:21), but the patriarch's blessings of his other eleven sons are overlooked (Heb 11:21; see also Gen 49:1-28; Sir 44:22-23). Both Genesis and Hebrews ignore Dinah, the daughter of Jacob and Leah (Gen 30:21; 46:15), in the account of the blessings. The feature that seems to qualify Jacob and Joseph as exemplars of faith is that both of them prophesy that the Israelites will return to their ancestral land (Gen 48:21; 50:24); both insist that their bones be returned to Canaan for burial (Gen 50:5, 25; see also Heb 11:22).

---

48. Williams, *Sisters in the Wilderness*, 245.

49. Elsa Tamez, "The Woman Who Complicated the History of Salvation," in *New Eyes for Reading*, ed. John S. Pobee and Bärbel von Wartenberg-Potter (Oak Park, IL: Meyer Stone Books, 1986), 5–17, at 14.

Jewish Feminist Interpretations of the Aqedah

The Canadian Jewish poet Elizabeth Brewster reimagines the Aqedah from Sarah's perspective, beginning with the observation that "Sarah would never have consented to sacrificing Isaac" and speculating that she "perhaps felt a thrill of sympathy for Hagar and that other boy, mixed with fury at God and Abraham." The Israeli-Canadian writer Edeet Ravel reflects on the meaning of the Aqedah through a biblical anecdote related in her novel *Ten Thousand Lovers*:

The sacrifice of children was a common practice in ancient times. At a certain point, though, it no longer seemed the right thing to do. This emerging view is taken up by the Bible, which stipulates that the sacrifice of children will no longer be permitted. To make its point, the Bible presents a morality play, an enactment of this new Thou Shalt Not. That way you can actually see the prohibition acted out, you have a story to help you understand it and remember it and internalize it. You don't just get a statement, as you do with all the other laws, because this thing . . . is the one thing (the Bible seems to be saying) you can really stop doing.

In the story God tells Abraham to sacrifice his child and Abraham gets ready to obey: he builds an altar, he ties up his child, he puts his child on the altar, and he raises his hand to slay his child. But the angel of God calls to him from heaven and says: "Do not bring your hand down upon the child." Here it is. You can see it: it's very clear. A child on the altar, a knife in the air, an angel saying no. Do not bring down your hand on the child.

(*Sources*: Elizabeth Brewster, *Burning Bush* [Toronto: Oberon Press, 2000], 65, 66; Edeet Ravel, *Ten Thousand Lovers* [London: Review, 2003], 372–73.)

Mary Ann Beavis

In contrast to the earlier argument that Jesus is superior to Moses (3:1-19), here Moses is held up as a paradigm of faith from his birth to the crossing of the Red Sea (11:23-29). The role of Moses' mother and sister in fearlessly shielding him "by faith" from "the king's edict" (and that of the midwives who refused to kill the newborn Hebrew boys) is obscured by the use of the term "parents," literally "fathers" (πατέρων) (Heb 11:23). In Jewish tradition, Moses' sister Miriam is said to have prophesied that a deliverer who would lead Israel to freedom would be born of her parents.[50]

TRANSLATION MATTERS

Some ancient manuscripts of Hebrews add another sentence after v. 23: "By faith Moses, when he was grown up, killed the Egyptian, because he observed the humiliation of his people" (αδελφων, literally, "brothers"). This interpolation would make more sense after v. 26, which refers to Moses' fearlessness in the face of the king's anger, provoked by his murder of an Egyptian. In Exodus, Moses' killing the Egyptian and flight to Midian take place immediately after the story of his rescue from the Nile by the princess (Exod 2:5-15).

Similarly, the role of Pharaoh's daughter, a figure extolled in later Jewish literature and given the name *Batya* ("daughter of God"; Lev. Rab. 1:3) for rescuing the infant from the Nile and adopting him, is minimized. In Hebrews, Moses' faith is illustrated by his refusal to be called her son (11:24).

In Islam the woman who rescues Moses from the Nile is called Aasiyaa and is said to be Pharaoh's wife, not his daughter. In the Hadith (sayings of Mohammed) she is known as one of four great women, with the Virgin Mary, Kadijah (the prophet's first wife), and Fatima (the prophet's daughter).

For the homilist, Moses' heroism resides in his self-sacrifice (11:25-26a), in anticipation of the future salvation effected through the messiah ("Christ"). Pamela Eisenbaum observes that "it is unlikely the author means that Moses envisioned Christ; rather he projects the current situation onto the past";[51] however, in view of Moses' reputation as a prophet it seems likely that the homilist would regard him as inspired by a vision of Christ, "looking ahead to the reward" (11:26). Hebrews' portrayal of the early career of Moses as a fearless visionary who gives up the wealth of Egypt to share in the suffering of his people for the sake of "him who is invisible" (11:27) is at variance with the story in Exodus, where Pharaoh's rage is provoked by Moses' murder of an Egyptian, and the flawed hero, "afraid," flees because "he [Pharaoh] sought to kill Moses" (Exod

---

50. Exod. Rab. 1.26; b. Soṭah 12b-13a.
51. Pamela Eisenbaum, "Hebrews," in *The Jewish Annotated New Testament*, ed. Amy-Jill Levine and Marc Zvi Brettler (New York: Oxford University Press, 2011), 422 n. 26.

2:11-15). Hebrews 11:27, however, notes that Moses was "unafraid of the king's anger." The next two verses (Heb 11:28-29) round off the Moses story with reference to the first Passover (Exod 12:1-28; 12:43–13:10) and the crossing of the Red Sea (Exod 14:1-31, tales that juxtapose violence and liberation: the firstborn of Israel are spared, but the Egyptian firstborn are destroyed; the Israelites cross the seabed and are saved, but when the Egyptians follow, they drown.

Postcolonial biblical and literary feminist scholars draw our attention to this theological dilemma, "one's (Hebrew) life is saved at the expense of killing the others (Canaanites)," violence versus liberation, sanctioned by the Judeo-Christian God YHWH. Many First Nations scholars call for a reading from the other side. For Robert Allen Warrior the exodus is a narrative of genocide against the inhabitants of Canaan for the sake of liberating the former slaves of Egypt.[52] Unfortunately, the God whom the European colonialists worshiped also sanctioned the sailing of merchant ships for the conquest of the First Nations, the original inhabitants of the Americas (North, Central, and South). Laura Donaldson, a biblical scholar of Cherokee descent, critically discloses an ugly colonial history when she examines the exodus story, illustrating both colonialist and anticolonialist characteristics embedded in Exodus as well as how nationalism and ethnocentrism are entangled in the story of Moses, who is called to his leadership role by a warrior Lord.[53] In their quest for liberty and freedom (the founding ethos of nation building for both the United States and Canada), European settlers stole native people's lives, liberty, and dignity. While critically examining liberation theologies (e.g., *minjung* theology and African American theology), and at the same time recognizing the Bible's ambivalent and contradictory nature, I have argued in *Story and Song* that the Canaanite side of the story should be taken seriously in order to investigate the dangerous tie between Western imperialism and Christian texts that allows certain groups to dominate others.[54] Instead of reading the Passover and the crossing of the Red Sea (Heb 11:28-29) as parallel stories, unrelated to each other, we as contem-

52. Robert Allen Warrior, "A Native American Perspective: Canaanites, Cowboys, and Indians," in *Voices from the Margin: Interpreting the Bible in the Third World*, ed. R. S. Sugirtharajah (Maryknoll, NY: Orbis Books, 1991), 287–95, at 279.

53. Laura E. Donaldson, *Decolonizing Feminisms: Race, Gender, and Empire-Building* (Chapel Hill: University of North Carolina Press, 1992), 102–17.

54. HyeRan Kim-Cragg, *Story and Song: A Postcolonial Interplay between Christian Education and Worship* (New York: Peter Lang, 2012), 32.

porary readers should be able to read and treat them as two sides of one coin, a story of deliverance and conquest, with attentiveness to all the complexities involved. Warrior's warning is alarming: "As long as people believe in the Yahweh of deliverance, the world will not be safe from Yahweh the conqueror."[55]

Our Stories Are Our Scripture
For Hebrews 11

Just Another Dog Tale

Back when dogs spoke up at
   meetings were polite hung
   tails up back wall of council
   lodge ever a ruckus

Usual yappy small dogs big dog
   growls intimidate so dogs
   cower cringe made sure later
   to lie how other

Dogs were "told off good" even
   brags about important things
   said as if they were chief
   celebrity that

Time then Nanabush played
   trick set fire so much smoke
   in panic dog delegates
   grabbed tails to this day

Mix up must be reconciled that
   is why when strange dogs
   meet first thing they do is
   check out if proper

Dog is wearing proper tail sniff
   backside but careful not all
   dogs have original owned
   designated tails

Annharte

The rehearsal of the Moses-Exodus narrative is followed by a brief reference to the fall of the walls of Jericho "by faith" (11:30). The only hero of the book of Joshua mentioned in the list is "Rahab the prostitute" (Josh 2:1-21; 6:17), who is saved "by faith" because of her peaceable reception of the Israelite spies. As Carol Mosser notes, the homilist's singling out of Rahab is surprising, especially when figures like Joshua and Caleb are left out: "The great captain of the conquest has deliberately been passed over. A Canaanite prostitute stands in his place."[56] Moreover, she is placed deliberately at the "climactic center" of the hero list; the rapid summary of Israelite history from Judges to the exile that follows (11:32-40) is its denouement. Mosser's explanation is that there is

---

55. Warrior, "Native American Perspective," 251.
56. Carol Mosser, "Rahab Outside the Camp," in *The Epistle to the Hebrews and Christian Theology*, ed. Richard Bauckham, Daniel R. Driver, Trevor A. Hart, and Nathan MacDonald (Grand Rapids, MI: Eerdmans, 2009), 383–404, at 394.

something about Rahab's situation that has a greater relevance to the addressees than any of the other heroes; in particular, she "left the camp" of Jericho and abandoned it to destruction (see also Heb 13:13). Mosser regards this as an exhortation to the audience to flee pre-70 Jerusalem to save themselves from the Roman onslaught.[57] This hypothesis seems overly literal in view of the homilist's preference for the heavenly city over earthly existence (Heb 11:10, 16; 12:22; 13:14). It is more likely that Rahab's belief in the inevitability of Israel's conquest of the land (see also Josh 2:10) and her abandonment of a city fated for destruction (see also Heb 12:25-28) explain why she is singled out as an example by the homilist, who envisions a celestial promised land as the hoped-for destination of the audience (Heb 11:6).

Unquestionably, Rahab is highly extolled in Hebrews and elsewhere in the Bible as well as through early Jewish and Christian traditions (see box: "By Faith Rahab"). She is, however, a problematic figure, to say the least, in postcolonial feminist circles. Musa Dube, among the chief postcolonial New Testament scholars, characterizes the story of Rahab as "a script about the domestication of the promised land. She reflects the colonizer's desire to enter and domesticate the land of Canaan."[58] Laura Donaldson, using her critical indigenous lens, sees Rahab's story as the Israelite version of Pocahontas. In the narrative of the colonization of America, Pocahontas served as an example of a good Indian woman who accepted, legitimated, and facilitated the settlement of Europeans. Rahab, Donaldson feels, serves the same role in the story of the conquest of the promised land. Another Cherokee scholar, Rayna Green, coins the term "Pocahontas Perplex."[59] This "perplex" can be applied to other biblical women. Orpah, for example, is often demonized as the bad Moabite who did not turn to God as did Rahab or her sister-in-law Ruth. The biblical texts that venerate Rahab's faith may, Donaldson warns, be in danger of becoming rhetoric that "displace[s] questions of colonialism, racism, and their concomitant violence."[60] This warning, if taken seriously, may help guide us to "the unsettling place of questioning some of the foundational myths that [we] cherish and hold dear to [our] hearts, such as the exodus,

57. Ibid., 403–4.

58. Musa Dube, *Postcolonial Feminist Interpretation of the Bible* (St. Louis, MO: Chalice Press, 2000), 77.

59. Kwok Pui-lan, *Postcolonial Imagination and Feminist Theology* (Louisville, KY: Westminster John Knox, 2005), 117.

60. Donaldson, *Decolonizing Feminisms*, 62.

By Faith Rahab

In early Jewish and Christian tradition Rahab is remembered as a hero, proselyte, and ancestor (Sifre Num. 78; Num. Rab. 8; Jas 2:25). Not only is she mentioned in Matthew's genealogy of Jesus (Matt 1:5), but she is counted as a foremother of the prophets Jeremiah, Ezekiel, and Huldah (b. Meg. 14b; Midr. Shemuel, cited in *Jewish Encyclopedia*, <http://www.jewishencyclopedia.com/articles/12535-rahab> [February 13, 2012]). In early Christian literature she is often portrayed as a type of the church, e.g.:

> Rahab, who is a type of the church, suspended the scarlet thread from her window as a sign of salvation, to show that the nations would be saved through the Lord's passion. . . . The house of Rahab and all those with her were saved through the scarlet sign when Jericho was destroyed and burned and its king, a type of the devil, slain. So when this world is destroyed by fire and the devil who now has dominion over the world is overthrown, no one will be preserved for eternal salvation if that one is not found inside the house of the ecclesia which is marked with the scarlet sign, that is, with the blood of Christ.

(*Source*: Gregory of Elvia, quoted in Origen's *Tractate on the Books of Holy Scripture* 139; Heen and Krey, *Ancient Christian Commentary*, 202; other examples include Theodoret of Cyr, *Interpretation of Hebrews* 11; Irenaeus, *Haer.* 4.20.12; Hilary of Poitiers, *Tractate of the Mysteries* 2.9.154–56.)

Mary Ann Beavis

the covenant, the promised land, and the chosen people," all of which are pertinent and integral to the themes of Hebrews.[61]

If Rahab is the climactic figure in the heroes list, the other "heroes" cited briefly in the next verse are anticlimactic to the feminist reader: the weak and hesitant Gideon (Judg 6:11-18, 36-40); Barak, who refuses to confront the army of Sisera without the prophet-judge Deborah at his side and whose victory is secured by the hand of the woman Jael (Judg 4–5); the lustful and selfish Samson (Judg 14–16); Jephthah, who foolishly vows to sacrifice his daughter (Judg 11:1-40); David, a treacherous and adulterous husband and negligent father (2 Sam 3:13-16; 6:23; 11:2-27; 13–18); his changeable and manipulative mentor Samuel (1 Sam 10:1; 11:14-15; 13:8-14; 15:10-35; see also 16:1-13); "and the prophets" (11:32). The homilist goes on to summarize their mighty deeds performed

---

61. Kwok, *Postcolonial Imagination*, 121.

"through faith" (διὰ πίστεως) (11:33-34), culminating in a reference to "women [who] received their dead by resurrection" (11:35a; see also 1 Kgs 17:17-24; 2 Kgs 4:18-37). The list of triumphs is followed by a lengthier list of the sufferings endured by the prophets of Israel: torture (e.g., 2 Macc 6:18–7:42); mocking; flogging; "chains and imprisonment" (e.g., Jer 37:11-21; 20:1-12; 2 Chr 16:7-10; 1 Kgs 22:24-27; 4 Macc 12:3 LXX); stoning (e.g., 2 Chr 24:20-21; Tertullian, *Scorpace* 8; see also 2 Kgs 21:13); being "sawn in two" (see also Mart. Isa. 5:11-14); death by the sword (e.g., Jer 2:30; 26:20-23; 1 Kgs 19:10, 14); wearing animal skins (e.g., 1 Kgs 19:13, 19; Zech 13:4; see also Matt 7:15); wandering in deserts, mountains, caves, and holes in the ground (e.g., Judg 6:2; 1 Sam 23:14; 1 Kgs 17:1-7; 19:3-9; 2 Kgs 2:25; 1 Macc 2:28, 31; 2 Macc 5:27; 10:6). Most of these sufferings are paralleled by accounts of early christian martyrs, including Jesus and John the Baptist: verbal abuse (e.g., Matt 27:29-31, 41-42; Luke 23:11), scourging (e.g., Matt 20:19; Acts 22:24; 2 Cor 11:24), imprisonment (see also Mark 1:16; 6:17; Acts 8:7; 9:2; 12:4-5; 16:23; 22:4; Rom 16:7; 2 Cor 11:23; Phil 1:9, 23), stoning (Acts 7:58-59; see also 14:9; 2 Cor 11:25), death by the sword (e.g., Acts 12:2), and enduring harsh conditions (e.g., 2 Cor 11:25-28). Several references indicate that the addressees had experienced such sufferings to some degree: abuse and persecution (Heb 10:33; 13:13), support of prisoners (10:34; 13:3), and torture (13:3), although they had not yet experienced bloodshed (12:4). The ancient heroes did not receive "what was promised," i.e., the "better" heavenly rest/homeland/city; they still await the divine perfection that will be achieved together with "us" (ἡμῶν) (11:40)—the members of the community.

Paraenesis: Ethical Implications (12:1-29)

The ethical implications of the pilgrimage of faith are introduced by the famous words, eloquently rendered in the AV:

> since we are surrounded by so great a cloud of witnesses, let us lay aside every weight, and the sin which so easily ensnares us, and let us run with endurance the race that is set before us, looking unto Jesus, the author and finisher of our faith, who for the joy that was set before Him endured the cross, despising the shame, and has sat down at the right hand of the throne of God. (12:1-2)

This passage has informed the Christian doctrine of the communion of saints, defined by feminist theologian Elizabeth A. Johnson as

> an ongoing connection between the living and the dead, implying that the dead have found new life thanks to the merciful power of God. It

¹Therefore, since we are surrounded by so great a cloud of witnesses, let us also lay aside every weight and the sin that clings so closely, and let us run with perseverance the race that is set before us, ²looking to Jesus the pioneer and perfecter of our faith, who for the sake of the joy that was set before him endured the cross, disregarding its shame, and has taken his seat at the right hand of the throne of God.

³Consider him who endured such hostility against himself from sinners, so that you may not grow weary or lose heart. ⁴In your struggle against sin you have not yet resisted to the point of shedding your blood. ⁵And you have forgotten the exhortation that addresses you as children—

also posits a bond of companionship among living persons themselves who, though widely separated geographically, form one church community. Since the range of those who seek God is as broad as the human race itself, it furthermore affirms a link between all who have been brushed with the fire of divine love and witness to this in their lives.[62]

As noted earlier, the term translated by the AV (and the NRSV) as "witnesses" is μαρτύρων or "martyrs" (see below "Martyrs and Martyrdom"), a meaning that captures the experience of the audience of Hebrews and the sense of solidarity they are encouraged to share with their heroes and heroines of the past and with Jesus, the "author and finisher" (NRSV "pioneer and perfecter") "of our faith."

As James Thompson notes, the homilist presents Jesus not as the object of faith but as "the ultimate *example* of faith, the culmination of the list of heroes in chapter 11."[63] The image of the spiritual journey as a "race" or competition (ἀγών) carries through the athletic metaphors that punctuate the homily (see also 5:14; 10:32-34; 12:3, 12-13) to present Jesus as one who has endured the rigors of the contest not simply for the sake of individual triumph but as the first of many to complete the marathon of faith. The audience is exhorted to look to the victory of Jesus, who endured the ultimate "hostility against himself from sinners" so that they will not "grow weary or lose heart" in their own struggle with sin (12:3), which has not yet involved resistance to the point of bloodshed (12:4)—a trial Jesus has already endured and overcome.

62. Elizabeth A. Johnson, *Friends of God and Prophets: A Feminist Theological Reading of the Communion of Saints* (New York: Continuum, 1999), 7–8.

63. Thompson, *Hebrews*, 248.

Heb 12:1-29 (cont.)

"My child, do not regard lightly the
discipline of the Lord,
or lose heart when you are
punished by him;
[6]for the Lord disciplines those
whom he loves,
and chastises every child
whom he accepts."
[7]Endure trials for the sake of discipline.
God is treating you as children; for what
child is there whom a parent does not
discipline? [8]If you do not have that discipline in which all children share, then
you are illegitimate and not his children.
[9]Moreover, we had human parents to
discipline us, and we respected them.
Should we not be even more willing to
be subject to the Father of spirits and
live? [10]For they disciplined us for a short
time as seemed best to them, but he

Martyrs and Martyrdom

In Christian terms the word
"martyr" (μάρτυς) literally means
"witness" in the sense of one
who bears testimony to Jesus,
although the Jewish Scriptures
attest to both men and women
who were ready to die rather
than renounce Torah (e.g., 1
Macc 1:62-63; 2 Macc 6:8-11,
18-31; 7:1-42; 4 Macc 1:1–18:24).
There is evidence in the NT that
some Christians were persecuted
and even executed for their faith,
at the hands of both Jewish and
Gentile authorities (e.g., Mark
13:12; see also Mark 10:39; Acts
6:5–8:2; 12:1-2; 22:20; Heb
10:32-39; 12:4; Rev 2:13; 17:6;
20:4). The Roman historian
Tacitus (*Ann.* 15.44; ca. 55–120
CE) relates the torture and
killing of many Christians by the
emperor Nero, who blamed
them for the great fire of Rome
(64 CE). Early Christian writers
Melito of Sardis (see also
Eusebius, *Hist. Eccl.* 4.26) and
Tertullian (*Apol.* 5.3-5) refer to
the persecution of Christians
during the reign of Domitian
(81–96 CE). Many scholars think
this event informs the imagery
of Revelation (see also Irenaeus
of Lyons, *Haer.* 5.30) and that the
sufferings experienced by the
seven churches of Asia Minor
(including John's exile on
Patmos and the martyrdom of
Antipas [Rev 2:13]) were the
result of the refusal of the
followers of Jesus to recognize
the imperial cult.

The first evidence of an official
policy of suppressing
Christianity occurs in the reign
of Trajan (98–117), when Pliny
the Younger requests the
emperor's advice about whether
to execute two Christian
"deaconesses" who had been
brought before him for judgment
(*Ep.* 10.96). Although sporadic
persecutions broke out in
various parts of the Roman
world, the major crises occurred
during the reigns of Marcus
Aurelius (ca. 177), Decius and
Valerian (mid-third century),
and Diocletian (early fourth
century). As the persecution of
Christians accelerated before the

disciplines us for our good, in order that we may share his holiness. ¹¹Now, discipline always seems painful rather than pleasant at the time, but later it yields the peaceful fruit of righteousness to those who have been trained by it.

¹²Therefore lift your drooping hands and strengthen your weak knees, ¹³and make straight paths for your feet, so that what is lame may not be put out of joint, but rather be healed.

¹⁴Pursue peace with everyone, and the holiness without which no one will see the Lord. ¹⁵See to it that no one fails to obtain the grace of God; that no root of bitterness springs up and causes trouble, and through it many become defiled. ¹⁶See to it that no one

reign of Constantine (306–337), the term "martyr" came to refer to one who died for the sake of Christ.

Although early Christian martyrs were admired, some teachers (e.g., Clement of Alexandria, Mensurius of Carthage) cautioned that martyrdom should not be sought out but borne only when absolutely necessary. Unfortunately, many martyrs throughout history have been executed by other Christians on charges of heresy, notably during the Reformation, when Catholics were executed by Protestants and Protestants by Catholics. Today ecumenical dialogue and cooperation are enjoyed by many churches, but in parts of the world where Christians and other groups are in the minority they may be and are persecuted and sometimes killed for their religious beliefs or political views.

(*Source*: See also Mary Ann Beavis, *Mark* [Grand Rapids, MI: Baker Academic, 2011], 162; Johnson, *Friends of God*, 71–79.)

Mary Ann Beavis

The Communion of Saints in Cross-Cultural Perspective

In Asian Confucian culture the connection between the living and the dead is strong. The life of the dead depends on the faithful fulfilment of the duty of the living, and the well-being of the living depends on the blessing of the dead, who watch over their descendants as "a cloud of witnesses" (12:1). This is the origin of the ancestral veneration ritual, and the faithful observance of anniversaries of the death of loved ones also has its place within this worldview.

Russell Yee, a Chinese American liturgical scholar who

becomes like Esau, an immoral and godless person, who sold his birthright for a single meal. [17]You know that later, when he wanted to inherit the blessing, he was rejected, for he found no chance to repent, even though he sought the blessing with tears.

[18]You have not come to something that can be touched, a blazing fire, and darkness, and gloom, and a tempest, [19]and the sound of a trumpet, and a voice whose words made the hearers beg that not another word be spoken to them. [20](For they could not endure the order that was given, "If even an animal touches the mountain, it shall be stoned to death." [21]Indeed, so terrifying was the sight that Moses said, "I tremble with fear.") [22]But you have come to Mount Zion and to the city of the living God, the heavenly Jerusalem, and to innumerable angels in festal gathering, [23]and to the assembly of the firstborn who are enrolled in

has worked on contextualized and inculturated worship projects by exploring Asian cultures in relation to worship practice, puts it this way: "Ancestor rituals are deeply entrenched because of the belief that deceased ancestors must be met and supplied with provisions for their afterlife journey, or else they (with their evil spirits) can and will cause trouble for those still in life."

Ancestor rituals involve a gathering of all the family members (usually at the eldest son's home), where women (often the wives of the sons) prepare and lay out food on the table in front of the portraits of the dead loved ones. When things are ready (all laid out in order and with suitable decorum), the male family members (excluding women) perform the ritual, which includes gestures that suggest they are actually feeding the spirits of the departed. This ritual was (not surprisingly, but unfairly) targeted by Christian missionaries as barbaric, backward-looking, and therefore needing to be abandoned. While challenged and denounced by the Western orthodox approach to worship, these practices still bear significance for people of Asian descent in Asia and in the North American diasporas.

Greer Anne Wenh-In Ng probes the meaning of this reality: "To what extent is it permissible or faithful for Christians of East Asian Confucian background living in North America to retain some form of veneration of ancestors and of family members who have died? How do they properly venerate ancestors without being made to feel they are somehow not being true to their Christian faith and practice?" Providing some possible answers to those questions, Ng further encourages us to think about

heaven, and to God the judge of all, and to the spirits of the righteous made perfect, [24]and to Jesus, the mediator of a new covenant, and to the sprinkled blood that speaks a better word than the blood of Abel.

[25]See that you do not refuse the one who is speaking; for if they did not escape when they refused the one who warned them on earth, how much less will we escape if we reject the one who warns from heaven! [26]At that time his voice shook the earth; but now he has promised, "Yet once more I will shake not only the earth but also the heaven." [27]This phrase, "Yet once more," indicates the removal of what is shaken—that is, created things—so that what cannot be shaken may remain. [28]Therefore, since we are receiving a kingdom that cannot be shaken, let us give thanks, by which we offer to God an acceptable worship with reverence and awe; [29]for indeed our God is a consuming fire.

how culture, liturgy, and the Bible intersect with each other.

As regards remembering past heroes of faith (including respected members of the family), the churches have been inconsistent over the centuries. For example, Vatican decrees in the seventeenth and eighteenth centuries prohibited the practice of ancestor veneration as pagan. This prohibition was reversed by the papal instruction of 1935–1936 that acknowledged both ancestor veneration and the Confucian cult as legitimately performed by Catholics. The key to unlock this tangled and ugly Christian colonial history, Ng argues, is to engage in a pastorally sensitive and pedagogically deliberate conversation. We may hope that this conversation can identify the issue as "a problem mainly for those whose religious history and experience is grounded in an exclusive and proselytizing monotheism rather than for those who have always lived in cultures characterized by religious pluralism," while upholding positive examples of "expanding the Christian concept of the communion of saints to include one's ancestors."

One should also note that the practice of honoring ancestors is deeply rooted in biblical, Jewish, and Christian traditions as well as in many non-Western cultural traditions in Asia, Africa, and elsewhere. The homilist's vision of the cloud of witnesses can be more effectively communicated with an informed understanding of Asian and other cultural practices. A particular cultural practice can be a window through which we can see better what is inside the text in Hebrews. After all, we are searching for wisdom, which is embedded in culture and in life-giving elements that are woven into religious meaning and Christian practice.

Consideration of a variety of cultural practices surrounding the recognition of the presence and role of the spirits of the departed in our present lives can help us understand certain passages in Hebrews and the liturgy developed to mark All Saints Day. It may also help us understand the pastoral and cultural implications for our practice of ministry, while promoting ritually and culturally diverse faith relevant to the twenty-first century.

(*Sources*: Russell Yee, *Worship on the Way: Exploring Asian North American Christian Experience* [Valley Forge, PA: Judson Press, 2012], 78; Greer Anne Wenh-In Ng, "The Asian North American Community at Worship: Issues of Indigenization and Contextualization," in *People on the Way: Asian North Americans Discovering Christ, Culture, and Community*, ed. David Ng [Valley Forge, PA: Judson Press, 1996], 147–75, at 151, 153, 156.)

HyeRan Kim-Cragg

The homilist then returns to the theme of parental *paideia* ("elementary education") as a means of enabling the addressees to cope with their sufferings (12:5-11); here the instruction offered by the divine parent is likened not to the gentle "milk" of the mother or wet nurse (see also 5:12c-13) but to the "discipline" meted out by parents to their children. The Wisdom teaching of Prov 3:11-12 is used to illustrate God's care for his offspring (Heb 12:5b-6). The Greek of the citation literally refers to God's paternal correction of his "sons"; however, the Wisdom literature frequently cites the maternal role in the formation of children,[64] a feature of ancient education noted by the homilist: "Moreover, we had human parents [πατέρας] to discipline us, and we respected them" (Heb 12:9; see also 11:23). The NRSV translation obscures the harshness of the language used to describe the chastisements endured by the "sons" of the Lord, which include not just "punishment" (ἐλεγχόμενος; 12:5) but also "lashes" (μαστιγοῖ; 12:6); however, the word consistently translated in these verses as "discipline," παιδεία (12:5, 7, 8, 11; see also 6, 10), refers to the formation of the whole person on the path to maturity.[65]

64. Prov 1:8; 4:3; 6:20; 10:1; 15:20; 17:25; 19:26; 20:20; 23:22, 25; 29:15; 30:11, 17; 31:1; see also Exod 20:12; Deut 5:16.
65. See Thompson, *Hebrews*, 121; on the education of girls in antiquity, see Pomeroy, *Goddesses, Whores, Wives, and Slaves*, 136–37, 170–76.

Women and Athletics

Although sports were mostly the purview of men in antiquity, in Hellenistic times education in athletics began to be available to women. Sarah Pomeroy notes:

Apart from some races at Olympia segregated from the men's events, and foot-races in honor of Hera at Elis for maidens classified by age, women in Greece did not personally partici-pate in athletic competi-tions until the first century A.D., when their names begin to appear in inscrip-tions. An inscription erected

at Delphi honoring three female athletes from Tralles proclaims that one of them, Hedea, won prizes for singing and accompanying herself on the cithara at Athens, for footracing at Nemea, and for driving a war chariot at Isthmia.

Spartan women in particular were renowned for their physical fitness.
(*Source:* Sarah B. Pomeroy, *Goddesses, Whores, Wives, and Slaves: Women in Classical Antiquity* [New York: Schocken, 1995], 137; 36; see also Plate 13.)

Mary Ann Beavis

It should be remembered, however, that the physical discipline of children was part of the Wisdom tradition, as it was of the ancient Medi-terranean cultural ethos. The approach to primary education for a child presumed in a text like Prov 13:24; 23:13-14 and in other examples of Wisdom literature (e.g., Sir 30:1, 9-12) is based on a fundamental distrust and fear of the (boy-)child. To deal with this, the boy-child was separated from maternal care at the age of seven or eight so that he would acquire masculine social norms.[66] This becomes even more problematic for feminists who are searching for a Sophia who is supposed to be life-giving, guiding, and nurturing of the whole person, when we read in Sirach that Sophia is identified with the fear of God (1:12). Even though one may argue that this fear is not about creating terror but about glory and exultation, the joy of life, it is difficult not to see patterns that connect *paideia* with a discipline that deliberately creates fear in the child in order to prevent evil.[67] "For the fear of the Lord is wisdom and discipline,

66. John J. Pilch, "'Beat His Ribs While He Is Young' (Sir 30:12): A Window on the Mediterranean World," *BTB* 23 (1994): 101–13.

67. Charles F. Melchert, *Wise Teaching: Biblical Wisdom and Educational Ministry* (Harrisburg, PA: Trinity Press International, 1996), 154.

fidelity and humility are his delight" (Sir 1:27) can be easily interpreted to mean "For the fear of the Lord is wisdom and discipline; infidelity and disobedience lead to the *paideia* of punishment."

Like their model Jesus, the addressees are children and heirs of God, so they are temporarily undergoing the kinds of *paideia* he endured, an emblem of their legitimacy (12:8). Another *qal waḥomer* argument makes the point: if "fleshly" (σαρκὸς) parents are to be respected, the "father of spirits" (πνευμάτων) should be obeyed all the more so that one may attain "the peaceful fruit of righteousness" (12:9-11). The image of the desirable qualities imparted by Sophia as "fruit" (benefits) is a commonplace of the Wisdom tradition.[68] The discourse on the divine parent's *paideia* of his children concludes with a return to the athletic imagery of 12:1-4, heavily influenced by Wisdom language.[69] The exhortation to "make straight paths for your feet" (see also Prov 4:26) implicitly compares faltering members of the community to runners whose limbs are "put out of joint" during the race and holds out the promise of healing for those who stay the course. To the ancient audience the link between athletics and *paideia* would have been clear, since physical training was considered intrinsic to the education of the whole person.

From a feminist standpoint the portrayal of God as a father who exerts "painful" discipline on his children in order to show his "love" for them (Heb 12:5-6) for their own "good" (12:10) is disturbingly redolent of the kind of "divine child abuse" decried by feminist theologians.[70] While, as noted above, this view of parenting is typical of ancient—and specifically biblical—attitudes to childrearing,[71] there is some recognition that excessively harsh treatment of children can have negative consequences (e.g., Eph 6:4; Col 3:21).

The teachings that follow (Heb 12:14-17) concern relationships within the community and resemble the kinds of Jewish-Christian Wisdom

---

68. E.g., Job 22:21; Prov 3:14; 8:19; 11:30; 13:2; 22:4; Wis 3:13, 15; Sir 1:20; 6:19; 27:7; 37:25, 26; see also Jas 3:17.

69. E.g., Sir 2:12; 25:23; Job 4:3; Isa 35:3.

70. Joanne Carlson Brown and Carole R. Bohn, eds., *Christianity, Patriarchy, and Abuse: A Feminist Critique* (Cleveland, OH: Pilgrim Press, 1989), 26–27.

71. E.g., Prov 22:15; 23:13, 14; 29:15; see also 2 Macc 6:12; 7:33; 10:4; 4 Macc 10:10; see also Heen and Krey, *Ancient Christian Commentary X*, 213–16.

Paideia and Feminist Pedagogy

The teaching of endurance for the sake of discipline (12:7) and of subjection to parents and to God the Father (12:9) in the name of achieving holiness can have antieducational results from a feminist pedagogical point of view. Greer Anne Wenh-In Ng addresses this issue through the teaching of the follower of Confucius, Dong Zhongxu, who lived sometime during the Han dynasty (202 BCE–220 CE) and developed a hierarchical and patriarchal system of knowledge that demands the obedience of children to their parents and of wives to their husbands. About a thousand years later, during the Song dynasty in the eleventh century, this discipline of obedience to parents was established, codified, systematized, and made mandatory by law as part of the neo-Confucian teaching of filial piety. A thousand years of long-standing teaching of discipline and obedience yielded another thousand years of longsuffering (not to mention resilience and subversion) for children and women. These traditions need to be revisited, along with biblical texts such as Hebrews, and reinterpreted, using the hermeneutic of suspicion. Jesus, after all, would teach us to transgress unjust legal systems and to have courage to teach what is true in their stead.

(*Sources*: Greer Ann Wenh-In Ng, "From Confucian Master Teacher to Freirian Mutual Learner: Challenges in Pedagogical Practice and Religious Education," *Religious Education* 95 [2000]: 308–19, at 315–16; Ai Ra Kim, *Women Struggling for a New Life: The Role of Religion in the Cultural Passage from Korea to America* [Albany: State University of New York Press, 1995]; see bell hooks, *Teaching to Transgress: Education as the Practice of Freedom* [New York and London: Routledge, 1994]; Parker Palmer, *The Courage to Teach: Exploring the Inner Landscape of a Teacher's Life* [San Francisco: Jossey-Bass, 2000].)

HyeRan Kim-Cragg

teachings found in the letter attributed to James.[72] Members are to pursue peace, holiness, and the grace of God, individually and for one another (12:14-15a). The warning against the growth of a "root of bitterness" (12:15b) echoes Moses' warning against members of the assembly of Israel

---

72. Thomas W. Leahy, "The Epistle of James," in *The New Jerome Biblical Commentary*, ed. Raymond E. Brown, Joseph A. Fitzmyer, and Roland E. Murphy (Englewood Cliffs, NJ: Prentice Hall, 1990), 909–16, at 909–10.

Esau's Repentance— Another View

An early commentary on Hebrews by Theodore of Mopsuestia (ca. 350–458) offers a rhetorically and exegetically sensitive interpretation of Esau that does not preclude sincere repentance for those who have strayed from the community:

> Through these words he does not wish to preclude the chance of repentance, but to teach that it is not possible for those who do not receive correction at the present time to receive it later. . . . For he has not been eager to say contradictory things, especially in so close proximity. Anyone could figure this out from the examples that he uses. For first he made mention of Esau, who partly was disheartened when he did not obtain the blessing, but partly abided the decision even after this event owing to the malice of his character. Then when he repented of his assent to sin, he did not obtain the blessing. For he was not asking for repentance, but for the blessing that had been given to his brother in accordance with the worthiness of his character. It was impossible that the blessing would again be taken away and given to him again. Also, however, it is possible to discover that his tears were not altogether unprofitable. His father seems to have grieved thereafter for his careless son and seems to have given him some blessings. So he does not wish to preclude repentance through these words.

(*Source*: *Fragments on the Epistle to the Hebrews* 12, in Heen and Krey, *Ancient Christian Commentary*, 221–22.)

Mary Ann Beavis

who are tempted to turn against their God (Deut 29:18). Such persons are implicitly compared to Esau, the twin brother of Jacob "who sold his birthright for a single meal" (Heb 12:16; see also Gen 25:29-34) and was subsequently deprived of his father's blessing, despite his "tears" (Heb 12:17; see also Gen 27:38). Although Esau is mentioned earlier (Heb 11:20) as one of the sons who received Isaac's blessing, here he is deplored as a profane fornicator (πόρνος), reflecting the tendency of Jewish tradition to portray him as a reprehensible character in contrast to the righteous Jacob (see also Rom 9:13).[73] The message of Esau for the audience is that, like him, they will not be given a chance to "repent," i.e., those who stray will

---

73. See Eisenbaum, "Hebrews," 424 n. 16.

not be accepted back into the community even if they beg to be readmitted (Heb 12:17), i.e., they will "fail to obtain the grace of God" (12:15).

The vivid contrast between the earthly Sinai and the heavenly Zion that follows (Heb 12:18-24) is the climax both of the section (10:19–12:29) and of the homily as a whole. The culmination of the exodus-like journey of faith of the "cloud of witnesses" (12:1) comprising the community of biblical heroes, members of the "church" (ἐκκλησία; 12:23), and their forerunner and mediator, Jesus (12:24), is set against the numinous spectacle witnessed by the Israelites in Moses' time (12:18-20). The homilist vividly portrays the most awe-inspiring aspects of the Sinai theophany (Exod 19:1-25; see also Deut 4:10-15), where God reveals his covenant with Israel (Exod 19:5; Deut 4:13) in "a blazing fire, and darkness, and gloom, and a tempest, and the sound of a trumpet" (Heb 12:18-19a; see also Exod 19:16, 19), the overwhelming voice of God (12:19b; see also Exod 19:16). The inaccessibility of the holy mountain is emphasized: even an animal that touched the mountain was subject to stoning (Heb 12:20; Exod 19:12-13), and Moses himself "trembled with fear" (Heb 12:21; see also Deut 9:19).

Although it is a scene of judgment, the vision of the heavenly "rest" of the faithful (see also Heb 3:7-19; 11:1, 13-16)—"Mount Zion and . . . the city of the living God, the heavenly Jerusalem" (Heb 12:22; see also 11:10, 16; 13:14)—is one of joy and bliss, over against the fearfulness and gloom of the Sinai theophany. The "firstborn who are enrolled in heaven" are probably the "witnesses" (see also 12:1)—"the spirits of the righteous made perfect"—whose names are inscribed in a heavenly book (12:23; see also Exod 32:32; Ps 69:28; Dan 12:1; Rev 20:12). The reference to Jesus, "mediator of a new covenant," and his "sprinkled blood," compared to the blood of the murdered Abel (Heb 12:24; see also 11:4), is the culmination of the "two covenants" motif introduced in Heb 7:22. Like Abel's "greater" sacrifice (11:4), Jesus' blood, sprinkled in covenant ratification, "speaks a better word" (12:24) than the blood of the first martyr, Abel. The first covenant, associated with Moses and Mount Sinai, is obviated by the new covenant, associated with the messiah, Jesus, and Mount Zion. As argued earlier, the new covenant of Hebrews resonates with the tradition of the "eternal covenant" associated with David and his descendants: "I have made a covenant with my chosen one, I have sworn to my servant David: 'I will establish your descendants forever, and build your throne for all generations'" (Ps 89:3-4).

It should be noted that Hebrews' Sinai/Zion motif is not a case of playing "Judaism" off against "Christianity" to the former's detriment.

Rather, the homilist draws creatively from two streams in the prophetic literature, one that exhorts Israel to return to the law revealed through Moses[74] and one that anticipates the joyous return of the exiles from Babylon to Jerusalem ("Zion"), which is often depicted in utopian terms.[75] Second Isaiah's idyllic portrayal of postexilic Jerusalem is reminiscent of the description of the heavenly Zion in Heb 12:22-24:

> For the LORD will comfort Zion;
>   he will comfort all her waste places,
> and will make her wilderness like Eden,
>   her desert like the garden of the LORD;
> joy and gladness will be found in her,
>   thanksgiving and the voice of song. . . .
> So the ransomed of the LORD shall return,
>   and come to Zion with singing;
> everlasting joy shall be upon their heads;
>   they shall obtain joy and gladness,
>   and sorrow and sighing shall flee away. . . .

Hebrews 12:22-24 and the Global "Here and There"

Catherine Keller's discussion of "the here and there" resonates with the homilist's concepts of the earthly Jerusalem and the city that is to come. For Keller the "here and there" is "the strange spatiality of the postmodern globe." In the same way the homilist sees the audience of Hebrews as belonging to both worlds. Keller's concept of "here and there" is temporal as well as spatial. She sees the present as something that is urgently unfolding to the currently emerging future, as "*eschatological* orientation." In the interstitial space of here and there is the messianic vision, the hopeful promise, and the heavenly anticipation of the destination upon which these early Christian communities have fixed their gaze. (*Source*: Catherine Keller, "The Love of Postcolonialism," in *Postcolonial Theologies: Divinity and Empire*, ed. Catherine Keller, Michael Nausner, and Mayra Rivera [St. Louis, MO: Chalice Press, 2004]), 221–42, at 223, 229.)

HyeRan Kim-Cragg

74. E.g., Jer 26:4, 20; Mic 6:4; Mal 4:4; see also Dan 9:9-10, 13.
75. E.g., Isa 1:27; 2:3; 4:3-5; 8:18; 12:6; 33:20; 51:3, 11, 16; 52:1; Joel 3:16; Obad 21; Mic 4:2, 7, 8; Zech 1:17; 2:10; 8:3; 9:9.

Our Stories Are Our Scripture
For Hebrews 12

Comes around Goes off Again

A widow when cleaning a large
salmon discovered how
generous was his milt so was
conceived

A lover pale handsome as he
came to be beside her in bed
one morning soon after
lonesomeness

Got the best part for he was so
very attractive so much so
another lady took to stealing
him away

Compliant he went off as new
conquest but always
defended the widow when
his current amour

Would make fun humiliate her a
public showdown was
eventual next thing on
agenda had widow

Doing dance making chant how
she supposed him for herself
then he changed back being
just semen

Annharte

Daughter Zion

Reflecting the vulnerability of
women in wartime, the Jewish
Scriptures often personify
Jerusalem as a woman
("daughter Zion"), who
alternatively suffers, laments,
and rejoices in accordance with
the fortunes of the holy city in
the Babylonian empire (2 Kgs
19:21; Ps 9:14; Isa 1:8; 10:32; 16:1;
37:22; 52:2; 62:11; Jer 4:31; 6:2, 23;
Lam 1:6; 2:1, 4, 8, 10, 13, 18; 4:22;
Mic 1:13; 4:8, 10, 13; Zeph 3:14;
Zech 2:10; 9:9). Both lamentation
and rejoicing were liturgical
roles of women in ancient Israel
(e.g., Lam 1:4; 2 Chr 35:25; Jer
9:20; Exod 15:20-21; Judg 11:34;
Jdt 16:1; see also Luke 23:27). In
the NT the arrival of the
messiah, Jesus, is celebrated in
terms borrowed from this
tradition: "This took place to
fulfill what had been spoken
through the prophet, saying,
'Tell the daughter of Zion, Look,
your king is coming to you,
humble, and mounted on a
donkey, and on a colt, the foal of
a donkey'" (Matt 21:4-5; John
12:15; see also Zech 9:9).

Mary Ann Beavis

I have put my words in your mouth,
    and hidden you in the shadow of my hand,
stretching out the heavens
    and laying the foundations of the earth,
    and saying to Zion, "You are my people." (Isa 51:3, 11, 16)

As Thompson observes, "The author's purpose is not to engage in a
polemic with Judaism or to denigrate Israel's sacred institutions, but,

A Jewish Perspective
(Heb 12:18-22)

Hebrews 12:18-22 deals with the Israelite experience at Mount Sinai in a way that took me aback when I first encountered it in rereading Hebrews. The opening statement, "You have not come to something that can be touched . . ." led me to expect a contrast between the externals of the Sinai experience, "a blazing fire, and darkness . . ." and the presence of God at its center. The Hasidic masters of the last two centuries of Jewish spiritual tradition have often drawn this contrast, noting that the people who "witnessed the thunder and lightning, the sound of the trumpet, and the mountain smoking . . . stood at a distance" (Exod 20:18) rather than drawing near to the deeper and transcendent reality of God beyond all these appearances.[77]

Instead, Hebrews contrasts the earthly Sinai with the heavenly Jerusalem: a strange contrast to my mind. In Jewish tradition Sinai and Jerusalem are not typically pitted against one another. Rather, they are juxtaposed as highlights of the Jewish journey with God: "'On the day of his wedding': Sinai. 'On the day of the gladness of his heart': Jerusalem" (Song 3:11, Exodus Rabbah Pequdei 52).

Justin Jaron Lewis

like the ancient orators, to use the *synkrisis* to demonstrate the greatness of the Christian experience in comparison to all alternatives."[76]

Unfortunately, the threatening quality of the exhortation that follows (Heb 12:25-29) undermines the celestial vision of the heavenly Zion. The ominous reference to "the one who is speaking" (12:25a) refers both to the "earthly" voice of God that spoke from Sinai (12:19) and to the divine voice that warns the audience from heaven (12:25b). The homilist finds God's current message to the community in prophecy: "Yet once more I will shake not only the earth but also the heaven" (12:26; see also Hag 2:6). As the earth was shaken in the Sinai theophany, God's final advent ("yet once more") will dissolve the created cosmos, leaving only the heavenly reality. The homilist's worldview has affinities both with popular Platonism, in which the world of sense-perception was seen as temporal and ephemeral and "reality" was seen as invisible, archetypal, and eternal, and with some strains of biblical eschatology, e.g.: "Lift up your eyes to the heavens, and look at the earth beneath; for the heavens will vanish like smoke, the earth will wear out like a garment, and those who live on it will die like gnats; but my salvation will be forever, and my deliverance

---

76. Thompson, *Hebrews*, 267.

will never be ended" (Isa 51:6; Ps 102:24-28; see also Rev 21:1-4; 2 Pet 3:12-13). The imminence of the unshakable realm (βασιλεία) is cited as a reason for joy on the part of the community, whose service to God should consist of reverence and awe (12:28). A final verse comprises the end of the warning: "for indeed our God is a consuming fire" (12:29). Here the homilist vividly invokes the biblical association of divinity with fire (Deut 4:24).[78] The implication of a fiery dissolution of the "shakable" elements to be replaced by the eternal, heavenly realm has affinities with the Stoic-influenced eschatology expressed in 2 Pet 3:10-13:

> But the day of the Lord will come like a thief, and then the heavens will pass away with a loud noise, and the elements will be dissolved with fire, and the earth and everything that is done on it will be disclosed. Since all these things are to be dissolved in this way, what sort of persons ought you to be in leading lives of holiness and godliness, waiting for and hastening the coming of the day of God, because of which the heavens will be set ablaze and dissolved, and the elements will melt with fire? But, in accordance with his promise, we wait for new heavens and a new earth, where righteousness is at home.

Harold Attridge notes that the decisiveness of this warning has led some interpreters to speculate that vv. 25-29 comprised the original ending of Hebrews.[79] As he further observes, however, ending on a note of warning and judgment would run contrary to the homilist's practice of balancing admonition with encouragement (see also 2:14-16; 4:14-16; 6:9-12; 10:32-39).[80]

Interpretive Essay: Atonement Theology—Another View

In an attempt to reconstruct atonement theology as one that advocates on behalf of victims and the oppressed rather than reinforcing victimization and a twisted concept of sacrifice, Andrew Sung Park highlights the work of the Spirit in the guise of the Paraclete, a name derived from the

---

77. The late Slonimer Rebbe, Shalom Noaḥ Berezovsky, *Netivot Shalom* 1 (Jerusalem: Yeshivat Beit Avraham Slonim, 5757 [1997]), 11–12, citing unspecified "holy books."

78. See also Deut 4:33; 5:24-26; 9:3; 1 Kgs 18:24; 2 Kgs 1:12; Job 1:16; Pss 50:3; 68:2; Jer 5:14; Heb 1:7; Acts 2:3.

79. Attridge, *Hebrews*, 383.

80. Ibid.

Greek παράκλητος.[81] This word is used most prominently in the Johannine writings to refer to the intercessory role of Jesus Christ, a Christology similar to that of the homilist. Park makes a distinction, however, between the Holy Spirit and the Paraclete, based on trinitarian theology but built further on a triune atonement theology from Asian American perspectives: "The Paraclete is also more personal than the Holy Spirit in a number of the New Testament passages. While the Holy Spirit, like the Spirit of God in the Hebrew Bible, is energy or a force, the Paraclete is a person," he writes.[82] Referring to John 14:16, where Jesus says, "and I will ask the Father, and he will give you another Advocate [Paraclete]," implying Jesus is the first and primary Paraclete, Park argues that the Paraclete works as "the extension of Jesus' resurrection" and is "the wounded healer" who is among us to "comfort the comfortless, to advocate for the rights of victims, to uplift the discouraged, to help the helpless. . . . The

81. Andrew Sung Park, *Triune Atonement: Christ's Healing for Sinners, Victims, and the Whole Creation* (Louisville, KY: Westminster John Knox, 2009), 60–72.
82. Ibid., 62.

Paraclete is the Spirit that is at work in the community."[83] His perspective seems to support a reading of Hebrews in which the role of the Paraclete was critical for the audience, who were struggling with the delay of the parousia, the second coming of Jesus, and had to be comforted by the notion that the Paraclete, the extension of Jesus' resurrection, had already arrived to be with them. Indeed, the word "paraclete" literally means one who "has been called to be on their side."

As appealing as this interpretation appears, feminist sensibilities are alerted to the fact that παράκλητος is a masculine noun in Greek, while the Spirit in Hebrew, רוח, is feminine, and the Spirit in Greek, πνεῦμα, is neuter. One may question to what extent (if at all) the male counselor can "advocate" for and "comfort" female victims, in line with the doubt expressed in Rosemary Radford Ruether's famous question, "Can a male Savior save women?"[84] Her question points to the heart of Christology. For her the Christ symbol is beyond maleness because it signifies the messianic humanity, with a plurality of people working together for justice and struggling to change the systemic injustice of patriarchy. Unless, as Don Schweitzer puts it, "the trinitarian language of God as Father and Jesus as only-begotten Son" is recognized as symbolic discourse that must be "deliteralized in terms of its gender and hierarchical parent-child imagery,"[85] Ruether's second question, "Can Christology be liberated from patriarchy?" begs our response and haunts our feminist consciousness.[86] While the masculine noun "paraclete" cannot and should not encompass all the aspects and dimensions of the Spirit's work as comforter, helper, and advocate, an argument for its comprehensive use can be and has been made. The dangerous result is the legitimation of the perspective represented by the Vatican declaration against the ordination of women, *Inter Insigniores* (1976), in which the imitation of Christ is reduced to only one element, namely, male sex.

In the case of the passage in John 16:7, "for if I do not go away, the Advocate will not come to you," feminist readers may wonder if a male

83. Ibid., 67–68.

84. Rosemary Radford Ruether, *To Change the World: Christology and Cultural Criticism* (New York: Crossroad, 1981), 45–56.

85. Don Schweitzer, *Contemporary Christologies: A Fortress Introduction* (Minneapolis: Fortress Press, 2010), 39–40.

86. Rosemary Radford Ruether, "Can Christology Be Liberated from Patriarchy?," in *Reconstructing the Christ Symbol*, ed. Maryanne Stevens (Mahwah, NJ: Paulist Press, 1993) 7–29.

representation of the Paraclete reflects a preference for separation over connectedness. Research into human development demonstrates that men advance in maturity through separation, while women tend to grow best through relation and intimacy.[87] Mary Grey, opposing a mystification and idealization of suffering, unpacks the word "atonement" as "at-one-ment," implying a "fundamental drive to unity and wholeness, which sparks itself off the creative-redemptive process" in order to draw alternative meanings of death toward reconstructing atonement theology.[88] For her, death in general, and the death of Jesus in particular, a necessary event for at-one-ment theology, has multiple meanings that include disintegration, separation, and absence of growth and change.

Referring to the same text of John 16:7, Grey agrees that the separation of Jesus from his disciples was necessary. She further argues, however, that this separation has to be understood together with Jesus' emphasis on connection and interconnectedness: "Holding together the pain of loss and separation is the deeply-felt experience of interdependence and community."[89] In the Johannine discourse in which this text is found (John 15:26–16:33), most of Jesus' words are about abiding love and the wisdom of interconnectedness. The many Johannine references to the Paraclete (14:16, 26; 15:26; 16:7) illustrate the mutuality and interrelationship between God and God's people in Jesus, the true vine (15:1, 5). The work of the Paraclete, as the Spirit of Truth, is placed at the center of this relationship. The Western view, with its stress on separation demanded by society, emerging from the male-centered notion of development and growth, needs to be challenged by this biblical and theological insight into the wisdom of wholeness that is achieved only through communal relationship and mutual respect.

HyeRan Kim-Cragg

---

87. Carol Gilligan, *In a Different Voice: Psychological Theory and Women's Development* (Boston: Harvard University Press, 1982).

88. Mary Grey, *Feminism, Redemption, and the Christian Tradition* (Mystic, CT: Twenty-Third Publications, 1990), 160.

89. Ibid., 187.

Hebrews 13:1-25

Wisdom and Community

The final exhortations in Heb 13 fall into four main parts: (1) teachings on relationships within the community (13:1-6); (2) warnings against false teachings (13:7-17), echoing the doctrinal instruction of the body of the letter; (3) personal requests from the author(s) (13:18-21); and (4) an epistolary postscript (13:22-25). In view of the many linkages between the doctrinal section of the chapter (13:7-17) and the rest of the homily, it seems likely that the chapter is not an appendix but an integral part of the discourse, conveying a "take-home message" to the audience and, in good homiletic style, concluding on a positive and encouraging note. The postscript does, however, appear to be a later addition, appended to the homily to bring it into conformity with the Pauline letters.

Teachings on Relationships within the Community (Heb 13:1-6)

After the ominous tone of 12:25-29, with its warnings of judgment and fiery cosmic dissolution, the homilist's concluding remarks begin with a benign exhortation to φιλαδελφία, "friendly love" (13:1), a term that relates specifically to the affection between siblings; here it is an appropriate term for the fondness among the "brothers and sisters" (ἀδελφοί) of the

173

Heb 13:1-6

[1]Let mutual love continue. [2]Do not neglect to show hospitality to strangers, for by doing that some have entertained angels without knowing it. [3]Remember those who are in prison, as though you were in prison with them; those who are being tortured, as though you yourselves were being tortured. [4]Let marriage be held in honor by all, and let the marriage bed be kept undefiled; for God will judge fornicators and adulterers. [5]Keep your lives free from the love of money, and be content with what you have; for he has said, "I will never leave you or forsake you." [6]So we can say with confidence,

"The Lord is my helper;
    I will not be afraid.
What can anyone do to me?"

church (ἐκκλησία), commonplace in the NT.[1] The value of familial love is extended to φιλοξενία, hospitality—literally, "love of strangers"—as James Thompson notes, a time-honored practice that "enabled early Christians to travel from city to city and created a web of interconnected communities."[2] The homilist reminds the audience that by welcoming strangers they are following biblical precedent: "for by doing that some have entertained angels without knowing it" (Heb 13:2). This reference to hospitality is closely related to the experience of pilgrims, exemplified by the heroes and heroines of faith portrayed in Heb 11:1-40. Faith as a journey of "strangers and foreigners on the earth" (11:13) toward the promised heavenly inheritance (see 11:33-38) requires courageous acts of hospitality. Here hospitality is far from "charity," understood as handouts to the needy. Rather, those who are called to offer hospitality are themselves identified as being in need of hospitality. The emphasis on hospitality, the love of strangers, is not meant to dismiss or devalue love for oneself and loved ones. For the homilist these two dimensions of love go together, which is compatible with and supportive of the Golden Rule taught by Jesus: "'to love one's neighbor as oneself,'—this is much more important than all whole burnt offerings and sacrifices" (Mark 12:33-34).

The problem with "charity" as it is often practiced is the assumption that in the act of giving, the power of the one who gives remains un-

1. See Rom 12:10; 1 Thess 4:9; 1 Pet 1:22; 1 Pet 2:17; 3:8; 2 Pet 1:7; 1 John 2:10; 3:10; 4:20, 21.

2. See Rom 12:13; 1 Pet 4:9; *Didachē* 12:1-2; see Gen 19:1-3; Judg 19:19-21; Job 31:32. James W. Thompson, *Hebrews*, Paideia Commentaries on the New Testament (Grand Rapids, MI: Baker Academic, 2008), 278.

changed while the status of those who receive also remains unchanged, their agency dismissed, their suffering and need remote and removed from the giver. Letty M. Russell has advocated a theology of hospitality, recognizing the limitations of a "hermeneutic of the other" that promotes the "distancing, dualistic language of otherness."[3] She recognizes the contribution of postcolonial scholarship in helping her acknowledge "ways in which white, Euro-American colonialism and imperialism have helped to structure the world in terms of those who 'have' and those who 'need.'"[4] Her theology of hospitality is relevant to this particular section in which the homilist tries to impart the final teaching that over-arches the entire homily; it points to the grounding of the community in familial love, φιλαδελφία, caring for those who are close to them but not losing sight of their solidarity with other communities (φιλοξενία), while acclaiming God's everlasting and faithful love through Jesus Christ, who is "the same yesterday and today and forever" (13:8).

Commentators often cite the story of the three "men" who visit Abraham and Sarah to announce the birth of Isaac (Gen 18:1-15), in which the visitors are offered rest and refreshment by the ancestral couple and receive the blessing of offspring.[5] Other scriptural accounts of those who entertained angels "unawares" include Gen 19:1-3; Judg 6:11-18; 13:3-23; and, most prominently, the book of Tobit, in which the angel Raphael, disguised as the man Azariah, a distant relative (Tob 5:13), is welcomed by the afflicted Tobit, who consequently receives the multiple blessings of healing, an appropriate wife for his son, progeny, and the restoration of his fortunes.

The community is urged to maintain solidarity with other "estranged" members of the christian community—"those who are in prison"—empathizing with their bondage and torture as if it were their own (13:3; 10:32-34), perhaps an encouragement to visit believers in prison and offer them material support and legal assistance.[6]

---

3. Letty M. Russell, *Just Hospitality: God's Welcome in a World of Difference*, ed. J. Shannon Clarkson and Kate M. Ott (Louisville, KY: Westminster John Knox, 2009), 25.

4. Ibid.

5. E.g., Harold Attridge, *The Epistle to the Hebrews: A Commentary*, Hermeneia (Philadelphia: Fortress Press, 1989), 386; Craig R. Koester, *Hebrews*, AB 36 (New York: Doubleday, 2001), 563; Thompson, *Hebrews*, 278; Alan C. Mitchell, *Hebrews*, SP 13 (Collegeville, MN: Liturgical Press, 2009), 293.

6. See Pamela Eisenbaum, "Hebrews," in *The Jewish Annotated New Testament*, ed. Amy-Jill Levine and Marc Zvi Brettler (New York: Oxford University Press, 2011), 406–26, at 420, note on Heb 10:34; see also Lucian of Samosata, *Peregrinus* 12–13.

The Prison Diary of Perpetua

This excerpt from the diary of Perpetua, a young woman martyred in Carthage ca. 202–203, poignantly illustrates the experience of an imprisoned believer and the kinds of support offered her by members of her community:

> After a few days we are taken into the dungeon, and I was very much afraid, because I had never felt such darkness. O terrible day! O the fierce heat of the shock of the soldiery, because of the crowds! I was very unusually distressed by my anxiety for my infant. There were present there Tertius and Pomponius, the blessed deacons who ministered to us, and had arranged by means of a gratuity that we might be refreshed by being sent out for a few hours into a pleasanter part of the prison. Then going out of the dungeon, all attended to their own wants. I suckled my child, which was now enfeebled with hunger. In my anxiety for it, I addressed my mother and comforted my brother, and commended to their care my son. I was languishing because I had seen them languishing on my account. Such solicitude I suffered for many days, and I obtained for my infant to remain in the dungeon with me; and forthwith I grew strong and was relieved from distress and anxiety about my infant; and the dungeon became to me as it were a palace, so that I preferred being there to being elsewhere.

(*Source*: "Appendix: The Martyrdom of Perpetua and Felicity," trans. R. E. Wallis, *The Ante-Nicene Fathers*, vol. 3: *Latin Christianity, Its Founder, Tertullian* ([Buffalo, NY: Christian Literature Publishing Co., 1887]), 700 [*Passion* 1.3].)

The command to "let marriage be held in honor by all, and let the marriage bed be kept undefiled" (Heb 13:4), accompanied by a warning that God will judge "fornicators and adulterers," may be designed to deflect pagan accusations that christians indulged in illicit sexual practices and other atrocities as part of their worship,[7] charges that figured in the persecution of believers. While familial love (φιλαδελφία) and the love of strangers (φιλοξενία) are recommended (13:1-2), the love of money (φιλάργυρος) is disparaged, a commonplace topos in the Wisdom litera-

---

7. Stephen Benko, *Pagan Rome and the Early Christians* (Bloomington: Indiana University Press, 1984), 54–78.

ture.[8] The denigration of money is, however, more than a pious sentiment since some community members have experienced the actual expropriation of their possessions (10:34). The sapiential preference for dependence on God rather than material wealth is underlined by scriptural reassurances (Heb 13:5b, 6): "I will never leave you or forsake you" (see Deut 31:6, 8; Josh 1:5); "The Lord is my helper; I will not be afraid. What can anyone do to me?" (see Ps 118).

Hebrews 13:5 in Feminist Perspective

In delineating a feminist hermeneutic of hospitality, Letty M. Russell provides an insight into "the denigration of money" from the perspective of the role played by North American imperialism (empire, as she calls it). North American imperialism needs to change, she says, and provide a space in which people around the world can "speak back to empire [while] hearing and heeding the call to be just in our concrete social and political practices." In the words of Mary Jo Leddy, money is what drives us (North Americans). "Our made-in-the-West materialism," she writes, "has the potential to diminish and distort the human spirit just as much as historical materialism destroyed the desire for hope and meaning in the lives of those who lived under communism." In the context of Hebrews, the audience to which the homilist reaches out is made up of those who are having difficulty "keeping their lives free from the love of money" (13:5) because either they have so much or they have so little; they are trapped in the sin of materialism. This sin is embedded in and feeds into "the culture of money," which must be dismantled and transformed into "radical gratitude," within what Leddy refers to as "the great economy of grace." The alternative to the sinful order can be described as "as more is given, more is received," the opposite of "more money drives us more." This countercultural teaching (similar to that of the parable of the loaves and fishes) is deeply theological in that it points to God who is the creator of all; there is nothing we have that does not come from God. It is also deeply ethical and relational in that whatever we have is given at the mercy (labor) of someone else, and our act of sharing (or not) has consequences for the well-being of others. Leddy sums up her argument as follows: "To dwell in gratitude is to begin to

---

8. E.g., Prov 8:10; Eccl 5:9; Sir 31:5-7; 11:18-19; 21:5; 31:5-11; Wis 5:8; 7:8; 8:5; see also Luke 12:13-21; 1 Tim 6:10.

recognize that other people are not simply objects to be disposed of or even objects of our concern." In this regard Jacques Derrida's reflections on "ethics as hospitality" and his dictum that "ethics is hospitality" are illuminating. In terms of the relationality of hospitality, Gayatri Chakravorty Spivak moves us beyond the human arena by inviting us to dream: "Today it is planetarity that we are called to imagine." Against the Christian dualism of the doctrine of the *creation ex nihilo*, she claims: "For nature, the sacred other of the human community is . . . bounded by the structure of ethical responsibility." Catherine Keller, supporting Spivak's claim but spinning it religiously, puts the relational character into sharp relief: "If all existence is within and beyond its alienations covenantally bound, *religare*, 'reconnected,' . . . then all bodies *matter*."

(*Sources*: Russell, *Just Hospitality* [see n. 2 above], 37, 45, 46; Mary Jo Leddy, *Radical Gratitude* [Maryknoll, NY: Orbis Books, 2002], 20, 66, 67; Jacques Derrida, *On Cosmopolitanism and Forgiveness, Thinking in Action* [London and New York: Routledge, 2001], 16–17; Gayatri Chakravorty Spivak, *Death of a Discipline* [New York: Columbia University Press, 2003], 72, 74; Gayatri Chakravorty Spivak, *A Critique of Postcolonial Reason: Toward a History of the Vanishing Present* [Cambridge, MA: Harvard University Press, 1999], 382; Catherine Keller, "The Love of Postcolonialism," in *Postcolonial Theologies: Divinity and Empire*, ed. Catherine Keller, Michael Nausner, and Mayra Rivera [St. Louis, MO: Chalice Press, 2004], 221–42, at 240.)

HyeRan Kim-Cragg

Warnings against False Teachings (Heb 13:7-17)

A warning against being "carried away by all kinds of strange teachings" (13:9) is embedded in a section that interweaves ethical exhortation and the distinctive cultic doctrines of the body of Hebrews (13:7-17). The section is defined by references to "leaders" (ἡγουμένων) who "spoke the word [τὸν λόγον] to you" (13:7), who continue to attend to the "souls" of the community, and who "will give an account [λόγον]," presumably to God, of their spiritual state (13:17). The term used for "leaders" in these verses is seldom employed in the NT (Luke 22:26; Acts 15:22); perhaps significantly, it is also used in 1 Clement (1.3; 21.6), the earliest extra-biblical document to quote Hebrews (see introduction). The exhortation for the audience to imitate the "faith" of the leaders (13:7) places the

⁷Remember your leaders, those who spoke the word of God to you; consider the outcome of their way of life, and imitate their faith. ⁸Jesus Christ is the same yesterday and today and forever. ⁹Do not be carried away by all kinds of strange teachings; for it is well for the heart to be strengthened by grace, not by regulations about food, which have not benefited those who observe them. ¹⁰We have an altar from which those who officiate in the tent have no right to eat. ¹¹For the bodies of those animals whose blood is brought into the sanctuary by the high priest as a sacrifice for sin are burned outside the camp. ¹²Therefore Jesus also suffered outside the city gate in order to sanctify the people by his own blood. ¹³Let us then go to him outside the camp and bear the abuse he endured. ¹⁴For here we have no lasting city, but we are looking for the city that is to come. ¹⁵Through him, then, let us continually offer a sacrifice of praise to God, that is, the fruit of lips that confess his name. ¹⁶Do not neglect to do good and to share what you have, for such sacrifices are pleasing to God.

¹⁷Obey your leaders and submit to them, for they are keeping watch over your souls and will give an account. Let them do this with joy and not with sighing—for that would be harmful to you.

leadership in the company of the heroes and heroines of Heb 11:4-40, engaged in the pilgrimage of faith through their "way of life" (see the references to Jesus as "pioneer" [ἀρχηγὸν] in 2:10; 12:2).

The liturgical-sounding formula "Jesus Christ is the same yesterday and today and forever" (13:8) recalls the sophialogical portrayal of Christ as the "reflection of God's glory and the exact imprint of God's very being" (Heb 1:3; compare Wis 7:25-26). Here the statement of Christ's eternity is not so much a christological statement as an assertion of the stability of authentic doctrine, which is grounded in the teaching of Jesus and has been passed on to the community (2:3), from the "milk" of elementary teaching to the "solid food" of advanced instruction (5:12).

Warnings against erroneous teachings of various kinds are commonplace in the NT;[9] the term used here to describe the unauthorized teaching is ξέναις, referring not to the bizarre content of the doctrine but to its source outside the community. The image of being "carried away" echoes the nautical image of "drifting away" (Heb 2:1), a temptation that besets the community (10:25). The "foreign" teaching has something to do with "regulations about food"; this may be a literal reference to "Jewish

9. Heb 13:9; see, e.g., Eph 4:14; Col 2:8; 1 Tim 3:1-7; 6:3-4; 1 John 2:18-17; Jude 3-11.

Our Stories Are Our Scripture
For Hebrews 13

Chilam Balam[12] conversation quiz

Ever notice the sun is a huge fried
egg stuck in the sky to give
people

Natural light philosophy how cross
sign is a corn or first tree brings
rain

Sharpen well the eyes sculpture face
to read great ones stone stories

Why bother imitate howl of
coyote white rattle making
sound weasel

Await figure playing flute bone
heart blessing just green
jaguar blood

Riddle bite into thirteen layers
of corn tortilla listen up
conch shell call

Annharte

dietary laws or to the issue of meat offered to idols" (see Acts 15; 1 Cor 8),[10] or, as Thompson suggests, "Whereas 'grace' (*charis*) is the summary for the benefits of Christ described in 7:1–10:18, 'foods' is most likely a metonymy for the earthly alternatives that do not bring stability (see 9:9; 12:16)."[11] For the homilist the nourishment that truly sustains the believer is sound teaching (see comment on 5:12).

The alimentary language continues with a reference to "an altar from which those who officiate in the tent have no right to eat" (13:10), the heavenly altar of Christ's metaphorical sacrifice. The Day of Atonement sacrifice was not eaten, but other Israelite sacrifices were consumed by the priests and/or by those who offered them, e.g., the peace offering (Lev 3:1-17; 7:11-34), the guilt offering (Lev 7:1-6), and the grain offering (Lev 2:1-10). Although this verse invites a eucharistic interpretation, it seems more consistent with the homilist's association of food and teaching to see it as a reference to the spiritual sustenance offered by the teaching of the leadership—and by the content of the homily—which is inaccessible to those who remain loyal to the earthly cult ("those who officiate in the tent"). The sacrificial metaphor continues with an analogy between the Day of Atonement ritual in which the carcasses of the sacrificed animals were "burned outside the camp" (13:11; Lev 16:27)

10. Eisenbaum, "Hebrews," 425, note on 13:9.
11. Thompson, *Hebrews*, 281.
12. Title of prophetic codices (Mayan).

Outside the Camp

The biblical concept "outside the camp" is given a surprising twist here. In the Torah, "outside the camp" means outside the community and away from the holiness of the sanctuary or temple. It is a place associated with marginalization or exclusion, the place of lepers (Lev 13:46; Num 5:3-4; 12:14-15) and the dead (Lev 10:4-5; 24:14, 23; Num 15:36; see also Num 31:19). Sacrifices are offered not outside the camp but in the precincts of the sanctuary. Portions of some sacrificial animals are burned outside the camp (Exod 29:14; Lev 4:12, 20; 8:17; 9:11; 16:27; see also Lev 6:11 [MT Lev 6:4]), but this is not part of the sacrifice itself, simply a way of disposing of what is *not* offered to God. Thus conflating Jesus' "sacrifice for sin" of "his own blood" with his suffering "outside the camp" combines two images that Torah and Jewish tradition keep distinct from, indeed opposed to, one another.

Joined with the call to "go to him outside the camp," this transgressive combination expresses the most profound and challenging of Christian values: readiness to transcend all boundaries in solidarity with those who are disempowered and excluded.

Justin Jaron Lewis

and the atoning death of Jesus, who suffered "outside the city gate" (Heb 13:12). Consistent with the pilgrimage theme, the addressees are exhorted to follow him "outside the camp" and share in his suffering (13:13) and are reminded of their true destination; this is not the earthly Jerusalem, outside whose precincts Jesus was crucified, but "the city that is to come," the celestial Zion (12:22-24).

A Jewish Perspective (Heb 13:11-13)

Hebrews 13:11-13 retreats from the triumphalist tone of the earlier rhetoric about Jesus as the true high priest. Envisioning Jesus not in the holy of holies but in the profane setting "outside the camp" perhaps reflects a ruefully realistic awareness of the situation of early Jesus-followers as a marginal group.

Corresponding to their heavenly destination, the kinds of "sacrifice" commended to the community are immaterial: praise to God, confessing God's name, doing good, and sharing possessions (Heb 13:15-16).[13] Such

---

13. See Pss 4:6; 50:14, 23; 106:12; 115:17; Prov 21:3; Amos 4:5; Tob 8:19.

a view of sacrifice is deeply in tune with the theology of Christian Eucharist, although the homilist does not seem to relate these two things at all. The very fact of the eucharistic act as sacramental is manifest in the sharing of meals, as a way of experiencing the presence of Christ, μυστήριον, by identifying bread and wine with his body and blood, an action that gains its meaning only in the act of sharing as people of God, followers of Jesus.

This Greek word μυστήριον, difficult to translate in English, is used in liturgical theology to refer to the acts in which God is disclosed to us, in the same way as Jesus tells the disciples, "To you has been given the secret [μυστήριον] of the kingdom of God" (Mark 4:11).[14] Though it is impossible to fully understand μυστήριον, the secret and unrevealed nature of God's presence is tangibly grasped and experienced in the work of the people in praising, confessing, and sharing together. The participation of all members of the community in offering such spiritual sacrifices implicitly confers priestly status on them all, brothers and sisters, women and men. Nevertheless, the addressees are directed to "obey" and "submit to" the leaders, who will be called to a reckoning (ὡς λόγον) regarding the souls of the community, presumably at the last judgment (Heb 13:17; see also 4:13; 6:2; 9:27; 10:27; 12:25-29). The addressees are threatened with harm if the leaders are obliged to render their account to God "with sighing" rather than "with joy." As with previous instances of rhetorical bullying and manipulation (see comments on 6:1-12; 10:26-31), the homilist's insistence that the audience members "submit" and "obey" not only for their own good but in order to spare the feelings of the leaders is problematic from a feminist standpoint. Here the audience is placed in the position of dependent wives, children, and slaves, expected to obey and submit to patriarchal leadership (see Col 3:18-25; Eph 5:22–6:9; 1 Pet 3:1, 7), and subjected to emotional blackmail: not to be duly submissive and obedient would cause the *leaders* pain and hurt the disobedient themselves in some unspecified way: "Let *them* do this with joy and not with sighing—for that would be harmful *to you*" (Heb 13:17b). It is easy to imagine that some members of the community—including leaders—were tired of being subjected to suffering and deprivation in the service of a judgmental God for an invisible future reward.

---

14. See James F. White, *Introduction to Christian Worship*, 3rd ed. (Nashville, TN: Abingdon, 2000), 181.

Hebrews and Household Codes

It is important not to overgeneralize the influence of household codes in the first century as expressed in NT texts (Col 3:18-25; Eph 5:22–6:9; 1 Pet 3:1, 7). Sarah Tanzer has observed that "in the Roman Empire the patriarchal household coexisted (though perhaps uneasily) with emancipatory ideas about women that allowed for greater freedom and independence of women." It is fair to say, however, that the homilist's pastorally forceful advice in Hebrews, which is comparable to other household code texts, aims to "establish the authority of the ruler of the household (husband, fathers, masters), [which is] far-reaching [and extends to] the church understood on the model of the household, with Christ as ruler." Such codes of order, "a common ethic of the Hellenistic world" rather than specifically Christian are, however, perhaps also understood as evidence of how disruptive and subversive this emerging group, called Christians (Acts 11:26), would have been, as Kathleen Corley argues. In the Roman Empire's colonial system, she continues, the ruling colonialists were focused on "the stability of the imperial state: slaves are to submit to their masters, women to their husbands, and all are to submit to the elders of the church and, ultimately, to Rome." After all, "these new foreign religions attracted women and slaves [and were therefore vulnerable to] accusations of immorality and the intent to subvert Roman political and social authority." (*Sources:* Sarah J. Tanzer, "Ephesians," in *Searching the Scriptures*, vol. 2: *A Feminist Commentary*, ed. Elisabeth Schüssler Fiorenza [New York: Crossroad, 1994], 325–48, at 332; Kathleen Corley, *Private Women, Public Meals: Social Conflict in the Synoptic Tradition* [Peabody, MA: Hendrickson, 1994], 351.)

HyeRan Kim-Cragg

Personal Requests from the Author(s) and Epistolary Postscript (Heb 13:18-25)

The last eight verses of Hebrews have an epistolary flavor. They fall into two sections: 13:18-21, beginning with a request from the writers to "pray for us" and concluding with a final "amen" (ἀμήν), a transliterated Hebrew word meaning "let it be so" that often appears at the end of NT letters.[15] Although the term is sometimes used in other parts of such

---

15. E.g., Rom 16:27; 1 Cor 16:24; 2 Cor 13:14; Phil 4:23; Eph 6:24; Col 4:18; 1 Thess 5:28; 2 Thess 3:18; Phlm 25; 1 Tim 6:21; 2 Tim 4:22; Titus 3:15; 1 Pet 5:14; 2 Pet 3:18; 1 John 5:21; Jude 25; Rev 22:21.

Heb 13:18-25

[18]Pray for us; we are sure that we have a clear conscience, desiring to act honorably in all things. [19]I urge you all the more to do this, so that I may be restored to you very soon.

[20]Now may the God of peace, who brought back from the dead our Lord Jesus, the great shepherd of the sheep, by the blood of the eternal covenant, [21]make you complete in everything good so that you may do his will, working among us that which is pleasing in his sight, through Jesus Christ, to whom be the glory forever and ever. Amen.

[22]I appeal to you, brothers and sisters, bear with my word of exhortation, for I have written to you briefly. [23]I want you to know that our brother Timothy has been set free; and if he comes in time, he will be with me when I see you. [24]Greet all your leaders and all the saints. Those from Italy send you greetings. [25]Grace be with all of you.

letters in expressions of praise or as an affirmation of divine attributes,[16] in Hebrews the "amen" is used only here, indicating the conclusion of the document (although some manuscripts add a second "amen" at the end of v. 25), in the manner of a formula at the end of a liturgy.[17] A postscript follows (13:22-25), adding personal details and instructions and identifying the genre of the document as "a word of exhortation" (λόγου τῆς παρακλήσεως) or homily.

Throughout Hebrews the homilist characteristically uses the first-person plural self-referentially, most often including him- or herself with the addressees (e.g., "therefore *we* must pay greater attention to what *we* have heard, so that *we* do not drift away from it," 2:1), sometimes addressing the audience in the second-person plural as separate from him- or herself (e.g., "take care, brothers and sisters, that none of *you* may have an evil, unbelieving heart that turns away from the living God," 3:12). The authorial "I" occurs only four times in the document: once in a rhetorical question interjected into the catalogue of heroes of faith ("what more shall I say?" 11:32); the other three in the concluding verses (13:19, 22, 23).[18] The shift between "we," "you," and "I" in the concluding verses has interesting implications for the authorship of the document, as the italicized pronouns in the final two subsections illustrate:

16. E.g., Rom 1:25; 9:5; 11:36; 2 Cor 1:20; Gal 1:5; Eph 3:21; 1 Tim 1:17; 1 Pet 5:11.

17. BDAG 53.

18. For a complete list of instances in which the author uses these pronouns, see Adolf von Harnack, "The Authorship of the Epistle to the Hebrews," *LCR* 19 (1900): 448–71, at 455.

Pray for *us;* we are sure that we have a clear conscience, desiring to act honorably in all things. *I* urge you all the more to do this, so that *I* may be restored to you very soon.

Now may the God of peace, who brought back from the dead our Lord Jesus, the great shepherd of the sheep, by the blood of the eternal covenant, make *you* complete in everything good so that *you* may do his will, working among *us* [some authorities read "you"] that which is pleasing in his sight, through Jesus Christ, to whom be the glory forever and ever. Amen.

I appeal to *you,* brothers and sisters, bear with *my* word of exhortation, for *I* have written to you briefly. *I* want you to know that *our* brother Timothy has been set free; and if he comes in time, he will be with me when *I* see you. Greet all *your* leaders and all the saints. Those from Italy send *you* greetings. Grace be with all of *you.*

Whereas in vv. 18-21 both the first-person plural ("pray for us") and first-person singular ("I urge you all the more") are used, vv. 22-25 use the first-person singular exclusively to refer to a single author. The list of personal requests begins with the formula "pray for us" (13:18; see also 1 Thess 5:25; 2 Thess 3:1), indicating collective authorship (see also 2 Cor 1:1; Phil 1:1; Col 1:1; 1 Thess 1:1; 2 Thess 1:1), or that a single author is speaking on behalf of a larger community to which he or she belongs. The request for prayer in the first-person singular (13:19-20) would support the latter hypothesis, implying that the homilist wishes to return from a host community to a home community. Another possibility is that the "I" is a reference to the scribe to whom the letter was dictated (see Rom 16:22), or an indication of a change in handwriting from the scribe's to the author's (see Gal 6:11; 1 Cor 16:21; Col 4:18; 2 Thess 3:17). In the former case it would be the scribe who was separated from his or her home community and wished to return; in the latter it would be the author who dictated the homily. The benediction (13:20-21) uses the Johannine-sounding title "the great shepherd of the sheep" (John 10:2, 11, 12, 14, 16; see also 1 Pet 2:25; 5:4) in conjunction with the central motif of the homily, "the blood of the eternal covenant," juxtaposing the messianic shepherd title (see Ezek 34:23; 37:24) with the divine promise to the Davidic line.[19] Otherwise, the language of the benediction is similar to Paul's.[20]

---

19. 2 Sam 23:5; 2 Chr 13:5; 21:7; 23:3; Ps 89:3; Isa 55:3; Jer 33:21; Sir 47:11.
20. E.g., Rom 15:33; 16:20; 2 Cor 13:11; Phil 4:9.

Harold Attridge sees vv. 22-25 as akin to the conclusions of other early Christian letters containing "a brief set of remarks that comment on the letter itself [and] give pertinent instructions or information about the sender or his emissaries."[21] These remarks differ from vv. 18-21 in that the author refers to him- or herself solely in the first-person singular ("I appeal to you . . . I have written to you . . . I want you to know") and makes specific references to the well-known Pauline missionary Timothy,[22] implying that he had recently been released from prison and would be traveling with the author to see the addressees: "he will be with me when I see you" (Heb 13:23b). The greeting to "all the leaders" (see 13:7, 17) and "all the saints" is offered not only by the author but by "those from Italy" (13:24), a phrase that could mean that a group of Italians was sending greetings home or that the greeting was from a home community in Italy—perhaps Rome—to a community elsewhere. As Attridge notes, of the two possibilities "the construal of the phrase as a reference to Italians away from home is slightly more natural and less problematic."[23] The final farewell matches the wording of Titus 3:15b verbatim.

Feminist Reflections on Multiple Authorship

The exegetical work of multiple subject locations fluidly moving from "I" to "we," to "he," back to "I," entails a notion of agency that is in tension with that of the audience to which this homily is addressed. In other words, when a single author, I, is speaking on behalf of a larger community to which he or she belongs, the notion of agency and the subject's location are stressed. Yet when the audience members are forced to "submit to" and "obey" their leaders (Heb 13:17), they become passive objects. Also, when the benediction uses "the great shepherd of the sheep" (13:20), this unidentified group, as the sheep, are asked to pray for the leaders, since it is assumed that they need to be restored by the leaders (13:18). In both cases the leaders are the agents of the group's well-being while the audience members become the passive recipients: "Let them

21. See 1 Thess 5:27; Titus 3:12-14; Col 4:7-8; Eph 6:21-22; 2 Tim 4:20-21; 1 Clem. 65.1. Attridge, *Hebrews*, 408.

22. Acts 16:1; 17:14, 15; 18:5; 19:22; 20:4; Rom 16:21; 1 Cor 4:17; 16:10; 2 Cor 1:1, 19; Phil 1:1; 2:19; 1 Thess 1:1; 3:2, 6; 2 Thess 1:1; Phlm 1:1; Col 1:1; 1 Tim 1:2, 18; 6:20; 2 Tim 1:2.

23. Ibid., 410.

[leaders] do this with joy and not with sighing—for that would be harmful to you" (13:17-18).

Here the postcolonial notion of the subaltern may be helpful, especially to those who identify themselves as being in a polarizing situation, a community with positive agents and passive objects. The term "subaltern," which is similar but not identical to the concept of *minjung*, discussed earlier, has broadened our understanding of those at the margins as "a name for the general attribute of subordination . . . whether this is expressed in terms of class, caste, age, gender, and office or in any other way." Many postcolonial and subaltern studies writers contend that these particular groups should be agents, although it is difficult to identify and impossible to locate who is who, just as we have difficulty identifying the authors and audiences of Hebrews among "I," "he," and "we." They are the subjects of their own life, yet objects who are "continually pulled back into the status quo." The imposition of the status quo code found in 13:17 can be viewed as a

Christianizing representation of the hierarchical Greco-Roman social morality. Perhaps this is a part of the canonization process, which is a colonial project in which the submissions of wives, children, and slaves intersect with the ruling offices of elites, priests, and male heads of the household.

No matter the possible speculations about who the author(s) and audience may be, it is clear that Hebrews presents "a new voice of Christianity, of a self-renewing Christianity continuing the polyglossia (not infrequently literally Pentecostal and accompanied by glossolalia, speech not of many languages but exceeding language itself)." (*Sources*: John Beaverly, *Subalternity and Representation: Arguments in Cultural Theory* [Durham, NC: Duke University Press, 1999], 26; Joerg Rieger, "Liberating God-Talk: Postcolonialism and the Challenge of the Margins," in *Postcolonial Theologies: Divinity and Empire*, 204–20, at 213; Catherine Keller, "The Love of Postcolonialism," 223.)

HyeRan Kim-Cragg

Although the greetings in vv. 18-25 have many affinities with the NT letters, especially those of Paul, the shift from the general (vv. 18-21) to the specific (vv. 22-25), the exclusive use of "I" in vv. 22-23, and the decisive-sounding "amen" in v. 21 suggest that the last four verses are a fragment from another letter, or a composition modeled on a Pauline letter, appended to the document to enhance its epistolary tone and to align it with the authoritative voice of Paul. In contrast, throughout the body of Hebrews "the author does not emphasize her or his identity but rather stresses God's continuing speech in scripture, the perfection made possible through Jesus in human life, and the undergirding of hope with faith in God."[24] This secondary Paulinization of Hebrews was an early step in the canonization process, which resulted in a collection of Scriptures that "sought not only to foster the authority of the local church officers and the organizational unity of the church but also to inculcate the kyriarchal pattern of submission that was the backbone of the imperial order."[25]

"Those from Italy" (Heb 13:24)

Ruth Hoppin uses the reference to "those from Italy" as part of her case that Priscilla, a prominent Italian believer, was the author of Hebrews:

Approaching a new set of signposts, we embark on a road to the city of origin. Too obvious to be missed, "They of Italy" . . . in Heb. 13.24 connects Hebrews with Rome. Italy denotes Rome, as it does in Acts 18.2. Only from Rome, a church center, would greetings likely be sent. Although the preposition ἀπὸ (from or away from) can refer to greetings sent either to or from Italy, it is used similarly in Acts 17.13, where "those in Thessalonica"

(οἱ ἀπὸ τῆς Θεσσαλονίκης) refers in context to Jews of Thessalonica in their own city. The same phrase, "they of Italy," in Acts 18.2 isn't really comparable. Referring to Priscilla and Aquila expatriate in Corinth, the phrase is "having come from Italy," not "they of Italy."

For further discussion of the Priscilla hypothesis, see the introduction, lviii–lix. (*Source*: Ruth Hoppin, "The Epistle to the Hebrews is Priscilla's Letter," in *A Feminist Companion to the Catholic Epistles and Hebrews* FCNTECW 8 [Cleveland, OH: Pilgrim Press, 2004], 147–70, at 165–66.)

Mary Ann Beavis

---

24. Cynthia Briggs Kittredge, "Hebrews," in *Searching the Scriptures, Volume Two: A Feminist Commentary*, 428–54, at 450.

25. Elisabeth Schüssler Fiorenza, "Transgressing Canonical Boundaries," in *Searching the Scriptures*, vol. 2: *A Feminist Commentary*, ed. Elisabeth Schüssler Fiorenza (New York: Crossroad, 1994), 1–14, at 7.

Interpretive Essay: Hospitality: A Two-Edged Sword?

As a contributing voice, I am interested in highlighting marginal characters in the biblical text.[26] Since the homily almost never speaks of women, I would like to remember once again the women characters evoked by Heb 13:2. Using a narrative approach,[27] particularly characterization, I will reread the roles of the women characters brought to mind by the hospitality command. I will explore the characters from a postcolonial and liberationist perspective as I relate the role of the biblical characters to the roles of a particular group of present readers: Filipina domestic workers. As a biblical student in Louvain, Belgium, I had the opportunity to accompany a Filipino/a migrant workers' charismatic prayer group through Bible study and Bible sharing. Some of them work as domestic helpers in different parts of Belgium. My contribution is an attempt to provide an echo of their voices.

Introduction

Readers of Hebrews, especially those who care about women in the Scriptures and the influence of the Scriptures on women, will affirm Mary Rose D'Angelo's observation: "Women are included in Hebrews, but only marginally."[28] Only Sarah and Rahab are mentioned explicitly (11:11-12, 31). In this contribution I will reread the stories evoked by Heb 13:2: "Do not neglect to show hospitality to strangers, for by doing that some have entertained angels without knowing it." It seems to me that there is a need to remember the role of women in these evoked stories since this command, now taken as a word of God, can be seen as twofold: women provide hospitality, but they are also in need of hospitality.

---

26. See Ma. Marilou S. Ibita, "Fostering Narrative Approaches to Scripture in Asia: The Primary Task of Explicit Recognition," *EAPR* 46 (2009): 124–41, at 130–31, where I discuss the importance of the messages of minor characters in the biblical stories and the challenges they pose.

27. See, for example, Kenneth Schenck, "Hebrews as the Re-presentation of a Story: A Narrative Approach to Hebrews," in *Reading the Epistle to the Hebrews: A Resource for Students*, ed. Eric F. Mason and Kevin B. McCruden, RBS 66 (Leiden and Boston: Brill, 2011), 171–88.

28. Mary Rose D'Angelo, "Hebrews," in *The Women's Bible Commentary*, ed. Carol A. Newsom and Sharon H. Ringe (Louisville, KY: Westminster John Knox, 1992), 364–67, at 365.

As noted in the commentary, the value of loving one's family (Heb 13:1) is extended to "love of strangers" by means of the command to be hospitable (13:2). Bruce J. Malina and John J. Pilch explain that in the practice of hospitality in the ancient Mediterranean world "the outsider is 'received' and socially transformed from stranger to guest."[29] Both men and women are involved in the practice of hospitality. Recalling some of the biblical narratives of hospitality and the women's roles, however, particularly in food preparation and at meals, I see that the command of hospitality, with all its implications, is like a double-edged sword for both the biblical women and present-day Filipina domestic workers.

Hospitality and Some Biblical Women

I will divide my discussion of hospitality in the biblical narratives into two parts. First, I will describe the women characters in the stories who provide hospitality to angelic visitors and some people recognized as sent by God. Then I will also review these stories and some others that show women in need of hospitality.

1.1 PROVIDING HOSPITALITY

In the stories that more clearly connect the practice of hospitality with entertaining angels in the rest of the Scriptures (Gen 18:1-15, 19:1-3;[30] Judg 6:11-18; 13:3-22, and the book of Tobit),[31] food is an important feature of hospitality. Men feature prominently, but women have important roles to play too.

The primary narrative that comes to mind in connection with Heb 13:2 is Gen 18:1-15. In the first part of the story Abraham is characterized as actively providing food, along with a servant (Gen 18:1-8). Sarah is described as being asked to prepare the cakes (Gen 18:6). After the meal is over, however, Sarah is thrust into the limelight. The visitors ask for her, and Abraham indicates where she is (18:9). She physiologically bears the

---

29. See Bruce J. Malina and John J. Pilch, *Social-Science Commentary on the Book of Acts* (Minneapolis: Fortress Press, 2008), 214.

30. Genesis 19 does not include a meal, even though Lot welcomes the angelic visitors in Gen 18. As host, however, Lot tries to protect his angelic visitors at the expense of his daughters (19:7). While the daughters were spared (19:12, 16) at the destruction of Sodom, Lot's wife was not (19:26).

31. See also David A. deSilva, *Perseverance in Gratitude: A Socio-Rhetorical Commentary on the Epistle "to the Hebrews"* (Grand Rapids, MI: Eerdmans, 2000), 488.

blessing that comes after the matriarch and patriarch have extended hospitality to the visitors. Sarah's having a son is considered a measure of time in connection with the return of the visitors (18:10). The old age of the couple is highlighted with an additional piece of information: "it had ceased to be with Sarah after the manner of women" (18:11). Moreover, there is a description of Sarah's response, her laughter and her musings (18:12). While the Lord speaks again to Abraham in a way that reprimands Sarah (18:13), the promise of a son is reiterated (18:14). Furthermore, in v. 15 there is direct communication between Sarah and the Lord: "But Sarah denied, saying, 'I did not laugh'; for she was afraid. He said, 'Oh yes, you did laugh.'"

The story of Gideon entertaining an angel (Judg 6:11-18) does not mention any woman, but Judg 13:3-22 describes the unnamed wife of Manoah speaking to an angel twice (13:3-6, 9) before the angel speaks to Manoah (13:11-18). She is given a voice to relate this to her husband, detailing the content of her conversations with the angel (13:6-7), who finally appears to Manoah; after their conversation, Manoah offers a food sacrifice to the Lord. While Manoah realizes too late that this is the angel of the Lord (v. 21), the wife knows it from the beginning (v. 6). She corrects her husband's misunderstanding and allays his fear: "If the LORD had meant to kill us, he would not have accepted a burnt offering and a grain offering at our hands, or shown us all these things, or now announced to us such things as these" (13:23). The episode also ends with the "woman" in focus: "The *woman bore* a son, and *named* him Samson" (13:24).

In the book of Tobit[32] the angel Raphael disguises himself as Azariah, a relative (Tob 5:13). He is heartily welcomed by Tobit (5:14) and he journeys with Tobias to Ecbatana (chaps. 6–12). While Tobit's kinsman Raguel is elaborately described as extending hospitality, Edna, his wife, also takes an active part in welcoming the visitors. She asks about their identity (7:4) and weeps along with Raguel and Sarah, their daughter, upon recognizing Tobias. While only the men recline at table, Sarah and Edna are called in when Tobias insists, right before the meal, that he wishes to marry Sarah.[33] Edna's role in preparing her daughter for her

---

32. The role of Anna, Tobit's wife, in preparing the food for her family is both implicit (2:1) and explicit (2:11-14) but is downplayed when Azariah appears.

33. See Susan Marks, "Present and Absent: Women at Greco-Roman Wedding Meals," in *Meals in the Early Christian World: Social Formation, Experimentation, and Conflict at the Table*, ed. Dennis E. Smith and Hal E. Taussig (New York: Palgrave Macmillan, 2012), 123–48.

eighth marriage is highlighted (7:13-15). As the story nears its end, the importance of hospitality and meals is also underscored when Azariah reveals that he is the angel Raphael, who accepted the hospitality offered to him and ate and drank, even if only in a vision (Tob 12:19).

In these scriptural stories that feature women's role in providing hospitality we see that women are, to some extent, capable of providing the food needed for their guests. There are some examples, however, in which women serve as hosts not to angelic visitors but to people recognized sooner or later as sent by God. For instance, we have the story of the wealthy woman who provided meals for Elisha (2 Kgs 4:8-37). There is also the example of those who provide hospitality even if they themselves are in need. During the drought predicted by Elijah, the prophet survives hunger through the help of the widow of Zarephath (1 Kgs 17:8-17). Because she feeds him (at his insistence), she and her son are saved from dying of hunger, and her words are very telling: "As the Lord your God lives, I have nothing baked, only a handful of meal in a jar, and a little oil in a jug; I am now gathering a couple of sticks, so that I may go home and prepare it for myself and my son, that we may eat it, and die" (17:12). This indicates that not all hosts can afford to provide for guests, yet they endeavor to give them their all.

The command to be hospitable in Heb 13:2 also shows the influence of the Wisdom tradition concerning hospitality. Reflecting the influence of Greco-Roman banquet practices, Sirach contains several pointers on table etiquette,[34] mostly addressed to men (Sir 13:8-11; 27:29-31; 29:21-28; 30:25; 31:12-31; 32:1-13). In these texts the role of women in providing hospitality, such as food preparation, is implicit and silenced, despite the descriptions of rich banquets.[35] We note, however, that Proverbs pictures Lady Wisdom as providing rich food and drink (9:1-6). Wisdom's feast contrasts with a banquet set by a ruler, which includes deceptive food that does not truly satisfy, causing diners to vomit the little they have ingested (see Prov 23:1-8).

Meals as a form of hospitality abound in the Christian Scriptures, even if there are no instances of providing food to angelic visitors. Instead there

---

34. On Sirach and table etiquette, see Ursula Rapp, "You Are How You Eat: How Eating and Drinking Behaviour Identifies the Wise According to Jesus Ben Sirach," in *Decisive Meals: Table Politics in Biblical Literature*, trans. Martin Rumscheidt, ed. Kathy Ehrensperger, Nathan MacDonald, and Luzia Sutter Rehmann, LNTS 449 (New York: T & T Clark, 2012), 42–61.

35. For the role of women in preparing meals and at banquets, see the various articles in Smith and Taussig, *Meals*.

are characters who provide hospitality to Jesus and his followers, especially traveling missionaries. Many of these stories are found in Luke, where Jesus does mighty deeds and instructs before, during, and after a meal.[36] Even in these meals, however, the hosts are mostly men.[37] Nevertheless, Luke 8:1-3 notes that women provided for Jesus. Martha also waited at table for Jesus (Luke 10:38-42), as did Peter's mother-in-law (Mark 1:31).

Other prominent missionaries among the Christ-believers are helped by hospitality extended by women. Peter, after being freed from prison, takes refuge in the house of Mary, the mother of John Mark (Acts 12:12-17). Paul and the gatherings of Christ-believers were hosted by some women: Lydia (Acts 16:14-15);[38] Prisca/Priscilla and Aquila (1 Cor 16:19; Rom 16:3-5; Acts 18:2-3, 18); Philemon and Apphia (Phlm 2); and Phoebe (Rom 16:1-2).[39] As in the Pauline assemblies and the audience of Hebrews, it was through the practice of hospitality by the different communities that itinerant missionaries could spread the Gospel.[40]

Overall, this short review of the practice of hospitality shows that in these meal scenes, even if men are presented prominently, the roles women play are also important in entertaining visitors, including angels. The visitors seem to pay equal attention to both the female and male characters. The women characters, however, bear the physical marks or effects of providing hospitality to these visitors. Sarah becomes pregnant and bears a son just as the wife of Manoah does. The younger Sarah (in the book of Tobit) is freed from the demon that killed her seven husbands, and she has to leave her parents as a consequence of her marriage to Tobias. The advice on hospitality in the Wisdom tradition speaks mainly to men only as banqueters, while the women's role is silenced—apart from Lady Wisdom's playing the role of host. In the Christian Scriptures,

---

36. See Ma. Marilou S. Ibita, "Dining with Jesus in the Third Gospel: Celebrating Eucharist in the Third World," *EAPR* 42 (2005): 249–61. For a comprehensive treatment of meal scenes in the Christian Testament, see Dennis E. Smith, *From Symposium to Eucharist: The Banquet in the Early Christian World* (Minneapolis: Fortress Press, 2003).

37. Luke 9:29, Levi; 7:36 and 11:37, a Pharisee; 14:1, a leader of the Pharisees; 19:5-7, Zacchaeus.

38. See Richard S. Ascough, *Lydia: Paul's Cosmopolitan Hostess*, Paul's Social Network: Brothers and Sisters in Faith (Collegeville, MN: Liturgical Press, 2009), 29–35.

39. See Joan Cecelia Campbell, *Phoebe: Patron and Emissary*, Paul's Social Network: Brothers and Sisters in Faith (Collegeville, MN: Liturgical Press, 2009), 92.

40. See deSilva, *Perseverance in Gratitude*, 487–88; Knut Backhaus, "How to Entertain Angels: Ethics in the Epistle to the Hebrews," in *Hebrews: Contemporary Methods, New Insights*, ed. Gabriella Gelardini, BibInt 75 (Leiden: Brill, 2005), 149–75, at 163.

despite the absence of stories about meals offered to angels, Jesus and the traveling missionaries benefit from women's hospitality.

Needing Hospitality

The wife of Manoah and the women of Tobit do not necessarily need hospitality themselves, since they are not travelers. Nevertheless, if we look at the obverse of being a host we realize that women are also guests in need of hospitality in the context of the larger narratives.

The stories of the two Sarahs contrast with each other. The Sarah of Tobit, as Tobias's wife, is welcomed and blessed (Tob 11:17). In Genesis 18, however, we recall that the setting is Mamre. Even as they played host to the angelic visitors, Abraham, Sarah, and their household were nomads in need of hospitality themselves. As wanderers, they were in a precarious situation. The unfolding of the Abraham saga tells us that by the time of Gen 20 they have arrived in the Negev. Here Sarah is once again in sexual danger and in need of protection (Gen 20:1-18; see also 12:10-20) because of Abraham's attempt to save his own life.

Turning to the Christian Testament, we have stories of women pilgrims who continue to play the role of hosts despite being in need of hospitality themselves. The women followers of Jesus from Galilee would have needed accommodation when they arrived in Jerusalem for Passover and after the crucifixion (Mark 15:40-41; Matt 27:55-56; Luke 23:49). Paul, a recipient of many people's hospitality, asks the believers in Rome to receive Phoebe because she is "a servant of the church which is at Cenchreae . . . a benefactor of many and of myself as well" (Rom 16:1-2). One wonders whether Prisca and Aquila "risked their necks for Paul's life" (Rom 16:4) as they traveled with him.

These texts remind us that women are not only providers of hospitality; they are also in need of hospitality so that they are safe and enabled to fulfill the tasks they must do even if they are not in their own homes. The two Sarahs are also depicted in the biblical texts, however, as harsh mistresses of their own women slaves. In Gen 16; 21:8-20, Sarah treats the Egyptian Hagar and her son Ishmael harshly. Likewise, in Tobit, Sarah is unkind to her maids, resulting in one taunting her and cursing her (Tob 3:8-9). These stories present the women as complex characters. Without carefully rereading their roles in the male-centered narratives we will lose the chance to critically reread stories that also represent aspects of the lives of present-day women.

Hospitality and Filipina Domestic Workers

Similarly to the biblical women whose stories we find echoed in Heb 13:2, the command of hospitality functions like a double-edged sword to Filipinas, both as hosts and as guests.

2.1 FILIPINAS AS PROVIDERS OF HOSPITALITY

Hebrews 13:2 challenges and affirms lowland Filipino/a Christians.[41] It affirms our basic family-orientedness,[42] treating others hospitably as family members and providing hospitality marked by meals:

> We Filipinos are *meal-oriented (salu-salo, kainan)*. Because Filipinos consider almost everyone as part of their family *(parang pamilya)*, we are known for being gracious hosts and grateful guests. Serving our guests with the best we have is an inborn value to Filipinos, rich and poor alike. We love to celebrate any and all events with a special meal. Even with unexpected guests, we Filipinos try our best to offer something, meager as it may be, with the traditional greeting: "Come and eat with us" *(Tuloy po kayo at kumain muna tayo)*. [43]

Filipinas learn when very young to do the basics of work at home. Generally speaking, cooking and food preparation are considered women's work in the Philippines. Usually women cook every day for their families' needs. When preparing for guests it is very common for women to cook and serve foods that are to the guests' liking. Moreover, it is not unusual for unexpected guests or even strangers who find themselves in a Filipino home to be treated like family and given something to eat and drink to make them feel at home,[44] even if it means that the host

41. See José M. deMesa, *And God Said, "Bahala na!": The Theme of Providence in the Lowland Filipino Context*, Maryhill Studies 2 (Quezon City: Publishers' Printing Press, 1979), Foreword: "The Lowland Christian Groups—Cebuano, Tagalog, Ilokano, Ilongo, Bikolano, Waray-Waray, Pampango and Pangasinan."

42. See Episcopal Commission on Catechesis and Catholic Education, *Catechism for Filipino Catholics* (Manila: ECCCE, 2005), no. 34.

43. DeMesa, *And God Said*, 37.

44. For a more nuanced explanation of the dining process that shows the interrelationship between meal-partakers in a Filipino setting, see Ma. Marilou S. Ibita, "Conversation with the Story of the Lord's Supper in 1 Corinthians 11:17-34: Engaging the Scripture Text and the Filipino Christians' Context," *1 and 2 Corinthians: Text and Contexts*, ed. Yung Suk Kim (Minneapolis: Fortress Press, 2013), 97–115. See also Carmen Santiago, "The Language of Food," in *The Culinary Culture of the Philippines* (Manila: Bancom Audiovision, 1976), 133–39.

needs to procure these things from a nearby store, perhaps taking a loan at the store for the food products.

2.2. Filipinas in Need of Hospitality

Early training in housework, especially cooking and food preparation, helps rural and urban women find work in small, medium, and large-scale food businesses. In the same way, it provides an increasingly large workforce in the field of hospitality and services both in the Philippines and abroad. Since the 1970s[45] a significant number of Filipinas, including many who are well educated but are also skilled in housework, women who are hard working, with a deep sense of love for family and wanting to take them out of poverty,[46] have begun to work overseas as domestic helpers.[47] The Filipina who is used to being a host has turned into something else. Unlike the biblical women who are pilgrims and wanderers, Filipinas have become not only pilgrims but migrant workers in need of hospitality, safety, and protection in their workplaces in host countries.[48] This is the second challenge of Heb 13:2.

45. See Kathleen Nadeau, "Out-Migration from the Philippines with a Focus on the Middle East: A Case Study," *EAPR* 45 (2008); see http://idjames.org/2012/06 /out-migration-from-the-philippines-with-a-focus-on-the-middle-east-a-case-study/, accessed July 15, 2015.

46. These factors also exposed the Filipinas to becoming mail-order brides, a subject that is out of our framework here. See, e.g., http://www.articlesbase.com/dating -articles/7-golden-characteristics-of-philippine-girls-and-filipino-women-550569. html, accessed July 15, 2015. A random internet search for "Filipina mail order bride" on 25 October 2012 resulted in 245,000 hits in 0.31 seconds. Trafficked and prostituted women referred to as "hospitality girls" are another related issue that cannot be addressed here. See http://feminism.eserver.org/gender/sex-work/trafficking-of -women.txt, accessed July 15, 2015.

47. The gender issue in migration worldwide, for both documented and undocumented workers, including Filipinas, is huge and cannot be treated here. Filipino/a migrant workers are found in many white- and blue-collar jobs, but domestic work dominates. The 2010 Philippine Overseas Employment Administration record shows that 1,703 men and 94,880 women are recorded as "household service workers." For more information see http://www.poea.gov.ph/ar/ar2010.pdf, accessed July 15, 2015.

48. The latest electronically available official report from the Philippine Overseas Employment Administration claims that about 4,030 land- and sea-based migrant workers left the Philippines every day in 2010 (ibid.). Saudi Arabia remains the top destination, followed by the UAE, Hong Kong, Qatar, Singapore, Kuwait, Taiwan, Italy, Bahrain, and Canada. For a brief overview of the case of domestic workers worldwide, see Gloria Moreno-Fontes Chammartin, "Domestic Workers: Little Pro-

The obligation to provide hospitality, as the biblical narratives show, is a double-edged sword, and this is even clearer in the case of migrant workers. On the one hand, they are hailed as new heroes/heroines and "new evangelizers." They are the new heroes/heroines as they economically help their home country through their remittances. Migrant workers, very many of them domestic workers, are also described in the church as "new evangelizers,"[49] much like the first generation of itinerant Christ-believers. This challenge and task are tested in places where Christianity is not the majority religion and others where it has been the majority but is losing ground.

Being "new evangelizers" takes many forms. Margaret Magat explains that in Italy, for example, this includes the private and the public sphere, from teaching young Italian wards how to pray the rosary to inviting employers to join in religious and cultural celebrations that also serve as an occasion for sharing Filipino cuisine.[50] Nevertheless, a critical look at the migrant as new evangelizer is also necessary. As Magat observes, "The image of the Filipino migrant as the 'new evangelizer' has been largely accepted and not questioned by the women collaborators I interviewed."[51] Magat critically describes this trend:

> The image of the migrant worker as the new evangelizer can be compared to . . . the one propagated by the Philippine government: that the workers, or overseas contract workers (OCWs), are the "bagong bayani" or the new heroes of the Philippines for bringing in remittances that aid their country. Some women are proud of this label and the supercilious treatment they received when they returned for infrequent

---

tection for the Underpaid," at http://www.migrationinformation.org/Feature/display.cfm?ID=300, accessed July 15, 2015.

49. For a short overview on migration and new evangelization, see Bishop Gilbert A. Garcera, DD, on "Filipino Migrants as New Evangelizers," http://www.familiam .org/pcpf/allegati/1593/4_Garcera_ENG.pdf, accessed July 15, 2015. For a critical view of this, see Margaret Magat, "Teachers and 'New Evangelizers' for their Faith: Filipina Domestic Workers at Work in Italy," *Paedagogica Historica: International Journal of the History of Education* 43 (2007): 603–24, at 618–20. This perspective on migrants as new evangelizers continues in the Synod of Bishops, XIII Ordinary General Assembly, "The New Evangelization for the Transmission of the Christian Faith," *Lineamenta* 13, available at http://www.vatican.va/roman_curia/synod/documents /rc_synod_doc_20110202_lineamenta-xiii-assembly_en.html#_ftn49 (accessed July 15, 2015): "Migrants must not simply be evangelized but be trained themselves to be evangelizing agents."

50. Magat, "Teachers," 619.

51. Ibid., 620, 623–24.

visits to the Philippines, while others I talked to dismissed it and saw it as a ploy for the government to cover up its failures to generate jobs, which would make migration for work unnecessary.[52]

On the other hand, migrant workers, including Filipina domestic workers, are also in need of hospitality. During the Jubilee of Migrants and Itinerant People, Pope John Paul II opened his message with Heb 13:1-2, saying: "The passage from the Letter to the Hebrews, which we heard a few moments ago, links the exhortation to offer hospitality to the guest, the pilgrim and the stranger with the commandment of love, which sums up the new law of Christ."[53] This underscores the point that migrant workers are also people to be ministered to by the church.

The hospitality extended to Filipina domestic helpers varies widely and their level of integration within the host country is not uniform. Despite some who are lucky enough to find good jobs and good employers, it is not uncommon for them to be subjected to harsh working conditions as well as physical (and sexual), verbal, and psycho-emotional abuse, being unpaid or underpaid, hunger, discrimination, lack of support in cases of breaking contracts with abusive employers or being victims of illegal recruiters and other issues in dispute. The cases of undocumented workers are even worse.[54] Sometimes instances of abuse lead to the deaths of domestic workers.[55]

One thing that helps Filipina migrant workers cope is their religious commitment and its varied expressions, especially when they are far from home. Participating in Sunday Eucharist is key. This celebration is usually followed by table fellowship in the form of a potluck Filipino meal, an occasion for the Filipina migrant workers, such as the domestics I met in Brussels, to receive hospitality from each other. A few studies have also been conducted on the role of religion among Filipina domestic workers in Hong Kong and how their hospitality toward each other, such as food sharing, helps them to survive and cope with the challenges they have to

52. Ibid., 618.

53. John Paul II, "Jubilee of Migrants and Itinerant People," June 2, 2000, available at http://www.vatican.va/holy_father/john_paul_ii/homilies/2000/documents/hf_jp-ii_hom_20000602_jubilmigrants_en.html, accessed July 15, 2015.

54. http://www.hrw.org/world-report-2012/world-report-2012-landmark-victory-domestic-workers, and http://www.hrw.org/world-report-2012/world-report-2012-landmark-victory-domestic-workers, accessed May 28, 2015.

55. See also Lisa Law, "Home Cooking: Filipino Women and Geographies of the Senses in Hong Kong," *Cultural Geographies* 8 (2001): 264–83, at 268, available at http://cgj.sagepub.com/content/8/3/264.full.pdf, accessed July 15, 2015.

face.[56] It is through their Christian faith and at church that migrants, including Filipina domestic helpers, find comfort in the midst of the sacrifices they make for the well-being of their families and as their nation's economic lifeline. Yet there are also times when their faith is inadequate to help them critically assess their difficult and unjust situations.[57] While the church helps many migrant workers to cope with challenges abroad, often the emphasis is on resilience, faith witnessing, and especially self-sacrifice.[58]

This brief discussion has shown that, given the multiple burdens the Filipina domestic workers carry to support themselves, their families, their nation, and also their church, it is very important that their rights be continuously upheld by the church, the Philippine government,[59] and their host countries.

Conclusion

In sum, the command not to neglect hospitality in Heb 13:2 beckons us to recall the scriptural stories of women who provided hospitality and were also in need of hospitality. There are many similarities between the demand and the need for hospitality in the lives of women in biblical narratives and in the present lives of Filipina domestic workers, even if there are some differences in detail. They all model hosts who extend

56. See ibid., 267–81; Gemma Tulod Cruz, "Pilgrims in the Wilderness: Religion and Filipino Women in the Context of Migration," *EAPR* 46 (2009), n.p., available at http://www.eapi.org.ph/resources/eapr/east-asian-pastoral-review-2009/volume-46-2009-number-4/pilgrims-in-the-wilderness-religion-and-filipino-women-in-the-context-of-migration, accessed July 15, 2015.

57. Magat, "Teachers," 611–17.

58. See ibid., 623: "It is the task of priests like Father Nonong and Father Bati whenever possible to encourage the Filipinos in Italy and elsewhere to look at their service jobs with all their manifest and hidden difficulties as an opportunity to live their faith." It is interesting to note that the second Filipino saint to be canonized (on October 21, 2012), the martyr St. Pedro Calungsod, is hailed as a patron of overseas Filipino migrants. See Noel Sales Barcelona, "Migrants Celebrate St. Pedro Calungsod's Canonization," *CBCP News*, October 29, 2012, http://www.cbcpnews.com/cbcpnews/?p=6307, accessed July 15, 2015.

59. The Philippines is the second country to ratify the Domestic Workers Convention that protects their rights. See the section, "The Domestic Workers' Convention: Turning New Global Standards Into Change on the Ground" in "World Report 2012: A Landmark Victory for Domestic Workers," at http://www.hrw.org/world-report-2012/world-report-2012-landmark-victory-domestic-workers, accessed May 28, 2015. To date, only twenty-two countries have ratified this convention. The United States is not one of them; neither is Canada.

hospitality, with some doing so even at their own expense. Some of them can inflict harm on other women (as the two Sarahs did), yet they are also women in need of hospitality. They share some of the dangers and abuses that pilgrims and migrants must face and overcome. They are women of faith who journey in life: the biblical women are pilgrims along the way, while the Filipinas are mostly migrant workers who long to return home. Rereading the biblical stories and reading or hearing about the stories of migrant women makes us realize that the command to hospitality has a twofold effect on women who want to take this message seriously both as hosts and as pilgrims or migrants in need of hospitality.

The command in Heb 13:2 is beautifully illustrated in a mandala by the Indian painter Lucy D'Souza Krone called "Table of Nations," in which everyone is pictured as both host and guest:

> The mandala shows a six-cornered star with the eucharistic gifts of bread and wine in the center. People of many nations have gathered around the round table. They bring gifts and fruits typical of their

countries. The upper point of the star points to Jesus, who has raised his hands in blessing. His clothes are the color of fire, indicating his love for God and for us. On the right side of the painting, symbolizing the East, people from Asia are seated. The man in red comes from Israel, and is followed by children from the Middle East and Africa. A woman from Europe sits, with her children, opposite Jesus. From the West come South and North Americans; finally there are a boy from Germany and a Maasai girl from Tanzania.

The points of the star are directed at women who hold their babies in their arms and men who look at us and invite us to join the celebration with the children gathered here. All this takes place in God's beautifully created cosmos, with sun, moon, and stars. In the painting we see five loaves of bread and two fish. Jesus, as the light of the world and the bread of life, invites us to celebrate together with all—at the table of the Lord, which is the table of the nations.[60]

Ma. Marilou Ibita

60. "Tisch der Nationen," at http://www.lucy-art.de/galerie.htm, accessed July 15, 2015. Translated from German by Andreas Krone.

Afterword

Biblical commentaries do not usually feature conclusions, but this distinctive series invites reflection on the task of writing a feminist, multi-vocal commentary. As both an author and one of the editors of the series I can attest that it has been a rewarding and a challenging experience.

From a feminist exegetical standpoint, two contributions of the commentary stand out. One is the realization that Hebrews is, indeed, a submerged tradition of Sophia. Although Hebrews never uses the term "wisdom," it is the New Testament writing that most resembles the book of Wisdom, and its Christology, cosmology, ethics, and perspective on sacred history echo many sophialogical themes. The second is the approach to the problem of sacrifice, an aspect of the biblical tradition that has been thoroughly critiqued by feminist scholars. It is undeniable that Hebrews has given strong canonical grounds for the interpretation of sacrifice as intrinsic to Christian soteriology and ethics. As argued in the body of the commentary, however, traditional theological associations of sacrifice with suffering, self-denial, death, and abjection are foreign to ancient understandings of sacrificial rituals. For the biblical tradition, including Hebrews, the basic meaning of the Latin term *sacrificio*, "make sacred," captures the significance of the ritual better than the English term with its many negative associations. This means not that sacrifice should be embraced as a feminist theological category but that it needs to be understood on its own terms as celebratory and relational.

Commentary writing is usually a solitary task, and sharing the work, and the credit, with others is a novelty in a field that valorizes the individual exegete, toiling not only to illumine the text but to advance her academic career. For me as a biblical scholar, co-authoring with HyeRan Kim-Cragg, a Korean-Canadian postcolonial feminist theologian with expertise in pastoral theology of worship and religious education, has added richness and depth to the exposition, revealing dimensions of the text and of scholarship that were invisible to me, a European-Canadian historical-critical exegete. Likewise, the contributions from Filipina (Maricel and Marilou Ibita), Jewish (Justin Jaron Lewis), and proto-feminist historical (Nancy Calvert Koyzis) perspectives, and feminist Bible study sessions with the Friends of Sophia, all brought scholarly, cultural, religious, and experiential wisdom to the task, and the finished product is immeasurably better for it.

From my standpoint as a feminist biblical scholar, the thirteen poems by Marie Annharte Baker pose the most stimulating challenge to the feminist exegetical and theological enterprise. The title of this collection, "Our Stories Are Our Scriptures," as noted in the introduction, draws attention to the fact that many inhabitants of this continent know the Scriptures of the Middle East and its environs much better than we know the sacred stories native to the Americas—if we know them at all. Rather, the Jewish and Christian Scriptures have become our stories, and we have tended to assume their universal relevance. This is not to diminish the efforts of First Nations Christians who endeavor to be faithful both to the Bible and to their native cultures and spiritualities. Nevertheless, as feminist biblical scholars and theologians we need to listen attentively and respectfully to the wisdom of the stories of our own lands, and their First Nations interpreters, in their own right.

Mary Ann Beavis

Works Cited

Adelman, Penina V. *Miriam's Well: Rituals for Jewish Women Around the Year*. Fresh Meadows, NY: Biblio Press, 1986.

Ahn, Byung-Mu. *A Story of Minjung Theology*. Seoul: Theological Institute, 1987.

Alsup, John E. "Atonement." In *Harper's Bible Dictionary*, edited by Paul J. Achtemeier. San Francisco: HarperSanFrancisco, 1985.

Althaus-Reid, Marcella, and Lisa Isherwood. *Controversies in Feminist Theology*. London: SCM Press, 2007.

Anderson, Bernhard W. "Covenant." In *Oxford Companion to the Bible*, edited by Bruce M. Metzger and Michael D. Coogan, 138–39. New York/Oxford: Oxford University Press, 1993.

Ascough, Richard S. *Lydia: Paul's Cosmopolitan Hostess*. Paul's Social Network: Brothers and Sisters in Faith. Collegeville, MN: Liturgical Press, 2009.

Ashcroft, Bill, Gareth Griffiths, and Helen Tiffin. *The Empire Writes Back: Theory and Practice in Post-Colonial Literature*. London and New York: Routledge, 1989.

Attridge, Harold. *The Epistle to the Hebrews: A Commentary*. Hermeneia. Philadelphia: Fortress Press, 1989.

Bacon, Francis. "De Dignitate et Augmentis Scientiarum." In *The Philosophical Works of Francis Bacon*, edited by John M. Robertson, 413–638. London: Routledge; New York: Dutton, 1905.

Bagnall, Roger S., and Raffaela Cibiore, with Evie Ahtaridis. *Women's Letters from Ancient Egypt, 300 BC–800 AD*. Ann Arbor: University of Michigan Press, 2006.

Baker, Marie Annharte. *Imprint and Casualties: Poets on Women and Language, Reinventing Memory*. Edited by Anne Burke. Readings from the Living

Archives of the Feminist Caucus of the League of Canadian Poets. Vol. 2. Fredericton, NB: Broken Jaw Press, 2000.

———. *Indigena Awry.* Vancouver, BC: New Star Books, 2012.

Balentine, Samuel. E. *The Torah's Vision of Worship.* Minneapolis: Fortress Press, 1999.

Barker, Margaret. "Atonement: The Rite of Healing." Paper presented at the Society for Old Testament Study, Edinburgh. 1994. http://www.marquette .edu/maqom/atonement.html, accessed January 12, 2012.

Bartow, Charles. *God's Human Speech: A Practical Theology of Proclamation.* Grand Rapids, MI: Eerdmans, 1997.

———. "Performance Study in Service to the Spoken Word in Worship." In *Performance in Preaching: Bringing the Sermon to Life,* edited by Jana Childers and Clayton J. Schmit, 211–23. Grand Rapids, MI: Baker Academic, 2008.

Baskin, Judith R. "Menorah." In *Oxford Companion to the Bible,* edited by Bruce M. Metzger and Michael D. Coogan, 512. New York/Oxford: Oxford University Press, 1993.

Bateman, Herbert W., IV. "Psalm 110:1 and the New Testament." *BSac* 149 (1992): 438–53.

Bauckham, Richard, Daniel R. Driver, Trevor A. Hart, and Nathan MacDonald, eds. *The Epistle to the Hebrews and Christian Theology.* Grand Rapids, MI, and Cambridge: Eerdmans, 2009.

Beavis, Mary Ann. "2 Thessalonians." In *Searching the Scriptures.* Vol. 2: *A Feminist Commentary,* edited by Elisabeth Schüssler Fiorenza, 263–71. New York: Crossroad, 1994.

———. "The Aqedah, Jephtha's Daughter, and the Theme of Child Sacrifice in the Word of Canadian Women Authors." In *Feminist Theology with a Canadian Accent: Canadian Perspectives on Contextual Feminist Theology,* edited by Mary Ann Beavis, Elaine Guillemin, and Barbara Pell, 253–70. Ottawa: Novalis, 2006.

———. "Hebrews and Wisdom." In *Mark, Manuscripts and Monotheism: Essays in Honor of Larry W. Hurtado,* edited by Chris Keith and Dieter T. Roth. London: Bloomsbury, 2014.

———. "The New Covenant and Judaism." *TBT* 22 (1984): 24–30.

———. "A Study of the Relation of the Old and New Covenants in the Epistle to the Hebrews, in the Light of Scholarship 1938–1980." MA thesis, University of Manitoba, 1981.

Bell, John L. *The Singing Thing: A Case for Congregational Song.* Chicago: GIA Publications, 2000.

Bellis, Alice Ogden. *Helpmates, Harlots, and Heroes: Women's Stories in the Hebrew Bible.* Louisville, KY: Westminster John Knox, 2007.

Benjamin, Don C. "Israel's God: Mother and Midwife." *BTB* 19 (1989): 115–20.

Benko, Stephen. *Pagan Rome and the Early Christians.* Bloomington: Indiana University Press, 1984.

Berger, Teresa. *Gender Differences and the Making of Liturgical History: Lifting a Veil on Liturgy's Past*. Farnham, UK, and Burlington, VT: Ashgate, 2011.

————. *Women's Ways of Worship: Gender Analysis and Liturgical History*. Collegeville, MN: Liturgical Press, 1999.

Bidlack, Beth. "Antoinette Brown Blackwell: Pioneering Exegete and Congregational Minister." In *Strangely Familiar: Protofeminist Interpretations of Patriarchal Biblical Texts*, edited by Nancy Calvert-Koyzis and Heather Weir, 151–70. Atlanta, GA: SBL, 2009.

Bodington, Gracilla. *St. Paul's Epistle to the Hebrews: Explained in Simple and Familiar Language*. London: James Nisbet, 1846.

Brenner, Athalya, ed. *A Feminist Companion to Wisdom Literature*. FCB 9. Sheffield: Academic Press, 1995.

Bright, John. *An History of Israel, with an Introduction and Appendix*. Louisville, KY: Westminster John Knox, 2000.

Brown, Antoinette L. "Exegesis of 1 Corinthians, XIV., 34, 35; and 1 Timothy II., 11,12." *OQR* 4 (1849): 358–73.

Brown, Joanne Carlson. "Divine Child Abuse?" *Daughters of Sarah* 18 (1992): 24–28.

Brown, Joanne Carlson, and Carole R. Bohn, eds. *Christianity, Patriarchy, and Abuse: A Feminist Critique*. Cleveland: Pilgrim Press, 1989.

Brown, Michael. "Biblical Myth and Contemporary Experience: The *Akedah* in Modern Jewish Literature." *Judaism* 31 (1982): 99–111.

Buchanan, George Wesley. *To the Hebrews*. AB 36. Garden City, NY: Doubleday, 1972.

Burke, Anne, ed. *Imprint and Casualties: Poets on Women and Language, Reinventing Memory*. Readings from the Living Archives of the Feminist Caucus of the League of Canadian Poets. Vol. 2. Fredericton, NB: Broken Jaw Press, 2000.

Burke, David G. "Cherub, Cherubim." In *Oxford Companion to the Bible*, edited by Bruce M. Metzger and Michael D. Coogan, 107–8. New York and Oxford: Oxford University Press, 1993.

Camagay, Ma. Luisa T. "Ang Kababaihan at Pambansang Kamalayan." *Philippine Social Sciences Review, Gender Issues in Philippine Society* 50 (1995): 1–14.

Campbell, Joan Cecilia. *Phoebe: Patron and Emissary*. Paul's Social Network: Brothers and Sisters in Faith. Collegeville, MN: Liturgical Press, 2009.

Carcopino, Jerome. *Daily Life in Ancient Rome: The People and the City at the Height of the Empire*. Harmondsworth: Penguin, 1991.

Charles, Elizabeth Rundle. *Within the Veil: Studies in the Epistle to the Hebrews*. London: SPCK, 1891.

Charlesworth, James H. *The Old Testament Pseudepigrapha*. Vol. 2. New York: Doubleday, 1985.

Chung, Hyun-Kyung. *Struggle to Be the Sun Again: Introducing Asian Women's Theology*. Maryknoll, NY: Orbis Books, 1991.

Claasens, Juliana M. "Praying from the Depths of the Deep: Remembering the Image of God as Midwife in Psalm 71." *RevExp* 104 (2007): 761–75.

———. "Rupturing God-Language: The Metaphor of God as Midwife in Psalm 22." 2005. http://home.nwciowa.edu/wacome/ClaassensBakhtin2005.pdf, accessed December 16, 2011.

Cody, Aelred. *Heavenly Sanctuary and Liturgy in the Epistle to the Hebrews: The Achievement of Salvation in the Epistle's Perspectives.* St. Meinrad, IN: Grail, 1960.

Cohen, Shaye J. D. "The Significance of Yavneh: Pharisees, Rabbis, and the End of Jewish Sectarianism." *HUCA* 55 (1984): 27–53.

Cohen, Shaye D. "The Letter of Paul to the Galatians." In *The Jewish Annotated New Testament*, 332–44. New York: Oxford University Press, 2001.

Corrington, Gail Patterson. "The Milk of Salvation: Redemption by the Mother in Late Antiquity and Early Christianity." *HTR* 4 (1989): 393–420.

Craddock, Fred B. "The Letter to the Hebrews." In *The New Interpreter's Bible*, 121–73. Nashville, TN: Abingdon, 1998.

D'Angelo, Mary Rose. "Hebrews." In *The Women's Bible Commentary*, edited by Carol A. Newsom and Sharon H. Ringe, 364–67. London: SPCK; Philadelphia: Westminster/John Knox, 1992.

———. *Moses in the Letter to the Hebrews.* SBLS 42. Missoula, MT: Scholars Press, 1979.

Datuin, Flaudette May V. "Reclaiming the Southeast Asian Goddess: Examples from Contemporary Art by Women (Philippines, Thailand and Indonesia)." Translated by Izumi Nakajima. *Image and Gender* 6 (2006): 105–19.

deConick, April. *Holy Misogyny: Why the Sex and Gender Conflicts in the Early Church Still Matter.* New York: Continuum, 2011.

de Groot, Christiana, and Marian Ann Taylor. *Recovering Nineteenth-Century Women Interpreters of the Bible.* SemeiaSt 38. Atlanta, GA: SBL, 2007.

Delaney, Carol. *Abraham on Trial: The Social Legacy of Biblical Myth.* Princeton, NJ: Princeton University Press, 1998.

Del Maestro, M. L., trans. *Revelations of Divine Love of Julian of Norwich.* New York: Doubleday, 1977.

deSilva, David A. "The Epistle to the Hebrews in Social-Scientific Perspective." *ResQ* 36 (1994): 1–21.

———. *Perseverance in Gratitude: A Socio-Rhetorical Commentary on the Epistle "to the Hebrews."* Grand Rapids, MI: Eerdmans, 2000.

De Troyer, Kristin. "Blood: A Threat to Holiness or (Another) Holiness?" In *Wholly Woman, Holy Blood: A Feminist Critique of Purity and Impurity*, edited by Kristin De Troyer, Judith A. Herbert, Judith Ann Johnson, and Anne-Marie Korte, 45–65. Harrisburg, PA: Trinity Press International, 2003.

———. "Preface." In *Wholly Woman, Holy Blood: A Feminist Critique of Purity and Impurity*, edited by Kristin De Troyer, Judith A. Herbert, Judith Ann Johnson, and Anne-Marie Korte, xi–xii. Harrisburg, PA: Trinity Press International, 2003.

Dever, William G. *Did God Have a Wife? Archaeology and Folk Religion in Ancient Israel*. Grand Rapids. MI: Eerdmans, 2005.

Dietrich, Gabriele. *One day i shall be like a banyan tree*. Belgaum: Dileep S. Kamat, 1985.

Donaldson, Laura E. *Decolonizing Feminisms: Race, Gender, and Empire-Building*. Chapel Hill: University of North Carolina Press, 1992.

Donaldson, Terence L. *Jews and Anti-Judaism in the New Testament*. London: SPCK, 2010.

Douglas, Mary. "Atonement in Leviticus." *JSQ* 1 (1993–94): 109–30.

Dube, Musa W. "Go Therefore and Make Disciples of All Nations (Matt. 28:19a): A Postcolonial Perspective on Biblical Criticism and Pedagogy." In *Teaching the Bible: The Discourse and Politics of Biblical Pedagogy*, edited by Fernando F. Segovia and Mary Ann Tolbert, 224–46. Maryknoll, NY: Orbis Books, 1998.

———. *Postcolonial Feminist Interpretation of the Bible*. St. Louis, MO: Chalice Press, 2000.

Duck, Ruth. *Gender and the Name of God: The Trinitarian Baptismal Formula*. New York: Pilgrim Press, 1991.

Dunnill, John. *Covenant and Sacrifice in the Letter to the Hebrews*. SNTSMS 75. Cambridge: Cambridge University Press, 1993.

Dyer, Bryan R. "'A Great Conflict Full of Suffering': Suffering in the Epistle to the Hebrews in Light of Feminist Concerns." *McMaster Journal of Theology and Ministry* 12 (2010–11): 179–98.

Eberhart, Christian. *The Sacrifice of Jesus: Understanding Atonement Biblically*. Minneapolis: Fortress Press, 2011.

Eisenbaum, Pamela. "Father and Son: The Christology of Hebrews in Patrilineal Perspective." In *A Feminist Companion to the Catholic Epistles and Hebrews*, edited by Amy-Jill Levine with Maria Mayo Robbins, FCNTECW 8, 127–46. Cleveland, OH: Pilgrim Press, 2004.

———. "Hebrews." In *The Jewish Annotated New Testament*, 406–26. New York: Oxford University Press, 2011.

———. *The Jewish Heroes of Christian History: Hebrews 11 in Literary Context*. Atlanta, GA: Scholars Press, 1997.

———. *Paul Was Not a Christian: The Original Message of a Misunderstood Apostle*. San Francisco: HarperOne, 2009.

Elkins, Heather Murray. *Worshipping Women: Re-Forming God's People for Praise*. Nashville, TN: Abingdon, 1994.

Ellingworth, Paul. *The Epistle to the Hebrews*. NIGTC. Grand Rapids, MI: Eerdmans, 2003.

Eskenazi, D. Tamara Cohn, and Andrea L. Weiss, eds. *The Torah: A Women's Commentary*. New York: Women of Reformed Judaism, 2008.

Fineman, Alisa. "U'vachein, And Then." In *Talking to Goddess: Powerful Voices from Many Traditions*, edited by D'vorah J. Grenn, 211–12. Napa, CA: The Lilith Institute, 2009.

Finger, Reta Halteman. "Liberation or Abuse." *Daughters of Sarah* 18 (1992): 37–38.

Friedlander, Gerald. *Pirke de-Rabbi Eliezer*. Skokie, IL: Varda Books, 2004.

Fuller, Russell. "Marriage." In *Oxford Companion to the Bible*, edited by Bruce M. Metzger and Michael D. Coogan, 496–97. New York and Oxford: Oxford University Press, 1993.

Gilligan, Carol. *In a Different Voice: Psychological Theory and Women's Development*. Boston: Harvard University Press, 1982.

Gold, Victor Roland, et al., eds. *The New Testament and Psalms: An Inclusive Version*. New York and Oxford: Oxford University Press, 1995.

Grey, Mary. *Feminism, Redemption, and the Christian Tradition*. Mystic, CT: Twenty-Third Publications, 1990.

———. *Sacred Longings: The Ecological Spirit and Global Culture*. Minneapolis: Fortress Press, 2004.

———. "'Who Do You Say That I Am?' Images of Christ in Feminist Liberation Theology." In *Images of Christ: Ancient and Modern*, edited by Stanley E. Porter, Michael A. Hayes, and David Tombs, 189–205. Roehampton Institute London Papers 2. London and New York: T & T Clark, 2004.

Hagner, Donald A. *Encountering the Book of Hebrews: An Exposition*. Grand Rapids, MI: Eerdmans, 2002.

Hahn, Scott. *The Kingdom of God as Liturgical Empire: A Theological Commentary on 1–2 Chronicles*. Grand Rapids, MI: Baker Academic, 2012.

Harrington, Daniel J. *What Are They Saying about the Letter to the Hebrews*. Mahwah, NJ: Paulist Press, 2005.

Hayes, Richard B. "'Here We Have No Lasting City': New Covenantalism in Hebrews." In *The Epistle to the Hebrews and Christian Theology*, edited by Richard Bauckham et al., 151–73. Grand Rapids, MI, and Cambridge: Eerdmans, 2009.

Heen, Erik M., And Philip D. W. Krey. *Ancient Christian Commentary on Scripture, New Testament X*. Downers Grove, IL: InterVarsity, 2006.

Henrix, Hans Herman. "The Covenant Has Never Been Revoked: Basis of the Christian-Jewish Relationship." 2010. http://www.jcrelations.net/The_covenant_has_never_been_revoked.2250.0.html#, accessed January 5, 2012.

Heschel, Abraham Joshua. *The Sabbath: Its Meaning for Modern Man*. New York: Farrar, Strauss, 1948.

Heyward, Carter. *Saving Jesus from Those Who Are Right: Rethinking What It Means to Be Christian*. Minneapolis: Fortress Press, 1999.

Hoppin, Ruth. "The Book of the Hebrews Revisited: Implications of the Theology of Hebrews for Gender Equality." http://www.womenpriests.org/scriptur/hoppin2.asp, accessed October 22, 2011.

———. "The Epistle to the Hebrews is Priscilla's Letter." In *A Feminist Companion to the Catholic Epistles and Hebrews*, FCNTECW 8, 147–70. Cleveland, OH: Pilgrim Press, 2004.

———. *Priscilla's Letter: Finding the Author of the Epistle to the Hebrews*. Fort Bragg, CA: Lost Coast Books, 1997.

Houts, Margo. "Atonement and Abuse: An Alternate View." *Daughters of Sarah* 18 (1992): 29–32.

Hyman, Paul, and Dalia Olfer, eds. *Jewish Women: A Comprehensive Historical Encyclopedia.* Jewish Women's Archive. 2009. http://jwa.org/encyclopedia /article/legal-religious-status-of-jewish-female, accessed July 15, 2015.

Ibita, Ma. Marilou S. "Dining with Jesus in the Third Gospel: Celebrating Eucharist in the Third World." *EAPR* 42 (2005): 249–61.

———. "Fostering Narrative Approaches to Scripture in Asia: The Primary Task of Explicit Recognition." *EAPR* 46 (2009): 124–41.

Isaacs, Marie. *Sacred Space: An Approach to the Theology of the Epistle to the Hebrews.* JSNTSup 73. Sheffield: JSOT Press, 1992.

Jagessar, Michael N., and Stephen Burns. *Christian Worship: Postcolonial Perspectives.* Sheffield: Equinox, 2011.

Jay, Nancy. "Sacrifice as Remedy for Having Been Born of a Woman." In *Immaculate and Powerful: The Female in Social Image and Social Reality,* edited by C. W. Atkinson, 283–309. Boston: Beacon, 1985.

———. *Throughout Your Generations Forever: Sacrifice, Religion, and Paternity.* Chicago and London: University of Chicago Press, 1992.

Joh, Wonhee Anne. *Heart of the Cross: A Postcolonial Christology.* Louisville, KY: Westminster John Knox, 2006.

Johnson, Elizabeth A. *Friends of God and Prophets: A Feminist Theological Reading of the Communion of Saints.* New York: Continuum, 1999.

———. *She Who Is: The Mystery of God in Feminist Theological Discourse.* New York: Crossroad, 1996.

———. "Wisdom Was Made Flesh and Pitched Her Tent Among Us." In *Reconstructing the Christ Symbol: Essays in Feminist Christology,* edited by Maryanne Stevens, 96–116. New York and Mahwah, NJ: Paulist Press, 1993.

Johnson, Luke T. *The Writings of the New Testament: An Interpretation.* Philadelphia: Fortress Press, 1986.

Johnson, Richard W. *Going Outside the Camp: The Sociological Function of the Epistle to the Hebrews.* JSNTSup 209. London and New York: Sheffield Academic Press, 2001.

Johnson, Todd, ed. *The Conviction of Things Not Seen: Worship and Ministry in the 21st Century.* Grand Rapids, MI: Brazos Press, 2002.

Käsemann, Ernst. *The Wandering People of God: An Investigation of the Letter to the Hebrews.* Minneapolis: Fortress Press, 1984.

Kato, Julius-Kei. *How Immigrant Christians Living in Mixed Cultures Interpret Their Religion: Asian-American Diasporic Hybridity and Its Implications for Hermeneutics.* Lewiston, NY: Edwin Mellen Press, 2011.

Kavanagh, Aidan. *The Shape of Baptism: The Rite of Christian Initiation.* New York: Pueblo, 1978.

Kee, Howard Clark. "The Formation of Christian Communities." In *The Cambridge Companion to the Bible,* 2nd ed., edited by Bruce Chilton, 481–682. Cambridge: Cambridge University Press, 1997.

Keller, Catherine. *God and Power: Counter-Apocalyptic Journeys*. Minneapolis: Fortress Press, 2005.

———. "The Love of Postcolonialism." In *Postcolonial Theologies: Divinity and Empire*, edited by Catherine Keller, Michael Nausner, and Mayra Rivera, 221–42. St. Louis, MO: Chalice Press, 2004.

Kim, David Kyuman. "Enchanting Diasporas, Asian Americans, and Passionate Attachment of Race." In *Revealing the Sacred in Asian and Pacific America*, edited by Jane Naomi Iwamura and Paul Spickard, 327–40. New York: Routledge, 2003.

Kim, Elaine H., and Chungmoo Choi. *Dangerous Women: Gender and Korean Nationalism*. New York: Routledge, 1998.

Kim, Nami. "My/Our Comfort *Not* at the Expense of 'Somebody Else's.'" *JFSR* 21 (2005): 75–94.

Kim, Yung Suk, and Jin-Ho Kim, ed. *Reading Minjung Theology in the Twenty-First Century: Selected Writings by Ahn Byung-Mu and Modern Critical Responses*. Eugene, OR.: Wipf and Stock, 2013.

Kim-Cragg, HyeRan. "Becoming a Feminist Christian: A Korean-Canadian Perspective." In *My Red Couch: And Other Stories on Seeking a Feminist Faith*, edited by Claire Bischoff and Rachel Gaffron, 183–89. Cleveland, OH: Pilgrim Press, 2005.

———. "Between and Beyond Asian-ness: A Voice of a Postcolonial Hybrid Korean-Canadian in the Diaspora." In *What Young Asian Theologians Are Thinking*, edited byLeow Theng Huat, 90–102. The CSCA Christianity in Southeast Asia Series No 7. Trinity Theological College, 2014.

———. *Story and Song: A Postcolonial Interplay between Christian Education and Worship*. New York: Peter Lang, 2012.

———. "Women and Confucianism: A Korean-Canadian Postcolonial Feminist Perspective." In *Introduction to Asian Feminist Perspectives on Religions: Toward Interfaith Dialogue*, edited by Asian Women's Resource Centre for Culture and Theology (AWRC), 84–103. Kuala Lumpur, Malaysia: AWRC, 2008.

King, Karen L., ed. *Images of the Feminine in Gnosticism*. Harrisburg, PA: Trinity International, 1988.

Kittredge, Cynthia Briggs. "Hebrews." In *Searching the Scriptures*. Vol. 2: *A Feminist Commentary*, edited by Elisabeth Schüssler Fiorenza, 428–54. New York: Crossroad, 1994.

Klirs, Tracy Guren et al. *The Merit of Our Mothers: A Bilingual Anthology of Jewish Women's Prayers*. Cincinnati, OH: Hebrew Union College Press, 1992.

Kolarcik, Michael. *The Psalms*. Toronto: Regis College, 2003.

Koren, Sharon. "Contemporary Reflection." *Parashat Va-eira*. In *The Torah: A Women's Commentary*, edited by D. Tamara Cohn Eskenazi and Andrea L. Weiss, 351–52. New York: Women of Reformed Judaism, 2008.

Kraemer, Ross. *Her Share of the Blessings: Women's Religions among Pagans, Jews, and Christians in the Greco-Roman World*. New York: Oxford University Press, 1993.

————. "Women's Authorship of Jewish and Christian Literature in the Greco-Roman Period." In *"Women Like This": New Perspectives on Jewish Women in the Greco-Roman World*, edited by Amy-Jill Levine, 221–42. Atlanta, GA: Scholars Press, 1991.

Kwok, Pui-lan. *Postcolonial Imagination and Feminist Theology.* Louisville, KY: Westminster John Knox, 2005.

Laffey, Alice. "The Priestly Creation Narrative: Goodness and Interdependence." In *Earth, Wind & Fire: Biblical and Theological Perspectives on* Creation, edited by Carol J. Dempsey and Mary Margaret Pazdan, 24–34. Collegeville, MN: Liturgical Press, 2004.

Leahy, Thomas W. "The Epistle of James." In *The New Jerome Biblical Commentary*, edited by Raymond E. Brown, Joseph A. Fitzmyer, and Roland E. Murphy, 909–16. Englewood Cliffs, NJ: Prentice Hall, 1990.

Lee, Jung-Young. "A Life In-Between: A Korean-American Journey." In *Journeys at the Margin: Toward an Autobiographical Theology in American-Asian Perspective*, edited by Peter C. Phan and Jung Young Lee, 23–39. Collegeville, MN: Liturgical Press, 1999.

Lehne, Susanne. *The New Covenant in Hebrews.* JSNTSup 44. Sheffield: JSOT Press, 1990.

Lerner, Gerda. *The Creation of Feminist Consciousness From the Middle Ages to Eighteen Seventy.* New York: Oxford University Press, 1993.

Liew, Tat-siong Benny. *What Is Asian American Biblical Hermeneutics? Reading the New Testament.* Honolulu: University of Hawaii Press, 2008.

MacDermot, Violet. *The Fall of Sophia: A Gnostic Text on the Redemption of Universal Consciousness.* Great Barrington, MA: Lindisfarne, 2001.

Malina, Bruce J. *The New Testament World: Insights from Cultural Anthropology.* London: SCM Press, 1983.

Malina, Bruce J., and John J. Pilch. *Social-Science Commentary on the Book of Acts.* Minneapolis: Fortress Press, 2008.

Marin, Moisés Mayordomo. "Construction of Masculinity in Antiquity and Early Christianity." *Lectio Difficilor* 2. 2006. http://www.lectio.unibe.ch/06_2/marin_construction.htm, accessed February 9, 2012.

Marks, Susan. "Present and Absent: Women at Greco-Roman Wedding Meals." In *Meals in the Early Christian World: Social Formation, Experimentation, and Conflict at the Table*, edited by Dennis E. Smith and Hal E. Taussig, 123–48. New York: Palgrave Macmillan, 2012.

McCall, Leslie. "The Complexity of Intersectionality." *Signs: Journal of Women in Culture and Society* 30 (2005): 1771–1800.

McVann, Mark. "Family Centeredness." In *Biblical Social Values and Their Meaning: A Handbook*, edited by John J. Pilch and Bruce J. Malina, 70–73. Peabody, MA: Hendrickson, 1993.

Melchert, Charles F. *Wise Teaching: Biblical Wisdom and Educational Ministry.* Harrisburg, PA: Trinity Press International, 1996.

Miller, Charles H. "Italy." In *Harper's Bible Dictionary*, edited by Paul J. Achtemeier, 438. San Francisco: HarperSanFrancisco, 1985.

Miller-McLemore, Bonnie J. "Practical Theology and Pedagogy: Embodying Theological Know-How." In *For Life Abundant: Practical Theology, Theological Education, and Christian Ministry*, edited by Dorothy C. Bass and Craig Dykstra, 170–90. Grand Rapids, MI: Eerdmans, 2008.

Mitchell, Alan C. *Hebrews*. SP 13. Collegeville, MN: Liturgical Press, 2009.

Moffatt, James. *A Critical and Exegetical Commentary on the Epistle to the Hebrews*. New York: Scribner's, 1924.

Moltmann, Jurgen. "Sabbath: Finishing and Beginning." *LP* 7 (April–June 1998): 4–5.

Morrison, Michael D. *Who Needs a New Covenant? Rhetorical Function of the Covenant Motif in the Argument of Hebrews*. Princeton Theological Monograph Series. Eugene, OR: Pickwick, 2008.

Mosser, Carol. "Rahab Outside the Camp." In *The Epistle to the Hebrews and Christian Theology*, edited by Richard Bauckham, Daniel R. Driver, Trevor A. Hart, and Nathan MacDonald, 383–404. Grand Rapids: Eerdmans, 2009.

Murray, Robert. *The Cosmic Covenant: Biblical Themes of Justice, Peace and the Integrity of Creation*. Piscataway, NY: Gorgias Press, 1992.

Myerhoff, Barbara. *Number Our Days*. New York: Dutton, 1978.

Nagano, Paul M. "A Japanese-American Pilgrimage: Theological Reflections." In *Journeys at the Margin: Toward an Autobiographical Theology in American-Asian Perspective*, edited by Peter C. Phan and Jung Young Lee, 63–79. Collegeville, MN: Liturgical Press, 1999.

Neyrey, Jerome H. "Dyadism." In *Biblical Social Values and Their Meaning: A Handbook*, edited by John J. Pilch and Bruce J. Malina, 49–52. Peabody, MA: Hendrickson, 1993.

———. "Group Orientation." In *Biblical Social Values and Their Meaning: A Handbook*, edited by John J. Pilch and Bruce J. Malina, 88–91. Peabody, MA: Hendrickson, 1993.

Ng, Greer Anne Wenh-In. "Pastoral Care in the Context of North American Asian Communities." In *Injustice and the Care of Souls: Taking Oppression Seriously in Pastoral Care*, edited by Sheryl A. Kujawa-Holbrook and Karen B. Montagno, 73–88. Minneapolis: Fortress Press, 2009.

Oden, Thomas C., and Christopher A. Hall. *Ancient Christian Commentary on Scripture*. Vol. 2: *Mark*. Downers Grove, IL: InterVarsity, 1998.

O'Loughlin, Thomas. *The Didachē: A Window on the Earliest Christians*. Grand Rapids, MI: Baker Academic, 2010.

Pagels, Elaine. *The Gnostic Gospels*. New York: Random House, 1979.

Palmer, Parker. *Let Your Life Speak: Listening for the Voice of Vocation*. San Francisco: Jossey-Bass, 2000.

Park, Andrew Sung. *Triune Atonement: Christ's Healing for Sinners, Victims, and the Whole Creation*. Louisville, KY: Westminster John Knox, 2009.

————. *The Wounded Heart of God: The Asian Concept of Han and the Christian Doctrine of Sin.* Nashville, TN: Abingdon, 1993.

Pfitzner, Victor C. *Hebrews.* ANTC. Nashville: Abingdon, 1977.

Phan, Peter C. "Betwixt and Between: Doing Theology with Memory and Imagination." In *Journeys at the Margin: Toward an Autobiographical Theology in American-Asian Perspective*, edited by Peter C. Phan and Jung Young Lee, 113–33. Collegeville, MN: Liturgical Press, 1999.

————. *Christianity with an Asian Face: Asian American Theology in the Making.* Maryknoll, NY: Orbis Books, 2003.

Pilch, John J. *Introducing the Cultural Context of the New Testament.* Hear the Word 2. Eugene, OR: Wipf & Stock, 2007.

————. "Parenting." In *Biblical Social Values and Their Meaning: A Handbook*, edited by John J. Pilch and Bruce J. Malina, 128–31. Peabody, MA: Hendrickson, 1993.

Plaut, W. Gunther. *The Torah: A Modern Commentary.* New York: Union of American Hebrew Congregations, 1981.

Plevnik, Joseph. "Honor/Shame." In *Biblical Social Values and Their Meaning: A Handbook*, edited by John J. Pilch and Bruce J. Malina, 94–104. Peabody, MA: Hendrickson, 1993.

Polen, Nehemia. "Leviticus, and Hebrews . . . and Leviticus." In *The Epistle to the Hebrews and Christian Theology*, edited by Richard Bauckham, Daniel R. Driver, Tervor A. Hart, and Nathan MacDonald, 213–28. Grand Rapids, MI: Eerdmans, 2009.

Pomeroy, Sarah B. *Goddesses, Whores, Wives, and Slaves: Women in Classical Antiquity.* New York: Schocken Books, 1995.

Powery, Emerson B. "The Gospel of Mark." In *True to Our Native Land: An African American New Testament Commentary*, edited by Brian R. Blount, 121–57. Minneapolis: Fortress Press, 2007.

Procter-Smith, Marjorie. "Feminist Interpretation and Liturgical Proclamation." In *Searching the Scriptures*. Vol. 1: *A Feminist Introduction*, edited by Elisabeth Schüssler Fiorenza, 313–25. New York: Crossroad, 1993.

————. *In Her Own Rite: Constructing Feminist Liturgical Tradition.* Nashville, TN: Abingdon, 1990.

Punt, Jeremy H. "The Letter to the Hebrews." In *A Postcolonial Commentary on the New Testament Writings*, edited by Fernando F. Segovia and R. S. Sugirtharajah, 328–68. The Bible and Postcolonialism Series 13. London: T & T Clark, 2007.

Puttick, Elizabeth. "Women in New Religious Movements." In *New Religious Movements: Challenge and* Response, edited by Bryan Wilson and Jamie Cresswell, 143–62. New York: Routledge, 1999.

Quindoza-Santiago, Lilia. "Roots of Feminist Thought in the Philippines." Translated by Thelma B. Kintanar. *Review of Women Studies* 6 (1996): 159–72.

Rapp, Ursula. "You Are How You Eat: How Eating and Drinking Behaviour Identifies the Wise According to Jesus Ben Sirach." In *Decisive Meals: Table Politics in Biblical Literature*, edited by Kathy Ehrensperger, Nathan MacDonald, and Luzia Sutter Rehmann, translated by Martin Rumscheidt, 42–61. LNTS 449. New York: T & T Clark, 2012.

Ravel, Edeet. *Ten Thousand Lovers*. London: Review, 2003.

Reid, Barbara E. "Sabbath, the Crown of Creation." In *Earth, Wind & Fire: Biblical and Theological Perspectives on* Creation, edited by Carol J. Dempsey and Mary Margaret Pazdan, 67–76. Collegeville, MN: Liturgical Press, 2004.

———. *Taking Up the Cross: New Testament Interpretations through Latina and Feminist Eyes*. Minneapolis: Fortress Press, 2007.

Reinhartz, Adele. "The Gospel of John." In *Searching the Scriptures*. Vol. 2: *A Feminist Commentary*, edited by Elisabeth Schüssler Fiorenza, 561–600. New York: Crossroad, 1994.

Rodkinson, Michael L. *Babylonian Talmud, Book 4: Tracts Pecharim, Yomah and Hagiga*. New York: Talmud Society, 1918.

Ruether, Rosemary Radford. "Can Christology Be Liberated from Patriarchy?" In *Reconstructing the Christ Symbol: Essays in Feminist Christology*, edited by Maryanne Stevens, 7–29. New York and Mahwah, NJ: Paulist Press, 1993.

———. *To Change the World: Christology and Cultural Criticism*. New York: Crossroad, 1981.

Runia, David T. *Philo in Early Christian Literature*. Philadelphia: Fortress Press, 1993.

Russell, Letty M. *Just Hospitality: God's Welcome in a World of Difference*. Edited by J. Shannon Clarkson and Kate M. Ott. Louisville, KY: Westminster John Knox, 2009.

Saleveo, Iutisone. *Legitimation in the Letter to the Hebrews: The Construction and Maintenance of a Symbolic Universe*. JSNTSup 219. Sheffield: Sheffield Academic Press, 2002.

Santiago, Luciano P. R. "The Development of the Religious Congregations for Women in the Philippines during the Spanish Period (1565–1898)." *The Journal of Sophia Asia Studies* 12 (1994): 49–71.

Schaberg, Jane D. *The Illegitimacy of Jesus*. Sheffield: Sheffield Academic Press, 1995.

———. "Magdalene christianity." In *On the Cutting Edge: The Study of Women in Biblical Worlds*, edited by Jane D. Schaberg, Alice Bach, and Esther Fuchs, 193–220. New York: Continuum, 2003.

Schenck, Kenneth. "Hebrews as the Re-presentation of a Story: A Narrative Approach to Hebrews." In *Reading the Epistle to the Hebrews: A Resource for Students*, edited by Eric F. Mason and Kevin B. McCruden, 171–88. RBS 66. Atlanta, GA: SBL, 2011.

———. *Understanding the Book of Hebrews: The Story behind the Sermon*. Louisville, KY: Westminster John Knox, 2005.

Scholz, Susanne. *Introducing the Women's Hebrew Bible*. London: T & T Clark, 2007.

Schroer, Silvia. "The Book of Wisdom." In *Searching the Scriptures*. Vol. 2: *A Feminist Commentary*, edited by Elisabeth Schüssler Fiorenza, 18–38. New York: Crossroad, 1994.

Schüssler Fiorenza, Elisabeth, ed. *Searching the Scriptures*. Vol. 1: *A Feminist Introduction*. New York: Crossroad, 1993.

———. *Searching the Scriptures*. Vol. 2: *A Feminist Commentary*. New York: Crossroad, 1994.

———. "Transgressing Canonical Boundaries." In *Searching the Scriptures*. Vol. 2: *A Feminist Commentary*, edited by Elisabeth Schüssler Fiorenza, 1–14. New York: Crossroad, 1994.

Schweitzer, Don. *Contemporary Christologies: A Fortress Introduction*. Minneapolis: Fortress Press, 2010.

Segovia, Fernando F., and Mary Ann Tolbert, eds. *Reading from this Place: Social Location and Biblical Interpretation in Global Perspective*. Minneapolis: Fortress Press, 1995.

Slee, Nicola. "Visualizing, Conceptualizing, Imagining and Praying the Christa: In Search of Her Risen Forms." *FemT* 21 (2012): 71–90.

Smith, Dennis E. *From Symposium to Eucharist: The Banquet in the Early Christian World*. Minneapolis: Fortress Press, 2003.

Snyder, Jane McIntosh. *The Woman and the Lyre: Women Writers in Classical Greece and Rome*. Carbondale: Southern Illinois University Press, 1989.

Sohn, Ruth H. "Post-biblical Interpretations." *Parashat Vayahk'heil*. In *The Torah: A Women's Commentary*, edited by D. Tamara Cohn Eskenazi and Andrea L. Weiss, 538–39. New York: Women of Reformed Judaism, 2008.

Spicq, Ceslas. *L'Epitre aux Hebreux*. 2 Vols. Paris: Gabalda, 1952–53.

Stern, Chaim, ed. *Gates of Repentance: The New Union Prayerbook for the Days of Awe*. New York: Central Conference of American Rabbis, 1996.

Stevenson-Moessner, Jeanne. "The Road to Perfection: An Interpretation of Suffering in Hebrews." *Int* 57 (2003): 280–90

Sugirtharajah, R. S. "From Orientalist to Post-Colonial: Notes on Reading Practices." *AsJT* 10 (1996): 20–27.

———, ed. *The Postcolonial Bible*. The Bible and Postcolonialism 1. Sheffield: Sheffield Academic Press, 1998.

———. *Postcolonial Criticism and Biblical Interpretation*. Cambridge and New York: Cambridge University Press, 2002.

Suh, Nam-Dong. *Development of Minjung Theology in Korea*. Seoul: Han'gilsa, 1983.

Swan, Laura. *The Forgotten Desert Mothers: Sayings, Lives, and Stories of Early Christian Women*. New York: Paulist Press, 2001.

Tamez, Elsa. "The Woman Who Complicated the History of Salvation." In *New Eyes for Reading*, edited by John S. Pobee and Bärbel von Wartenberg-Potter, 5–17. Oak Park, IL: Meyer Stone Books, 1986.

Taylor, Marion, and Agnes Choi, eds. *Handbook of Women Biblical Interpreters: A Historical and Biographical Guide*. Grand Rapids, MI: Baker Academic, 2012.

Taylor, Marion Ann, and Heather E. Weir. *Let Her Speak for Herself: Nineteenth-Century Women Writing on Women in Genesis*. Waco, TX: Baylor University Press, 2006.

Thompson, James W. *The Beginnings of Christian Philosophy: The Epistle to the Hebrews*. CBQMS 13. Washington, DC: Catholic Biblical Association of America, 1982.

———. *Hebrews*. Paideia Commentaries on the New Testament. Grand Rapids, MI: Baker Academic, 2008.

Valler, Shulamit. "Who Is *ēšet ḥayil* in Rabbinic Literature?" In *A Feminist Companion to Wisdom Literature*, edited by Athalya Brenner, FCB 9, 85–99. Sheffield: Sheffield Academic Press, 1995.

van Dijk-Hemmes, Fokkelien. "Traces of Women's Text in the Hebrew Bible." In *On Gendering Texts: Female and Male Voices in the Hebrew Bible*, edited by Athalya Brenner and Fokkelien van Dijk-Hemmes, 17–112. Leiden: Brill, 1991.

Vanhoye, Albert. "Heb 6,7-8 et le mashal rabbinique." In *The New Testament Age: Essays in Honor of Bo Reiche*, edited by William C. Weinrich, 2.527–32. Macon, GA: Mercer University Press, 1984.

Wagener, Ulrike. "Hebrews: Strangers in the World," In *Feminist Biblical Interpretation: A Compendium of Critical Commentary on the Books of the Bible and Related Literature*, edited by Luise Schottroff and Marie-Theres Wacker, 857–69. Grand Rapids, MI: Eerdmans, 2012.

Wallis, R. E. "Appendix: The Martyrdom of Perpetua and Felicity." In *The Ante-Nicene Fathers*, volume 3: *Latin Christianity, Its Founder, Tertullian*, 697–706. Buffalo, NY: The Christian Literature Publishing Company, 1887.

Wardle, Timothy Scott. "Continuity and Discontinuity: The Temple and Early Christian Identity." PhD dissertation, Department of Religion, Duke University, 2008.

Warrior, Robert Allen. "A Native American Perspective: Canaanites, Cowboys, and Indians." In *Voices from the Margin: Interpreting the Bible in the Third World*, edited by R. S. Sugirtharajah, 287–95. Maryknoll, NY: Orbis Books, 1991.

Weber, Hans-Ruedi. *Experiments with Bible Study*. Geneva: WCC, 1981.

Weissler, Chava. *Voices of the Matriarchs: Listening to the Prayers of Early Modern Jewish Women*. Boston: Beacon Press, 1998.

White, James F. *Introduction to Christian Worship*. 3rd ed. Nashville, TN: Abingdon, 2000.

Whitlark, Jason A. "'Here We Do Not Have a City That Remains': A Figured Critique of Roman Imperial Propaganda in Hebrews 13:14." *JBL* 131 (2012): 161–79.

Williams, Delores S. *Sisters in the Wilderness: The Challenge of Womanist God-Talk*. Maryknoll, NY: Orbis Books, 1994.

Wills, Kenneth. "The Form of the Sermon in Hellenistic Judaism and Early Christianity." *HTR* 77 (1984): 277–99.

Yim, Taesoo. *Minjung Theology towards a Second Reformation*. Hong Kong: Christian Conference of Asia, 2006.

Yonge, C. D. *The Works of Philo Judaeus, the Contemporary of Josephus, Translated from the Greek*. London: H. G. Bohn, 1933.

Index of Scripture References and Other Ancient Sources

Index of Subjects

General Editor

Barbara E. Reid, OP, is a Dominican Sister of Grand Rapids, Michigan. She holds a PhD in biblical studies from The Catholic University of America and is vice president and academic dean and professor of New Testament studies at Catholic Theological Union, Chicago. Her most recent publications are *Wisdom's Feast: An Invitation to Feminist Interpretation of the Scriptures* (Eerdmans, 2016) and *Abiding Word: Sunday Reflections on Year A, B, C* (3 vols.; Liturgical Press, 2011, 2012, 2013). She served as president of the Catholic Biblical Association in 2014–2015.

Volume Editor

Linda M. Maloney, PhD, ThD, is a native of Houston, Texas. She studied at St. Louis University (BA, MA, PhD), the University of South Carolina (MIBS), and Eberhard-Karls-Universität Tübingen, where she earned her ThD in New Testament in 1990 under the direction of Prof. Gerhard Lohfink. She has taught at public and private colleges, universities, and seminaries in the United States and was academic editor at Liturgical Press from 1995 to 2005. She is a priest of the Episcopal Church (USA) and lives in Vermont and California.

Authors

Mary Ann Beavis has master's degrees in religious studies and theology from the University of Manitoba and the University of Notre Dame and a PhD in New Testament studies from Cambridge University (UK). She is currently professor of religion and culture at St. Thomas More College, University of Saskatchewan (Saskatoon, Canada). Her areas of academic interest and expertise include Christian origins, feminist biblical interpretation, Christianity and Goddess spirituality, and religion and popular culture. She is the author of several single-author and edited books as well as many peer-reviewed journal articles, book chapters, and book reviews. She is the founding editor of the *Journal of Religion and Popular Culture*.

HyeRan Kim-Cragg is Lydia Gruchy Professor of Pastoral Studies at St. Andrew's College, Saskatoon, Canada. As a practical theologian, her main areas of teaching are religious education and worship. Influenced by postcolonial theory, feminist theology, and migration, her most recent book is *The Encounters: Retelling the Bible from Migration and Intercultural Perspectives*, co-authored with EunYoung Choi. Her most recent articles appear in *Liturgy in Postcolonial Perspectives, Church in the Age of Migration: A Moving Body*, and the journal *Religious Education*.